THE ENCYCLOPEDIA OF
MYTHOLOGY

GODS, HEROES, AND LEGENDS OF THE GREEKS AND ROMANS

ERIC FLAUM

WITH DAVID PANDY

COURAGE BOOKS

AN IMPRINT OF RUNNING PRESS
PHILADELPHIA, PENNSYLVANIA

Page 4: *Pallas Athene and the Centaur*, Botticelli, c. 1482.

A RUNNING PRESS/FRIEDMAN GROUP BOOK

Copyright © 1993 by Michael Friedman Publishing Group, Inc.

9 8 7 6 5 4 3

Digit on the right indicates the number of this printing.

Library of Congress Cataloging-in-Publication Number 93-70594

ISBN 1-56138-231-0

THE ENCYCLOPEDIA OF MYTHOLOGY
Gods, Heroes, and Legends of the Greeks and Romans
was prepared and produced by
Michael Friedman Publishing Group, Inc.
15 West 26th Street
New York, New York 10010

Editors: Dana Rosen and Benjamin J. Boyington
Art Director: Jeff Batzli
Designer: Lynne Yeamans
Layout: Kevin Ullrich
Photography Editor: Ede Rothaus

Typeset by Bookworks Plus
Color separations by Rainbow Graphic Arts Co., Ltd.
Printed in China by Leefung-Asco Printers Ltd.

Published by
Courage Books
An imprint of
Running Press Book Publishers
125 South Twenty-second Street
Philadelphia, Pennsylvania 19103

DEDICATION

For Davey—a gentleman, a scholar, and a friend—and also for Samantha, in the nick of time.

ACKNOWLEDGMENTS

Thanks once again to Karla, who made this all possible, and to Dana and Ben for their patience and professionalism. Special thanks to Marilyn and Paul. Words alone cannot express our gratitude for all that they have done.

Biggest thanks of all go to Seija and Casey, who have supported this obsession all along. They make life a wondrous thing, and mere words cannot express my gratitude and love for the women of my life.

Additional thanks go to the friends and family who have supported and aided this project. Elise and Laban came through with helpful volumes, as did Elyse and Tom, while Tom Robbins and a friend named Biff helped bring mythology to life for me.

Unrelated love and thanks go out to KL, Mr. Butch (and the Chairwoman), C-Man, Grohos, Heather, Frank, Bob, Margaret and Kal (whose coffee table is getting mighty crowded!), and all those Decaturs, Flaums, Messingers, and Siccttes.

In memory of Georg Vilhelm Alexander Raustiala ("Isi") 1919–1992.

TABLE OF CONTENTS

Maps of the Classical World ✦ 6

Introduction ✦ 9

An Encyclopedia of
Greek Mythological Characters ✦ 10

Founding Fathers
and Other Famous Forebears ✦ 166

The Pantheon in Greek and Roman ✦ 166

Roman Mythological Characters ✦ 167

Bibliography ✦ 172

Index ✦ 173

Tanais River

Olbia

CHERSONESUS

B L A C K   S E A

COLCHIS

Sinope

PAPHLAGONIA

Byzantium
Chalcedon

GALATIA

Cyzicus

Parnassus

PHRYGIA

▲ *Mount Nysa*

Mallus

CARIA

CILICIA

SYRIA

LYCIA

Salamis

Cyprus

Paphos

Sidon

PHOENICIA

Samaria

Joppa

Alexandria

The Evolution of Place Names in the Classical World

NAME	FORMERLY KNOWN AS
Megara	Nisa
Scamander River	Xanthus River
Thebes	Cadmea
Troy	Illium
Venice	New Troy

NAME	LATER KNOWN AS
Dia	Naxos
Samothrace	Dardania

INTRODUCTION

Every civilization, in the process of establishing a cultural identity and in the pursuit of explaining the world's mysteries, has given rise to a mythological canon of some sort: the Hopi and their trickster god Masau'u; the Hindus and Siva, the goddess of destruction and rebirth; and the English and Americans and their heroes Robin Hood and Jesse James, noble thieves who stole from the rich to give to the poor.

Yet of all the mythologies that have ever been, that of the Greeks stands out as unique because it is so well known. Practically everyone has some snippet of Greek mythology in his or her mind. It would be rare to find a high school graduate who does not have a vague idea of who Venus was, does not remember that Midas was rich, or does not know that Poseidon had something to do with the sea. The reason is simple: the Greek myths have been an important part of Western European culture for such a long time, and have had a great impact on religion, the arts, and everyday thought. They were created by the Greeks (in some cases before Greece was Greek), and then shamelessly plagiarized by the Romans. These myths scandalized some medieval churchmen, had the distinction of being condemned by Martin Luther, and were still in vogue at the Versailles of Louis XIV. Today, courses in mythology still attract large numbers of students in both college and high school. The Greek myths are in short, timeless.

In any book on mythology it is important to introduce some order, especially in a book such as this, in which the only order is its alphabetical listing of names. In the most classical ordering of Greek mythology, there are four kinds of myths. First, there is the true myth, the attempt to explain a natural event such as a rumbling volcano to a prescientific world that has no rational means of explaining natural phenomena. That is why the Greeks put the Cyclopes under Mt. Aetna in Sicily and decided that the mountain's rumbling represented the monsters' attempts to escape. Second, there are, to borrow a word from the Norse, the saga myths, essentially factual events from Greek history that have been colored by the imaginations of numerous ancient storytellers. Such is the mythology that surrounds the siege of Troy, a real event from the late second millennium B.C. Third, there are fairy tales—*märchen*, to use the scholarly term—stories created simply for the delight they bring in the telling. One example is the story of Pygmalion, a sculptor who created a statue so beautiful that he fell in love with it and was rewarded for his devotion when Aphrodite turned the statue into the beautiful (and living) Galatea. Lastly, there are some myths that are psychological, designed to explain human behavior; the classic example is that of the self-love of Narcissus.

As a teacher I am always amazed by the ability of the Greek myths to delight students. Savvy, even cynical, Madonna-smitten teens still listen with rapt attention to stories about the birth of Athena, Phaëthon's fateful ride, or Perseus' adventures with the Gorgon's head.

This beautifully illustrated book lists an amazingly complete catalog of Greek and Roman mythological beings and creatures, listed by their Greek names, and includes a table at the back of the book listing those beings that are known by both Roman and Greek appellations. I encourage you to take some time, let your mind run over the list of gods, heroes, and monsters, and then turn to the entries that interest you. You will discover, as I have, facets of these creatures you never expected, and that, in turn, should lead you to other aspects of the never-ending appeal of Greek mythology.

Timothy R. Roberts, PhD
Lincoln University

Abderus   A volunteer who accompanied Heracles on his eighth labor: to capture Diomedes' mares. After Heracles captured the wild, man-eating horses, he left them under Abderus' charge. While Heracles was fighting Diomedes and his allies, the carnivorous mares ate Abderus. Heracles founded the city Abdera beside his tomb, and the athletic competitions held there never included chariot races.

Acacallis   The daughter of Pasiphaë and Minos, Acacallis became Apollo's first love. Apollo seduced her at Carmanor's house, for which Minos banished her to Libya. There Acacallis gave birth to Garamas, listed in some versions as the first mortal born.

Acamas   The son of Phaedra and Theseus, Acamas was the brother of Demophon, with whom he would eventually share the rule of Athens. While serving as an envoy of Diomedes' embassy at Troy, Acamas slept with Laodice and fathered a child upon her. That child, Munitus, was entrusted to Aethra, Acamas' grandmother and one of Helen's attendants. Acamas later returned to Troy as a member of the Greek alliance and was one of those who hid inside the Trojan Horse.

When Troy fell, Aethra and young Munitus escaped to a Greek camp, where Acamas and Demophon recognized their grandmother. Agamemnon allowed Aethra to be repatriated (in exchange for the brothers' portion of Trojan booty). During the voyage back to Greece, Munitus was bitten by a snake and died.

Acastus   The son of King Pelias, Acastus purified Peleus after the latter accidentally killed Eurytion. Acastus' wife, Cretheis, tried to seduce Peleus, who spurned her. Cretheis responded by accusing Peleus of having tried to ravish her, and insisted that Acastus kill him. Acastus then took Peleus out for a hunt and abandoned him without any means of defense. The Centaurs found Peleus but uncharacteristically spared him.

Peleus eventually returned to Acastus' kingdom and, with help from Zeus, avenged himself. After killing Acastus, Peleus mutilated the body of Cretheis in revenge for her part in his suffering.

Achelous   A river god who was the eldest son of Tethys and Oceanus, Achelous performed a second purification of Alcmaeon for the latter's murder of his own mother. After Achelous purified Alcmaeon, he also gave Alcmaeon his daughter, Callirrhoë, in marriage.

Achelous is also said to have fought with Heracles for the affections of Deianeira, assuming the shapes of a bull, a speckled serpent, and a Minotaur-like man before Heracles eventually defeated him, snapping off one of his horns in the process.

In different versions of this story it is suggested that Achelous' horn was traded back to him, was given to Oeneus as a bridal gift, or was taken by Heracles, who filled it with fruits from the Hesperides and took it to Tartarus during his twelfth labor.

Achilles   The seventh son born to Peleus and his wife, Thetis, Achilles had six brothers who died during Thetis' attempts to make them invulnerable. Thetis was close to successfully completing the process with Achilles when Peleus snatched the infant away, leaving only his ankle vulnerable. In some versions Thetis dips the child in the river Styx, leaving only the portion of his ankle where she held him untouched by the waters. In either case, Peleus replaced the child's ankle with one that had belonged to Damysus, a notoriously swift giant. Shortly thereafter Thetis ran off with the child.

Thetis then entrusted the child to Cheiron the Centaur, and returned to the sea. Under the tutelage of Cheiron, Achilles mastered many skills; he was best known for the speed with which he ran. In some versions it is suggested that Achilles was so fast he was able to catch wild stags on foot.

When the events that led to the Trojan War began to unfold, Thetis learned that if Achilles were to fight in Troy the Greeks would be guaranteed victory and Achilles

The Centaur Cheiron Teaches Young Achilles Archery, Giuseppe Crespi, 17th–18th **century.**

would be a hero, but that Achilles was also sure to die. Thetis disguised Achilles as a girl and hid him with Lycomedes on Scyros. Despite the disguise, Achilles conceived one or two sons with Lycomedes' daughter, Deidameia.

Agamemnon sent Odysseus, Nestor, and Ajax to find Achilles, and once his identity was revealed (through trickery), Achilles vowed to lead the Myrmidon army against Troy. Placed in charge of the Hellenic fleet, Achilles brought with him Patroclus, his closest ally and fighting companion. Along the way they mistakenly attacked the Mysian kingdom of Telephus, thinking it was Troy, and wounded Telephus.

Before departing for Troy, Achilles had been warned by Thetis to avoid killing any son of Apollo, since if he were to do so Apollo was sure to kill him in revenge. Achilles engaged Mnemon to keep an eye out for any of Apollo's progeny and to make sure that Achilles was aware of their presence. When the Greeks passed by Tenes' kingdom, however, and Tenes (a son of Apollo) hurled rocks at their ships, Achilles struck him dead. Achilles then killed Mnemon for having failed to remind him of Tenes' lineage, and made extensive sacrifices and tributes in honor of Tenes.

Achilles had another regret during the course of the voyage to Troy: the use of his name by Agamemnon's messengers in their successful retrieval of Agamemnon's daughter, Iphigeneia, who was to be sacrificed. In versions where Iphigeneia is not sacrificed, Achilles is credited with rescuing her, and there are even some versions in which he is said to marry her and father Neoptolemus upon her instead of Deidameia.

In some descriptions of the initial battle of the Trojan War, Achilles is the second Greek to set foot on Trojan soil, while in others he is the very last Greek to enter the fray. In either case, Achilles soon killed Cycnus, another of Apollo's sons. Achilles went on to slay Troilus, about whom it was prophesied that Troy would not fall if he were to reach his twentieth birthday. The slaying of Troilus in a sanctuary put Achilles in further disfavor of the gods. (They were already displeased with him because he was frequently verbally contemptuous of them and failed to give them the respect shown by the other Greeks.)

Earlier in the war, when Achilles fell in love with Polyxena, a daughter of Hecabe, he had sent Automedon to speak with Polyxena's brother Hector. The Trojan prince sent word back to Achilles that he could have Polyxena only if he betrayed the Greeks, or at least

Achilles and Troilus, **red-figured hydria, 4th century** B.C.

killed Great Ajax. In the next battle, Achilles sought out Hector and attempted to make it clear to him that he had no intention of betraying the Greeks or Ajax. While the two were engaged, Helenus, a brother of Hector, shot an arrow into Achilles' hand (allegedly with divine guidance) and temporarily removed the Greeks' fiercest warrior from the fighting.

During the sack of Lyrnessus, one of many neighboring cities that were decimated by Achilles' troops, Achilles killed Eëtion, the King of the Cilicians and captured two young women—Chryseis and Briseis—and a divine horse called Pedasus, which he added to his divine team.

Chryseis was claimed as a spoil of war by Agamemnon, who let Achilles keep Briseis. When the gods forced Agamemnon to return Chryseis to her father, Agamemnon decided that he was entitled to Briseis. Achilles announced that he would no longer support the Greek cause and that he would leave the very next day.

That night Protesilaus' ship was set on fire and Achilles rejoined the fighting when he saw his close friend Patroclus single-handedly

holding off the Trojans. Thetis provided Achilles with a new set of armor and Agamemnon returned Briseis to him. In the battle that ensued, Patroclus was killed and Achilles fought to avenge his companion. Achilles caused the Trojans to retreat, splitting their ranks and leaving them vulnerable to attack. Achilles encountered Hector during the Trojan retreat and now was ready for the combat Hector had proposed earlier, just before Achilles had removed himself from the fighting.

In an attempt to tire Achilles out, Hector ran around the walls of Troy with Achilles in pursuit. Achilles caught him on the third lap and killed him. Achilles took Hector's armor and, in a show of great disrespect, dragged the Trojan's corpse behind his chariot.

Achilles buried Patroclus and sacrificed many horses, hounds, and Trojans (some of whom were sons of Priam) in his friend's honor. Achilles also continued to drag Hector's corpse around until Apollo and Hermes intervened and insisted that Priam be allowed to offer a ransom for it. Priam offered its weight in gold, but Achilles again expressed his desire for Polyxena. Priam said Achilles

Ambassadors Sent to Achilles by Agamemnon in Order to Persuade Him to Fight,
Ingres, 1801.

island on which sacrifices could be made in Achilles' honor, and Thetis and the Muses mourned for more than two weeks before having Achilles' body burned on the eighteenth day. Funeral games were held in his honor, and his ashes were eventually mixed with those of Patroclus and placed inside the golden urn, crafted by Hephaestus, that Dionysus had given to Thetis and Peleus as a wedding gift.

There are many variations on Achilles' afterlife. In some versions it is suggested that he eventually was married to Helen, while in others he is unhappily confined in Tartarus. In other versions Thetis snatched Achilles' soul from his funeral pyre and took it to Leuce, near the mouth of the Danube. In any case, Achilles is best known as the greatest hero of the most celebrated of mythological wars.

. . . a prophecy concerning your son Achilles, who is now with Cheiron the Centaur and is fed by water-nymphs though he should be at your breast. When he comes to the Elysian Fields, it has been arranged that he shall marry Medea the daughter of Aeëtes . . .
—Hera, The Voyage of Argo,
Apollonius of Rhodes

could marry Polyxena only if he could convince the Greeks to leave without Helen, and paid Achilles the gold as a temporary measure.

As the battle continued, Achilles killed the Amazon Queen Penthesileia, although in some versions it is suggested that Penthesileia first slew Achilles, who was revived by Zeus at Thetis' request. When Thersites, a common Greek soldier, accused Achilles of having violated Penthesileia's corpse, Achilles struck him so hard that all of Thersites' teeth were broken and his ghost went directly to Tartarus. Achilles then went to Lesbos, where he made sacrifices to Apollo, Artemis, and Leto and was purified by Odysseus for the murder of Thersites.

Late in the war, Achilles was slain after he was struck by an arrow fired by Paris. In some versions it is suggested that Apollo steered this arrow, while in others it is claimed that Apollo actually assumed the shape of Paris and shot the arrow himself. The arrow struck Achilles in the ankle (his sole vulnerable spot), and Achilles howled in pain and suffered greatly before succumbing. A battle then raged over his corpse, and Ajax and Odysseus eventually rescued it for a proper burial.

After Achilles' death, his ghost made repeated visits to the Greek forces to remind them of his dying wish: that Polyxena be sacrificed on his tomb. In most versions, it is suggested that this was because Achilles' death was orchestrated by or somehow involved Polyxena, who might have revealed the secret of Achilles' vulnerable heel to Paris, who, with Deiphobus, murdered Achilles. Once the Trojan War had come to an end, however, the Greeks, particularly Agamemnon, were reluctant to spill any more blood. The spirit of Achilles paid visits to many of his allies, imploring them to make sure he received the tribute due him.

Agamemnon was being influenced by his mistress Cassandra, who was Polyxena's sister. Calchas and others agreed that Achilles' request could not be denied, and Neoptolemus served as priest at the sacrifice of Polyxena. There are some versions, however, in which the Greeks are depicted as having left Troy before being forced by Achilles' ghost to sacrifice Polyxena.

A great number of tributes were made to Achilles, even by those gods who had conspired to kill him. Poseidon offered up an

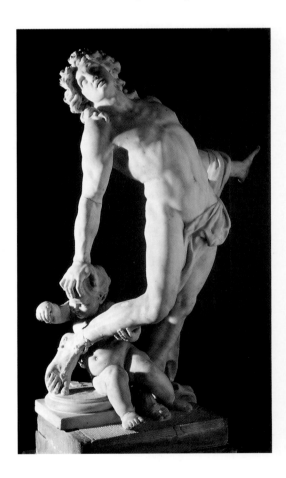

The Dying Achilles, **Christopher Veyrier, 1683.**

Acrisius A son of Abas and Aglaia who shared control of Argolis with his twin brother, Proetus, Acrisius married Aganippe, with whom he had a daughter, Danaë. An oracle had warned Acrisius that he would not sire any sons, but that a grandson would end his life. He then imprisoned Danaë to prevent her becoming pregnant, but Zeus "came upon her in a shower of gold" and impregnated her. Not believing that his daughter's condition was divinely brought about, Acrisius assumed that Proetus had fathered the child as part of the fight for control of their kingdom.

When Danaë delivered the child, Acrisius locked her and her newborn son, Perseus, inside a wooden ark and cast it into the sea. (They were rescued in due time.) Acrisius then fought Proetus to a draw, and they eventually agreed to split their kingdom in two.

Many years later, after Perseus had killed Medusa, Acrisius heard of his grandson's accomplishments and fled Argolis for fear that Perseus would seek revenge for the earlier treatment of Danaë. Unfortunately, Acrisius fled to Larissa, where Perseus had come to attend Polydectes' funeral games. When Perseus made an errant throw with his discus, it struck Acrisius in the foot, which caused complications that led to his death.

Actaeon The son of Aristaeus and Autonoë, Actaeon had the misfortune of accidentally seeing Artemis nude while she was

Achilles Kills Hector, Rubens, c. 1630.

bathing outside of Orchomenus. As punishment for this—no one but the nymphs of the valley was allowed to see the goddess naked—she turned him into a stag. Actaeon then ran off in a panic and was ripped to pieces by his own pack of hounds.

Admetus The King of Pherae who sought to marry Pelias' coveted daughter, Alcestis. Pelias declared that no one would be allowed to marry Alcestis unless they defeated him in a chariot race. Admetus, with the help of Apollo and Heracles, yoked a wild boar and a lion to his chariot to answer the challenge. Unfortunately, Admetus failed to include Artemis in his subsequent sacrifices, and on his wedding night Artemis punished Admetus by turning Alcestis into a twisting mass of hissing vipers.

Apollo aided Admetus a second time when he returned Alcestis to human form, with the stipulation that Admetus forfeit his life or arrange for one of his family members to take his place. When neither of Admetus' elderly parents was willing to take their son's place, Alcestis took the poison that had been

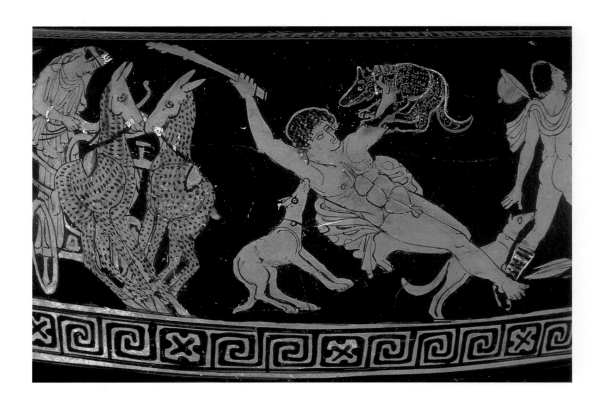

The Death of Actaeon, **red-figured krater, 5th century** B.C.

Actaeon, **Paul Manship, 1925.**

intended for Admetus and went to Tartarus, but Persephone, impressed with her actions, sent Alcestis back to the land of the living.

Some versions of this story have Admetus running away from Hades when he comes to take him to the underworld and Alcestis volunteering to take his place.

Admetus also participated in the hunt for the Calydonian Boar and, while still a prince, served aboard the *Argo.*

Adonis Aphrodite caused King Cinyras to lie with his own daughter, Smyrna. When Cinyras realized what he had done and went to kill the princess, Aphrodite turned Smyrna into a myrrh tree; the king split this tree in half, and Adonis emerged from the split. Aphrodite then concealed the baby boy in a chest and entrusted him to Persephone.

Eventually Aphrodite and Persephone came to fight over the handsome young Adonis' affections, and Zeus sent the Muse Calliope to decide the issue. Calliope ruled that each of the women should have access to him for one third of the year, and the remaining third would be Adonis' to spend alone. Persephone's dissatisfaction with Calliope's ruling, and her affection for Adonis, made Ares jealous. As a result, Ares turned himself into a boar and killed Adonis.

After Adonis' murder, Aphrodite became enraged, since he was now spending the entire year with Persephone. Aphrodite brought her complaint to Zeus, who ruled that Adonis' year would now be split in half; one part would be spent in the underworld, the other among the Olympians.

Adonis and Aphrodite conceived Golgos, the founder of Cyprian Golgi, and Beroë. And some say that it was Adonis, and not Dionysus, who was Priapus' father.

In alternate versions of Adonis' story it is suggested that his parents were Phoenix and Alphesiboea, and that he was actually killed by Apollo in the form of a boar.

Adrasteia
An ash nymph who was the sister of Io and the daughter of Melisseus, Adrasteia was one of the nymphs to whom Mother Earth entrusted the baby Zeus to be raised and protected from his father, Cronus. It was believed that obeisance before Adrasteia was a sign of humility and that Prometheus' failure to pay her the proper respect helped lead to his extreme punishment.

Adrastus
The King of Argos whose daughters, Aegeia and Deipyla, were widely courted by those wishing to share in his power. Adrastus interpreted a prophesy from the Delphic Oracle to mean he should choose Polyneices and Tydeus, each of whom had been banished from his respective homeland and had some claim to a throne. Adrastus promised to return each of them to his throne, beginning with Polyneices. Adrastus mustered together his four chieftains—Capaneus, Hippomedon, Amphiaraus, and Parthenopaeus—who in combination with his sons-in-law constituted the seven champions in Aeschylus' *Seven Against Thebes*.

Amphiaraus rightly foresaw that only Adrastus himself would survive the attack, during which Polyneices and Eteocles slew one another in singular combat and Amphiaraus fell into a gaping hole in the earth caused by Zeus. Adrastus escaped on the winged horse Arion, which had been given him years earlier by Heracles.

When Creon, the new ruler of Thebes, declared that none of the fallen Argives would be allowed a proper burial, Adrastus convinced Theseus to attack the city and punish Creon, whom he eventually imprisoned.

Later, when the sons of those slain at Thebes, collectively known as the Epigoni, set out to avenge their fathers' defeat, Adrastus' son Aegialeus was killed in the initial skirmish.

Teiresias the seer correctly predicted that Adrastus would die from grief upon hearing the news but that his passing would make way for the Epigoni's successful conquest of Thebes.

Aeacus
A son of Aegina and Zeus. Hera was so angered by Aeacus' birth that she cast a drought over Aegina's homeland of Oenone. Aeacus beseeched his father to rescue Oenone, which he did by repopulating the island with the Myrmidons.

Aeacus was a pious ruler and a great military commander. He named his kingdom Aegina, in honor of his mother, and made it nearly impregnable. Aeacus also assisted Apollo and Poseidon in the building of Troy's walls. In some versions it is suggested that this had to do with a prophesy that warned that Troy's walls would fall repeatedly unless a mortal participated in their construction. When the wall was breached for the first time, Apollo predicted that Troy would fall repeatedly, and that Aeacus' heirs would stand among the city's captors. (This was proven true when Telamon was among those who conquered the city in the Trojan War.)

Aëdon
The daughter of Pandareus who married Zethus and bore him only one child, a son named Itylus. Aëdon was jealous of her sister Niobe, who had many children, and attempted to kill Sipylus, the oldest. Instead, she accidentally killed Itylus and was transformed into a nightingale by Zeus.

Aeëtes
The son of Helius and Perse, Aeëtes became the King of Colchis. He first married Asterodeia, who bore him Chalciope and Medea, and later married Eidyia, with whom he conceived Apsyrtus. Among the treasures of Aeëtes' kingdom was the Golden Fleece, which had been shorn from the winged ram that Phrixus had ridden to Colchis. It fell to Aeëtes to decide whether or not Jason and the Argonauts might obtain the Fleece without a struggle.

When Jason arrived, he made a peaceful request for the fleece; Aeëtes not only dismissed this request, but threatened to cut out Jason's tongue and cut off his hands. Aeëtes then reconsidered, and suggested that Jason might earn the right to claim the Fleece were he to accomplish a series of seemingly impossible tasks.

Jason was aided in his efforts by Eros, who caused Aeëtes' daughter Medea to fall in love with him. Medea gave Jason potions that allowed him to accomplish the tasks assigned him by Aeëtes. When Aeëtes told Medea of

Venus and Adonis, **Titian, 1554.**

his intentions to renege on the deal with Jason, Medea alerted Jason and provided him with a potion to soothe the hundred-eyed dragon that guarded the Golden Fleece. Jason then escaped with both the Fleece and Medea.

In some versions, Aeëtes himself pursues the *Argo*. In these accounts, he is delayed when Medea murders his son Apsyrtus and tosses the butchered remains into the sea piece by piece, knowing her father will feel obliged to retrieve them all for proper burial. Other versions, however, suggest that Aeëtes remained in Colchis while Apsyrtus and others pursued the *Argo*. When word filtered back that Jason and Medea had made it safely back to Greece with the assistance of Aeëtes' enemy King Alcinous, Aeëtes spoke to all the Greeks, demanding that justice be served, but received no support.

Aeëtes remained king despite this affair, and ruled for more than a decade until his throne was usurped by Perses, who was most likely Aeëtes' brother. Shortly after this happened, Medea left Jason and worked her way home to Colchis with a son, Medeius. Upon their arrival, Medeius killed Perses and reestablished Aeëtes as King of Colchis.

[Aeëtes] has it in his power to be a deadly and relentless enemy. He claims to be a son of Helios; his Colchian tribesmen are innumerable; and his terrifying voice and powerful build might well be envied by the god of war himself. No, it would be no easy thing to take the fleece without permission of [Aeëtes], guarded as it is from every side by such a serpent, a deathless and unsleeping beast, offspring of Earth herself.
—Argus, The Voyage of Argo,
Apollonius of Rhodes

Aegeus

The eldest son of Pandion and Pylia, Aegeus succeeded his father to the Athenian throne despite his brother Lycus' claims that he was of illegitimate birth. Constantly fearful of plots against him, Aegeus exiled Lycus, and grew suspicious of his brother Pallas' fifty sons, whom he believed were intent on pressing their father's claims to his throne. Aegeus eventually ambushed them when their friendship with Minos' son Androgeus caused him to fear that Minos himself might become involved in their conflict.

Aegeus was married twice, first to Melite and then to Chalciope, but neither was able to provide him with a child. He went to the Delphic Oracle, which led him to visit his friend Pittheus in Troezen. Along the way he encountered Medea, who was on the verge of killing her sons by Jason. Unaware of her

intentions, Aegeus promised Medea protection in Athens and proceeded on his way.

When Aegeus reached Troezen, Pittheus made him drunk and allowed him to sleep with his daughter Aethra. Poseidon also had slept with Aethra, but he granted Aegeus paternity when it was learned that she was pregnant. When a son was born to Aethra, Aegeus kept his birth secret since he feared the plotting of his fifty nephews.

The child was named Theseus and was reared by Pittheus; the boy remained ignorant of the identity of his true father for some time. Meanwhile, Medea arrived in Athens, and Aegeus gave her refuge. In time, the two were married, and Medea subsequently bore Aegeus another son, Medus.

When Theseus, now full-grown, came to Athens, Medea tried to poison him to prevent him from claiming what she hoped Aegeus would pass along to Medus. Theseus survived and attempted to punish Medea for her actions, but Aegeus aided her escape.

The ambush of Pallas' sons took place around this time, and it counted Minos' son as one of its victims. In order to maintain a peace with Minos, Aegeus was forced to make yearly sacrifices to Minos' monstrous stepson, the Minotaur. Once Theseus arrived in Athens, however, Aegeus convinced him to try to put a stop to these tributes. Theseus was successful, but upon his return he forgot to fly the white signal flag that would inform his father of his success. When Aegeus saw a black flag flying on the ship as it approached port, he either fell or leapt into the sea that was eventually named for him. It is said that this tragic miscommunication was Ariadne's revenge on Theseus for having abandoned her after she had helped him overcome the Minotaur.

Aegina

A daughter of Asopus and Metope and the twin of Thebe, Aegina was carried off by Zeus, who then had his way with her. Her father, Asopus, caught up with them at a moment when Zeus was unarmed. Asopus rescued Aegina, but was seriously wounded (and lamed) by one of Zeus' thunderbolts for doing so, and Zeus ended up taking Aegina off to Oenone, where she became pregnant with Aeacus.

Aegisthus

The son of Pelopia, Aegisthus was conceived when his grandfather, Thyestes, raped Pelopia, his own daughter. After the rape, Thyestes fled, just as Atreus arrived in Sicyon looking for him. Believing Pelopia to be the daughter of the king at whose court she was in attendance, Atreus married her and

brought her back to Mycenae, where Aegisthus was born.

Because the child was conceived during the course of a rape, Pelopia (unaware that the rapist had been her father) abandoned her baby. The child was rescued by goatherds, for whom it was named (Aegisthus means "goat strength"), and was then reclaimed by Atreus, who believed it to be his own.

When Aegisthus was seven years old, Atreus had Thyestes imprisoned, and sent "his" son to kill his nemesis. But Thyestes escaped Aegisthus' attack and recognized the sword the boy held as the one he had left behind during his rape of Pelopia. Thyestes explained to Aegisthus his true parentage and sent him to bring Pelopia to him. Pelopia committed suicide when she learned the truth, and Thyestes then dispatched Aegisthus to kill Atreus.

After Thyestes was ousted from Mycenae, he took Aegisthus to Argos and the court of King Cylarabes. When Agamemnon and his allies set out for Troy, Aegisthus remained behind and sought to avenge his father's treatment by scheming with his ally Nauplius to enter into a relationship with Agamemnon's unhappy wife, Clytaemnestra. Aegisthus became Clytaemnestra's lover, and was well positioned to take control of Agamemnon's kingdom.

When the news came that Troy had fallen and Agamemnon was on his way home, Aegisthus and Clytaemnestra set the trap that resulted in the murder of Agamemnon. Aegisthus decapitated Agamemnon after Clytaemnestra entrapped him (in some versions she is credited with Agamemnon's murder), and Clytaemnestra then slew Cassandra.

Because Agamemnon was a hero of the Trojan War, his murder is often portrayed as one of the more heinous acts in the mythological canon. But Clytaemnestra's first husband had been killed by Agamemnon, and she herself had been taken as a spoil of that victory. In some cases, her brothers, the illustrious Dioscuri, are said to have been killed in their attempt to retrieve her. And Aegisthus' father's throne had been usurped by the very same man, with the help of Clytaemnestra's father. So while the murders of Cassandra and Agamemnon were by no means exemplary actions, they were not the greedy, cold-blooded atrocities they were implied to be in some Greek dramas.

Aegisthus reigned over Mycenae for seven years, although it is widely regarded that Clytaemnestra was the more forceful of the two. When Agamemnon's son, Orestes,

Orestes and Aegisthus, **red-figured krater, 5th century** B.C.

returned to avenge his father's murder, it seems that Aegisthus fell blindly into Orestes' trap. On the one hand, it is surprising that Aegisthus would be caught unaware, since it had been prophesied that if he went ahead with his plan to kill Agamemnon, Orestes would avenge his father's death. But on the other hand, in some versions it is suggested that Aegisthus killed a baby he believed to be Orestes, but who was in fact the son of a nurse who had replaced the royal infant with her own child.

Aegyptus One of the twin sons of King Belus and Anchinoë. Aegyptus and his brother Danaus quarreled over their father's kingdom, and Aegyptus eventually proposed the mar-

riage of his fifty sons to Danaus' fifty daughters. This story is the basis of Aeschylus' *The Suppliants,* in which Danaus' daughters, known collectively as the Danaids, flee to Argos instead of entering into marriages they consider unholy. (While some Hellenic tribes encouraged marriages between first cousins, the Danaids believed such unions improper.) Aegyptus sent his sons to Argos to retrieve their brides, which resulted in forty-nine of the fifty being slain on their wedding night. Upon hearing of his sons' fates, Aegyptus fled to Aroe, where he died.

Aeneas The son of Aphrodite and Anchises, the King of the Dardanians, Aeneas was the cousin of Priam, the King of Troy,

with whom he had cordial but strained relations. Aeneas accompanied Paris when he went to stay with Menelaus, whose wife, Helen, Paris hoped to seduce. Despite his role in Helen's abduction and his friend Achates' death at the hands of the Greeks, Aeneas remained neutral throughout the early years of the Trojan War.

Late in the war, Achilles led Greek troops on raids about Mount Ida and drove Aeneas and his army back to Lyrnessus. The Greeks conquered the city of Lyrnessus, but Aeneas managed to escape and was then willing to join the Trojan alliance. Aeneas' escape at this time, as well as a few other close calls, was aided by Olympians who sought to keep him safe. Because he was Aphrodite's son, Aeneas

Ulysses and Aeolus from The Ulysses Cycle, Alessandro Allori, 1560.

received help from a number of deities, some of whom knew of Aeneas' fate to father a royal line that would eventually rule Troy.

There are several variations on Aeneas' role in the fall of Troy; the most reliable account tells of Aeneas being taken captive by Neoptolemus and held for ransom, which the Dardanians promptly paid. Aeneas later fathered Ascanius, who would rule Troy. In those versions where Astyanax, the son of Hector, survived the fall of Troy, Aeneas agreed to let him serve as king on the condition that Ascanius would succeed him.

In the versions where Aeneas escapes during the fall of Troy, he is credited with tricking Odysseus and Diomedes into taking a false copy of the Palladium, a statue of Athene invested with great religious importance. Once the Greek forces departed, Aeneas took the genuine article to Italy. In some versions Aeneas carries his elderly father out of Troy on his shoulders, earning Agamemnon's respect and their freedom. It is usually agreed, however, that Aeneas lived to an old age and saw his heirs take control of Troy as the prophesies had suggested.

Despite his secondary role in Greek mythology, Aeneas became one of the most

famous characters in all of Roman mythology when Virgil chose to focus his epic, *The Aeneid*, on Aeneas' travels after his departure from Troy. Aeneas traveled southwest from Troy, stopping briefly at Drepane, where Anchises died. After Anchises' funeral rites were held, Aeneas again set sail, but was driven to Carthage, in northern Africa, by a storm. There he was welcomed by Dido, Queen of Carthage, who fell in love with him and became his mistress (because of manipulation by Venus and Juno). Eventually Aeneas resumed his journey, by order of Jupiter—the gods knew that Aeneas' destiny was linked directly to the future of Rome, and they did not want him to establish himself in the city destined to be Rome's enemy.

After leaving Carthage, Aeneas went to Cumae, from whence he visited the Sibyl and made a visit to the Underworld. Later, when he reached the mouth of the Tiber River, he became involved in a war with the Rutulians and eventually slew their leader, King Turnus. *The Aeneid* ends with this event, and does not mention other stories about Aeneas, such as the founding of Lavinium, his struggles against local peoples, and his disappearance in a storm.

> *I sing of arms and the man who, fated to be an exile, was the first to sail from the land of Troy and reach the coast of Lavinium in Italy. He suffered greatly on sea and land because of the anger of Juno, and he endured much in warfare, before he could build a city and install his gods in Latium. From him came the Latin race, the lords of Alba Longa, and the lofty city of Rome.*
> —The Aeneid, *Virgil*

Aeolus

The oldest of Hellen and Orseis' sons, Aeolus seduced and impregnated the prophetess Thea. Poseidon helped Thea hide her condition from her father, Cheiron, by turning her into a mare. When this mare dropped its foal, Poseidon transformed the foal into a baby. The daughter was named Arne, and given to Desmontes to raise.

Aeolus is also the name that Arne then gave to one of her twins, whose father was Poseidon. These children were abandoned by Arne's stepmother, Desmontes, but were rescued and entrusted to Metapontus and Theano. (Theano led Metapontus to believe that the boys were his sons.)

Theano eventually bore a pair of twins of her own and grew jealous when Metapontus continued to favor their adopted sons. When her true sons were fully grown, Theano convinced them to attack their stepbrothers, but Aeolus and his brother, Boeotus, slew them

first (in self-defense), bringing on Theano's suicide shortly thereafter.

Aeolus and Boeotus then set out to rescue their mother, Arne, who was being terribly mistreated by Desmontes. They killed Desmontes and brought Arne back to Icaria, where King Metapontus married her and adopted the twins. The marriage was not particularly successful, and Metapontus attempted to replace Arne with Autolyte. In the ensuing fight, Boeotus accidentally killed Autolyte, and the twins left the region.

Aeolus set sail and took possession of the islands that bear his name in the Tyrrhenian Sea. He made his home on Lipara and married Enarete, with whom he had twelve children. Growing up in isolation, his children (six boys and six girls), were unaware of the taboo against incest and indulged in sexual relations until their father learned what was going on. Canache, the eldest, committed suicide at her father's request, and the rest were separated geographically.

From his remote island chain, Aeolus became known as the Warden of the Winds, from which he controlled the seagoing breezes. When Odysseus escaped from the Cyclopes, he landed on the island of Aeolus, where he was entertained nobly for an entire month. On the last day of Odysseus' stay, Aeolus gave him a bag of winds to be used in case of emergency. Odysseus' crew opened it, blowing the ship back to Aeolus' island. Aeolus informed Odysseus that the gods had made it clear that no such help should have been given and that it was now up to them to use their oars to get home. As Aeolus was dying, Zeus decided that he didn't want him confined in Tartarus and set him upon a throne within the Cave of the Winds, where he remains for eternity.

Aerope

Most famous for being the mother of Agamemnon and Menelaus, with Atreus as the father. Aerope's father, King Catreus, banished her, most likely because of a prophesy that suggested that one of his children would take his life. Instead of killing her, Catreus was persuaded by Nauplius to sell Aerope and her sister Clymene to him as slaves. Nauplius treated them well, marrying Clymene and making it possible for Aerope to marry Atreus.

Though married to Atreus, it was, unfortunately, his brother, Thyestes, with whom Aerope was in love. When the brothers fought for control of Mycenae, Thyestes consented to lie with Aerope on the condition that she steal Atreus' golden-fleeced lamb for him. Aerope did so. (When Atreus' third marriage is discussed, it is mentioned that he had executed his previous wife, Aerope. It seems likely that her abetting Thyestes led Atreus to kill her.)

Aesacus

The son of Priam and Arisbe, daughter of the seer Merops, Aesacus learned how to interpret dreams from his grandfather. He also fell in love with Asterope, who died young. In his grief, Aesacus made repeated attempts to end his life by leaping off a cliff into the sea. The gods eventually took pity on Aesacus and turned him into a diving seabird, so that he could repeat the act endlessly.

Aeson

The son of Tyro and Cretheus, the founder of Iolcus. When Cretheus died, Aeson was the rightful heir to the Iolcan throne, but his stepbrother, Pelias, had other ideas. Pelias imprisoned Aeson and usurped his throne.

Pelias would have killed Aeson were it not for Tyro's intervention, but it was necessary for Aeson's wife, Polymele, to hide the birth of their son, Diomedes, who was taken from Iolcus to be raised by Cheiron the Centaur.

Aethra

The daughter of Pittheus, Aethra was set to marry Bellerophon until he was banished from their home and. Aethra remained a virgin even though it was apparent that Bellerophon was not coming back. Years later, when Pittheus' friend Aegeus complained that he had been unable to conceive any children, Pittheus arranged for Aegeus to lie with Aethra. Shortly after that Athene sent Aethra to the isle of Sphaeria where Poseidon overpowered and violated her. When Aethra realized she was pregnant, Poseidon conceded paternity of the child to Aegeus, who told

Aethra to keep the child's existence secret because his relatives might try to kill it.

The child born to Aethra was Theseus, who was raised by Pittheus and taught by Connidas. When Theseus kidnapped the young Helen, it was Aethra who cared for her. Several years later, when Helen ran off to Troy with Paris, she took Aethra with her. While in Troy Aethra was entrusted with the care of the child her grandson Acamas had fathered on Laodice. When Troy fell, Aethra managed to escape with the boy, Munitus, to the Greek camp, where Acamas and his brother Demophon recognized their grandmother and rescued her and Munitus.

Aetolus

The son of Endymion and Iphianassa, Aetolus accidentally killed Apis during a chariot race held at Arcas' funeral games for Azan. Aetolus was banished across the Gulf of Corinth, where he eventually killed Dorus and established his own kingdom, which he named Aetolia.

Agamemnon

The leader of the Greek forces in the Trojan War. While Agamemnon was regal in action and appearance, it is often suggested that the Trojan War would have been lost had it not been for the assistance he received from Odysseus, Athene, and others.

Agamemnon was the son of Atreus and Aerope, the grandson of Pelops, and the brother of Menelaus. When Agamemnon and Menelaus reached manhood they became allied with Tyndareus, the King of Sparta, who enabled them to defeat their uncle Thyestes and reclaim the throne he had taken from their father. Agamemnon, as the elder of the two brothers, now ruled the wealthiest of all royal houses and received tributes from kings throughout Greece. Agamemnon's first war involved a battle with Tantalus, the King of Pisa, who was a cousin. Agamemnon killed Tantalus, sacked Pisa, and claimed Tantalus' wife, Clytaemnestra (a daughter of Tyndareus), for himself. Clytaemnestra's brothers, the Dioscuri, then marched against Agamemnon and his Mycenaean troops and (in some versions) were killed.

Menelaus went on to marry Helen, Clytaemnestra's sister, though there are different explanations as to how their marriage came about. In some versions, Tyndareus was concerned about the reaction of those who would not win Helen's hand in marriage, and made all of the suitors vow to protect and defend whoever Helen's husband might turn out to be. Tyndareus then announced that Menelaus was his choice and abdicated the

Briseis Led to Agamemnon, **Giambattista Tiepolo, 18th century.**

Spartan throne to his new son-in-law, establishing Agamemnon and Menelaus as leaders of the Hellenic community.

After Paris seduced Helen and she ran off with him, Menelaus went to Agamemnon and demanded that they prepare for war. Agamemnon insisted that peaceful solutions be attempted; when those failed, and counterclaims demanding the return of Priam's sister Hesione were set, Agamemnon assembled all of those who had promised Tyndareus to defend the "lucky" suitor. Agamemnon was put in charge of the Hellenic land forces; Odysseus, Palamedes, and Diomedes became his lieutenants, and Great Ajax and Phoenix served similar positions under Achilles.

Fleets of Greek troops set out for Troy, only to be left floundering when the winds died. A prophecy proclaimed the need for Agamemnon to sacrifice a daughter if the Greeks wished to reach Troy under his command. Without the sacrifice, there would be no winds, and the fleet would not reach Troy. The alliance made it clear that Agamemnon's failure to sacrifice his daughter would result in his being replaced by Palamedes. A detail was sent back to Argos to trick Clytaemnestra into letting Iphigeneia go with them. Agamemnon tried to warn his wife of their intentions by sending her a secret message, hoping that she would not let Iphigeneia leave. Menelaus intercepted the message and Iphigeneia left Argos by sea. In many versions it is suggested that Iphigeneia was sacrificed, though there are several variations in which Artemis, or even Achilles, rescues her.

For the next decade, Agamemnon's role in the Trojan War is comparable to that of Zeus in most of mythology: he is omnipresent and involved to varying extents with nearly all aspects of the war. It is therefore nearly impossible to include descriptions of all of Agamemnon's activities during the course of the decade-long conflict.

One of the most noteworthy of the events Agamemnon was directly involved in was Achilles' temporary withdrawal from the Greek alliance, which occurred when Agamemnon was forced to return Chryseis to her father. Having lost his spoil, Agamemnon reclaimed Briseis, whom he had originally given to Achilles. This situation was eventually resolved when Achilles chose to return to battle for reasons of his own and not because of the many messengers Agamemnon sent to assuage his anger. Following Achilles' return to battle, Agamemnon sent Briseis back to Achilles with assurances that he had not slept with her.

As the Trojan War proceeded, Agamemnon was forced to respond to the demands of his troops, attacks by the enemy, and proclamations from a long list of seers and oracles. Agamemnon was told to obtain one of Pelops' bones, bring Neoptolemus to the battlefield, and steal Athene's Palladium, which was being safeguarded within the walls of Troy. In the end, it took Odysseus' Trojan Horse plan to defeat the Trojans.

Troy was pillaged and looted, its inhabitants raped and/or murdered. Agamemnon took the best of the city's spoils for himself, including Cassandra, one of Priam's daughters. In an attempt to endear himself to his new mistress, Agamemnon unsuccessfully attempted to prevent the sacrifice of Cassandra's sister Polyxena.

Another argument in the aftermath of Troy's fall revolved around Agamemnon's desire to make sacrifices to Athene. Others, Menelaus and Odysseus among them, wished to head for Greece as soon as possible, hoping to avoid yet another delay. Agamemnon, Diomedes, and Nestor made their sacrifices to Athene and enjoyed a safe and swift voyage home, while those who ignored Agamemnon's wishes were either greatly delayed in reaching Greece or never arrived there at all.

When word of Agamemnon's imminent arrival reached Clytaemnestra, she adorned herself to welcome her long-departed husband and trick him into a sense of security. Cassandra, Agamemnon's new mistress and a seer doomed to make accurate prophesies but not be believed, predicted their awaiting doom, but Agamemnon and the others failed to heed her words. Once Agamemnon entered his home, a net was cast over him and he quickly received two deadly blows with a sword; a third blow decapitated him. Aegisthus is usually credited with at least the first two thrusts, although in some plays it is suggested that these deeds were committed by Clytaemnestra.

Orestes and Electra, two of Agamemnon's

Agamemnon, gold funerary mask, 16th century B.C.

children by Clytaemnestra, eventually avenged their father's death by killing Aegisthus and their mother. Agamemnon's ghost went to Tartarus, where it eventually encountered Odysseus, who was still struggling to make it home nearly ten years after the fall of Troy. It was Agamemnon who warned Odysseus to keep his arrival home in Ithaca secret so that he might surprise the many suitors who were courting his wife, Penelope.

> So Agamemnon, rather than retreat
> Endured to offer up his daughter's life
> To help a war fought for a faithless wife
> And pay the ransom for a storm-bound fleet.
> —Chorus, Agamemnon, Aeschylus

> Low lies the kindly guardian of our State,
> Who fought ten years to win
> Redress for woman's sin;
> Now by a woman slain.
> —Chorus, Agamemnon, Aeschylus

> . . . with eyes and head like Zeus who delights in thunder, like Ares for girth, and with the chest of Poseidon; like some ox of the herd preeminent among the others, a bull, who stands conspicuous in the huddling cattle; such was the son of Atreus as Zeus made him that day, conspicuous among men, and foremost among the fighters.
> —The Iliad, Homer

Agave   A Maenad who was the daughter of Cadmus and Harmonia, and the mother of Pentheus. When Pentheus attempted to put an end to the revelry Dionysus had inspired on Mount Cithaeron, Agave was among those who attacked him and was personally responsible for wrenching off his head.

Agave later married Lycotherses, the King of Illyria, whom she eventually discovered was battling her father. Agave killed him as well, and handed control of his kingdom over to Cadmus.

Agelaus   The herdsman to whom Priam entrusted the infant Paris to be exposed on Mount Ida. The boy was suckled there by a bear for five days before Agelaus returned and retrieved him. In some versions it is suggested that the infant's mother, Hecabe, bribed Agelaus to spare the child and raise it himself.

Agenor   The husband of Telephassa (also known as Argiope) and the father of several sons—Cadmus, Phoenix, Cilix, Thasus, and Phineus—and Europe, a daughter who was beloved by Zeus. When Zeus carried Europe off, Agenor sent his sons to find her, and for-

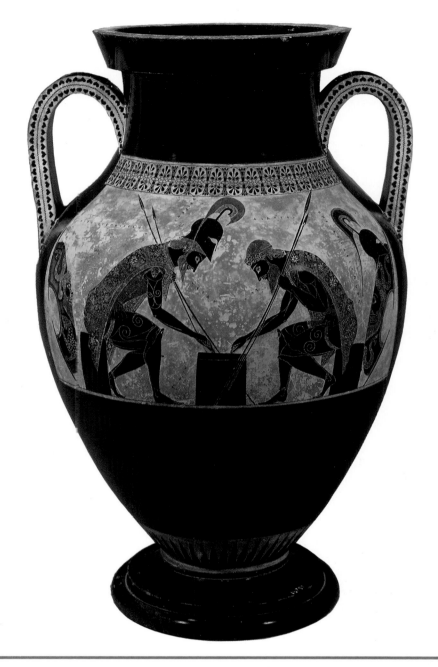

Ajax and Achilles Playing Dice, black-figured amphora, Exekias, 6th century B.C.

bade them to return without her. Europe never returned, and neither did the sons. Agenor might have been a twin brother of Belus, with Libya and Poseidon as their parents.

Aglauros   The eldest daughter of King Cecrops of Athens and Agraulos, and the sister of Herse and Pandrosos, Aglauros was entrusted by Athene with a basket containing the young Erichthonius, who was half-human, half-serpent. Later, Hermes bribed Aglauros to help him endear himself to Herse. When Aglauros did nothing to earn the gold she'd taken from Hermes, he turned her to stone.

After her death, Aglauros' mother and sisters peered into the basket Athene had given her and were so horrified by what they saw that they leapt to their deaths.

Agraulos   Wife of King Cecrops, by whom she bore Aglauros, Herse, and Pandrosos. After Hermes turned Aglauros to stone, Agraulos and her remaining two daughters looked into the basket Athene had entrusted to Aglauros. When they saw the half-man, half-serpent Erichthonius, the women screamed in fear and leapt to their deaths from their home on the Acropolis.

Another version has Agraulos leaping to her death in accordance with an oracle that suggested her doing so would save Athens, which was under attack at the time.

Aias   Another transliteration, used in many contemporary translations, of the names of the characters who are best known as Great Ajax and Little Ajax.

Ajax The name of two great warriors—Great Ajax and Little Ajax—who joined the Greek forces in the Trojan War. These two characters were unrelated, but were allies and are occasionally confused with one another. The son of Telamon and Periboea is the one who is usually referred to as Great Ajax. Although a more accurate translation of their name is Aias, Ajax is the name by which these characters are best known.

Great Ajax was born in Salamis, where it was said Heracles covered the newborn with his invulnerable lion's pelt, which suggests an explanation for the belief that Ajax's body, with the exception of his armpit and possibly his neck, was impervious to arrows. Eventually Ajax succeeded his grandfather, Alcathous, as the King of Megara. Great Ajax is described as standing head and shoulders above everyone else, and is said to have been second only to Achilles in courage, strength, and good looks. Ajax's impenetrable shield, made from the hides of seven bulls, was said to be able to deflect any projectile.

Despite his high rank in the Greek alliance—Ajax served as an assistant to Achilles, one of the few Greek leaders with whom he appears to have had a passable relationship—Ajax found himself at odds with its leaders. Ajax's disregard for authority also extended to the Olympians, whom he spoke of with callous disregard and whose advice and assistance he often declined due to his adherence, as a Lelegian, to a pre-Hellenic goddess that existed long before the upstart Olympians came to be worshiped. Ajax is often described as a self-obsessed, arrogant brute who showed great disregard for family as well as for those dependent upon him, such as his crews. Unlike Achilles or Diomedes, Ajax was not the beneficiary of any divine intervention.

When Ajax engaged Hector in an epic battle that eventually ended in a draw, Ajax recognized Hector's prowess (and vice versa), and the two exchanged gifts that would, ironically, play a role in the recipients' eventual deaths. When the fighting resumed, Ajax threw a huge stone at Hector, but Zeus revived him and invested him with enough strength to retreat to safety.

When Achilles withdrew from the fighting, Ajax replaced Achilles as the premiere warrior for the Greeks. It was Ajax who defended and rescued Patroclus' body with the help of Menelaus. And when Achilles himself was mortally wounded, it was Great Ajax who defended his corpse, killing Glaucus in the process and carrying Achilles' body through enemy forces with the help of Odysseus.

Aias and Achilles, detail of "François Vase," c. 570 B.C.

Ajax's rescue of Achilles' corpse was one of his finest deeds, but it also set the stage for his undoing. When Agamemnon decided to give Achilles' divine armaments, which Ajax thought should be awarded to him, to Odysseus and Menelaus, Ajax made plans to avenge himself upon all three. But when Athene, who favored the Greeks, learned of Ajax's intentions, she struck him with madness and caused him to "avenge" himself on a pair of white-footed rams he mistook for two of his three enemies. A third beast was bound to a pillar, flogged, and subjected to extensive verbal abuse.

When Ajax regained his senses and realized what he had done, he knew that he was bound to suffer the wrath of those he had "sacrificed." After this realization, Ajax called on Zeus to direct Teucer to his corpse and then attempted to take his own life by falling on his sword, but his impervious skin caused the sword to bend in the shape of a bow. (This was the sword that Hector had given Ajax following their battle.)

Ajax eventually realized that he could accomplish his goal by forcing the sword in through his armpit. Zeus led Teucer and Tecmessa to his body, but Menelaus announced that they could not give it a proper burial and that it must be left as carrion for the birds. Agamemnon eventually struck a compromise by allowing Ajax to be buried in a coffin (treatment given to suicides, victims of lightning strikes, and other unusual deaths) at Cape Rhoeteum, preventing the savaging of Ajax's remains but also denying him the honor of a cremation.

There are a handful of variations concerning some of the details of Ajax's undoing. In some versions it is suggested that Ajax and Odysseus fought over possession of the Palladium (a sacred statue of Athene) after the fall of Troy. In other versions it is claimed that Ajax did not commit suicide but that the

Trojans or, more likely, some of the Greeks, killed him with lumps of clay since he was impervious to steel. The use of clay in acts of murder—by blocking up one's respiratory functions—was thought by some to absolve them of the guilt associated with blood crimes. This would point to Greek conspirators since the Trojans would not be thinking in terms of blood guilt during the course of a war.

It is said that Achilles' weaponry might have been lost by Odysseus during his journey home, and that it eventually washed ashore at the foot of Ajax's tomb. During the reign of the Emperor Hadrian, it is said that waves caused Ajax's tomb to open. His bones were enormous in size, and it was said that his kneecaps were used as discuses. (Hadrian saw to it that Ajax's remains were reinterred in a safer place.)

It is worth noting that once Ajax's soul took up residence in the underworld, his was the only ghost who stood aloof from Odysseus during his visit to Tartarus.

Little Ajax, the son of Oïleus and Eriopis, was a Locrian and the half-brother of Medon. Despite his small stature this hero was considered to be the best spear-thrower among all of the Greeks, and was second in quickness of foot only to Achilles. Little Ajax was known for the linen corselet he wore, and for a tame serpent, longer than a man, that followed him about as if it were a hound. Ajax also was a high-ranking leader in the Greek alliance.

Little Ajax is best known for the events that transpired during the sack of Troy. He discovered Priam's daughter Cassandra, who was seeking refuge in the temple of Athene and guarding the Trojan Palladium, and took possession of both Cassandra and the icon. Agamemnon, however, made it clear that he desired Cassandra for his own, and Odysseus accused Ajax of having violated Cassandra in the temple. Calchas insisted that Athene be placated for this transgression, and Odysseus proposed that Ajax be stoned to death.

Little Ajax managed to escape, and quickly went to swear a solemn oath at Athene's altar that he had not committed such transgressions. (Cassandra herself never supported Odysseus' claims regarding the rape.) Ajax expressed his sorrow for removing the Palladium from Athene's sanctuary, promised to atone for his crime, and then set out for home. His ship was wrecked upon the Gyraean Rocks, and Ajax had nearly managed to reach shore when Poseidon struck his trident upon the rocks, causing Ajax to drown.

Little Ajax was buried on the island of Myconos, and his countrymen were instructed

Ajax Carrying the Body of Achilles, **black-figured amphora, Antimenes, 6th century** B.C.

to send a tribute of two girls to Troy each and every year for one thousand years to atone for Ajax's alleged violation of Athene's sanctuary (the alternative was famine and pestilence). The girls were required to spend one year as priestesses in Athene's sanctuary before returning home. It is estimated that if the Locrians had continued the tribute for its proscribed length, the last young girls would have returned from Troy some time in the middle of the third century B.C.

It is generally agreed that Ajax's "attack" on Cassandra was an Odyssean lie, and that, much like Great Ajax, Little Ajax was undone by Odysseus' treachery. Unfortunately, it is for this incident that Ajax is best remembered, despite ten years of vigilant service to the Greek alliance.

> . . . *when he had girt his body in all its armour, he strode on his way, as Ares the war god walks gigantic going into the fighting of men whom the son of Kronos has driven to fight angrily in heart-perishing hatred. Such was [Aias] as he strode gigantic, the wall of the Achaians, smiling under his threatening brows, with his feet beneath him taking huge strides forward, and shaking the spear far-shadowing.*
> —The Iliad, *Homer*

> *Swift Aias son of Oïleus led the men of Lokris, the lesser Aias, not great in size like the son of Telamon, but far slighter. He was a small man armoured in linen, yet with the throwing spear surpassed all Achaians and Hellens.*
> —The Iliad, *Homer*

Alalcomeneus
Alalcomeneus was one of many characters described as the first man to appear on earth, by Lake Copais in Boeotia. He was Zeus' counselor in his quarrel with Hera, and tutored the young Athene. The latter credit represents the patriarchal dogma that women were incapable of wisdom without it being imparted by a male figure.

Alcaeus
The son of Androgeus and the brother of Sthenelus, Alcaeus is thought by some to have been the son of Malis. Alcaeus was the founder of the Lydian dynasty, and was given the island of Paros by Rhadamanthys. When Heracles agreed to end his siege of Minos' kingdom, Alcaeus and Sthenelus became his slaves as a condition of the surrender.

Alcathous
One of Pelops and Hippodaemeia's more successful children, Alcathous eventually came to rule Megara. In

Death Scene from the Myth of Alcestis, from a sarcophagus, Hellenistic period.

some versions it is suggested that he won his throne by avenging the death of Megareus' son Euippus, who had been killed by the Lion of Cithaeron. In addition to being made Megareus' heir, Alcathous was married to the king's daughter, Euaechme. In other versions, however, Alcathous arrived in Megara shortly after Nisus had overrun and ransacked the city, leaving a veritable ruin which Alcathous then rebuilt.

Alcathous fathered Ischepolis, Callipolis, Iphinoë, Automedusa, and Periboea. When Callipolis heard the news of Ischepolis' death during the hunt for the Calydonian Boar, he flung his father's sacrifices from the altar in a gesture of mourning. Unfortunately, Alcathous had not heard the news regarding his eldest son's death and believed his son to have committed a truly impious act, for which he struck him dead.

Alcestis

The most beautiful of Pelias' three daughters, Alcestis was the sister of Evadne and Amphinome. When numerous suitors vied for Alcestis' hand, Pelias ruled that he would allow her to marry only the man who could yoke a wild boar and a lion to a chariot. Admetus, the King of Pherae, accomplished this task with the assistance of Apollo and Heracles.

On the wedding night, Admetus accidentally omitted Artemis from his prayers, a mistake for which the goddess turned Alcestis into hissing vipers. Apollo intervened on Admetus'

behalf and returned Alcestis to her original form, with the condition that Admetus would have to forfeit his life unless he could find a relative willing to die in his place. When Admetus' parents refused, Alcestis volunteered and committed suicide by drinking poison.

When Alcestis arrived in Tartarus, Persephone ruled that no wife should die in place of her husband and sent Alcestis back to the living. Other versions depict Admetus running away from Hades when it was his time to die, leaving Alcestis to volunteer to take his place; in these versions, Heracles rescues her after having completed his labors.

Alcinous

The King of the Corcyrian island of Macris, Alcinous was married to Arete. When Jason and Medea stopped in his kingdom during their escape from Aeëtes with the Golden Fleece, the Colchians asked Alcinous to turn Medea and the Fleece back over to them. Alcinous promised a ruling the next day, and told Arete that night that he would send Medea back if she were a virgin, but allow her to continue on with Jason if they had consummated their relationship. Arete favored the Argonauts and warned them of Alcinous' impending decision. That night Jason and Medea slept together. The next day Alcinous announced his decision.

Alcinous and Arete were the parents of Nausicaa, who offered refuge to Odysseus after his raft was destroyed by Poseidon. Alcinous heaped gifts upon Odysseus and provided him

with a first-rate ship for safe passage to Ithaca. Poseidon, who had spent the better part of a decade trying to prevent Odysseus from returning home, punished the crew of Alcinous' ship by striking the ship with the flat of his hand and turning it and the entire crew to stone.

Upon learning of the fate of the crew, Alcinous immediately sacrificed twelve bulls to Poseidon, who was now threatening the safety of Alcinous' two biggest harbors. Alcinous also swore to avoid such well-intentioned hospitality toward strangers in the future.

Alcmaeon

The son of Amphiaraus and Eriphyle, and the brother of Amphilochus, Alcmaeon was loath to join the Epigoni in their attempt to avenge their fathers' deaths. Like his father, Alcmaeon had to be convinced by Eriphyle (who had been bribed to do so) to lead an army against Thebes.

After the Epigoni conquered Thebes, Alcmaeon overheard Thersander's boasts of his role in the victory, including his bribery of Eriphyle (the original bribery had been accomplished by Thersander's father, Polyneices). Incensed, Alcmaeon consulted with Apollo, who agreed that his mother deserved to die. Unfortunately, Alcmaeon understood this agreement to indicate Apollo's approval of the act and personally murdered his own mother.

After a stop in Thesprotia, Alcmaeon went to Psophis, where Phegeus, the king of that land, purified him and gave him his daughter, Arsinoë, in marriage. But the

Erinnyes continued to hound Alcmaeon, and made Psophis barren.

Alcmaeon was then told to seek a second purification, this time from the river god Achelous, who subsequently gave Alcmaeon his own daughter, Callirrhoë, in marriage. After a year of marriage, Callirrhoë told her husband that he would not be admitted to her chambers again until he brought her the magic robe and necklace with which Eriphyle had been bribed, and which Alcmaeon had presented to his first wife, Arsinoë. So Alcmaeon returned to Psophis and told Phegeus and Arsinoë that he needed the gifts to give to Apollo to finally be rid of the Erinnyes' torment. One of Alcmaeon's servants revealed his master's true intentions, which led to Phegeus instructing his sons to kill Alcmaeon.

Arsinoë did not know the reason for her brothers' attack on her husband and would not believe them once they had explained. She cursed her brothers with a violent death; this curse was fulfilled by Alcmaeon's two sons by Callirrhoë, who had prayed to become fully grown within a day's time.

Alcmena

Also known as Alcmene, Alcmena was engaged to Amphitryon, whom Alcmena's father, Electryon, had left in charge of Argos while he went to fight the Teleboans and Taphians. Alcmena's eight brothers were killed in the fighting, and Amphitryon accidentally killed Electryon on his return, in an argument over compensation. Amphitryon and Alcmena fled to Thebes, where they were married. Alcmena made it a condition of Amphitryon's purification for the death of Electryon that he avenge the deaths of her brothers.

While Amphitryon was away on his mission of vengeance, Zeus impersonated him and lay with Alcmena for three dayless nights. Zeus' intention was to create a powerful mortal; the result was Heracles. When Zeus' wife, Hera, became enraged, Alcmena abandoned her newborn son. After Hera was tricked into suckling the infant Heracles (investing him with immortality), Alcmena reclaimed him and raised him along with her other son, Iphicles, whose father was Amphitryon.

When Eurystheus banished Heracles from Argolis, Alcmena accompanied him to Pheneus, but returned to Argolis after her son's apotheosis. When Eurystheus responded by expelling Alcmena and the Heraclids, a war ensued. (The Heraclids emerged victorious.) In some versions, Alcmena is said to have ordered Eurystheus' execution; in others she gouges the eyes from his severed head.

When Alcmena died, Zeus arranged for her to be taken to the Islands of the Blessed, where she was rejuvenated and married to Rhadamanthys, one of the three judges of the newly dead. In some versions, however, it is suggested that Alcmena and Rhadamanthys were married during the course of their natural lives.

Alcyone

The daughter of Aeolus and Aegiale, Alcyone was very happily married to Ceyx. When the two began calling one another Hera and Zeus, the real gods became angry and drowned Ceyx. Alcyone followed her husband into the sea, and both were subsequently transformed into kingfishers.

Aletes

The son of Clytaemnestra and Aegisthus, Aletes believed Oeax's rumor that Orestes and Pylades had been killed during their mission among the Taurians. As a result, Aletes assumed the Mycenaean throne, and was greatly surprised when Orestes returned alive. Orestes killed Aletes, which avenged his family's treatment at the hands of Aletes.

Aleus

A King of Tegea, Aleus was married to Neaera, with whom he conceived three sons, Cepheus, Lycurgus, and Amphidamas, and one daughter, Auge. Warned by an oracle that Neaera's brothers would die by the hand of a son of Auge, Aleus insisted that Auge remain chaste. Auge served as a priestess, but lost her virginity to Heracles. Auge became pregnant, a condition for which Aleus was ready to kill her. Instead, he gave her to King Nauplius to kill, but Nauplius sold her into slavery.

In some versions, Aleus is said to have locked Auge and her infant son into a sealed ark and cast them into the sea, at which point they were rescued by Nauplius.

The Aloeides

The name given to Otus and Ephialtes, the giant sons of Iphimedeia, who had been impregnated by Poseidon in an indirect way. These boys were later adopted by Aloeus, from whom they derived their name. At some point, the brothers swore to ravish Artemis and Hera, respectively, and declared war on Olympus. Their first step was to capture Ares, bind him, and hide him with their stepmother, Eriboea. (Ares was imprisoned in a bronze jar for thirteen months, until Hermes released him.) The Aloeides then began their assault on Olympus by piling Mount Pelion upon Mount Ossa, and attempting to pile both of these on top of Mount Olympus. This caused a great deal of concern among the

Zeus Visits Alcmena with the Help of Hermes, red-figured bell krater, Asteas, c. 350–325 B.C.

Olympians because a prophesy had stated that no other man, nor any gods, would be able to kill them.

During the course of their engagement, Otus received word from Artemis to meet at Naxos, but Ephialtes did not receive similar word from Hera. The two then fought over who would ravish Artemis first—Otus, because he had vowed to, or Ephialtes, because he was the oldest. In the fight that ensued, the Aloeides killed one another, relieving the Olympians of their siege.

As punishment for their actions, the Aloeides were sent to Tartarus, where they were bound with cords of living vipers and tied to a pillar atop which Styx sat to remind them of their unfulfilled oaths.

Alope

The beautiful daughter of King Cercyon, Alope was seduced by Poseidon and became pregnant, subsequently abandoning the son born of that union. When her father recognized the infant's swaddling clothes in the course of negotiating an argument between the two shepherds who had rescued the child, he imprisoned Alope and had the infant abandoned once again. The baby, who was named

Hippothous, was later rescued by one of the same two shepherds, and eventually took possession of Cercyon's Arcadian throne after he was deposed (and killed) by Theseus. Because of Theseus' ousting of Cercyon, the hero is thought to have ravished Alope and possibly to have been the true father of Hippothous.

In other versions, Alope dies in prison, where Poseidon, having been the cause of her problems in the first place, transforms her body into a spring that is then named for her.

Alpheius

A son of Thetis, Alpheius fell in love with Artemis, the virgin goddess. When Alpheius pursued her, Artemis and her nymphs muddied their faces so that he could not determine which one was the goddess. Confused, Alpheius departed, with the mockery of Artemis and her nymphs filling his ears. Alpheius also pursued Arethusa, a chase that ended in her transformation into a spring and his into a river.

Althaea

The wife of Oeneus and the mother of Toxeus and Meleager (whose father is sometimes thought to have been Ares), Althaea was told by the Fates that Meleager would survive only as long as one of her firebrands went unused, so she hid it so that her son might live a long life.

Once fully grown, Meleager participated in the hunt for the Calydonian Boar, after which he found himself fighting two of his uncles. Meleager killed these uncles and Althaea cursed him to lose in battle with her remaining two brothers and to be unable even to take up arms against them. Cleopatra eventually persuaded Meleager to defend himself, at which point the Furies reminded Althaea of the brand. She threw it into the fire, and Meleager was killed. Both Althaea and Cleopatra hanged themselves when they came to understand the repercussions of their actions.

Althaemenes

A son of Catreus, Althaemenes went with his sister Apemosyne to Rhodes when it was prophesied that he or one of his siblings would kill his father. When Apemosyne was violated by Hermes and reported this to Althaemenes, he responded by blaming her and kicking her to death.

Eventually, Althaemenes killed his father in a case of mistaken identity. When he learned what he had done, Althaemenes asked that he be swallowed up by the earth, at which time a wide chasm opened beneath him and ended his life.

Amaltheia

A goat nymph who suckled the infant Zeus in Crete while he was being hidden from his father, Cronus, Amaltheia helped care for the baby along with Adrasteia and a golden mastiff sculpted by Hephaestus.

One of many she-goats mentioned as being Pan's mother, Amaltheia was eventually set among the stars by a grateful Zeus once he had ascended to Cronus' throne. Her image was Capricorn, and it was one of her horns, borrowed by Zeus, that became the bountiful Cornucopia given to the daughters of Melisseus (Adrasteia and Io).

Amazons

A race of fearless female warriors who fought alongside, or against, the greatest mortal heroes. Daughters of Ares and the Naiad Harmonia (though Aphrodite or Ares' daughter Otrere is sometimes described as their mother), the Amazons worshiped their father as the god of war and Artemis as the goddess of virginity and female strength.

The Amazon civilization was a matriarchal society in which the women did the fighting and governing, the men were assigned household chores, and those male babies that were not killed outright were said to have had their arms and legs broken to incapacitate them. The Amazons' warlike ways contributed to a reputation for their having no regard for justice or decency.

The Amazons were originally based around the river Tanais, which was named for the son of Lysippe, one of their queens. From there, the Amazons expanded their empire, which eventually extended far into the west-

Battle of the Amazons, **detail of marble relief on a sarcophagus, 4th century** B.C.

The Battle of the Amazons, Rubens, before 1619.

ern Mediterranean landmasses. Troy fell to the Amazons, as did Syria. Also, the Amazons established such cities as Smyrna, Cyrene, Myrine, and Ephesus, the last of which was the site of the temple of Ephesian Artemis, one of the seven wonders of the ancient world.

The Amazons settled among the Caucasian Mountains near the River Mermodas in Asia Minor. There they allied with the all-male Gargarensians and allowed their young to mingle once each year, enjoying "promiscuous intercourse" to repopulate both communities. In some versions it is suggested that male babies born to the Amazons were not killed or mutilated, but were given to the Gargarensians, while all female newborns remained with the Amazons.

There were actually two different tribes known as Amazons; the second resided along the southern edge of the Mediterranean in Libya. It was this Amazon tribe that Dionysus allied with in Egypt to fight the Titans and restore King Ammon to his throne. They were successful, but when Dionysus returned years later the Amazons fought him and were defeated. Some sought refuge in the temple of Artemis, while others were slaughtered at Panhaema on Samos. Heracles also encountered these Amazons while crossing over to the Iberian peninsula on the way to his tenth labor.

The Libyan Amazons were led by Myrine, who led her armies to victories against the people of Atlantis, Lesbos, Samothrace, and

Thrace. The Amazons added the tribe of Gorgons (not to be confused with Medusa and her sisters) to their list of conquests, but were so busy celebrating the victory that they failed to notice that the three thousand Gorgons they were holding as prisoners had retrieved their weapons. A massacre of Myrine's followers took place, but Myrine herself escaped.

Some descriptions of Libyan Amazon encounters with Heracles tell of his prisoners escaping to Asia Minor, seeming to suggest that these refugees then became the ancestors of the other group of Amazons.

. . . the Amazons of the Doeantian plain were by no means gentle, well-conducted folk; they were brutal and aggressive, and their main con-

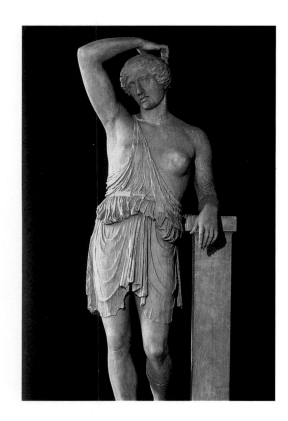

Wounded Amazon, **Roman copy after Greek sculpture, Kresilas, 5th century B.C.**

cern in life was war. War, indeed, was in their blood, daughters of Ares as they were and of the Nymph Harmonia, who lay with the gold in the depths of the Acmonian Wood and bore him girls who fell in love with fighting.
—The Voyage of Argo, *Apollonius of Rhodes*

Amphiaraus

An Argive who participated in the hunt for the Calydonian Boar, Amphiaraus blinded the Boar with an arrow near the culmination of the hunt. He is also listed as one of the Argonauts, but does not figure prominently in their voyage.

Amphiaraus married King Adrastus' sister, Eriphyle, and proved reluctant when asked to join his brother-in-law's attack on Thebes. Amphiaraus rightly foresaw that only Adrastus would return alive, but was eventually coerced to participate by his wife, who had been secretly bribed by Polyneices, whose throne the warriors were hoping to reclaim.

Amphiaraus attempted to escape when it was apparent that the battle was lost, and was about to be killed when his chariot fell into a crack that Zeus had thunderbolted into the earth alongside the river Ismenus. Amphiaraus subsequently reigned, alive among the dead, along with his charioteer, Baton.

Amphilochus

A son of Amphiaraus and Eriphyle, Amphilochus was the brother of Alcmaeon. Because their father, Amphiaraus, had been one of the champions who had marched on Thebes in Adrastus' ill-fated assault, Amphilochus was anxious to join the Epigoni and avenge the loss of his father; Alcmaeon, however, was reluctant. Amphilochus attempted to convince his brother to join them, and the two eventually agreed to defer to their mother, Eriphyle, who had been bribed to tell the brothers that they should join the Epigoni. Years later, when Alcmaeon learned of this bribery, he killed his mother.

Amphilochus also participated in the Trojan War, after which he traveled by land to Colophon with Calchas, Podaleirius, and others. Calchas died there, and Amphilochus and Mopsus jointly founded a city, which they named Mallus, in Cilicia. Amphilochus went on to found yet another city, but returned after a year with the expectation that Mopsus would allow him to resume his role as co-ruler. The two fought and referred their grievance to the Mallians, who suggested a battle to the death. This battle resulted in the deaths of both men, whose funeral pyres were placed so that their spirits could not exchange any unpleasantries during their cremations.

It is said that the souls of the two combatants became friendly as the smoke from the pyres intermingled. A common oracle was established for the two of them, and it quickly came to be known as the most truthful of all such shrines.

Amphion

Twin brother of Zethus, Amphion was born to Antiope after she was seduced by Zeus. Embarrassed by the situation, the twins' uncle, Lycus, abandoned them on Mount Cithaeron, where they were discovered by cattlemen who decided to raise them.

One day their mother, unknown to them, came to their home seeking refuge from Lycus' wife, Dirce, who mistreated her greatly. When Amphion and Zethus were finally made aware that Antiope was their mother, they killed Dirce by tying her (by her hair) to the horns of a wild bull.

The twins eventually expelled Laius from Thebes, and built the lower city. Amphion married Niobe, and the two conceived a great number of children (as many as fourteen). When Niobe belittled Leto for having given birth to only two children, Apollo and Artemis repaid Niobe's insults with the slaughter of nearly all of her children. Amphion took vengeance on the gods' Delphic priests and was killed by Apollo and then cruelly punished in Tartarus.

Amphitrite

A Nereid who became known as a sea goddess because of her marriage to Poseidon, whose courtship she initially spurned. After running off to the Atlas

The Salt Cellar **(Poseidon and Amphitrite), Benvenuto Cellini, 1540–1544.**

Amphitrite, Max Klinger, late 19th century.

Mountains, Amphitrite was approached by Poseidon's messengers One of those messengers, Delphinus the dolphin, eventually convinced her to return with him, and she married Poseidon, with whom she had three children: Triton, Rhode, and Benthesicyme.

Amphitryon

The nephew of Electryon, the King of Troezen, Amphitryon served as regent in Mycenae while Electryon was off in battle. (Amphitryon was also engaged to Electryon's daughter Alcmena at that time.) During his brief rule, Amphitryon paid a ransom to regain cattle that had been stolen from Electryon. When the king returned and learned that Amphitryon had paid for what was already his, an argument ensued. Amphitryon threw his club in anger at one of the cows. The club ricocheted off the cow's horn, striking and killing Electryon. For this, Amphitryon was banished to Thebes, where he was followed by Alcmena.

In Thebes, Amphitryon was purified by Creon, who then asked him to rid the land of the Teumessian Vixen. Creon then requested that Amphitryon battle his enemies, the Teleboans and Taphians. In this fight Amphitryon was allied with Cephalus. Their cause was aided by Comaetho, the daughter of the Teleboan King Pterelaus, who fell in love with Amphitryon. She killed her own father to win Amphitryon's favor, which helped Amphitryon's forces prove victorious, but was condemned to death for committing patricide.

Despite all of these adventures, it is for his role as the adoptive father of Heracles that Amphitryon is best known. While Amphitryon was off fighting the Teleboans, Zeus impersonated him and lay with Alcmena in order to create a great mortal who had the power to defend the Olympians from the giants. When Teiresias the seer told the real Amphitryon what had transpired in his absence, he vowed never to touch his wife again for fear of incurring Zeus' jealousy.

Amphitryon helped rear Heracles and was treated as if he were the boy's actual father. Amphitryon taught Heracles the art of chariot driving, while others instructed him in their own specialties. When Heracles was still a youth, he killed a teacher who treated him harshly; Amphitryon grew concerned about the boy's powers and sent him to live on a cattle farm until he was eighteen.

Amphitryon died while fighting the Minyans (a fact that makes his presence in Euripides' *Heracles* quite remarkable). Despite his death, Thebes prevailed, with a great deal of help from Heracles.

> *Is there a man living who has not heard of me—*
> *Amphitryon of Argos, whose bed welcomed*
>   *Zeus?*
> *Son of Alcaeus, grandson of Perseus; and father*
> *Of Heracles. I have lived there in Thebes ever*
>   *since*
> *The crop of Sown Men sprang full-grown out of*
>   *the earth . . .*
>   —Amphitryon, Heracles, *Euripides*

> *Do not be vexed, Amphitryon, it is you I count*
> *My father, not Zeus*
>   —Heracles, Heracles, *Euripides*

Amycus

The brother of the Bebrycan King Mygdon, who was killed by Heracles during the course of his ninth labor, Amycus, a son of Poseidon, assumed his dead brother's throne and led the Bebrycans to victory over Lycus after Heracles' departure.

During the course of his rule, Amycus extended his kingdom to the river Hypius, near which the *Argo* stopped on its way to Colchis. Amycus, who took great pride in his boxing skills, challenged the Argonauts to put forth their best fighter, Polydeuces. Their bout was a long, closely contested struggle, until Polydeuces struck Amycus with an impressive flurry of punches that ended with a series of fatal blows. The Argonauts routed Amycus' troops, who sought to avenge their leader's death, and then sacked Amycus' palace before resuming their journey.

> *'Listen, sailormen, to something you should*
> *know. No foreigner calling here is allowed to*
> *continue his journey without putting up his fists*
> *to mine. So pick out your best man and match*
> *him against me on the spot.'*
>   —Amycus, The Voyage of Argo, *Apollonius*
>   *of Rhodes*

Amymone

One of the Danaids, Amymone had the misfortune of stumbling upon a satyr in the woods one day. The satyr attempted to molest her, but she was rescued by Poseidon. Amymone's father, Danaus, in hope of ending a drought in Argos, had specifically asked his daughters to ingratiate themselves to Poseidon; Amymone did so and bore the god a son, Nauplius.

Amyntor

The father of Astydameia, whom Heracles sought to marry. When Amyntor refused the proposition, Heracles killed him and carried Astydameia off and fathered Tlepolemus on her.

Amyntor was also the father of Phoenix, whose mother was Cleobule. Amyntor punished Phoenix for having violated Phthia by blinding him and cursing him to remain childless for the rest of his life.

Anchises

The son of Capys and Aegesta, Anchises, the half-brother of Aegestes and the grandson of Ilus, became the King of the Dardanians. After Zeus caused Aphrodite to fall in love with Anchises, the two lay together on Mount Ida. Anchises did not realize she was a deity until after they had slept together; once he discovered her identity, he was quick to boast. Zeus aimed one of his fatal lightning bolts at him, and Aphrodite deflected it. The bolt struck Anchises a glancing blow and rattled him so badly that he was never able to stand fully upright again. Aphrodite eventually gave birth to Aeneas but lost her passion for Anchises and went on to take other lovers.

Androgeus

The son of Minos and Pasiphaë and the winner of each and every contest in the All-Athenian games. Because of Androgeus' resulting popularity and his friendship with Pallas' rebellious sons, King Aegeus grew concerned. Looking to avoid a threatening alliance, the king ambushed Androgeus at Oenoë. Androgeus fought valiantly, but was eventually overcome; Minos later prayed to Zeus to avenge his son's death, and the god responded by bringing down a plague of earthquakes and famine on all of Greece.

In some versions it is suggested that Androgeus was killed by Poseidon's white bull before Theseus captured it.

Andromache

The wife of Hector, Troy's most valiant defender. When Hector was killed near the culmination of the Trojan War, Andromache was claimed by Neoptolemus as a spoil of war.

Andromeda

The daughter of King Cepheus of Joppa and Cassiopeia. When Cassiopeia boasted that both she and Andromeda were more beautiful than the

Perseus Rescuing Andromeda, **Pierre Puget, 1684.**

Nereids, Poseidon moved to avenge the insult by sending a sea monster to attack Philistia, the capital of Joppa. When Cepheus was informed by an oracle that the only way to save his kingdom was by sacrificing Andromeda to the monster, he chained her to a rock to await her death.

Andromeda was rescued by Perseus, who was returning home with Medusa's head. Perseus promised to marry her, and Andromeda insisted on an immediate wedding, which led to a battle between her savior on one side and her parents and Phineus, the man to whom she had been engaged, on the other. Perseus killed many of Phineus' men and turned the rest to stone by showing them Medusa's severed head. When Poseidon placed Cepheus and Cassiopeia's images among the stars, Athene responded by

Aeneas' Flight from Troy Carrying His Father Anchises, **Carle van Loo, 1729.**

Hercules and Antaeus, **Antonio Pollaiolo, 1470s.**

Antaeus A Libyan King and the half-brother of Busiris, the King of Egypt, Antaeus was reputed to be the son of Poseidon and Mother Earth. Antaeus forced strangers to participate in wrestling competitions, and killed them. He saved the skulls of his victims, sustained himself on lion meat, and slept on the hard ground to keep strong.

In time, Heracles came along and challenged Antaeus to a wrestling match. When Heracles finally realized that Antaeus' secret strength was that he was revived whenever he came into contact with the ground, the hero held Antaeus up in the air until his strength waned. He then cracked Antaeus' ribs and held him aloft until he died.

Anteia The daughter of Iobates, Anteia (also known as Stheneboea) was originally married to Proetus. When Bellerophon came as a supplicant to Proetus' court, Anteia fell in love with him; when he spurned her advances, she accused him of seducing her and demanded that her husband kill him. Fearful of killing a guest, Proetus sent Bellerophon to Anteia's father, King Iobates, who eventually learned the truth. Anteia's fate after the revelation is unclear.

Antenor The brother-in-law of Priam and an intermediary between the Trojans and Greeks during the negotiations for Hesione. It was with Antenor that Menelaus, Odysseus, and Palamedes stayed when they came to request the return of Helen from Priam, and it was Antenor who dissuaded Priam from immediately killing Agamemnon's "messengers."

Later, Priam sent Antenor to negotiate a peace with Agamemnon. Antenor then helped the Greeks obtain the Trojan Palladium, a prized statue of Athene, in return for their promise to give him half of Priam's treasure and to set him up as the new King of Troy.

Once the Trojan Horse was brought within the walls of Troy, Antenor lit the signal beacon atop Achilles' tomb to inform the Greek troops in hiding that it was time to return. Antenor then reentered the city and gave word to the Greeks inside the Trojan Horse that it was safe to emerge.

Antenor and his family were allowed to go free, and were provided passage aboard Menelaus' ship. They eventually settled on the coast of the Adriatic, and Antenor came to rule a group of refugees whose king, Pylaemenes, had fallen at Troy. He led them to victory over the Euganei in northern Italy, where Antenor took control of a city he renamed New Troy, but eventually changed to

placing Andromeda's in a more honorable constellation.

Anius The illegitimate son of Apollo and Rhoeo, Anius was born after his mother, who had been cast out to sea by her father, was rescued by Rhadamanthys.

Anius married Dorippe, with whom he conceived three daughters, Elais, Spermo, and Oeno. During a visit to Delos, Dionysus granted each of Anius' daughters the ability to create basic staples with a prayer and a touch. Elais could turn anything into oil, Spermo corn, and Oeno wine.

At the onset of the Trojan War, Agamemnon caught wind of Anius' daughters' abilities and sent Menelaus and Odysseus to request their services. Blessed with prophetic powers by Apollo, Anius correctly predicted that it would be ten years until the fall of Troy, in which case they might as well stay with him for nine years before proceeding on. Odysseus and Menelaus chose to ignore Anius' prophesy and kidnapped his daughters. Dionysus, angered by the treatment given those whom he had endowed with special powers, turned the sisters into doves, in which form they became known as the Winegrowers.

Venice. It is possible that Antenor founded Padua as well.

Anticleia

The daughter of Autolycus, and the mother of Odysseus by Sisyphus, whose sole motive for laying with Anticleia was to avenge himself on her father. Anticleia was dead by the time Odysseus visited Tartarus during his long journey home from Troy. The two spoke together, and Anticleia brought Odysseus news from home but purposely avoided telling him about Penelope's many suitors.

Antigone

The daughter of Oedipus, and the sister of Eteocles, Polyneices, and Ismene, Antigone figures prominently in a number of Greek tragedies.

Following the suicide of their mother, Iocasta, and the banishment of their father, Antigone and her sister, Ismene, were entrusted to Creon. When he declared that none of Thebes' attackers, including Polyneices, were worthy of proper burial, Antigone defied him and buried her brother herself. Creon then sent his son Haemon, to whom Antigone had been engaged, to bury her alive in her brother's tomb as punishment. Instead, Haemon secretly married her and the two conceived a son, whose existence was kept secret. Years later, Creon recognized a mark on the child and had him killed, despite Heracles' attempts to stop the murder. As a result, Haemon killed Antigone and then himself.

In Sophocles' play *Antigone*, she is executed for her defiance, and her betrothed, Haemon, takes his own life shortly thereafter. Sophocles portrays Antigone as a woman who is as obsessed with her martyrdom as she is with ensuring that her brother receives a proper burial.

> *"No woman," they say, "ever merited her doom less, none ever was to die so shamefully for deeds so glorious as hers. When her own brother had fallen in bloody strife she would not leave him unburied to be devoured by carrion dogs or by any bird: does she not deserve the meed of golden honor?"*
>
> —Haemon, Antigone, *Sophocles*

Antilochus

The son of Nestor and either Anaxibia or Eurydice, Antilochus was exposed on Mount Ida following his birth. The infant was suckled by a bitch and was eventually raised by his father. Relatively young when Nestor left for the Trojan War, Antilochus grew to manhood during his father's absence and eventually set out for Troy to join the Greek forces, despite Nestor's objections.

Achilles was particularly impressed with the youth and argued in his defense; Nestor gave his consent on the condition that he be allowed to appoint Chalion as the boy's guardian.

Antilochus was one of the youngest, swiftest, and most handsome and courageous of all the Greeks, and he quickly endeared himself to his allies. Nestor had been warned that an Ethiopian would take Antilochus' life; this turned out to be Memnon, who initiated an attack on Nestor. Antilochus came to his father's defense and died as a result. Achilles immediately avenged Antilochus' death by killing Memnon.

> *Antilochus was the first to kill a chief man of the Trojans. . . . Throwing first, he struck the horn of the horse-haired helmet, and the bronze spear-point fixed in his forehead and drove inward through the bone; and a mist of darkness clouded both eyes and he fell as a tower falls in the strong encounter.*
>
> —The Iliad, *Homer*

Antinous

The most shameless and ill-behaved of the one hundred twelve suitors for the hand of Penelope. When Odysseus returned to Ithaca, he first entered his home disguised as a beggar. All of the suitors abused him, but none worse than Antinous, who threw a footstool at Odysseus. When Irus, a real beggar, challenged Odysseus to a boxing match, Antinous put up the prizes for the winner.

Odysseus returned the next day and proved his strength by stringing his huge bow, a feat that none of the other suitors had been able to accomplish. Now ready to reveal himself, Odysseus made an impossibly difficult shot through the rings of a dozen ax handles, then sent his next arrow straight into Antinous' throat.

Antiope

Daughter of Nycteus and Thebe, Antiope fled to the kingdom of Sicyon after being seduced by Zeus. The Sicyon King married her, which led to a war between him and Nycteus. Antiope's father was killed in the fighting, but her uncle Lycus led the Theban forces to victory and brought Antiope back home. There Antiope gave birth to Amphion and Zethus, whom Lycus and his wife, Dirce, exposed on a mountain.

The infant twins were rescued by cowherds and raised to manhood. Antiope, cruelly mistreated by Dirce, eventually escaped and sought refuge with her sons. When Dirce came and took Antiope away, their adoptive father revealed to the boys that Antiope was

Jupiter and Antiope, van Dyck, c. 1617–1618.

Venus and Cupid, Lamert Sustris, c. 1560.

their mother. Amphion and Zethus then freed Antiope and killed Dirce by tying her to the horns of a bull by her hair.

There are other versions of Antiope's story in which her father is said to be Asopus, and in which she is seduced by the King of Sicyon disguised as Lycus, to whom Antiope was married. As a result of this seduction, Lycus divorced Antiope and married Dirce. The twins carried out their murder of Dirce in a manner similar to that described above, and Dionysus avenged her death by sending Antiope raging madly about. In this version, Phocus cured Antiope and married her.

Aphidnus
After Theseus abducted the young Helen, he entrusted her to Aphidnus, an old friend. Together with Theseus' mother, Aethra, Aphidnus raised Helen to maturity. When Helen was rescued by her brothers, the Dioscuri, Aphidnus somehow avoided their wrath and remained Helen's adoptive father.

Aphrodite
The goddess of desire, Aphrodite was conceived when Cronus threw Uranus' genitalia into the sea. Aphrodite rose naked from the foam and stepped ashore at Cythera. Grass and flowers sprang up wherever her feet touched the earth, and the Seasons clothed her. There are more conventional descriptions of Aphrodite's conception and birth, but in most accounts, Zeus is described as Aphrodite's adoptive father and the concept of her watery birth is maintained. (The goddess of desire's connection with water may be one reason seafood has been considered an aphrodisiac.) As a goddess, Aphrodite had only one divine duty: to make love and to inspire others to do so as well.

Aphrodite was desired by all and had her choice of partners. She was also the patroness of smithcraft and the mechanical arts and was married to Hephaestus, the most famous craftsman of all. Her three children—Phobus, Deimus, and Harmonia—were, however, fathered by Ares, the god of war, with whom Aphrodite was having an affair. Hephaestus grew jealous of his wife's adulterous relationship with Ares, and set a trap for the two of them. Once he had them caught in his net, Hephaestus summoned all the gods to pass judgment. In the end, the gods denied Hephaestus' requests for punishment; most of the female deities refused to take part and the males were swayed by Aphrodite's beauty. She "thanked" Hermes for his help by sleeping with him and bearing Hermaphroditus.

Even Zeus, her adoptive father, was attracted to Aphrodite, but he exhibited rare self-restraint. Instead of consummating his desire, Zeus punished Aphrodite for arousing him by making her fall in love with the mortal Anchises, with whom she eventually conceived Aeneas.

When King Cinyras boasted that his daughter Smyrna was more beautiful than Aphrodite, the goddess punished him by causing him to sleep with Smyrna. The result of this union was the conception of Adonis. As Adonis grew to be a beautiful youth, Aphrodite fought with Persephone over the young man's affections. In the end, Adonis ended up spending one half the year with Persephone and the other half with Aphrodite, with whom he conceived Golgos, Beroë, and perhaps Priapus.

Aphrodite, despite casually causing jealousy in others, was not immune to it herself. When she caught Ares in bed with Eos, she cursed her lover with a constant longing for young mortals. When the Sirens refused to yield their virginity to either mortals or gods, Aphrodite is said to have turned them into birds. And when Teiresias judged Cale, one of the Charites, more beautiful than Aphrodite, the goddess turned Teiresias into an old woman.

When Eris instigated a fight by causing Aphrodite, Athene, and Hera to argue about which of them was the fairest, Paris was brought in to judge. Each of the three goddesses attempted to bribe him. Paris liked

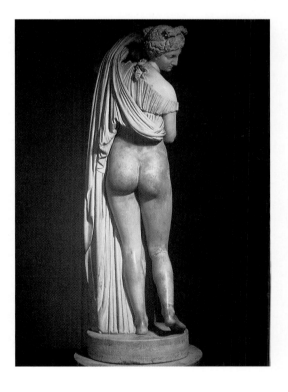

Aphrodite Callipyges, **Roman copy after Greek original, 5th century** B.C.

Venus Asking Vulcan for Arms for Aeneas, van Dyck, c. 1630.

Apollo A great and powerful deity, Apollo is one of the leading figures in all of mythology. The illegitimate son of Zeus and the twin brother of Artemis, Apollo played a prominent role in a host of famous tales. He was the son of Leto and Zeus, who had coupled in the form of quails and conceived twins. Hera hounded Leto, who eventually found refuge on the island of Delos, where the delivery of Apollo on Mount Cynthus was assisted by his nine-day-old twin sister.

Apollo matured with astonishing rapidity and quickly became involved in Olympian affairs. He became best known for his oracles, his interest in music, and his interest in diseases. Apollo never married, but took an endless series of lovers, upon whom he fathered many sons. Apollo assisted a great number of mortals in response to the involvement of other deities.

After Apollo, Hera, and Poseidon led the Olympians in a failed revolt against Zeus, Apollo and Poseidon were made to serve as bond servants in the hire of the Trojan King Laomedon. Their primary task in his employ was the construction of a wall around the city of Troy. Poseidon built the walls with Aeacus' help while Apollo played his lyre and fed the flocks. Apollo also predicted that Aeacus' sons would be among the captors of Troy.

The reference to Apollo playing the lyre while Poseidon worked on the wall reflects Apollo's patronage of music and his pride in his own abilities. Apollo had obtained this lyre as compensation for cows the young Hermes had stolen from him. Hermes, the inventor of this particular kind of lyre, also gave Apollo a musical pipe he had invented in exchange for a golden staff. Apollo pitted his skills against those of the satyr Marsyas, who had gained renown after finding a charmed flute of Athene. The contest was a close one until Apollo challenged Marsyas to duplicate on the flute what the god played on his lyre. When Marsyas lost, Apollo flayed him alive and nailed his skin to a tree.

Apollo and Artemis were quite protective of their mother and were often involved in her defense. When Niobe bragged that she had more children than Leto, Apollo and Artemis killed all but two of Niobe's children; and when Tityus attempted to violate Leto in a sacred grove, Apollo killed him with Artemis' assistance.

Quite often, Apollo's name arises in connection with the many lovers he took and the

Aphrodite's bribe—a promise to make Helen fall in love with him—and judged her the most beautiful. A related myth details Aphrodite's anger at the Spartan King Tyndareus, who had neglected her in his sacrifices. She punished him by causing the marriages of his three daughters—Helen, Clytaemnestra, and Timandra—to end in adulterous discord.

In gratitude for Paris' support, Aphrodite caused her son Eros to guide Paris to Greece and Tyndareus' daughter Helen, and set into motion the final steps leading to the Trojan War. Aphrodite rescued Paris from Menelaus during a duel; she was subsequently wounded by Diomedes when the battle resumed.

> *. . . when Aphrodite finds the orchard gate*
> *Pushed wide, and sweet, ripe bodies there,*
> *she makes it known, Till every man that passes,*
> *sick with longing, aims*
> *Heart-melting glances at such virgin loveliness.*
> —Danaus, The Suppliants, *Aeschylus*

> *Great is my power and wide my fame among*
> *mortals and also in heaven; I am the Goddess*
> *Cypris: All men that look upon the light of the*
> *sun, all that dwell beneath the Euxine Sea and*
> *the boundaries of Atlas are under my sway: I*
> *bless those that respect my power, and disap-*
> *point those who are not humble toward me.*
> —Aphrodite, Hippolytus, *Euripides*

Apollo Among the Shepherds, Gottlieb Schick, 1806–1808.

children those relationships produced. On Mount Oeta, Apollo scared off the Hamadryads and lay with Dryope, conceiving Amphissus in the process. He fathered, among others, Philammon on Chione, Corybantes on Thalia, Mopsus on Teiresias' daughter Manto, Miletus on Aria, Aristaeus on Cyrene, and Linus on Psamanthe.

Apollo also was the first god to romance a member of the same sex, when he fell in love with a beautiful young Spartan prince named Hyacinthus, who was also the object of others' affections. When it became clear that Apollo would win the boy's affections, the West Wind (one of the other suitors) responded by blowing a discus Hyacinthus had thrown back into his skull, killing him. Where Hyacinthus' blood fell, flowers sprouted from the ground and were named in his honor.

There were also several occasions when Apollo's romantic interests were not consummated. Apollo pursued a mountain nymph named Daphne who was rescued by Mother Earth just as the god was about to catch her. Apollo duelled with Idas over Marpessa until Zeus intervened and asked Marpessa to choose. Marpessa selected Idas and wisely explained that she knew if she chose Apollo he was sure to eventually abandon her for someone else. After having become Coronis' lover, Apollo found out about her relationship with Ischys. While Apollo killed Ischys, Artemis went after Coronis. Artemis killed Coronis, but Hermes was able to save her unborn child, Asclepius.

Apollo's role as Asclepius' father relates to his involvement with the art of medicine. Apollo frequently brought plagues upon communities that had displeased him, and also often cured the afflicted. When Apollo's jealousy of Orion (for having slept with Eos) caused him to trick Artemis into striking Orion dead, Asclepius attempted to revive him. Hades complained to Zeus, since Asclepius was taking victims away from him, and Zeus responded by slaying Asclepius. In revenge for Asclepius' death, Apollo killed the Cyclopes, for which Zeus wanted to banish Apollo to Tartarus forever. Leto pleaded in Apollo's defense and convinced Zeus to reduce his punishment to a year of hard labor in the service of King Admetus.

Apollo served Admetus humbly, and helped him win Alcestis as his wife. Apollo also participated in numerous conflicts, and played a prominent role in the Olympian defense against the giants. Despite the unpleasant dealings Apollo had had with the city's previous king, Laomedon, Apollo supported the city of Troy against the Greeks.

Minerva and Arachne, **Tintoretto, 1579.**

Apsyrtus

The son of Aeëtes, the King of Colchis, and his second wife, Eidyia, Apsyrtus was Medea's half-brother. In some versions it is suggested that when Jason and Medea stole the Golden Fleece and escaped in the *Argo*, Medea brought her brother along. When Aeëtes pursued them, Medea killed Apsyrtus and butchered him, throwing the pieces of his body into the sea one at a time, knowing that Aeëtes would stop to retrieve each of them for proper burial.

In other versions of the Argonauts' adventures, it was Apsyrtus who chased the *Argo*, which he caught up with in Brygia. When the local king arranged a truce to decide the fate of Medea and the Fleece, Apsyrtus was tricked by his sister into breaking that truce. This led to Jason killing Apsyrtus.

Arachne

A princess of Colophon whose skills as a weaver surpassed even those of Athene, Arachne was the winner of a weaving contest with the goddess. Fearing Athene's wrath, Arachne hanged herself, after which the goddess turned her into a spider and the noose into a web. Arachne scuttled up the web and escaped further wrath.

Areiopagus

A council of important magistrates that constituted the sole voice of the Athenian justice system, the Areiopagus was named for the court of deities that Ares assembled to prosecute Poseidon's son Halirrhothius for his rape of Ares' daughter Alcippe. The mortal Areiopagus continued to meet on the Hill of Ares, where it passed judgment on the city's most important cases.

Ares

The only son born to Zeus and Hera (though Hephaestus may also have been born to these two), Ares became the god of war, a deity who loved battle and conflict for its own sake. There are some versions of Ares' birth in which he is said to have been conceived by Hera when she touched a flower (some flowers were credited with a propensity for miraculous conceptions). Ares did whatever possible to incite war and turmoil, and was probably the most single-minded of all the deities. The strength of his sole focus made him sufficiently important to be established as one of the twelve ruling Olympians.

Ares never married, but he fathered a number of children on a variety of gods and mortals. Ares' greatest love was Aphrodite, with whom he had an ongoing affair despite her marriage to Hephaestus. After Hephaestus caught the lovers in a trap, the affair seems to have ended.

Despite his love of warfare, Ares was not strategically inclined, and he occasionally met with defeat. Athene defeated him twice (suggesting a link with two victories for Athens over the stronghold of Ares' worship, Thrace), and Aloeus' gigantic sons managed to imprison the god of war until Hermes learned of his predicament and liberated him.

Ares did not have a great number of allies, even among the Olympians. Hades was supportive of him since the wars Ares instigated kept him supplied with souls. Ares was often accompanied by his twin sister, Eris, the goddess of discord, and by his twin sons, Deimus and Phobus, whose names mean "panic" and "fear," respectively.

Although Ares always sought to settle things by force, he was forced into litigation over the death of Poseidon's son Halirrhothius, who had been trying to violate Ares' daughter Alcippe when the god of war struck him dead. Poseidon assembled a jury on the hill that bore Ares' name, and from which the highest court in the land, the Areiopagus, derived its name. In their first case, this court absolved Ares of any blood guilt.

Ares' name is invoked in nearly every mythological battle. He is said to have sided with the Trojans during their war with the Greeks, although his allegiance to any faction was never as great as his dedication to keeping such wars going. Having Ares' support in battle rarely guaranteed victory; it usually suggested only that a great deal of bloodshed would precede the outcome.

In Roman mythology, Ares is called Mars. Because the Romans were more warlike than the Greeks, he holds a more important position within the Roman pantheon than within the Greek. Mars is the father of Romulus and Remus, who were conceived after the god raped Rhea Silvia, and was said to have guided the young to emigrate from the Sabine cities and found new towns.

The best-known myth revolving around Mars concerns his involvement with Anna Perenna, a Roman goddess of the wood. When Mars fell in love with Minerva, he asked Anna to serve as intermediary between himself and the virgin goddess. Knowing that Minerva would never involve herself in a love affair with Mars, Anna disguised herself as the goddess at an evening rendezvous. When Mars recognized Anna Perenna, he became infuriated and berated her soundly.

"Nay, cease from this," she added, "rather let her win a mortal marriage and see her son fall in war, after vying with Ares in the might of his hands, and with the lightnings in the speed of his feet."

—Themis, Isthmian Odes, *Pindar*

Argonauts
The name given to the crew of the ship *Argo*, which was specifically constructed for Jason's quest to retrieve the Golden Fleece.

Argus
The earth-born, hundred-eyed herdsman assigned by Hera to watch over Io after the goddess turned her into a cow because of her affair with Zeus. Hermes was sent by Zeus to kill Argus, which he did by crushing him with a boulder after charming him with his flute. Hera honored Argus for his faithful service by placing his eyes in the tail of the peacock.

There was also a mortal named Argus who is best known as the builder of the *Argo*. This Argus also served as one of the Argonauts, and when the crew wished to appease Rhea, he carved her image and the crew offered prayers and sacrifices before traveling on. Wounded during the Argonauts' escape from Colchis, Argus was healed by one of Medea's potions.

Argus also was the name of Odysseus' faithful hunting hound who died of excitement when he recognized the disguised Odysseus upon his return from Troy.

Ariadne
A daughter of Minos and Pasiphaë, Ariadne had three siblings: a brother, Deucalion, a sister, Phaedra, and a half-brother, the Minotaur. After falling in love with Theseus when he came to slay the Minotaur, Ariadne gave him a magic ball of thread that would prevent him from getting lost within the Labyrinth. Theseus killed the Minotaur and rescued Ariadne, with whom he quickly escaped. When the ship stopped at the island of Dia (which later became known as Naxos), Ariadne was left behind.

While it is suggested in some versions that Theseus had taken a new mistress (possibly Aegle), or that there was concern about the scandal Ariadne's arrival in Thebes would cause, in others it is suggested that Dionysus caused Theseus to abandon Ariadne since he married her immediately thereafter. The marriage to Dionysus was a fruitful one, resulting in the births of Oenopion, Thoas, Staphylus, Latromis, Euanthes, and Tauropolus.

Different versions have Theseus outwrestling a humanized version of the Minotaur in the form of a general named Taurus, or defeating Ariadne's brother Deucalion after he succeeded Minos. In these versions it is suggested that Ariadne either died during childbirth on Dia or hanged herself; all versions state that Ariadne's death was caused by Dionysus, who was angry at her and Theseus for having lain together in one of his sacred groves.

Remember Ariadne, young Ariadne, daughter of Minos and Pasiphae, who was a daughter of the Sun. She did not scruple to befriend Theseus and save him in his hour of trial; and then, when Minos had relented, she left her home and sailed away with him.

—Jason, The Voyage of Argo, *Apollonius of Rhodes*

Mercury About to Slay Argus, Giacomo Amigoni, 1730–1732.

Sleeping Ariadne, **marble statue, c. 240** B.C.

Aristaeus
A son of Apollo and Cyrene, brother of Idmon, and half-brother of Diomedes. Hermes served as midwife at Aristaeus' birth, and Mother Earth fed and nurtured the child. Apollo himself instructed Aristaeus in his mysteries, while a group of nymphs taught him the culinary arts. Cyrene taught him the art of hunting, which Aristaeus went on to perfect on Mount Othrys. Once Aristaeus was grown, the Muses married him to Autonoë, a union that resulted in two children: Actaeon and Macris.

Aristaeus eventually settled in Tempe, where he became concerned when all of his bees (a powerful religious symbol) sickened and died for no apparent reason. Aristaeus' aunt, Arethusa, told him to capture and bind the seer Proteus to discover the reason for this. Proteus told him that it was because he had attempted to ravish Eurydice, who had been bitten by a serpent and killed when she tried to run away, before he had married Autonoë. To atone for this, Aristaeus made sacrifices to the Dryads and to Orpheus, Eurydice's husband, after which he was able to live the rest of his life in peace.

Arne
The daughter of Poseidon and Euippe (the name used for Thea in her horse form), Arne was originally delivered in the shape of a foal because her parents had coupled in the forms of horses. When the gods transformed her into a human infant, she was named Arne and entrusted to Desmontes. Once Arne was fully grown, Poseidon seduced and impregnated her. When Arne claimed that Poseidon was the father, Desmontes blinded and imprisoned her. Arne eventually delivered twins, which her stepmother exposed on Mount Pelion. These twins, Aeolus and Boeotus, survived, and later freed Arne.

There was also a princess named Arne who turned Siphnos over to Minos, who was avenging Androgeus' murder in Athens. Minos bribed Arne with gold, but she was unable to help because she was transformed by the gods into a jackdaw that was forever attracted to things that glittered.

Arsinoë
The daughter of King Phegeus of Psophis, Arsinoë was married to Alcmaeon when, after having killed his own mother, he came to Phegeus for purification. Despite his purification, the Erinnyes continued to torment Alcmaeon, causing him to continue his travels. He returned a year later, claiming that he needed the magic robe and necklace he had given Arsinoë to placate Apollo. When Phegeus learned that Alcmaeon actually wanted these artifacts to give to his new wife, Callirrhoë, the king dispatched Arsinoë's brothers to kill Alcmaeon, which they did. Unaware of their reasons for killing her husband, Arsinoë cursed her brothers to suffer violent deaths within the next phase of the moon. For this, Phegeus sold his daughter as a slave to the King of Nemea.

Artemis
The divine personification of the moon, Artemis represented and shared many of that celestial body's qualities. These aspects were eventually made manifest in her depiction as a chaste goddess who was the patroness of hunters, childbirth, fishermen, and unmarried girls.

Artemis and Apollo were the children of Leto and Zeus. Zeus' wife, Hera, cursed Leto to never deliver her children in the light of day, so it was not until Leto took refuge in a cave near Delos that Artemis was finally born. Nine days later the precocious youth aided her mother in the delivery of her late-arriving twin, Apollo. (This reflects her role as goddess of childbirth; also, women who died during delivery were said to have been killed by her arrows.)

Artemis' involvement with a wide variety of mythological characters revolves mostly around her chastity. When Actaeon was caught watching her bathe, she turned him into a stag that was then ripped to shreds by his own pack of hounds. When Alpheius fell in love with her, she disguised herself amongst her nymphs and drove him off by mocking him. And when Brontes the Cyclopes got too friendly with her she ripped from his chest a patch of hair that never grew back.

Artemis' connection with chastity also manifests itself in a wide range of stories in which young women are sacrificed in her name. And Artemis' belief in virginity was not limited to herself; she required perfect chastity of her companions, mostly nymphs. When Zeus seduced one of them, Callisto, Artemis turned her into a bear, whose image Zeus eventually set among the stars.

Artemis' role as a lover of the hunt is first described in the account of her childhood encounter with five enormous red female deers, of which she captured four. (The fifth went on to become the Ceryneian Hind.) Her love of the hunt also led to her friendship with Orion, another great hunter. When Apollo grew jealous of this friendship (possibly even fearful for his sister's virginity), he tricked Artemis into killing Orion. Artemis later set Orion's image among the stars. Artemis also hunted with her half-sister, Britomartis, another renowned female hunter, whom she deified

Artemis, bronze statue, c. 330–320 B.C.

after Britomartis gave her life to avoid losing her virginity to Minos.

When Artemis sent the Calydonian Boar to repay Oeneus for his failure to include her in his yearly sacrifices, she also saw to it that the hunt for the beast began under bad auspices and resulted in a good deal of murder and tragedy among Oeneus' family.

Revered, revered, hallowed daughter of Zeus,
hail Artemis, hail maiden of Leto and Zeus,
most beautiful of maidens by far. You dwell in
heaven in your noble sire's hall, in the house of
Zeus bedecked with gold. Hail most beautiful,
most beautiful of maidens in Olympus, hail
Artemis!
—Huntsmen, Hippolytus, *Euripides*

Ascalaphus

Hades' gardener, Ascalaphus testified that he had seen Core (Persephone) eat seven pomegranate seeds during her stay in Tartarus, and thus prevented her from completely escaping the underworld. Core's mother, Demeter, punished Ascalaphus by pushing him down into a hole and covering it with an enormous rock. Heracles eventually freed Ascalaphus during his visit to Tartarus, but Demeter responded by turning the former gardener into a short-eared owl, which was considered a bird of evil omen.

Asclepius

The son of Apollo and Coronis, Asclepius was either taken from his mother's dead body or abandoned by her on Mount Titthion. He was raised by Cheiron the Centaur, and learned the arts of healing and surgery and the use of drugs. He was considered the founder of medicine.

In the course of his experiments, Asclepius shared with Athene the blood of Medusa, which could be used either to raise the dead or to destroy life. Among Asclepius' patients was Heracles, who came to Asclepius in Eleusis to be healed after Hippocoön's sons wounded him. Asclepius is said to have resurrected a number of mortals, including Lycurgus, Capaneus, Tyndareus, Glaucus, Hippolytus, and Orion.

Asclepius and Hygieia (a daughter)
Feeding a Snake, funerary relief, 2nd
century B.C.

When the gods complained about Asclepius' actions, Zeus struck him dead with a thunderbolt. Asclepius was then brought back to life, which fulfilled Euippe's prophesy that he would become a god, die, and then reclaim his godhead.

But when, from flesh born mortal,
Man's blood on earth lies fallen,
A dark, unfading stain,
Who then by incantations
Can bid blood live again?
—Chorus, Agamemnon, *Aeschylus*

Asopus

The most prominent of the river gods, Asopus is usually believed to be the son of Oceanus and Tethys, though Poseidon and Pero, and Zeus and Eurynome, are also mentioned as his parents. Asopus married Metope, with whom he had two sons and anywhere from twelve to twenty daughters.

One of Asopus' daughters was Aegina, whom Zeus carried off. Asopus went in search of his daughter, and bribed Sisyphus for information concerning the whereabouts of Zeus and Aegina. With Sisyphus' help, Asopus was able to surprise Zeus unarmed and rescue Aegina from him. Zeus turned into a stone to avoid the spear Asopus threw at him, and it was this stone that eventually formed the basis for Sisyphus' eternal torment.

Shortly after rescuing Aegina, Asopus was struck by one of Zeus' well-directed thunderbolts and nearly killed. Asopus moved slowly ever after because of the injuries he sustained in this attack.

Asterius

The son of Tectamus and one of Cretheus' daughters, grandson of Dorus, and reigning King of Crete, Asterius married Europe after Zeus had fathered three sons by her: Minos, Rhadamanthys, and Sarpedon. Since Asterius and Europe never had children of their own, he adopted her sons and raised them as his own (Minos eventually assumed the Cretan throne).

Asterius is also the name of a giant, son of Anas, who ruled Caria along with his father before Miletus' arrival. Asterius was also another name for the Minotaur.

Astyanax

The son of Hector and Andromache, Astyanax was an infant at the time of the fall of Troy. Fearful of any heirs that might grow to avenge Hector's death, Odysseus insisted on systematic annihilation of all Priam's descendants. Calchas confirmed the need to kill Astyanax in particular since he foresaw that the child would avenge the loss of his parents and their city if he were allowed to reach manhood.

The specifics concerning Astyanax's death are uncertain. In some versions Odysseus tosses the infant from Troy's battlements, while in others Neoptolemus, who had claimed Astyanax's mother as a spoil of war, whirled the child by his foot and flung him onto the rocks. There are also versions in which Astyanax is old enough to leap to his own death upon hearing Calchas' pronouncements.

There are some versions of the fall of Troy in which Astyanax is said to have survived and become the King of Troy following the departure of the Greeks. Astyanax was overthrown by Antenor, but reclaimed his throne with the help of Aeneas, whose son Ascarius eventually succeeded Astyanax.

Astyoche
A name given to a number of different characters. The first Astyoche is a Danaid who had an affair with Pelops and subsequently gave birth to Chrysippus, who was eventually kidnapped by Laius. In some versions, Astyoche is the name of the daughter of Priam who married Telephus.

In yet other stories, Astyoche is named as the daughter of King Phyleus who is taken by Heracles as a spoil of war and upon whom he fathers Tlepolemus. There is also an Astyoche who married Erichthonius and bore Tros. Astyoche is also the name of one of Laomedon's daughters.

Atalanta
A daughter born to Clymene and Iasus, Atalanta was a great disappointment to Iasus, who had been hoping for a boy. This disappointment was so great that Iasus had the child exposed on the Parthenian Hill near Calydon. The infant was suckled by a bear and grew up among hunters. When she went to participate in the hunt for the Calydonian Boar, some men threatened to boycott the hunt if Atalanta were allowed to participate; Meleager nonetheless ruled in her favor.

Atalanta fought alongside Meleager, and she struck the Boar with one of her arrows as it charged Telamon and Peleus. Once the Boar had been vanquished, Meleager awarded its pelt to Atalanta. This act caused great controversy not only because his claim that she had drawn first blood was a dubious one, but because Meleager was a married man.

After the hunt, Atalanta was recognized by her father, Iasus, on the condition that she marry. Atalanta agreed to wed, but stated that anyone who wished to marry her must first beat her in a foot race (losers would forfeit their lives). After several suitors gave their lives in

Atalanta and Hippomenes, Guido Reni, c. 1620.

the effort to win Atalanta's hand, Melanion (also known as Hippomenes) enlisted the aid of Aphrodite, who provided Melanion with three golden apples that he dropped as he ran. Atalanta stopped to retrieve them, which delayed her long enough for Melanion to win the race and right to marry her.

One day Melanion convinced Atalanta to lie with him within Zeus' precinct, which angered the god greatly. Zeus turned them both into lions. Some say that Atalanta had been unfaithful to Melanion when she lay with Meleager, although it is possible that this happened before her marriage. The result of Meleager and Atalanta's union was Parthenopaeus, who was abandoned on the same hill on which Atalanta had been exposed, and survived in much the same way.

Athamas
The King of Orchomenus, Athamas was first married to Nephele, the cloud woman who was created in Hera's image to trap Ixion. It was at Hera's command that Athamas married Nephele, upon whom he fathered Phrixus, Leucon, and Helle. Athamas then fell in love with Ino, with whom he conceived Learchus and Melicertes. Nephele complained to Hera, but Ino's control led to

Athamas' decision to sacrifice Phrixus. Heracles intervened on Zeus' behalf and saved Phrixus.

While married to Ino, Athamas was entrusted with young Dionysus by Persephone, and asked to rear the child secretly. When Hera learned of Dionysus' existence she punished Athamas and Ino by driving them insane. This caused Athamas to mistake his son Learchus for a stag and kill him.

Dionysus blinded Athamas temporarily so that Ino could escape safely with Melicertes. When Athamas was eventually banished from Boeotia, an oracle told him to settle wherever wild beasts shared their dinner with him, which happened on the Thessalian Plain, where a pack of wolves shared their mutton with him. Athamas, who had regained his sanity shortly after Ino's departure, adopted his grandnephews Haliartus and Coronea and founded the city of Alos. It was said that Athamas again remarried, taking Themisto as his third wife, and raised a new family in Alos.

Athene
In the Pelasgian myths it is suggested that Athene was born beside Lake Tritonis in Libya, where she was nurtured by three nymphs. The identity of Athene's father is

uncertain; Zeus, Poseidon, and Itonus are all mentioned as potential fathers. The official version proposed by Athene's priests suggested that Zeus lusted after Metis, and forced himself upon her, after which it was prophesied that Metis would deliver a girl, but that any boy born to Metis by Zeus would grow to depose his father. Zeus responded to this prophesy by swallowing Metis. Shortly thereafter, he developed a headache, which led to Hermes fetching either Hephaestus or Prometheus. One of these characters then breached Zeus' skull and Athene sprang out fully armed.

Athene's interests and skills were many. She is credited with having invented the flute, trumpet, earthen pot, plow, rake, ox yoke, horse bridle, and chariot, as well as certain kinds of ships. She first taught the science of numbers, and was the patroness of the "womanly arts" (including cooking, weaving, and spinning). She was also the goddess of war and was often responsible for determining the fates of individuals engaged in combat. Despite these duties, she received no pleasure from battle and could be merciful; in fact, she often sought peaceful solutions to potentially violent situations.

Athene had a friend named Pallas, a girl with whom she often sparred. One day, the goddess accidentally killed Pallas with her spear; in memory of this friend, Athene put Pallas' name in front of her own, and because of this is often referred to as Pallas Athene. There are also some versions in which Pallas is said to have been a winged, goatlike giant who was Athene's real father; when he tried to violate her, Athene stripped his skin and took his wings. When Athene's warlike aspect was most prominent she was often referred to as Pallas.

Athene aided many of the causes nearest to Zeus' heart, and often came to take sides in matters in which Zeus himself could not, even though he might have wished to. Athene helped trick Hera into suckling the infant Heracles, and she was later helpful to the hero during the course of his labors. Athene favored the Argonauts and aided them throughout their voyage.

Athene was the only deity to stand her ground when Typhon attacked Olympus. Athene mocked Zeus for having run away and forced him to confront the monster in a battle that nearly cost him his throne. Athene was also at odds with Medusa the Gorgon, and helped Perseus when he was sent to retrieve her head. Perseus managed to decapitate Medusa, and eventually presented Athene with the Gorgon's head.

Athene was modest and took no lovers,

although her allegiances in mortal affairs were often based on romantic attachments. She was vain, but guarded her privacy. When Teiresias accidentally saw her bathing she blinded him, but compensated for that by giving him prophetic skills. Hephaestus was the only male who dared to try to violate her, and that was at the instigation of Poseidon. When Hephaestus attempted to force himself upon her, Athene pulled away at the last minute and his seed spilled upon her thigh. Athene wiped it off and tossed down the rag she had used in disgust. Through this act, Athene managed to impregnate Mother Earth with Hephaestus' seed; the result was the birth of Erichthonius, a hideous part-man, part-serpent. Athene eventually accepted the child back from Mother Earth and entrusted it to Aglauros.

***Athene,* bronze statue, 4th century** B.C.

Athene maintained an ongoing animosity toward Poseidon, with whom she had many conflicts. The two fought for preeminence of Athens, and when Athene prevailed Poseidon flooded the region as a parting gesture. Despite this, Athene and Poseidon found themselves supporting the Greeks at the outset of the Trojan War. This alliance would not survive, but it provided the Greek alliance with much-needed support while the Trojans enjoyed the favor of Hera, Aphrodite, Ares, and others.

Athene was an active participant in the Trojan War, rescuing those she favored and helping the Greek cause in many ways. When Great Ajax felt robbed of his share of Achilles' armor, he plotted the murders of Agamemnon, Odysseus, and Menelaus. Athene then made Ajax insane, a condition that eventually led to his death.

As the Greeks prepared for their final assault, they were warned that they needed to obtain Athene's Palladium, which was being kept in her sanctuary inside the walls of Troy. The Palladium was a statue of Athene that was said to have fallen from the sky, and was one of the most famous icons in all of mythology. While the Greeks treated the Palladium as a valuable relic and an object of prophetic need, in Virgil's *Aeneid* and other Roman mytholgies it is treated as something that combined the significance of the stone that Cronus had swallowed in place of the infant Zeus (which was installed at the altar of Apollo's Delphic Oracle) with the desirability of the Golden Fleece.

Athene also played a prominent role in the construction of the Trojan Horse, which she was said to have dreamed up, despite similar claims by Odysseus. The horse was dedicated to her, and her name was invoked by those who sought to trick the Trojans into bringing it into the city. Once the Greeks emerged from the Trojan Horse and began their final assault on the city, Athene remained a presence. When Odysseus and Menelaus engaged Deiphobus in bloody combat, it was Athene who allowed the Greeks to overcome their opponent, though Helen is occasionally credited with stabbing Deiphobus while he was engaged by Menelaus.

When Agamemnon's son, Orestes, avenged his father's death by killing Clytaemnestra and Aegisthus, Athene defended him against the Erinnyes. When they continued to hound Orestes long after he had been purified for his crimes, Athene assembled the Areiopagus, a court in front of which Orestes' case was tried. The eldest of the Erinnyes prosecuted the case, while Apollo allied with the aging Cronus and the Titans against Zeus and the other Olympians. As the leader of the unsuccessful revolt, during the course of which Menoetius was killed, Atlas was subjected to the most serious punishment: he was made to support the celestial globe upon his shoulders for all eternity.

Atlas achieved one brief respite from his burden when Heracles came to the Iberian peninsula in the course of his eleventh labor: the gathering of golden apples from Hera's tree. Atlas obtained the apples for Heracles and offered to bring them to Eurystheus for him, intending to slip away and be freed of his eternal punishment. Heracles pretended to fall for Atlas' ploy, and asked him to support the load for a brief moment while he prepared for the task. Atlas took back the burden, thinking it just for a moment, and Heracles went off, leaving Atlas back where he had started.

***Atlas, Heracles, and Athene with the Apples of the Hesperides,* marble relief, 5th century** B.C.

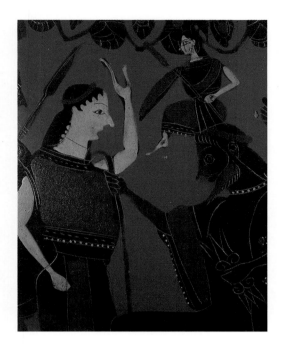

***Athene Emerging from the Head of Zeus,* black-figured amphora, 5th century** B.C.

defended. In the end, the jury was evenly divided and Athene cast the deciding vote in favor of Orestes' acquittal.

Athene also assisted Odysseus during his decade-long wanderings, and continued to do so once he had finally returned to his home in Ithaca. When the relatives of the suitors Odysseus had murdered attacked his palace, Athene intervened and directed the conflict toward a legal solution.

> *. . . Queen Athene, blest in battles,*
> *to whom Zeus gave holy authority*
> *To decide the issue of war . . .*
> —*Chorus,* Seven Against Thebes, *Aeschylus*

Atlas

Possibly the son of the Titans Eurynome and Phoebe or of Iapetus and the nymph Clymene, Atlas is most frequently described as being a son of Poseidon; it is also said that he had as brothers five sets of twins, among them Prometheus, Menoetius, and Epimetheus. Atlas and his family ruled over Atlantis, an enormous continent out beyond the Pillars of Heracles, a land that was said to have been bigger than Asia and Africa combined.

The family was perceived as becoming too greedy, which caused Zeus to allow the Athenian destruction of Atlantis, followed by a cataclysmic flood that deluged the entire kingdom in one day and one night. Atlas and Menoetius escaped, and subsequently became

***Atlas Bearing the Sky,* marble statue, Hellenistic period.**

> *The fate of Atlas grieves me—my own brother,*
> *Who in the far West stands with his unwieldy*
> *load*
> *pressing upon his back, the pillar of heaven and*
> *earth.*
> —*Prometheus,* Prometheus Bound, *Aeschylus*

Atreus

One of the many sons of Pelops and Hippodameia, Atreus was fated to battle his twin brother, Thyestes. When Hippodameia killed Chrysippus, the twins' stepbrother, Atreus fled the city of Elis, raising suspicions about what role he may have had in his stepbrother's murder.

Atreus wound up in Mycenae, as did Thyestes. They were welcomed by their nephew Eurystheus, whose mother, Archippe, had married Sthenelus. Eurystheus and Sthenelus died soon after the twins' arrival, and Atreus and Thyestes began to fight over control of Mycenae. Atreus, who had promised to sacrifice the very best of his flocks to Artemis, was tempted by Hermes with a horned, golden-fleeced lamb.

Atreus did sacrifice the magical beast to Artemis, but he kept the skin and had it stuffed, mounted, and hidden. When he and Thyestes fought for the throne, Atreus suggested that the possessor of such a magical beast should be king. Thyestes agreed, having already convinced Atreus' new bride, Aerope, who was infatuated with her brother-in-law, to steal it for him.

When Thyestes produced the divine lamb and was declared king, Atreus responded by suggesting that if he could make the sun go backwards the very next day he should be made king instead. Thyestes, believing this impossible, agreed, and the next day, Helius turned his chariot around in mid-flight and for the first and only time, set down in the east. (Atreus was known for his interest in astronomy, and it is likely that this story actually involves his prediction of a solar eclipse or some such phenomenon.)

Once Atreus was restored to the throne he banished Thyestes, but invited him back a short while later, pretending to be willing to share power with him. Atreus then slaughtered Thyestes' three sons, as well as a set of young twins, and served them to his brother at a banquet. When Thyestes was finished Atreus told him what he had eaten, for which Thyestes cursed his brother's house.

When Atreus began to worry how the gods would perceive his treatment of Thyestes, he consulted the Delphic Oracle regarding atonement. The oracle told him to seek out Thyestes and bring him home. Atreus went to Sicyon, from which Thyestes had just departed. While there, Atreus met Pelopia, the daughter of Thyestes, whom he believed to be the Sicyon King Thesprotus' daughter.

Atreus brought Pelopia back to Mycenae with him, and believed Aegisthus, the child she bore, to be his own. When the boy was seven years old, Atreus sent him to kill Thyestes, whom Atreus had since captured and jailed. Thyestes narrowly avoided young Aegisthus' sword, which he recognized as his own. (He had left it behind during his rape of Pelopia.) Thyestes instructed his son to bring Pelopia to him (his subsequent revelation to her of the truth of her rapist's heretofore unknown identity led to her suicide), and then to go kill Atreus, which the boy did. With Atreus dead, Thyestes became the King of Mycenae once again.

Atropos

One of the three Fates, Atropos, the most diminutive of the three, was the most feared since it was her shears that cut the thread of life. Atropos was also responsible for drawing up the invoice that Aeacus checked against the souls Hermes brought to Tartarus.

Auge

The daughter of Aleus and Neaera. When an oracle warned Aleus that a son of Auge would kill his brothers-in-law, Aleus insisted that Auge become a priestess and remain chaste. Auge retained her virginity until Heracles passed through town.

When a drought came over Tegea, Aleus sought out its cause and eventually discovered that Auge was pregnant. He handed her over to King Nauplius with instructions that she be drowned. Nauplius instead chose to sell her into slavery, and Auge was subsequently resold to Teuthras, a Mysian King. On the journey to Teuthras' kingdom, Auge delivered an infant son, which she abandoned on Mount Parthenius, where it was suckled by a doe, rescued, and named Telephus.

Augeias

The King of Elis who was the wealthiest man on earth as measured in flocks and herds, Augeias was the son of Helius and Naupiadame, although Eleius, Iphinoë, and even Poseidon are occasionally described as his parents. The half-brother of Aëetes, Augeias accompanied Jason on his peaceful request for the Golden Fleece. Aëetes responded to the request with scorn and failed to so much as acknowledge Augeias.

Augeias' stables were the subject of Heracles' fifth labor. Heracles was instructed to clean Augeias' enormous stables in a single day, which he did by diverting two rivers through them. Augeias ruled that Heracles had cheated, refused to pay him for his labors, and banished both Heracles and his own son, Phyleus, who had sided with Heracles and would later testify on his behalf.

Heracles mustered an army against Augeias, who was prepared for the attack and had many allies, including the Moliones and Amarynceus. This battle represents one of Heracles' rare defeats, but though his forces were repelled, the mighty Heracles managed to kill the Moliones as well as Augeias and his sons. In some versions it is suggested that only Augeias was killed, while in others the entire family is spared. In any case, Augeias' line continued for several generations.

Autolycus

A well-known thief who was the son of Hermes and Chione (and whose twin brother, Philammon, claimed Apollo as his father), Autolycus was able to transform beasts he had stolen, making them unrecognizable to their original owners. Sisyphus suspected Autolycus all along, and marked his beasts' hooves so that they could be identified no matter how their appearances were altered. Sisyphus used this trick to catch Autolycus red-handed, and during the arguments that ensued Sisyphus seduced Autolycus' daughter Anticleia, and the subsequent union resulted in the birth of Odysseus. (It was Autolycus who named the child.)

Autolycus joined the crew of the *Argo* at Sinope, along with Deileon and Phlogius, to fill vacancies created by members who had died or been abandoned along the way. The three had been stranded there during the course of their exploits with Heracles against the Amazons, and were glad for even the most remote possibility of returning to the Mediterranean. Autolycus is said to have taught Heracles the art of boxing.

Balius

One of two immortal, talking horses who drew Achilles' chariot at the siege of Troy. The other was Xanthus.

Bellerophon

Known as the son of Glaucus and the grandson of Sisyphus, Bellerophon may in fact have been the son of Poseidon. His name is derived from his hand in the death of a man named Bellerus. After Bellerus was slain, Bellerophon killed his brother, Deliades, and fled to the court of Proetus for refuge. At Tiryns Bellerophon was forced to avoid the romantic advances of Proetus' wife, Anteia. Out of revenge, she accused Bellerophon of having seduced her. Not wanting to shed the blood of his guest, Proetus sent Bellerophon to his father-in-law, Iobates, with a secret message telling him what had transpired and requesting that he kill his daughter's attacker. Because Iobates was similarly loath to kill a guest, he concocted a scheme in which Bellerophon was sent to kill the Chimaera.

Bellerophon Mounting Pegasus Fighting the Chimaera, **Rubens, early 17th century.**

On the advice of the seer Polyeidos, Bellerophon captured the winged horse Pegasus (with help from Athene, Poseidon, or both), and accomplished his task. Iobates then suggested that Bellerophon should fight the Solymians and their allies the Amazons, which he also did successfully. Bellerophon even defeated a group of Carian pirates on the way back to Lycia, but was ambushed by Iobates' men before he could return. After fighting off his ambushers, Bellerophon dismounted from Pegasus and advanced across the Xanthian Plain, bringing with him a flood (caused by Poseidon). When the Xanthian women hoisted their skirts and offered themselves to Bellerophon en masse (with the hope of getting him to stop his destruction of their homeland), Bellerophon ran away, and the flood receded with him.

Taking Bellerophon's response to the Xanthian women into consideration, Iobates realized that Anteia's original claims against him were not true. He gave Bellerophon his daughter Philonoë in marriage, and established him as the heir to the Lycian throne. It is said that during the course of his marriage to Philonoë, Bellerophon fathered Laodameia. Unfortunately, Bellerophon's change in fortune made him arrogant, and when he overstepped his bounds as a mortal and attempted to ride Pegasus to the top of Mount Olympus, Zeus sent a gadfly to sting the winged horse, who then threw his rider back to earth. Zeus kept Pegasus for his own, and Bellerophon, who had landed in a thorn bush, wandered the earth for the rest of his life—lame, blind, and accursed until the end.

Biadice

The wife of Cretheus, Biadice fell in love with her nephew, Phrixus. When he spurned her, she accused him of ravishing her, which contributed to the chain of events that led to Phrixus' father, Athamas, preparing to sacrifice him. (This sacrifice was interrupted by Heracles.)

Bias

Bias fell in love with his cousin, Pero, whose father, Neleus, had proclaimed that the only way for anyone to win her hand in marriage was to drive King Iphiclus' cattle out of Phylace. Bias' brother, Melampus, used his prophetic ability to win possession of the cattle, and Bias was able to marry Pero.

Later, shortly after the death of Pero, Bias married Iphianassa. Bias traveled with Neleus to Messene and helped conquer the city of Pylus, and was later killed by a nephew whose name is listed variously as Pylas, Pylus, or even Pylon.

Boreas' Abduction of Oreithyia, Francesco Romanelli, mid-17th century.

Boeotus

One of the twins born to Arne and abandoned to perish by Desmontes, Arne's stepmother. The twins were rescued by a shepherd and entrusted to Theano, whose husband, Metapontus, was angry that she had not provided him with heirs. When Theano gave birth to twins of her own, she grew jealous of the attention Metapontus—unaware of the fact that they were not really his own children—paid to Aeolus and Boeotus. When Boeotus and his brother slew the twins in self-defense in a battle brought about by their adoptive mother, Theano committed suicide. The brothers then went and rescued their real mother from Desmontes, whom they killed.

Metapontus married Arne and adopted the boys, but eventually tired of his second wife and attempted to replace her with Autolyte. In the ensuing battle with their father, the twins killed Autolyte. Boeotus fled Theano's kingdom with Arne, and the two took refuge in the palace of her father, also named Aeolus, upon whose death Boeotus was bequeathed the southern portion of his grandfather's kingdom, which he named for his mother.

Boreas

Another name for the North Wind, a being sometimes described as having characteristics similar to those ascribed to Ophion. Boreas is said to have been the son of Astraeus and Eos. Boreas is described variously as having serpents' tails for feet, as being a stallion who impregnated Erechtheus' mares, and most often, as a powerful wind such as the one that helped the Athenians destroy the fleets of King Xerxes.

When Boreas sought Erechtheus' permission to marry his daughter Oreithyia, Erechtheus was slow in making his decision. Boreas grew impatient, ravished Oreithyia on a rock beside the river Ilissus, and subsequently married her.

Briseis

The name of two women whose stories revolve around the Trojan War. The first Briseis was the beautiful daughter of Calchas who was left behind in Troy on the eve of the war. Calchas, who was allied with Agamemnon and the Greeks, asked Agamemnon to act on his behalf and ask Priam to release Briseis to prevent her becoming a prisoner of war. Briseis, who had been in love with Troilus, transferred her affections to Diomedes after her release from Troy.

The other Briseis was a daughter of Briseus. When her husband, Mynes, was killed by Achilles' forces, Briseis was captured by the Greeks. Agamemnon gave her to Achilles and kept Chryseis, another captive, for himself. Agamemnon was eventually forced to return

Chryseis to her father, which led him to reclaim Briseis; this became one of the factors in Achilles' decision to stop fighting alongside the Greeks. When Achilles finally rejoined the Greek forces, Agamemnon gave Briseis back to him with proof that she had remained inviolate.

Britomartis   A daughter of Leto, Britomartis was the inventor of hunting nets and a companion of Artemis. Minos pursued Britomartis for nine months, until she finally threw herself into the sea to preserve her virginity; she was subsequently deified by Artemis as Dictynna.

Broteas   An ugly child whose father was Tantalus and whose mother may have been Euryanassa, Eurythemista, Clytia, or Dione. When Broteas, who was a famous hunter, was disrespectful to Artemis, the goddess drove him insane, causing him to jump onto a lit pyre and be consumed by flames. In some versions it is suggested that Broteas' death was a suicide motivated by his hideous appearance.

Busiris   An Egyptian King whose realm suffered a drought of some eight or nine years, Busiris finally sent for the Greek seer Phrasius, who informed him that he needed to sacrifice one stranger to the gods each year. Phrasius became the first such sacrifice. When Heracles passed through Busiris' kingdom, he acted as if he would allow himself to be that year's victim but instead killed Busiris, his son Amphidamas, and their attendants.

Butes   The twin brother of Erechtheus and the brother of Philomela and Procne, Butes was the son of Pandion and Zeuxippe. After Pandion died of grief over his daughters' miserable fate, Butes became a priest of Athene and Poseidon.

Butes was best known for his beekeeping, and it was with this reputation that he is listed as one of the Argonauts. When the *Argo* passed by the land of the alluring Sirens, Butes jumped overboard and swam toward them. He was rescued by Aphrodite, who took him to Mount Eryx and made him her lover. (In some versions it is suggested that this was a ploy of Aphrodite to make Adonis jealous.) The result of their union was a son whose name was given to or taken from the mountain.

Cacus   The son of Hephaestus and Medusa, Cacus, a three-headed shepherd who puffed flames from his mouth and lived in a grisly cave decorated with the skulls and bones of his victims, was feared throughout the Aventine Forest. When Cacus made the mistake of stealing some of the cattle Heracles had taken from Geryon, Heracles slew him in revenge.

Cadmus   A son of Agenor and Telephassa, Cadmus was a brother of Europe, who was carried off by Zeus. When Agenor sent all of his sons to find Europe, Cadmus went with Telephassa to Rhodes and then to Thera and Edonia, where Telephassa died. Cadmus proceeded to consult the Delphic Oracle, where the Pythoness suggested he abandon his search and instead follow a cow until it collapsed from exhaustion. There, the Pythoness told Cadmus, he should found a city. This city was initially named Cadmea, but eventually came to be known as Thebes.

When some of Cadmus' men were killed by a great serpent while trying to obtain water, Cadmus responded by crushing the serpent's head with a rock. Athene, to whom Cadmus was preparing a sacrifice when the snake struck, told Cadmus to sow the serpent's teeth, from which fighting men would arise, prepared for battle. Once they rose, Cadmus tossed a rock amongst the Sown Men, also known as the Sparti. The rock incited a fight among the Sparti that left five survivors. The Sparti became Cadmus' generals and supported him well, but could not assuage Ares in his demands for vengeance for the death of the serpent. Cadmus was made to serve Ares as a bondman for a Great Year, which may in fact have comprised eight calendar years.

Heracles and Cacus, Baccio Bandinelli, 1527–1534.

Cadmus Killing the Dragon, black-figured kylix, c. 550 B.C.

After fulfilling his obligations, Cadmus received Athene's help in reclaiming control of his kingdom, and it was around this time that Cadmus married Harmonia. Their wedding was the first between mortals that was ever attended by Olympians, whose favor ensured Cadmus a long and successful reign. In his old age, Cadmus turned the throne of Thebes over to his grandson Pentheus. Cadmus and Harmonia retired to the land of the Encheleans, where their daughter Agave was living. The Encheleans made Cadmus their king, and he ruled until his and Harmonia's spirits were transformed into blue-spotted black serpents, fulfilling a prophesy of Dionysus. In this form they went to the Islands of the Blessed, while their bodies were buried in Illyria. Cadmus was succeeded on the throne by Illyrius, a son conceived during his later years.

Caenis/Caeneus

The daughter of Elatus, Caenis was a nymph who was raped by Poseidon. When Poseidon offered her a gift as recompense, Caenis expressed her desire to be an invulnerable fighter and claimed to be weary of being a woman. Poseidon transformed her into Caeneus, a man, and Caeneus eventu-

ally became a king and begot a son, Coronus. Caeneus participated in the hunt for the Calydonian Boar, and was present at the wedding of Peirithous and Hippodameia, where he killed a half-dozen Centaurs before being pounded into the ground and smothered. A sandy-winged bird emerged from Caeneus' corpse, which was subsequently found to have reverted to female form.

Calais

The twin brother of Zetes and the son of Boreas and Orethyia. Calais and Zetes were said to have grown wings when they reached manhood, and these attributes proved quite useful during their stint as Argonauts.

When Jason opted to leave Heracles behind following a stop at Pegae, Calais and Zetes supported their captain. Later, when the *Argo* reached Salmydessus, Calais and Zetes helped their brother-in-law, King Phineus, by chasing away the Harpies who had been hounding him. In return, Phineus provided the Argonauts with explicit directions to help them reach Colchis safely. While in Salmydessus, Calais and Zetes also freed their nephews, who had been imprisoned by Phineus' second wife, Idaea.

Calchas

The son of Thestor and the brother of Leucippe and Theonoë, Calchas was a seer who learned the art of prophesy from his father. Originally an ally of King Priam,

Cadmus and Harmonia Riding a Cart Drawn by Two Wild Boars, black-figured amphora, Diosphos, 6th century B.C.

Calchas was sent by the king to consult the Pythoness, who told Calchas to switch his allegiance to the Greeks and delay their siege since under any circumstances it would be a full decade before Troy would fall.

Calchas first swore an oath of friendship with Achilles, who then brought him to meet Agamemnon. Shortly after meeting the leader of the Greek forces, Calchas told Agamemnon that the only way he would be able to maintain his command and make progress with his becalmed fleet was through the sacrifice of his daughter Iphigeneia.

Calchas figured in most of the prophesies regarding things the Greeks needed to do in order for Troy to fall. Later, when the Trojans were tricked into bringing the Trojan Horse inside the city's walls, Calchas' name was invoked to explain the enormity of the horse and other strange aspects of the offering the Greeks had "left behind."

It was prophesied that Calchas would die when he encountered a seer greater than himself. When he encountered Mopsus, Calchas sought to engage him in a contest, and requested a seemingly impossible forecast from Mopsus. When Mopsus proved to be stunningly correct with his prediction, he in turn requested a seemingly simple prediction from Calchas, and challenged this prediction with one of his own, which was also correct. Calchas, it was said, died of a broken heart, and was buried by his companions.

Cale

One of the three Charites, Cale was said by Teiresias the seer to be more beautiful than her sisters or Aphrodite. When Aphrodite turned Teiresias into an old woman to punish him for not picking her, Cale took Teiresias with her to Crete and endowed her with a lovely head of hair.

Callirrhoë

The daughter of the river god Achelous, who married Callirrhoë to Alcmaeon after performing a second purification over him. After a year or so, Callirrhoë told Alcmaeon that he would be denied her favors until he retrieved Hera's magic robe and necklace, which he had given Arsinoë, his first wife.

After Alcmaeon returned to Arsinoë and was killed by her brothers, Callirrhoë prayed that her two sons by Alcmaeon might become fully grown in a day so that they could avenge their father's death. The gods granted this request, and the boys killed Phegeus and his sons. No king would purify Callirrhoë's sons, so they traveled west to Epirus, where they colonized a new settlement.

Callisto

A companion of Artemis, Callisto was seduced and impregnated by Zeus. Because Artemis required chastity from her followers and Callisto had broken this rule, Artemis transformed her into a bear so that she would be hunted down; Zeus saved her, however, and set her image among the stars.

In some versions of this story Zeus turns Callisto into a bear, Hera persuades Artemis to hunt her down, and Zeus places her among the stars before Artemis can complete her assignment.

Calydonian Boar

A beast sent by Artemis to punish Oeneus, the King of Calydon, for having omitted her from his annual sacrifices, the Calydonian Boar killed Oeneus' cattle and many of his laborers, and ruined all of his crops. The king responded by assembling a group of great heroes to hunt and slay the Boar.

Calypso

A daughter of Thetis and Oceanus, Nereus, or Atlas, Calypso lived on the island of Ogygia, one of the places where Odysseus washed up during his attempts to return home. Calypso welcomed Odysseus to her island and offered to share with him her food, drink, and bed. Odysseus was promised immortality and eternal youth as long as he stayed with Calypso.

Odysseus fathered the twins Nausithous and Nausinous upon Calypso (in some versions she is also described as the mother of Latinus), but despite the passage of time and the family he had assembled, Odysseus still longed for Ithaca. When Zeus sent Hermes to tell Calypso that it was time for Odysseus to be moving on, Calypso was left with no option but to comply. Calypso gave Odysseus the tools he needed to construct a raft and promised to stock it with enough supplies for him to reach home. Odysseus suspected some kind of trap, but Calypso vowed that she was telling the truth and eventually watched the father of her children sail for home.

Canache

The daughter of Aeolus and Enarete, Canache, together with her brothers and sisters, grew up in such isolation that she was unaware of the taboo against incest; as a result, Canache had an incestuous relationship with her brother Macareus. Some say that the fruit of their relationship was fed to dogs, while others suggest that this child was Amphissa, who was much beloved by Apollo.

Upon learning of his daughter's relationship with her brother, Aeolus sent Canache a sword, with which she dutifully took her life.

Capaneus

An Argive chieftain, Capaneus was one of the seven champions who participated in King Adrastus' march on Thebes. Capaneus led the assault on the city itself by mounting a scaling ladder, and was thunderbolted to death by Zeus. His death was the beginning of the turnaround that resulted in the Thebans' ability to withstand the Argive attack.

Because he was struck by lightning, Capaneus was buried separately, according to the superstition of the day. Capaneus' wife, Evadne, unable to end her life with her husband's remains, threw herself on the general pyre on which the other attackers were being burned.

Cassandra

One of Hecabe and Priam's many ill-fated daughters, Cassandra had the gift of prophesy combined with the curse that her predictions would never be believed. In some versions it is suggested that the prophetic skills are the result of an incident in which Cassandra and her twin brother, Helenus, were forgotten by their parents in one of Apollo's temples. When Hecabe returned to retrieve her twins, a pair of snakes were licking at their ears, an incident that invested them with foresight. There is another version, however, in which Apollo gave Cassandra the gift of prophesy in exchange for her sexual favors.

When Cassandra accepted Apollo's gift but refused to uphold her end of the bargain, Apollo added the proviso that her prophesies would remain accurate but would always be disbelieved. This was a factor in Priam's decision to imprison Cassandra when she began making predictions about the downfall of Troy.

Cassandra's husband, Eurypylus, was killed in combat, and Agamemnon eventually claimed Cassandra and took her back to Greece with him. On the way back to Greece, Agamemnon and Cassandra became the parents of twin sons, Teledamus and Pelops. Upon arriving in Argos, Cassandra entered a prophetic trance in which she glimpsed the bloody end that was her and Agamemnon's fate. Cassandra's warnings were ignored, as usual; Agamemnon was killed, and Cassandra and her twins were similarly dispatched.

Cassiopeia

The wife of Cepheus, an Ethiopian who was the King of Joppa, Cassiopeia was the mother of Andromeda. After Cassiopeia and Cepheus were killed for their mistreatment of Perseus, who had rescued their daughter, Andromeda, when they tried to sacrifice her, Poseidon set both Cepheus and Cassiopeia's images among the stars. (In repayment for her original insult of the Nereids, which had led to Andromeda almost being sacrificed, Cassiopeia was put in a position that

Destruction of Troy: Cassandra Being Taken by Ajax, **Roman wallpainting, 1st century** B.C.

Castor, **Roman copy after Greek statue,**
A.D. **1st–2nd century.**

makes her look foolish at certain times of the year.)

Castor

The son of Leda, either by Zeus or by Leda's husband, Tyndareus, the King of Sparta. Castor's twin brother was Polydeuces, and the two together were known as the Dioscuri. The pair are stock characters in Greek mythology, and figure in such all-star assemblages as the hunt for the Calydonian Boar and the voyage of the *Argo*.

Known best as a soldier and tamer of horses, Castor was also an Olympic prizewinner as a wrestler. It is said that Castor instructed the young Heracles in fencing, military weaponry, and strategy.

When Polydeuces was to be deified, he said he would accept only if Castor were rewarded in the same manner. The ruling council of the Olympians decided that the two would share the honor and split their time evenly between Olympus and Tartarus.

Catreus

As the eldest surviving son of Minos and Pasiphaë, Catreus succeeded his father as King of Crete. When it was prophesied that Catreus would be killed by one of his four children, his son Althaemenes and one of his daughters, Apemosyne, voluntarily left Crete to avoid fulfilling the prophesy. Once Catreus became king, he got rid of his remaining two daughters, Aerope and Clymene, by selling them as slaves to Nauplius, who married the latter and betrothed the former to Atreus.

As he began to grow older, Catreus realized that he had no heir, and went in search of Althaemenes. When he visited the Cameirans, with whom his son was staying, he was not immediately recognized, and a battle ensued. Althaemenes joined the side of his hosts, and threw the spear that killed his father, thus fulfilling the prophesy.

Cecrops

Famed for being the first king to recognize the rights of paternity, Cecrops—part man, part serpent—was the son of Mother Earth. Cecrops and his family lived together on the Acropolis, from whence Cecrops instituted the practice of monogamy and attempted to minimize the frequency of blood rituals.

Cecrops the Second was the son of Erechtheus and Praxithea, and fought with his three brothers over the succession to their father's throne. After Cecrops was selected by his brother-in-law Xuthus as the heir and his life was threatened by his brothers Metion and Orneus, he left Athens, going first to Megara and then to Euboea.

Centaurs

The children and descendants of Centaurus, the son of Ixion and Nephele who conceived the first Centaurs upon a herd of Magnesian mares. The resultant offspring were composite beings with the bodies of horses and the torsos and heads of humans, and became a favorite subject for generations of sculptors. Although some are credited with a good deal of wisdom, the Centaurs were usually depicted as an unruly, brawling lot. As stock characters,

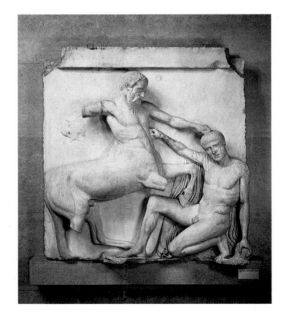

A Centaur Treads Down a Lapith,
Parthenon frieze, c. 440 B.C.

Centaurs figure prominently throughout the mythological canon in battles, brawls, rapes, and other unsavory acts.

When Peirithous and Hippodameia neglected to invite Ares and Eris to their wedding, the spurned gods caused the Centaurs to get drunk and begin a brawl that culminated in one Centaur, Eurytion, attempting to violate the new bride. In the battle that followed, the Centaurs inflicted overwhelming casualties on their enemies the Lapiths.

The Centaurs often served as the enactors of Zeus' divine wrath, by being sent to punish those who had offended him.

Cephalus

A son of Hermes, Cephalus married Erechtheus' daughter Procris. Cephalus was later seduced by Eos, and felt guilty for betraying his wife, but Eos convinced him that Procris' affections were, and always had been, easily bought. Cephalus eventually ran off with Eos, and encountered Procris, who was hiding from her current lover's wife under the name of Pterelas. When Cephalus fell in love with "Pterelas," who then revealed herself, they realized that each was equally guilty, and they were reconciled.

When Artemis grew annoyed with the frequency of their continuing adulteries, she caused Procris to become suspicious of Cephalus when he went out hunting. One night when Cephalus went out, Procris followed him to see where he was going, and was killed when he mistook her for an animal.

After this incident, Cephalus retired to Thebes, where he became allied with King Amphitryon; these two battled the Teleboans and the Taphians, and Cephalus loaned Amphitryon his hound Laelaps for the hunt of the Teumessian Vixen.

Despite being purified for the accidental slaying of his wife, Cephalus continued to be haunted by Procris' ghost, and eventually committed suicide by leaping into the sea at Cape Leucas.

Cepheus

The son of Anchinoë and the Arcadian King Belus, Cepheus eventually became the King of Joppa. Cepheus married Cassiopeia, and conceived Andromeda with her. The Joppan King was slain by Perseus following Perseus' intervention in Cepheus' sacrifice of his daughter.

Cerberus

A horrible, three-headed hound who served as Hades' guard dog in Tartarus, Cerberus is usually said to have been born to Echidne and Typhon. He patrolled the shore of the river Styx in the underworld, and

Heracles Fighting Cerberus, black-figured hydria, c. 530 B.C.

devoured both living intruders and fugitive ghosts.

Cerberus is best known for his role as the subject of Heracles' twelfth and final labor. When Hades told Heracles that he could take Cerberus back to the land of the living if he did so without using his club or arrows, Heracles grabbed Cerberus by the throat and dragged him up through a chasm that emerged in Mariandyne. Heracles first brought Cerberus to Mycenae to prove that he had accomplished the task, then sent the hound to guard one of Demeter's secret groves.

Cercopes A set of twins born to Oceanus and Theia who grew to become renowned cheats and liars, the Cercopes were given a variety of names, including Passalus and Acmon, Olus and Eurybatus, and Sillus and Triballus. Despite Theia's warning to stay clear of Heracles, the Cercopes' mischievous nature won out over her sage advice, and they insisted on disquieting his sheep.

Heracles caught the Cercopes, and carried them off to an uncertain fate. As they dangled upside down in his grasp, the Cercopes began to laugh at Heracles' buttocks, which had been blackened during the course of one of his recent labors. When Heracles learned what the Cercopes were laughing at, he shared their amusement and released them. There are also some versions in which the Cercopes are eventually turned to stone—or into apes— for attempting to deceive Zeus.

Cercyon The King of Arcadia, Cercyon was a particularly cruel man. When his daughter, Alope, was seduced by Poseidon, she abandoned the son born of that union. When Cercyon was asked to settle a dispute between two shepherds who had found a baby, he recognized the infant's swaddling clothes. Cercyon responded by imprisoning Alope and having the baby abandoned once again.

Cercyon also had an unpopular habit of challenging passersby to wrestle, and then crushing them to death. Theseus, in the course of making the road between Troezen and Athens safe, accepted Cercyon's challenge and killed the king by dropping him on his head. Theseus freed Alope and put her son, Hippothous (who had been rescued a second time by one of the shepherds), on the throne.

Ceryneian Hind One of five enormous hinds (female red deers) initially spotted by Artemis, who captured the other four. Swift and dappled, with brazen hooves and golden horns, these hinds were sometimes confused for harts. The Ceryneian Hind was the subject of Heracles' third labor.

Ceto The wife of Phorcys and the daughter of Pontus and Mother Earth, Ceto was the mother of the Phorcids.

Ceyx The nephew of Amphitryon, Ceyx was the husband of Alcyone. When these two took to calling each other Zeus and Hera, the real Zeus and Hera became angry and caused Ceyx to drown. Ceyx's ghost appeared to Alcyone, who threw herself into the sea, in imitation of which a pitying god transformed them both into kingfishers.

Chalciope The daughter of Asterodeia and King Aeëtes of Colchis, and the sister of Medea, Chalciope was the wife of Phrixus, whose arrival on a divine ram provided Colchis with the Golden Fleece later sought by the Argonauts.

When the *Argo* arrived in Colchis, it carried Chalciope's sons, Cytisorus, Argeus, Phrontis, and Melanion, whom the Argonauts had rescued after the young men had been shipwrecked. Chalciope was the first person Jason and her sons ran into during their initial, peaceful attempt to retrieve the Fleece. When Aeëtes made it clear that he would not willingly part with the Fleece, Chalciope conspired with Medea to help Jason accomplish the tasks Aeëtes had assigned him.

Chaos A key figure in most of the early creation myths, including the Pelasgian, Olympian, and Philosophical versions. Chaos is variously considered to have been the entity from which Eurynome rose naked; from which Mother Earth emerged; and which sprang from Darkness. Chaos later had a union with Darkness that resulted in Night, Day, and Air. When patriarchal factions began to take control of the politics of mythology, the God of All Things, a masculinized equivalent of Nature, was added to the list of Chaos' off-spring.

> . . . all Nature was all Chaos,
> The rounded body of all things in one,
> The living elements at war with lifelessness. . .
> —The Metamorphoses, *Ovid*

Charites Daughters of Zeus who were conceived immediately following his fight with Rhea. The original Charites included Pasithea and Cale, and Auxo and Hegemone were occasionally described as being Charites as well. The Charites eventually became a three-some, usually with Eurphosyne joining the two charter members (though some versions have her listed instead with Aglaia and Thalia).

Charon The ferryman who carried the dead across the river Styx into Tartarus, Charon was a miser who had to be bribed for his services, causing relatives to bury their dead with coins to guarantee passage. Orpheus charmed Charon in his unsuccessful attempt to rescue his wife, Eurydice, from the underworld, and Heracles, during his visit to Tartarus, terrified Charon into cooperating. (Hades later pun-

Charon Ferrying Souls Across the Styx, **marble relief from sarcophagus,** A.D. **3rd century.**

ished the boatman for a full year for his acquiescence to Heracles' demands.)

Charon is another classic stock figure of mythology. His task of ferrying the newly dead into Tartarus has inspired countless poetic references and literary metaphors.

Charybdis The daughter of Mother Earth and Poseidon, Charybdis was a voracious monster who was hurled by Zeus into the sea. Charybdis sucked in enormous amounts of water thrice daily, and then spewed it back out. She was said to reside on the cliff opposite Scylla; between them ran a waterway.

Cheiron One of the first generation of Centaurs, Cheiron is portrayed as a very fair, beneficent individual who was entrusted with the protection of several youthful characters destined for mythological fame.

Apollo entrusted Asclepius to Cheiron, who instructed the boy in the art of healing. Aeneas was also reared by Cheiron, and Pelias later entrusted Diomedes (who later came to be known as Jason), the son of Polymele and Aeson, to Cheiron.

Cheiron was helpful to others besides foundlings, among them Peleus, whose life he spared after Acastus abandoned Peleus during a hunt. Cheiron helped Peleus find the magic sword that Acastus had hidden, and also provided useful advice to Peleus preceding his wedding to Thetis. Thetis entrusted her son Achilles to Cheiron as she was leaving Peleus. Cheiron instructed the boy in the arts of riding, hunting, pipe playing, and healing.

As a friend of Heracles, Cheiron was put in an awkward position when a battle broke out between Heracles and the Centaurs. Cheiron felt obliged to align himself with the Centaurs, and in their defense he was wounded in the knee by one of Heracles' arrows. The wound was exceedingly painful, but his immortality prevented Cheiron from succumbing to the injury. It was around this time that Prometheus was freed of his eternal punishment and was seeking immortality. With Zeus' permission, Cheiron transferred his immortality to Prometheus, and died shortly thereafter.

In a very different version of Cheiron's conception, it is suggested that he was the child of Philyra and Cronus. Interrupted by Rhea during the course of his adulterous union with Philyra, Cronus turned himself into a stallion and galloped off. As a result, the child born to Philyra was half-man, half-horse.

Chimaera A fire-breathing she-goat with a lion's head, a goat's body, and a serpent's tail, the Chimaera is thought to have been the product of a union between Echidne and Typhon. In some versions of the story of the Sphinx it is suggested that the Chimaera and Orthus were its parents.

The Chimaera was eventually killed by Bellerophon, who, riding the winged horse Pegasus, riddled her with arrows from above. When the arrows alone proved incapable of finishing the Chimaera off, Bellerophon shoved lead in her mouth. Her fire-breath then melted the metal, causing it to sear her insides and kill her.

> *[Iobates] sent [Bellerophon] away with orders to kill the Chimaira none might approach; a thing of immortal make, not human, lion-fronted and snake behind, a goat in the middle, and snorting out the breath of the terrible flame of bright fire.*
> —The Iliad, *Homer*

Chrysaor When Perseus decapitated Medusa the Gorgon, Chrysaor and Pegasus emerged from her dead body. Chrysaor was the father of Geryon, whose mother was Callirrhoë. In some accounts of Heracles'

***Bellerophon, Riding Pegasus, Fights the Chimaera,* red-figured kylix, 6th century** B.C.

tenth labor (to obtain Geryon's cattle), three of Chrysaor's sons unite against Heracles and are killed in the ensuing battle.

Chryse

The wife of Dardanus, one of the earliest settlers in the area that would eventually become Troy, Chryse was the mother of the twins Idaeus and Deimas, who ruled over Arcadia until the time of the Deucalion Flood.

Chryseis

The daughter of Chryses, Chryseis (also known as Astynome) gave her father's name to her son, who subsequently became known as Chryses the Younger. After her father had eventually obtained Chryseis' freedom, Chryseis reported that Agamemnon had treated her quite well, and said that she wished to go back, particularly since she was carrying his child. Chryses the Younger was born shortly after her return.

Chryses

The father of Chryseis, a daughter who passed on her father's name to her son. Chryses the Younger was told that Apollo was his father, but in truth he was the son of Agamemnon, conceived when Chryseis was taken as a spoil of the Trojan War. Shortly before the war ended, Chryses the Elder went to Agamemnon to request the return of his daughter. Agamemnon was initially abusive and unrelenting, but changed his mind when Chryses invoked Apollo's aid, which resulted in scores of Greek deaths over the course of ten days. Agamemnon finally released Chryseis, who reported that she had been treated quite well and actually preferred to remain with the man whose child she was now carrying. Chryseis returned to Agamemnon and delivered Chryses the Younger.

Years later, when Orestes came to steal an icon from King Thoas, the elder Chryses told his namesake the truth of his paternity, revealing that Chryses the Younger and Orestes were half-brothers (as both were sons of Agamemnon). As a result, Chryses the Younger sided with Orestes.

There was also a son of Minos named Chryses who was killed by Heracles. Before his death, this Chryses fathered Minyas, who would go on to found his own Boeotian kingdom.

Chrysippus

A boy raised along with Pelops and Hippodameia's other children, Chrysippus is thought to be the product of an affair between Pelops and a Danaid named Astyoche. As a young boy, Chrysippus was introduced to Laius, who had recently been banished from Thebes and was taking refuge in Pelops' court. Laius fell in love with the child and abducted him when he returned to rule his homeland.

In some versions Chrysippus takes his own life in shame, while in others he remains alive until Hippodameia begins to worry that Pelops is favoring him over her true sons. When two of those sons refuse to kill Chrysippus, she murders him herself. In his dying breaths, Chrysippus identifies her as the culprit, and Hippodameia subsequently commits suicide.

Chrysothemis

A daughter of Agamemnon and Clytaemnestra, Chrysothemis managed to live in peace with Clytaemnestra and Aegisthus after they had killed Agamemnon, despite Electra's imprecations for Chrysothemis to rebuke them.

Cilla

The daughter of Laomedon and Strymo, Cilla was a sister of Priam. When Priam came to power in Troy, he was warned that an impending royal birth would lead to the city's destruction. When Cilla delivered a son, Munippus, Priam reacted by killing both Cilla and Munippus. The real threat to Troy, however, was Paris, who was born to Priam's wife later that same day.

Cinyras

The son of Paphus and the King of the Cyprians. When Cypriaus, Cinyras' wife, boasted that their daughter, Smyrna, was more beautiful than Aphrodite, the goddess responded by tricking Smyrna into sleeping with her father. When Cinyras realized what had happened, he chased after Smyrna. Aphrodite took pity on her and transformed her into a tree. Cinyras swung his sword at the tree, which split in two and produced the child Adonis.

Cinyras rose to command a great number of cities. When Agamemnon approached him in the course of assembling troops to fight the Trojans, Cinyras gave Agamemnon a prized breastplate and promised to contribute fifty ships to the Greek cause. When the time came to provide these forces, Cinyras sent one real ship and forty-nine small models. Agamemnon complained to Apollo, who struck Cinyras dead and caused his fifty daughters to take their lives by leaping into the sea.

Cinyras' death at the hand of Apollo contradicts those versions in which it is suggested that Cinyras took his own life shortly after the birth of Adonis.

Circe

A cruel misanthrope, Circe was the daughter of Helius and Perse, and the sister of Aeëtes and Pasiphaë. Circe married a

Circe Giving a Magic Potion to Odysseus, **black-figured lekythos, 5th century** B.C.

Colchian King, whom she killed in the hope of taking command of his kingdom; the king's subjects then banished Circe, forcing her to flee to Aeaea, the Island of Dawn, where Circe's niece Medea and Medea's lover, Jason, stopped during their escape from Colchis with the Golden Fleece. The lovers sought to be purified for a murder, but when Circe learned that the murder was the bloody and ruthless slaying of Medea's half-brother Apsyrtus, she sent the couple away.

On Aeaea, Circe became a much-feared enchantress with little love for humans. When Odysseus and his men stopped on the island, Odysseus sent out a reconnoitering party under Eurylochus' command. After Circe transformed all but Eurylochus into hogs, Eurylochus ran to warn Odysseus of what had happened; Odysseus then accepted a charm against Circe's magic from Hermes and soon had her at the end of his sword. Circe swore to treat Odysseus well and to return his men to their human forms as long as he was willing to sleep with her. Odysseus' stay on the island resulted in his fathering three sons on Circe: Agrius, Latinus, and Telegonus.

When Odysseus announced that it was time for him to leave, Circe not only consented but told him the steps he needed to take to be able to return home. She then provided Odysseus with a strong breeze to blow his ship toward Tartarus. She also prepared him for the dangers he would encounter while passing the land of the Sirens and helped plan his escape from them.

Cithaerian Lion

A beast that killed Megareus, the son of Megaria's King, the Cithaerian Lion was said to have been killed by Alcathous. In some versions, however, Heracles kills the beast, flays it, and wears its pelt from then on.

Cleopatra

The name of two tragic characters who met similar fates. The first Cleopatra, the daughter of Boreas and Oreithyia, married King Phineus, with whom she conceived two sons. Phineus later remarried, and eventually fell victim to the Harpies. Cleopatra committed suicide when she heard of his death, an act that seems unlikely considering Phineus had since taken a new wife.

The second Cleopatra is best known for her marriage to Meleager. When Meleager's passion for Atalanta during the hunt for the Calydonian Boar overcame his better judgment, he became embroiled in a fight with his uncles. Meleager dispatched two with ease, but was cursed by his mother to be unable to defend himself; Cleopatra nonetheless convinced him to take up arms against them, and Meleager was killed in the battle that followed. Both Cleopatra and Meleager's mother, Althaea—who had also conspired in her son's death—hanged themselves afterward.

Clotho

One of the three Fates, Clotho was responsible for spinning the thread of life.

When Tantalus killed his son Pelops and butchered him to feed the gods, Clotho rearticulated the pieces of the boy that Hermes had gathered together.

Clymenus

The name of two well-known mythological kings. The first Clymenus, King of Elis, married Epicaste and sired a daughter, Harpalyce, for whom he developed a growing passion. Clymenus eventually debauched Harpalyce, who murdered the child that resulted and served it to Clymenus as food. For her crime, Harpalyce was turned into a bird of prey, and Clymenus, in turn, hanged himself.

The second Clymenus was the Minyan King who was struck by a stone thrown by Menoeceus' charioteer. Mortally wounded, this Clymenus was carried back to Orchomenus, where he made his sons swear to avenge him. Led by the eldest son, Erginus, Clymenus' forces marched on Thebes and battled victoriously, securing an annual tribute to be made to them in Clymenus' honor.

Clytaemnestra

Best known as the daughter of Leda and King Tyndareus, Clytaemnestra is sometimes described as being the daughter of Zeus. Tyndareus made the mistake of neglecting the goddess Aphrodite, who punished him by causing all of his daughters—

Clytaemnestra, **John Collier, c. 1850–1934.**

Clytaemnestra, Helen, and Timandra—to have unhappy, adulterous marriages. Clytaemnestra also had two brothers who became known as the Dioscuri.

Clytaemnestra was first married to Tantalus, the King of Pisa, who was killed during the course of Agamemnon's attack on his kingdom. Agamemnon took Clytaemnestra as his wife and killed her brothers, the Dioscuri, when they came to rescue her. Clytaemnestra and Agamemnon became the parents of several children, including Orestes, Electra, Chrysothemis, and Iphigeneia.

When Agamemnon sailed for Troy, he left Clytaemnestra behind. Nauplius, a Greek enemy of Agamemnon, remained behind to incite trouble back home, and discovered that Clytaemnestra was open to advances from suitors. Nauplius informed Aegisthus, who also held a grudge against Agamemnon and saw an opportunity to take his woman and possibly even his kingdom.

When Agamemnon returned from Troy, Clytaemnestra pretended to welcome him, and lured him into a trap. She cast a net upon him,

Ulysses on the Island of Circe, **Giovanni Stradanus, c. 1523–1605.**

The Murder of Clytaemnestra, marble relief from sarcophagus, A.D. **2nd century.**

and Aegisthus struck him twice with his sword. Clytaemnestra completed the act by beheading him with an ax. She was not done, however, until Cassandra lay dead as well. Aegisthus and Clytaemnestra declared the day a holiday and assumed control of Agamemnon's kingdom. While Aegisthus was the titular ruler, it was Clytaemnestra who ran the show. She even prevented him from killing her daughter Electra, who maintained an ongoing hatred for the murderers of her father. Agamemnon's murder has always seemed one of the vilest deeds in Greek mythology, particularly as it is depicted in a number of famous dramas, but when one considers the circumstances under which Clytaemnestra became Agamemnon's wife, and his acquiescence in the matter of sacrificing Iphigeneia, her actions seem a bit more understandable.

Electra's sister Chrysothemis was the only one of Agamemnon and Clytaemnestra's children to remain with their mother, and Chrysothemis is usually portrayed as a neutral go-between for Electra and Clytaemnestra.

When Orestes learned of his father's fate, he swore to avenge Agamemnon's murder upon Aegisthus and came back to Argos. The depictions of the murders vary widely, but in the end Orestes, possibly with help from Pylades, killed Aegisthus and Clytaemnestra.

Clytaemnestra Comes to the Aid of Aegisthus, red-figured pelike, 6th century B.C.

Comaetho   The daughter of the Teleboan King Pterelaus, Comaetho fell in love with Amphitryon during the course of Pterelaus' battle against Amphitryon and his allies, and subsequently cut her father's golden lock of immortality. As a result, Pterelaus died and Amphitryon's side won the war. Instead of embracing Comaetho for her actions, however, Amphitryon sentenced her to death for committing patricide. (Comaetho's story is nearly identical to that of Scylla and her father, Nisus.)

Core   The original name of the daughter of Demeter and Zeus, who was abducted by Hades and became Persephone, Queen of Tartarus. Despite spending much more of her time as Core, it is only as Persephone that she continued to appear in mythology.

Coronis   The daughter of Phlegyas, King of the Lapiths, Coronis became one of Apollo's lovers. During this time she fell in love with Ischys, which was eventually consummated. When Apollo found out, he had his sister, Artemis, shoot a quiver's worth of arrows at Coronis. Although she died, her unborn child survived and was named Asclepius. In some versions of Coronis' story, it is stated that she was alive at Asclepius' birth and later exposed him on Mount Titthion.

In your eyes. But her unfaithfulness
Was closely witnessed by Apollo's bird
Who ran, or rather flew, to tell his master.
—The Metamorphoses, *Ovid*

Corythus

The son of Oenone and Paris, Corythus married Electra, who bore him Iasion at the same time she delivered Dardanus, whose father was Zeus. When Oenone became jealous of Paris' elopement with Helen, she sent Corythus to guide the Greek armies to Troy in the hope of contributing to her former lover's downfall. Corythus is also credited with taking in and raising two well-known foundlings—Auge and Heracles' son, Telephus, and Atalanta and Meleager's son, Parthenopaeus.

Creon

The son of Menoeceus, the brother of Iocaste, and the brother-in-law of Oedipus. When Creon made Oedipus aware of the "unbelievable" prophesies being made by Teiresias the seer, Oedipus accused Creon of plotting his overthrow as the King of Thebes. Creon and Oedipus were on the verge of blows, until it became apparent that Teiresias' prophesies were coming true.

In the aftermath of the ensuing bloodshed, Creon took control of the kingdom and assumed responsibility for Oedipus and Iocaste's daughters, Antigone and Ismene. It is said that Creon was initially willing to allow Oedipus to remain in the kingdom, until Oedipus cursed his own sons.

When Eteocles and Polyneices killed one another, Creon assumed command of the victorious Theban forces. Creon quickly ruled that the corpses of the losing side, particularly that of Polyneices, who had focused Adrastus' armies against Eteocles, could not be given proper burial. But Polyneices' sister Antigone insisted on giving her brother a proper burial. When she disobeyed Creon's command, he dispatched his son, Haemon, to bury Antigone alive. Haemon was loath to do this, since he had been engaged to Antigone. Instead the two were secretly married, and Antigone eventually bore Haemon a son, whom Creon recognized years later. Creon killed the child, which led to Haemon's killing of Antigone and himself. Creon was later imprisoned by Theseus after the latter overran Thebes.

There is another Theban King whose name was Creon, and the acts of these two Creons are sometimes confused. This other Creon was the father of Megara. It was this Creon to whom Alcmaeon and Manto's two children, Amphilochus and Tisiphone, were entrusted.

Heracles and the Cretan Bull, **relief from sarcophagus, Hellenistic period.**

Finally, there was also a Corinthian King named Creon. This king figures most prominently in the myths regarding Jason's attempts to divorce Medea in favor of Creon's daughter, Glauce. When Medea swore vengeance for Jason's betrayal, Creon banished her from his kingdom, but made the mistake of allowing her one day to leave. Medea then sent Glauce a golden robe and crown as a wedding present. When Glauce put the robe and crown on, they clung to her and torturously poisoned her to death. When Creon rushed to his daughter's aid, he too was killed.

Then know you, and know it well, that you
shall not live through many more courses of the
sun's swift chariot before one begotten of your
own loins shall have been given by you a corpse
for corpses, because you have thrust children of
the sunlight to the shades and ruthlessly lodged a
living soul in the grave but keep in this world one
who belongs to the gods infernal, a corpse
unburied, unhonored, all unhallowed.
—Teiresias, Antigone, *Sophocles*

Cretan Bull

The subject of Heracles' seventh labor, the Cretan Bull is also thought by some to have been the white bull that sired the Minotaur on Minos' wife, Pasiphaë. This creature may also be the same bull that ferried Europe to Crete.

A fire-breathing monster, the Cretan Bull ravaged a region of Crete along the river Tethris. After Heracles captured the beast and brought it to Mycenae as his seventh task, he gave it to Eurystheus, who dedicated it to Hera. But Hera hated Heracles and anything associated with him, and drove the Bull to Sparta and then back through Arcadia to Marathon. From there, Theseus finally dragged it to Athens, where it was sacrificed in Athene's honor.

Cretheis

The wife of Acastus and the mother of Sterope, Cretheis attempted to seduce Peleus. When Peleus rebuffed her, she told his wife, Polymela, that Peleus was planning on replacing her with Sterope; Cretheis also told her husband that Peleus had tried to seduce her. Polymela took her own life, and Acastus abandoned Peleus unarmed among the Centaurs, who surprisingly spared him.

Later, when Peleus married Thetis, he came back and (with Zeus' help) first killed Acastus and then completed his revenge by murdering and dismembering Cretheis.

Polyphemus the Cyclopes, **Giulio Romano, 16th century.**

father, and reincarcerated the Cyclopes and the Hundred-handed Ones. Cronus took his sister Rhea for his wife, and ruled from Elis. Mother Earth told Cronus that he was destined to be dethroned by one of his sons, so Cronus ate all of the children that Rhea bore him, including Hestia, Demeter, Hera, Hades, and Poseidon. Rhea tricked Cronus with the birth of their sixth child, whom she replaced with a stone (possibly carved) wrapped in swaddling blankets. Cronus swallowed the stone and believed himself safe.

Meanwhile the sixth child, Zeus, was being raised by Adrasteia. When Zeus came of age he caused Cronus to swallow an emetic that caused him to expel each of his children, as well as the stone that would become the centerpiece of the Delphic Oracle. Once Cronus' children were freed, a battle ensued. The Cyclopes and the Hundred-handed Ones were again freed, and Cronus and his Titan allies were overwhelmed. While Poseidon held Cronus in place with his trident, Zeus struck him dead with a thunderbolt.

It is interesting to note that Cronus' devouring of his own children represents a practice in which kings chose to extend their reign by sacrificing young boys in their place. Zeus' defeat of his father, and his general disinclination for human sacrifices, paved the way for kings to rule well into their old age if they were smart enough, strong enough, and lucky enough.

As the cult of Zeus took hold, Cronus' role was quickly downplayed, sometimes to the point where he was said to have been created by Eurynome as one of the Seven Planetary Powers. In this role, Cronus was the overseer of Saturn (his Roman name), with Rhea, his sister and wife, as his coruler.

Curetes The sons of Rhea who provided armed protection from Cronus for the newborn Zeus. The supreme Olympian later asked them to provide similar protection for Zagreus, but the Titans managed to lure Zagreus away from the Curetes and brutally murder him.

Some say that Curetes are actually the five male Dactyls: Heracles, Paeonius, Epimedes, Iasius, and Acesidas.

Cyclopes The sons of Mother Earth, the Cyclopes were giants who were particularly adept at construction and smithcraft. The Cyclopes are usually described as being three in number—Brontes, Steropes, and Arges, which translate to "thunder," "lightning," and "brightness," respectively. There are two particularly interesting explanations for their

Cretheus The founder of Iolcus, the husband of Tyro, and the father of Aeson, Cretheus also reared his nephews, Pelias and Neleus. When his uncle died, Pelias seized his throne, exiled Neleus, and imprisoned Aeson.

Cronus The son of the great god Uranus and Mother Earth. When Uranus imprisoned his and Mother Earth's earliest children (the

Cyclopes and the Hundred-handed Ones), Mother Earth asked Cronus for his help. Using a toothed sickle, Cronus ambushed his father and castrated him. He threw Uranus' severed parts into the sea, and Athene (who in some versions was born of Zeus), the Furies, and a host of giants and nymphs arose from the waters.

Cronus soon reverted to the ways of his

description as one-eyed monsters. Smiths were known to tattoo themselves with concentric rings in honor of the sun, the source of fire for their furnaces (the concentric circles are also part of the pattern used to make bowls, helmets, masks, etc.). It was also the practice of smiths to wear an eye patch over one good eye to prevent themselves from being made totally blind by flying sparks.

In some versions of early Olympian history, the Cyclopes and the Hundred-handed Ones are failed attempts by Mother Earth to create a race of mortals to populate the planet. When Uranus came to rule over Olympus he cast the Cyclopes into Tartarus. This was a major factor in Mother Earth's decision to help Cronus and the Titans overthrow Uranus. Unfortunately, Cronus turned out to be much like his father and quickly sent the Cyclopes back to the underworld. When Zeus made plans to overthrow Cronus, he too freed the Cyclopes and the Hundred-handed Ones. The Cyclopes gave Zeus his famous thunderbolts and were treated well by him until Apollo killed them to avenge the death of his son Asclepius, whom the Cyclopes had killed for bringing mortals back to life.

It was said that the ghosts of the Cyclopes went to dwell in the caverns of the actively volcanic Mount Aetna; this legend served to explain the smoke that frequently rose from that mountain. There were, however, descendants of the Cyclopes who lost all knowledge of smithcraft and became shepherds. These Cyclopes were said to be a miserable, lawless lot who lived as far from one another as possible. Their island home was one of the stops Odysseus made on his extended journey home from the Trojan War.

Cycnus
A name given to a wide range of mythological characters. Apollo and Hyria had a son named Cycnus who imposed three love-tasks on Phylius. When Phylius completed the three tasks, Cycnus requested yet another. His patience now exhausted, Phylius killed himself; in response, Cycnus leapt into the lake that was afterward known as the Cycnean lake, and was followed into it by his mother.

There was also a son of Ares and Pyrene named Cycnus. When Heracles challenged him to a duel (with Ares serving as Cycnus' second), Zeus threw a thunderbolt between the contestants and ordered that they stop.

There are similar versions of this story in which Cycnus is the son of Ares and Pelopia who took delight in challenging passersby to chariot duels. Cycnus emerged victorious until Heracles came along. The two met in a great

crash, and continued with hand-to-hand fighting. Heracles killed Cycnus before Zeus could interrupt, and Cycnus' corpse was despoiled by Heracles and his allies, but eventually given a proper burial by Ceyx.

Another Cycnus, the son of Poseidon and either Calyce or Harpale, was born in secret and exposed on a seashore, where he was discovered by fishermen. He grew to manhood and married Procleia, with whom he conceived Tenes. Procleia died and Cycnus married Phylonome, who fell in love with her stepson. Tenes rebuffed Phylonome's advances, and Phylonome responded by accusing him of trying to violate her. Cycnus believed his wife and exiled Tenes and his sister, Hemithea. When Cycnus eventually learned the truth, he had Phylonome buried alive and then set out to seek his children's forgiveness. Tenes was unresponsive at first, but eventually relented.

It is possible that this Cycnus was one of the two characters with that name whom Achilles is said to have killed during the course of the Trojan War and its related journeys. In one version it is suggested that Cycnus was killed fighting alongside Tenes when they encountered the Greeks on their way to Troy, and in others a character named Cycnus slays hundreds of Greeks in the first clash between Trojans and Greeks before Achilles strikes him down. Poseidon then responds by turning Cycnus' spirit into a swan.

Cyrene
The daughter of Hypseus, Cyrene despised domestic concerns and preferred to hunt and engage in physical contests. While Cyrene was wrestling with a lion, Apollo saw her for the first time and was greatly attracted to her. Apollo's companion Cheiron prophesied that the god would make her a great and powerful queen who would conceive a child with him. Apollo and Cyrene's first union resulted in the birth of Aristaeus, their second the birth of Idmon the seer. In some cases, Cyrene is also thought to have been the mother of Diomedes by Ares.

Cyzicus
The King of Arcton, Cyzicus invited the passing Argonauts to participate in the wedding banquet following his marriage to Cleite. The Argo sailed away that night, but was blown back by a storm. Neither group recognized the other, and a battle ensued during which Cyzicus and much of his army was overcome. This unfortunate incident is often said to have been brought about by Rhea in an effort to avenge herself on Cyzicus for having killed one of her sacred lions on Mount Dindymum.

Heracles and Cycnus, **black-figured amphora, 5th century** B.C.

Dactyls
Five males and five females that, according to some versions, sprang from the ground where Rhea had dug her nails into the soil while delivering Zeus. This origin contradicts the Dactyls' presence at events that took place before Zeus' birth, however, and there are some versions in which it is stated that the Dactyls' mother was Anchiale. The male Dactyls were smiths who discovered iron at Mount Berecynthus, and the females were emigrants to Samothrace, where they cast spells and introduced Orpheus to Rhea's mysteries.

In some cases, the Curetes are thought to have been the male Dactyls, though other names suggested include Acmon, Damnameneus, and Celmis, as well as Titias, Cyllenius, and Dascylus.

Daedalus
A master craftsman taught by Athene, Daedalus created many objects that figure prominently in a variety of myths. Daedalus' parentage is uncertain: Alcippe,

Daedalus and Icarus, Antonio Canova, 1779.

Merope, and Iphinoë are all mentioned at different times as being his mother; Daedalus' father, whoever he might have been, was almost certainly an Athenian.

Daedalus took as his apprentice his nephew Talos, the son of his sister Polycaste. When the twelve-year-old Talos' work began surpassing that of his uncle, Daedalus pushed him to his death from a roof. The possibility that Talos and his mother were involved in an incestuous affair is also mentioned as a factor in or rationalization for Daedalus' actions.

Daedalus was banished by the Areiopagus for his crime and eventually found himself on Cnossus. There he helped Minos' wife, Pasiphaë, consummate her unnatural desire for a white bull by building a hollow, cow-shaped vessel within which she could make herself available to the beast. When Minos learned the role Daedalus had played in Pasiphaë's conception of the Minotaur, he put Daedalus and his son, Icarus, into the center of the Labyrinth that Daedalus had created and that also contained Pasiphaë, the Minotaur, and its half-sister Ariadne.

After escaping the Labyrinth, Daedalus decided that his and Icarus' only hope of getting to freedom was by air, since Minos controlled a large portion of the Mediterranean. He fashioned a pair of wings for Icarus and himself, warning his son not to fly too high. Icarus didn't listen, and flew too close to Helius, whose heat caused the wax that held Icarus' feathers together to melt. Icarus fell to his death, and in many versions it is suggested that Polycaste's soul was responsible for shaping the events that caused this to happen. Daedalus' escape was one of a series of steps that eventually led to Theseus' invasion of Crete.

After his escape, Daedalus found himself in the court of King Cocalus of Camicus, where his skills earned him not only a warm welcome, but fame and fortune as well. Minos eventually tracked the inventor down and was on the verge of killing him when Cocalus' daughters intervened. They were so taken by the toys and gifts Daedalus had bestowed upon them that they aided in the murder of Minos. Despite the children's protests, Daedalus departed; he ended up in Sardinia with a group led by Heracles' nephew Iolaus.

Danaë The daughter of Acrisius, who had been warned that a grandson of his would kill him. Acrisius imprisoned Danaë so that no one could conceive the child that would kill him, but Zeus "came upon her in a shower of gold" and impregnated her with Perseus.

Danaë, Titian, c. 1545.

After Danaë delivered Perseus, Acrisius locked her and the child in a wooden ark and cast them out to sea. They were rescued off the island of Seriphos by a fisherman named Dictys, who brought them to his brother, King Polydectes. Mother and son took refuge in Polydectes' court, but it quickly became apparent that the king's motives were not entirely selfless. Polydectes constantly tried to force marriage on Danaë, who steadfastly refused.

When Perseus grew up and helped his mother rebuff Polydectes' advances, the king sent Perseus off on a seemingly impossible mission. While Perseus was away trying to remove the head of the Gorgon Medusa, Polydectes doubled his attempts to win Danaë, and she and Dictys went into hiding.

Perseus succeeded in his mission, returned, killed Polydectes and his allies, and established Dictys as king. Then Perseus, his new wife, Andromeda, a few allied Cyclopes, and Danaë all returned to Argos. In some versions Polydectes is portrayed as a peacemaker who marries Danaë under less forceful conditions. In all versions, however, it is at Polydectes' funeral games that Perseus fulfills the prophesy regarding Acrisius' death that caused him and Danaë to be cast out in the first place.

Danaids   The fifty daughters of Danaus. After being betrothed to their cousins, the sons of Aegyptus, the Danaids, who considered such a union improper, fled to Argos for pro-

tection. They were eventually forced into the marriage, but on their wedding night, at their father's instruction, all but one of them killed their new husbands. Hypermnestra spared her husband, Lynceus, in gratitude for his having spared her virginity.

The Danaids were credited with bringing the mysteries of Demeter to Peloponnesus and are thought to have been darkly complected people of Egyptian heritage. For the murder of their husbands, they are subject to eternal torments.

Danaus   One of the twin sons of King Belus and Anchinoë. When Belus died, Danaus' brother, Aegyptus, proposed a marriage between his fifty sons and Danaus' fifty daughters. Suspicious of his brother's motives, Danaus consulted an oracle that confirmed that Aegyptus had ulterior motives. With Athene's assistance, Danaus and the Danaids fled Greece, via Rhodes, to the kingdom of Argos. There the Argive King Gelanor resigned his position to avoid losing his life in any battle that might result from the dispute between the two brothers. (This story is the subject of Aeschylus' *The Suppliants.*)

When the mass marriage seemed inevitable, Danaus gave each of his daughters a sharp pin to hide in her hair and to use to stab her husband once night fell. All of the Danaids, with the exception of Hypermnestra, followed their father's instructions.

Danaus was outraged, and fought to have Hypermnestra executed. When an Argive judge sided with the daughter, she was reunited with Lynceus, who later killed Danaus and ruled in his place.

Daphne   A mountain nymph who was the daughter of the river god Peneius and a priestess of Mother Earth, Daphne was ardently pursued by Apollo. She cried out when the god was on the verge of catching her, and was rescued by Mother Earth, who left a laurel tree in her place.

Another Daphne, the daughter of Teiresias the seer, was captured by the Epigoni when they took Thebes. They sent her to

Apollo and Daphne, Bernini, 17th century.

Apollo, and she became his Pythoness. In some versions it is suggested that she remained a virgin and became a Sibyl.

> *A soaring drowsiness possessed her; growing*
> *In earth she stood, white thighs embraced by*
> *climbing*
> *Bark, her white arms branches, her fair head*
> *swaying*
> *In a cloud of leaves; all that was Daphne bowed*
> *In the stirring of the wind, the glittering green*
> *Leaf twined within her hair and she was laurel.*
> —The Metamorphoses, *Ovid*

Daphnis

The son of Hermes and a nymph, Daphnis was left by his mother to die in one of Hera's laurel groves. Daphnis grew to be a beautiful youth, was taught to play the pipes by Pan, and was beloved by Apollo. Daphnis hunted alongside Artemis and claimed a direct ancestral line to Helius.

Daphnis had sworn fidelity to a nymph named Nomia, whose rival, the Chimaera, seduced him. When Nomia learned of Daphnis' infidelity, she fulfilled a vow by blinding Daphnis, who subsequently spent the rest of his life singing sad songs. Daphnis eventually died, and was turned to stone by Hermes.

Dardanus

The son of Zeus and the Pleiad Electra, and the twin brother of Iasion, Dardanus claimed Corythus as his father. Dardanus married Chryse, and the two had twin sons, Idaeus and Deimas, who were destined to be parted by the Deucalion Flood. After the flood, Dardanus and Idaeus went to Samothrace, which they colonized and renamed Dardania.

When Dardanus heard of Iasion's death, he went to the Troad, where he was welcomed by Teucer at one of the settlements that would eventually become part of Troy. When Teucer died, Dardanus succeeded him, and settled on the side of Mount Ida. An oracle told him to move down the hill a bit, where he established yet another city named Dardania. This settlement was later merged with Ilium and Tros to form Troy.

There are versions of Dardanus' story in which Iasion goes to Samothrace while Dardanus goes to the Troad and begins his alliance with Teucer. In other versions Dardanus is described as a Phrygian King who gave his daughter in marriage to Teucer.

Dascylus

The son of Tantalus and the father of Lycus, Dascylus accidentally killed Titias at Priolas' funeral games. In the ensuing

Nessus Raping Deianeira, **Guido Reni, 1620–1621.**

battle, Heracles fought the Mysians and Phrygians on Dascylus' behalf.

There was also a son of Lycus named Dascylus, who was volunteered by his father to help guide the Argonauts safely to Colchis. Dascylus is also a name given to one of the Dactyls.

Deianeira

The daughter of Althaea and Dionysus or of Dexamenus, Deianeira was the sister of Meleager. When Meleager was killed, Deianeira and her sister Gorge were turned into guinea-fowl by Artemis. Dionysus pleaded with Artemis to undo her work, and the sisters were returned to their human forms.

When Heracles went to Tartarus during his twelfth labor, he met the ghost of Meleager, who asked Heracles to marry Deianeira. When Heracles returned from the underworld, he deflowered Deianeira, then left, promising to return and marry her. During Heracles' absence, Eurytion the Centaur tried to make Deianeira his wife, and was on the verge of marrying her when Heracles returned. Heracles killed Eurytion and Eurytion's brothers, and carried Deianeira off.

There are other versions in which Deianeira is being courted by Achelous as well as Heracles. The two suitors agreed to settle the matter through combat, and Heracles prevailed. Heracles and Deianeira eventually became the parents of Hyllus, and the three went to live in Trachis with Ceyx after Heracles accidentally killed the son of Architeles. On the way to Trachis, the Centaur Nessus attempted to carry Deianeira off as she was crossing the river Evenus. Nessus tried to violate Deianeira, and was shot by Heracles, who was following behind, from a distance of nearly a half mile. Before Nessus died he told Deianeira that his seed that had spilled on the ground, when mixed with his blood, would create a potion that would make Heracles eternally faithful to her.

Deianeira waited faithfully for her husband while he completed his labors. When Heracles sent Iole home ahead of his arrival, Deianeira grew jealous of her husband's new mistress. She sent Heracles a shirt that she had coated with Nessus' alleged love potion. This shirt caused Heracles great pain, and when he could no longer stand the torment, Heracles threw himself upon a funeral pyre, which led to his apotheosis.

Deianeira had learned too late about the true nature of Nessus' potion, and was unsuccessful in her attempt to get word to Heracles to prevent his wearing the garment. When she heard what had happened to her husband, Deianeira took her own life, either by hanging or with a knife.

For Deianeira, as I hear, hath ever an aching heart; she, the battle prize of old, is not like some bird lorn of its mate; she can never lull her yearning nor stay her tears; haunted by a sleepless fear for her absent lord, she pines on her anxious, widowed couch, miserable in her foreboding of mischance.
—Chorus, The Trachian Women, *Sophocles*

Deidameia

A daughter of Lycomedes, Deidameia met Achilles when he came to visit her father. This meeting eventually resulted in the birth of Pyrrhus, later known as Neoptolemus, who would play an influential role in the Trojan War. Deidameia and Achilles sailed off together and were blown by a storm to Scyros, where they were married.

Deidameia is also given as another name for Hippodameia.

Deiphobus

One of Priam and Hecabe's many sons, Deiphobus joined his brother Hector in attacking a stranger who turned out to be their brother Paris, whom Priam had abandoned at birth. When Paris' true identity was revealed, Deiphobus and all of his brothers welcomed Paris warmly and once Paris instigated war between Troy and Greece, Deiphobus fought valiantly in defense of his city.

Deiphobus is said to have played a role in the death of Achilles in those versions where Polyxena helped Deiphobus and Paris ambush the Greek hero. When Paris was killed in the war, Deiphobus became Helen's husband (her fourth).

When the Greeks emerged from the Trojan Horse and began their assault on the

***Omphalos (Navel of the World),* stone shrine from the Delphic Oracle, 5th century B.C.**

city of Troy, Menelaus and Odysseus went directly to Deiphobus' house, where they engaged in the bloodiest battle of the entire war. The conflict was not decided until Athene assisted in the slaying of Deiphobus. His corpse was mutilated and dragged about by the Greeks, and Aeneas later erected a monument in Deiphobus' honor on Cape Rhoeteum.

Delphic Oracle

The most famous of all oracles, the Delphic Oracle was originally a seat of worship to Gaea. With the ascendancy of the Olympian deities, worshipers of Apollo came to control the shrine. Delphi was thought to be located at the middle of the known world, and served as one of the few unifying elements of the fragmented Hellenic community. The Pythoness served as Apollo's chief priestess, and spent one month each year accepting visitors and answering their questions.

The centerpiece of the oracle was the stone that Cronus was tricked into swallowing in place of the infant Zeus. This stone was eventually set upon the altar of the oracle. The rich and powerful throughout Greece and the Mediterranean world came here for advice, leaving valuable treasures as payment for the Pythoness' utterances.

Delphyne

The serpent-tailed sister of Typhon, Delphyne guarded over Zeus' sinews during her brother's nearly victorious battle with the great deity. Pan scared the monstrous Delphyne and Hermes recovered the sinews and returned them to Zeus, thus bringing about the defeat of Typhon.

Demeter

A daughter of Cronus and Rhea, Demeter came to be one of the twelve ruling Olympians. She was most often recognized as the goddess of the harvest, representing a time when women controlled the mysteries of agriculture. Demeter was one of the Olympians initially swallowed by Cronus and later freed by Zeus. Zeus lay with Demeter on several occasions, and is credited with fathering Core, Iacchus, and possibly Dionysus. He also became jealous when he caught Demeter and Iasius together in a freshly plowed field during Cadmus and Harmonia's wedding. (The field is described as thrice-plowed, a description that refers to Demeter's involvement with the harvest.) Zeus killed Iasius with a thunderbolt, but not before Plutus was conceived. And although Demeter never married, she is described as initiating newlyweds in the "secrets of the couch."

Demeter's most famous role in mythology is that of the grieving mother, seen when Hades abducted her daughter Core and carried her off to Tartarus. Demeter searched far and wide for Core, and eventually was told by Triptolemus, one of King Celeus' sons, that one of his brothers had seen Hades carrying her daughter down through a crack in the earth into the underworld. Demeter complained about Core's abduction to Zeus, who eventually devised a compromise in which Core would be allowed to spend three quarters of the year with her mother and the remainder in Tartarus as Queen of the Underworld.

When Tantalus butchered his son Pelops and attempted to serve him to the gods,

Venus, Ceres, and Juno, **Raphael, 1517.**

Demeter, still dazed by the loss of Core, ate a piece of the child's left shoulder (she was the only god to partake). When Zeus revived Pelops, Demeter crafted an ivory replacement for the portion she had eaten.

Demeter also is described in some versions as creating the Lesser Mysteries for Heracles, since only Athenians were allowed to be introduced to the Greater Eleusian Mysteries.

Demophon   The son of Theseus and the brother of Acamas, Demophon succeeded his father to the throne of Athens, which he ruled around the time of the Trojan War.

Demophon and Acamas were important members of the Greek alliance for the entire Trojan War and were prepared to share in the spoils of the Greek victory when they encountered their grandmother, Aethra, one of Helen's attendants who had come to Troy with her from Sparta. Demophon and Acamas then asked Agamemnon to repatriate their grandmother, which he said he was willing to do if the brothers would renounce their portion of Troy's spoils. Demophon and Acamas grudgingly agreed, but first avenged themselves on Agamemnon (for his condition that they renounce their spoils) by insisting that Polyxena be sacrificed in accordance with Achilles' final wishes.

The brothers set sail for Athens but first landed in Thrace, where a princess named Phyllis fell in love with Demophon. He married her and became king, but quickly grew tired of Thrace. When Demophon announced that he was leaving to visit his mother, whom he had not seen in eleven years, Phyllis said that the king could not take such an extended leave. Demophon responded by swearing by each and every Olympian that he would be back within a year. Phyllis accompanied him a short distance and presented him with a casket that she said contained a charm. Phyllis warned her husband that he should open it only when he had abandoned all hope of returning.

Demophon, never intending to return, headed to Cyprus instead of Athens. A year later Demophon was still in Cyprus. Phyllis cursed him in the name of Rhea and committed suicide with poison. At the same time, Demophon decided to open the casket and examine its contents; whatever was in the casket drove him insane, and he galloped off on his horse in a panic. When Demophon hit his horse in the head with his sword, the horse stumbled; Demophon flew off, landed on his sword, and died.

Demophoön   The newborn son of King Celeus and Metaneira for whom Demeter served as wet nurse. To atone for having turned Celeus and Metaneira's son Abas into a lizard, Demeter promised to make Demophoön immortal. Just as the goddess was nearly done with the process, Metaneira inadvertently interrupted it and broke the spell, causing Demophoön's death.

Desmontes   A childless woman, Desmontes was entrusted with the care of Arne, daughter of Thea. When Arne delivered Aeolus and Boeotus, Desmontes abandoned the twins to die on Mount Pelion, where they were rescued by a shepherd. The twins later killed Desmontes in the process of rescuing their mother, whom Desmontes had been holding captive.

Deucalion   The King of Phthia whose name was eventually given to the same cataclysmic flood that is told of in the Bible and throughout the history of the pre-Christian Mediterranean. The son of Prometheus and the brother of Ariadne, Deucalion married Pyrrha and raised a family that included Orestheus, Amphictyon, and Hellen.

Deucalion and Pyrrha, Andrea del Minga, c. 1570–1572.

When Prometheus warned his son about Zeus' preparations to flood the earth and kill all mortals (because of his disgust with Lycaon's sons' attempt to feed their father their slaughtered brother), Deucalion built himself an ark and survived the flood. The ship landed on Mount Parnassus. (Mounts Aetna, Athos, and Othrys are all offered as alternate landing sites.)

Deucalion and Pyrrha were thankful for their safety and sorry for the near-destruction of their race. They conveyed these sentiments to Zeus, who sent Hermes and Themis to instruct the survivors to throw stones over their shoulders. The stones Deucalion threw

became men, and those Pyrrha threw became women, and "Thus mankind was renewed." As in Noah's story, it eventually became apparent that there were other flood survivors, including Megarus, Cerambus, and the inhabitants of Parnassus.

The other most noteworthy Deucalion was the son of the powerful King Minos. This Deucalion ascended to the throne of Crete after Minos' death, but eventually lost it and his life to Theseus.

. . . They left the temple
With floating robes and veiled heads, then
furtively

Dropped pebbles in their trail as they ran. . .
Pebbles grew into rocks, rocks into statues
That looked like men; the darker parts still wet
With earth were flesh, dry elements were bones,
And veins began to stir with human blood—
Such were the inclinations of heaven's will.
The stones that Deucalion dropped were men,
And those that fell from his wife's hands were
women.

—The Metamorphoses, *Ovid*

Dexamenus The King of Olenus to whose court Heracles went following the cleaning of Augeias' stables, Dexamenus was a Centaur whose twin daughters married the Moliones. Dexamenus was also the father of Deianeira, whom Heracles eventually married.

Dictys The brother of King Polydectes, Dictys rescued Danaë and her son Perseus after they were cast adrift in an ark by Acrisius. Dictys then brought them to his brother, who pressured Danaë for her favors. After the king sent Perseus to slay Medusa, and pressed his intentions even harder, Danaë and Dictys went into hiding. When Perseus returned with Medusa's head in hand, he turned the king and his allies to stone and established Dictys on the throne.

Diomedes The son of Tydeus and Deipyle, Diomedes was one of the Epigoni. After avenging his father's defeat at Thebes he joined the Greek alliance against Troy.

Diomedes served closely under Agamemnon, and was probably involved in the entrapment of Palamedes and the murder of Pandarus. He won the chariot race at Patroclus' funeral games, and when his cousin Thersites was killed by Achilles, Diomedes threw the corpse into the river Scamander.

Toward the end of the war, Diomedes was instrumental in retrieving Philoctetes, who was in possession of Heracles' bow. Diomedes also conspired with Odysseus to steal the Palladium, a sacred statue of Athene that was kept inside Troy and needed to pass from Trojan hands in order for the city to fall. In some versions of this story, Odysseus is about to kill Diomedes (after the latter obtained the Palladium by himself) in the hope of taking complete credit for obtaining the prize, while in others Diomedes stays in camp while Odysseus accomplishes the mission on his own.

Once Troy had fallen, Diomedes supported Agamemnon's desire to make a sacrifice to Athene, which was supposed to have assured him a safe voyage home. But Aphrodite had a score to settle with Diomedes and saw to it

Dionysus with the Nymph Leucotha, **marble relief, Hellenistic period.**

that his ship was wrecked along the Lycian coast. King Lycus would have sacrificed Diomedes to Ares were it not for his daughter Callirrhoë, who helped the Greek escape.

When Diomedes finally reached Argos, he discovered that his wife, Aegialeia, had fallen prey to Nauplius' schemes and had taken up with Cometes. Diomedes traveled on to Corinth, where he learned that his grandfather Oeneus needed assistance against a group wishing to oust him from power. Diomedes sailed to Aetolia and helped Oeneus secure his grip on the throne.

Diomedes spent the rest of his life in Italy, married to Euippe, the daughter of King

Daunus. Diomedes' success is said to have made Daunus jealous, causing him to murder his son-in-law. Diomedes was buried on one of the islands that were subsequently collectively named after him. (In some versions Diomedes is described as disappearing through an act of divine magic.) His golden armor was preserved by the priests of Athene, and he was worshiped as a god in areas of Venice and throughout much of southern Italy.

Several other mythological characters also had the name Diomedes. The first of these was the son of Ares and Cyrene who was the King of Thrace and owned the famous man-eating horses that were the object of Heracles' eighth

labor. Another Diomedes was the son of Aeson and Polymele who was abandoned, was subsequently raised by Cheiron, and later became known as Jason.

Dionysus

The son of Zeus and Semele, Demeter, Io, Dione, Persephone, or Lethe. The most common story regarding Dionysus' conception involves Zeus and Semele. When Hera convinced Semele to act in a way that angered Zeus greatly, and Zeus struck Semele dead with a lightning bolt, Hermes saved the six-month-old fetus Semele had been carrying and sewed it up inside Zeus' thigh. When Dionysus came to full term Hermes delivered him, an event reflected in the translation of Dionysus' name, which means "twice born," or "child of the double door."

On Hera's orders, the Titans tore the infant Dionysus to shreds and boiled his remains. Dionysus' grandmother Rhea rescued those remains, reconstituted the infant, and entrusted him to Persephone, who passed him along to King Athamas and his wife, Ino. They raised Dionysus as a girl (hence the frequent portrayal of him as a long-haired, effeminate youth), but Hera nonetheless eventually recognized him.

Zeus had Hermes transform Dionysus into a kid or a ram after Hera recognized him, and entrusted his son to the nymphs who lived on Mount Nysa, where they raised him in a cave. It was here that Dionysus invented wine, an accomplishment for which he is probably best remembered and most frequently celebrated. Hera eventually tracked Dionysus down to Mount Nysa and drove him insane, as she had Athamas and Ino. Dionysus then went on a mad, drunken rampage that took him to Egypt, where he allied with the Libyan Amazons against the Titans in an attempt to restore King Ammon to his throne.

Dionysus then went to India, which he is said to have conquered, where he introduced viniculture. On the return trip, Dionysus encountered the other Amazons, many of whom he slaughtered near Samos. Rhea purified him for the various murders he committed during the course of his rampage, and Dionysus moved on to Thebes, where a difference of opinion with King Pentheus resulted in much chaos and suffering among the Thebans. Dionysus then invited Minyas' daughters to revel with him, and drove them crazy when they refused. One of the daughters sacrificed her son (Hippasus) and all three were eventually turned into birds by Hermes. In some versions, it is said that Dionysus transformed them into bats instead.

Mostly because of the popularity of the wine-based worship he engendered, Dionysus grew in stature until he was allowed to sit at the right hand of Zeus as one of the twelve ruling Olympians. (Hestia, the only god to avoid taking sides in any wars or battles, gave up her place for him.) Once he had achieved this status, Dionysus went down to Tartarus and bribed Persephone to release his mother, Semele. Dionysus took Semele to Artemis' temple in Troezen, where she became the priestess Thyone.

Dionysus appears in numerous myths, and is often a stock character when inebriation plays a role. It is likely that many of the madnesses Dionysus inflicted on mythological characters might have been related to wine. Among his many escapades, Dionysus is said to have slept with Aphrodite. The fruit of their union was Priapus, an ugly child with enormous genitalia whose disfigurement had been caused by Hera, who disapproved of Aphrodite's promiscuity.

Dionysus was worshiped by the Centaurs, and was usually accompanied by countless Satyrs and Maenads.

Hermes with the Infant Dionysus,
Praxitales, 4th century B.C.

Dioscuri   The name by which the half-brothers Polydeuces and Castor were collectively known. Leda was their mother, and Zeus and King Tyndareus, Leda's husband, are each said to have fathered one of the twins. The Dioscuri were never separated in any adventure, and were the pride of Sparta. They carried off their cousins, the Leucippides, and fathered children upon them despite the Leucippides being engaged to Idas and Lynceus.

The Dioscuri fought in all of Sparta's battles and presided over games and competitions. (Polydeuces was particularly well known for his boxing skills.) The Dioscuri were said to be guardians of sailors in distress, and were eventually joined in that role by their sister, Helen. Before this, however, Helen was the cause of another of the Dioscuri's conflicts. They sought Helen after Theseus had abducted her, and led an army against Attica, which they ravaged until they learned her whereabouts. Despite their victory, the Dioscuri were welcomed in Athens because they had treated the common people well while displacing their rulers.

In some versions, the Dioscuri go to the defense of Clytaemnestra (their sister) when her first husband, Tantalus, is killed by Agamemnon. (In some of these accounts the Dioscuri are killed by Agamemnon and his forces, despite the fact that Agamemnon was allied with their father, Tyndareus.)

The Dioscuri figure in a number of other episodes and in several Greek dramas. They participated in the hunt for the Calydonian Boar, attended Peirithous and Hippodameia's wedding, during which war with the Centaurs broke out, and served as Argonauts.

In most versions the Dioscuri's end came when they resumed their dealings with Idas and Lynceus, whose fiancées they had stolen years earlier. When the pairs of brothers argued over the spoils of their alliance, a battle ensued that resulted in the death of all four. (In some versions, Polydeuces survives.)

Dirce   The wife of Lycus, Dirce was best known for her heartless mistreatment of her niece, Antiope. In some versions it is suggested that Dirce was angered by Antiope's pregnancy out of wedlock, while in others it is indicated that the twin sons of Antiope, Amphion and Zethus, were fathered by Dirce's husband, Lycus. Whatever the reason, Dirce imprisoned Antiope and abandoned her children to die. The twins survived, and later rescued Antiope and killed Dirce by tying her (by her hair) to the horns of a bull.

The Dioscuri, **black-figured amphora,**
5th century B.C.

Dryads   Oak nymphs who were the companions of Eurydice and to whom Aristaeus made sacrifices to atone for his role in Eurydice's death, the Dryads resided inside trees, and their lives ended with those of the trees they inhabited.

Dryope   The daughter of Dryops, Dryope was a nymph who tended her father's flocks in the company of her friends the Hamadryads. When Apollo became attracted to Dryope, he scared off the Hamadryads and had his way with her. Amphissus, the offspring of this union, eventually founded the city of Oeta and there built a temple dedicated to Apollo; he then installed Dryope as priestess, but the Hamadryads abducted her and left a poplar tree in her place.

Dryope is considered by some to have been Pan's mother by Hermes, and is also said to have fallen in love with Hylas along with her sister nymphs.

Echo and Narcissus, **Nicolas Poussin, before 1630.**

Eastern Demons
The six sons of Halia and Poseidon, the Eastern Demons were angered by Aphrodite and insulted her. When Aphrodite caused the young men to lose their senses, they ravished Halia. As punishment, Poseidon sank them all beneath the sea, where they became known as the Eastern Demons.

Echidne
The wife of Typhon, with whom she created or gave birth to a wide range of creatures, Echidne was one of the Phorcids. The upper half of Echidne was a lovely woman, the lower half a speckled serpent; she lived in a cave where she ate unsuspecting passersby and raised a frightful brood with Typhon. Echidne and Typhon are generally credited with being the parents of Cerberus, the Hydra, the Chimaera, Orphus, and, in many versions, the Sphinx, Ladon, and Scylla. In some versions, Echidne is said to have conceived the Sphinx and the Nemean Lion with her son Orphus. Echidne was killed in her sleep by Argus; Heracles is credited with taming or slaying many of her offspring.

Echo
A nymph who was seduced by Pan and subsequently gave birth to Iynx, Echo helped Zeus while he lay with the other nymphs by distracting Hera with long stories. As a result, Hera punished Echo by making it so that she could no longer speak except in foolish repetition.

Later, Echo was one of the many to fall in love with Narcissus and suffer his disdain. She spent the rest of her life pining away, until all that remained was her voice. When Narcissus took his own life, Echo grieved with him, and repeated his dying words.

Eëtion
The father of Andromache, Eëtion allied with the Trojans and married his daughter to Hector. During the Trojan War, Eëtion ransomed Priam's son Lycaon out of slavery so that the latter could resume fighting. Twelve days later, Lycaon was slain in battle.

Eëtion shared command of the Cilicians with Podes, and was killed by Achilles in the later stages of the decade-long engagement.

Electra
The daughter of Agamemnon and Clytaemnestra, Electra was the sister of Orestes, Chrysothemis, and Iphianassa. When Clytaemnestra and Aegisthus killed Agamemnon, Electra was quite vocal in her animosity toward them. Aegisthus was inclined to kill her, but Clytaemnestra insisted on sparing her.

In some versions, Electra sees to it that her infant brother, Orestes, is taken away when Agamemnon is killed. Electra then waits for him to come of age so that he can avenge his father's cold-blooded murder. In the meantime, Clytaemnestra sees to it that Electra is married to a peasant and lives in poverty so that she will be unable to threaten her and Aegisthus' reign. The peasant, aware of the difference in their stations, never touches Electra and provides her with as many comforts as his meager resources can provide.

When Orestes and his companion Pylades finally returned to Mycenae and killed Aegisthus, Electra convinced her brother to kill Clytaemnestra as well, despite the strict taboo against matricide. This caused Orestes and Pylades to run from the torments of the Erinnyes, which eventually took them to the Black Sea in an attempt to obtain the Taurians' wooden image of Artemis, which just happened to be under the care of Orestes and Electra's sister, Iphigeneia (who in these versions is still alive because Agamemnon's sacrifice of her was interrupted). Orestes, Iphigeneia, and Pylades eventually returned from the east and met up with Electra in Delphi, where she had gone to consult the oracle regarding rumors of their sacrifice.

Electra married Orestes' best friend, Pylades, and went to live in Phocis, his homeland. Electra and Pylades conceived Medon and Strophius the Second. There are many variations in this story, usually concerning the details of the period from Orestes' return to Mycenae to his murder of Aegisthus. Electra's role in her stepfather's murder is tentative at best, but most of the blame for Clytaemnestra's death is often directed toward her. At the least, Electra is said to have convinced Orestes to kill their mother, and it is often suggested that Electra devised and enacted the trap that brought Clytaemnestra into the fatal ambush.

Electryon
The son of Perseus, Electryon was the husband of Anaxo, with whom he conceived eight sons and a daughter named Alcmene. When Electryon went to war with the Taphians and Teleboans, he left his nephew Amphitryon as his regent, with the promise that if he served well he would be allowed to marry Alcmene.

When Electryon returned victorious— albeit without his eight sons, who were all killed in battle—he argued with Amphitryon for having paid a ransom for cattle that were rightly Electryon's. When Amphitryon angrily threw his club at a cow it struck the animal's horn and ricocheted, striking and killing Electryon.

Empusae Filthy, brazen-slippered demons with the hindquarters of an ass, the Empusae were daughters of Hecate who took sport in scaring off travelers, but could themselves be driven away easily with insulting words. These demons were greedily seductive and would disguise themselves as beautiful maidens in order to lie with men; once the men fell asleep, the Empusae would suck their blood.

Endymion The son of Zeus and the nymph Calyce, Endymion ousted Clymenus from his throne in Elis. Endymion married Iphianassa, with whom he had four sons, including Epeius—his successor—and Aetolus. He was eventually seen by Selene while sleeping in a cave on Mount Latmus; she fell deeply in love with him, and requested the gods to grant him eternal youth. They responded by causing him to fall into a dreamless, eternal sleep. Selene subsequently conceived fifty daughters by the sleeping Endymion.

In different versions of Endymion's story, the name of his wife is given as Hyperippe, Chromia, or Neis. There are also some versions in which it is suggested that Endymion's eternal sleep was either personally requested or given by Zeus as a form of punishment.

Eos The manifestation of dawn, Eos commanded a chariot that she would steer toward Olympus to signal the approach of her brother Helius. Eos also rode with Helius as he crossed the sky, in which form she was known as Hemera. Their sister Hespera (who may also have been another manifestation of Eos) served a similar function at the end of the day, marking Helius' arrival on the western shores and the onset of dusk. All were the children of Hyperion and Theia. Eos had another sister, Selene. (It should be noted that Eos is frequently referred to as Aurora, even in translations of certain Greek epics, as well as in the Roman classics.)

One day Aphrodite found Eos in bed with Aphrodite's lover Ares and cursed Eos so that she would have a constant longing for young mortals. This led Eos to seduce many young men, among them Orion, Cephalus, and Cleitus, all while she was married to Astraeus. As a result, the paternity of Eos' offspring is unclear, although Astraeus is usually credited with being the father of Boreas, the West and South winds, Phosphorus, and maybe all the remaining stars in Heaven.

Aurora, sleepless in the waking dawn,
Swung wide her purple gates and rose-tipped
light

Glowed through her stairs and halls; retreating
stars
Were closed in ranks by Lucifer who vanished
Even from his watchtower in the morning sky.
—The Metamorphoses, *Ovid*

Epaphus A son of Io, Epaphus is better known for simply being born (and for the manner of his conception) than for anything he ever did. His mother, Io, was punished for arousing Zeus' interest by Hera, who turned Io into a cow and had her chased around the Mediterranean by a gadfly. After Io escaped the gadfly, Zeus arrived and, with a single touch, took away the madness she had come to suffer. Epaphus, whose name means "child of a touch," was said to have been conceived by this act.

Epaphus was rumored to have been the divine bull Apis, who ruled over Egypt, and he may have fathered Libya in this form.

The child pastured amid flowers,
The Calf whom Zeus begot
Of the Cow, mother of our race,
Made pregnant by the breathing and caress of
Zeus;
Thence his true name was given,
His life fulfilled as it was foretold,

When his mother bore Epaphus, 'Child of a
touch.'
—Chorus, The Suppliants, *Aeschylus*

Epeius The son of Panopeus, Epeius was born a coward as punishment for his father's failure to live up to a vow. Epeius went on to become King of Olympia before losing that title to Pelops. A skilled craftsman, Epeius was an adept boxer despite his cowardice, and was a member of the Greek alliance.

Near the end of the Trojan War, Epeius was enlisted to build the wooden horse that the Greeks hoped to use to trick the Trojans and put an end to their decade-long war. With Athene's supervision, Epeius constructed a hollow horse of fir planks and fashioned a trap door through which the Greeks could enter and exit. On the other side of the trap door, Epeius carved an inscription that read: "In thankful anticipation of a safe return to their homes, the Greeks dedicate this offering to the Goddess [Athene]."

When Odysseus persuaded the bravest Greeks to hide within the horse he also managed to persuade (or bribe, threaten, or coax) Epeius to join them, particularly since Epeius alone knew how to operate the trap door through which they would have to emerge.

The Sleep of Endymion, Anne-Louis Girodet, 1783.

Epeius spent his time within the horse in an "ecstasy of fear," and finally sprang the secret passage open when Antenor signaled that the coast was clear. Despite his crucial role in the Trojan Horse affair, Epeius was always best known for his cowardice.

Ephialtes

The son of Iphimedeia by Poseidon (in an indirect way), and the twin brother of Otus. Ephialtes and Otus eventually came to be known as the Aloeides, and it is by this name that they are most well known.

Ephialtes was also one of the giants who battled Zeus and his Olympian allies. (The nature of his reincarnation or resurrection is unclear.) Ephialtes was engaged by Ares, who beat him to his knees. Apollo followed with an arrow that pierced Ephialtes' left eye, and Heracles finished the job with a similar shot to the right eye. "Thus died Ephialtes."

Epigoni

Sons of the seven champions who fell in Adrastus' attack on Thebes, the Epigoni swore to avenge their fathers by attacking Thebes again, but the Delphic Oracle told them that they would be victorious only if Alcmaeon, son of Amphiaraus, took command of their forces. Like his father, however, Alcmaeon was reluctant to join; he eventually deferred to his mother, Eriphyle, who was bribed to convince him to go (she had also been bribed to ensure his father's participation in the earlier assault).

Aegialeus, the son of Adrastus, led the first attack, and was killed. Meanwhile, Teiresias the seer had prophesied that Thebes would fall when the last of the seven champions died. When Adrastus, the sole survivor, died of grief upon learning his son's fate, most of the Thebans, assuming that the prophesy would come true, fled their homeland. The next day the Epigoni walked into a nearly deserted Thebes, which they occupied and looted, sending much of their bounty to Apollo at Delphi.

In addition to Alcmaeon, Thersander, and Aegialeus, the Epigoni included Amphilochus and possibly Diomedes.

Epimetheus

A brother of Atlas, Prometheus, and Menoetius, Epimetheus was convinced by Prometheus to ally with Zeus and the Olympians against his brothers, who were allied with Cronus and the Titans. As payment for this support, Zeus arranged for Epimetheus to marry Pandora. Epimetheus accepted her as his wife despite Prometheus' warning not to accept any gifts from Zeus lest all mankind suffer the consequences. It is not clear whether Epimetheus forgot his brother's advice or discounted it in light of Prometheus' fall from grace. Epimetheus tried to prevent Pandora from opening the jar of evils she had been entrusted with, but she eventually succumbed to the temptation and released the Spites upon the world.

Erechtheus

The son of Pandion and Zeuxippe, and part of a distinguished family that included his twin brother, Butes, another brother, Aegeus, and two sisters, Philomela and Procne. When Pandion died of grief over Philomela and Procne's tragic end, Erechtheus became the King of Athens. He married Praxithea and produced four sons—Cecrops, Metion, Orneus, Pandorus—and seven daughters—Protogonia, Pandora, Procnis, Creusa, Oreithyia, Chthonia, and Otionia.

Erechtheus led Athens into battle against Eleusis, during the course of which he sacrificed his youngest daughter, Otionia, in the hope of victory. Her sisters Pandora and Protogonia, having made a pact to act in unison, took their own lives. In addition, Erechtheus struck down his great-grandson, Eumolpus, as he fled from the decisive battle. Poseidon, Eumolpus' father, avenged the youth by ending Erechtheus' life.

Eriboea

One of the potential sacrifices to the Minotaur, Eriboea was lusted after by Minos. Theseus defended her from the king's advances and then slew the Minotaur in order to save both of their lives. As a gesture of gratitude, she invited him to her couch.

Later, Eriboea became the stepmother to the Aloeides. In the course of their attack on Olympus, the Aloeides captured Ares and confined him within a bronze vessel. They then entrusted this container to Eriboea, who was forced by Hermes to release Ares once her stepsons had been defeated.

Erichthonius

A child conceived upon Mother Earth with the semen that Athene had wiped from her thigh after Hephaestus had attempted to violate Athene. Mother Earth disavowed any responsibility for the child, so Athene accepted responsibility for it.

Erichthonius was part man and part serpent, and Athene hid the child in a basket that she entrusted to Aglauros, whose death eventually left Erichthonius without a guardian. Athene reclaimed Erichthonius, who later became the King of Athens. Athene gave Erichthonius two drops of Medusa's blood—one could kill, the other could cure any fatality. And in some versions Erichthonius is said to have helped Athene give Teiresias inward sight (in this case, understanding the language of prophetic birds) after the goddess had blinded him. Erichthonius is credited with introducing the use of silver, as well as the use of chariots. He was said to have been a prosperous ruler who owned three thousand mares, some of which were impregnated by Boreas when he took the form of a stallion.

Erichthonius is included among both Teucrian and Athenian lineages, and this is used to explain the connection between the settlers of the cities that eventually combined to create Troy. In honor of his role in creating the four-horse chariot, Erichthonius was eventually placed among the stars as the constellation Auriga.

Erigone

The name given to two different women, the first of whom was the daughter of Icarius, who was slain by drunken shepherds. Erigone was led to her father's body by his hound, Maera, and subsequently hanged herself after cursing the daughters of Athens to suffer similar fates until her father's death was avenged.

The second Erigone was the daughter of Clytaemnestra and Aegisthus. When Orestes returned to Athens and killed Erigone's parents, Erigone tried to sway the Athenians against Orestes. He was acquitted, but left Athens to cleanse himself of his act and escape the Erinnyes. Erigone's brother Aletes assumed the throne of Athens, but paid for it with his life when Orestes eventually returned.

Erigone's fate is unclear. In some versions she is on the verge of being killed by Orestes right after he slaughters Aletes, but is rescued by Artemis. In other versions it is suggested that Erigone went on to become Orestes' second wife and the mother of Penthilus and possibly Tisamenus. Finally, in a very different version of the story, Erigone, like her namesake, takes her life at the end of a rope following the Athenians' acquittal of Orestes.

Erinnyes

The name by which the Furies are more properly known. The Erinnyes were said to have arisen from the drops of blood that fell from Uranus after he was castrated by his son Cronus; in other versions they were the daughters of Mother Earth and Darkness or of Cronus and Eurynome or Night. The Erinnyes began their work at the entrance to Tartarus, where they screened out those who had yet to atone for their sins. The Erinnyes eventually became better known for their responsibility as the avengers of offenses against mothers by their children, and later came to be the punishers of all patricides and perjurers as well. Among the Olympians, the Erinnyes came to represent the concepts of retribution and vindictiveness, and the psychological domain of the guilty conscience. Over time, the Erinnyes' domain extended to the hearing of complaints regarding insolence by the young toward the old, children toward their parents, and hosts toward their guests.

While the Erinnyes were usually depicted as hideous female creatures who had wings and wore black robes, more exaggerated descriptions suggest that the Erinnyes had snakes for hair, the heads of dogs, blood-shot eyes, and coal-black bodies with bat wings. Because of the exclusively negative interaction they had with mortals, the Erinnyes were rarely referred to by name. Instead they were euphemistically called the Eumenides, "the kindly ones," a term Orestes is said to have coined when the Erinnyes were finally assuaged by his purifications following his murder of his mother.

The Erinnyes also tortured Oedipus, despite his being ignorant that the man he had killed on the road to Cadmus was his father; chastised Alcmaeon for the murder of his mother, Eriphyle, after he had been purified by Phegeus; and haunted the Amazon Queen Penthesileia for the accidental shooting of her sister Hippolyte.

The Erinnyes were usually said to have been three in number—Alecto, Tisiphone, and Megaera—but were occasionally depicted as a large flock of creatures, with the three named members leading the pack. The Erinnyes lived in Erebus, the darkest pit of the Underworld.

Eriphyle

The sister of Adrastus, King of Argos, and the wife of Amphiaraus. When Adrastus decided to lead seven champions against Thebes in the hope that they could return Polyneices to the throne, Amphiaraus was reluctant to join, but was convinced by Eriphyle, who had secretly been bribed by Polyneices. In exchange for Aphrodite's charmed necklace, which had belonged to Polyneices' ancestor Harmonia, Eriphyle agreed to convince her husband to support Adrastus.

Later, when the Epigoni rallied to avenge their fathers' deaths, Amphiaraus' son, Alcmaeon, proved hesitant to get involved, and Eriphyle was once again bribed, this time by Polyneices' son Thersander. Eriphyle convinced Alcmaeon to lead the Epigoni, which he did with great success. When Alcmaeon learned of Eriphyle's part in his and his father's persuasion, he became incensed and consulted Apollo. He took Apollo's agreement with his complaints to mean that the god condoned his killing her. Alcmaeon murdered Eriphyle, who managed to curse him in her dying breaths to be denied shelter for the rest of his life.

Eriphyle was also the mother of Amphilochus, another of the Epigoni.

The Erinnyes, **marble relief from sarcophagus,** A.D. **3rd century.**

Eris The twin sister of Ares and the daughter of Zeus and Hera. (Some versions imply that Hera's impregnation was caused by the touch of a flower.) Eris, who is also commonly referred to by her Roman name, Discordia, spread rumors and planted jealousies that would grow to cause the wars that were her brother's province.

Most often, Eris caused trouble when she was excluded from certain festivities. When she was not invited to the wedding of Peleus and Thetis, she sowed the seeds that would first bring about a feud and eventually lead to the Trojan War. And when Peirithous and Hippodameia neglected to invite Ares and Eris to their wedding, the twins retaliated by getting the Centaurs so drunk that they began a brawl that expanded into yet another war.

Eros The god of desire and sexual passion, Eros was a wild youth who gave no respect to age or station, but instead flew about on golden wings, randomly shooting arrows to make his targets fall in love or setting their hearts on fire with his torches.

In some versions of the creation of the Olympic universe it is suggested that Eros was the son of Night and was hatched out of the silver egg. In his earliest forms, Eros was known variously as Phanes, Ericepaius, and Protogenus Phaëthon. It is said that as Phanes he created the earth, sky, sun, and moon, but allowed Night to rule the universe until passing control on to Uranus.

Erymanthian Boar A fierce, enormous beast who menaced the northern regions of Peloponnesus, the Erymanthian Boar was captured alive by Heracles during the course of his fourth labor. To accomplish this feat, Heracles flushed the Boar from its hiding place and drove it into deep snow, where he mounted its back, rode it, and eventually chained it. While carrying the Boar back to Mycenae, Heracles learned of the assembling of the Argonauts and abandoned the beast. An unknown person subsequently killed and butchered the animal.

Eryx The son of Aphrodite and Butes the Argonaut who was conceived when Aphrodite slept with Butes in an effort to make Adonis jealous, Eryx became the King of Sicily. Eryx was widely praised for his skills as a wrestler

and boxer, and challenged Heracles to a fivefold contest. Heracles won the first four matches, and in the course of the fifth—wrestling—threw Eryx to the ground and killed him.

Eteocles The son of Oedipus, Eteocles fought with his brother Polyneices over their father's throne. Eteocles banished Polyneices, who went on to form an alliance with Adrastus. The latter two led an army against Thebes and sent Tydeus to demand that Eteocles relinquish his throne. Eteocles refused, and the battle made famous in Aeschylus' *Seven Against Thebes* ensued.

When Adrastus' forces gained an early advantage, Eteocles consulted the seer Teiresias, who told him that it would take the sacrifice of a Theban prince to ensure victory. Menoeceus volunteered, and the battle soon turned in Thebes' favor. As the fighting progressed, and many of the seven champions fell, Eteocles and Polyneices agreed to meet in singular combat, during which they mortally wounded one another. In many versions of this tale it is suggested that their deaths were the result of Oedipus' curse upon them.

> In this faith I will go and face him—I myself.
> Who has a stronger right than I? Chief and
>   Chief
> I'll match him, brother to brother, enemy to
>   enemy.
> —Eteocles, Seven Against Thebes, *Aeschylus*

Euippe The name given to the mare that Poseidon transformed Thea into before they coupled in the form of horses.

Eumaeus The servant of Odysseus to whom the wanderer came in disguise upon returning to Ithaca. When Odysseus revealed his true identity and attacked his wife's suitors, Eumaeus and another servant, Philoetius, fought alongside their master, and were responsible for removing Melantheus' extremities and feeding them to the dogs.

Eumenides The name given to the Erinnyes by Orestes after they were finally pacified by him. The name Eumenides means "kindly ones," and was used by other mortals who were afraid to even mention the Erinnyes' names lest they draw their attention.

Eumolpus An influential man who became instructed in the ways of the Eleusian Mysteries, and whose family controlled that priesthood for more than a millennium.

Aphrodite, Pan, and Eros, **marble sculpture, early 1st century** B.C.

In some stories it is suggested that Eumolpus was a son of King Celeus, and that when Eumolpus' brother Eubuleus saw Hades lead Core, daughter of Demeter, into the underworld, Eumolpus turned the tale into a lament, which his brother Triptolemus heard and shared with Demeter. The goddess rewarded Eumolpus, Triptolemus, and King Celeus by instructing them in her worship and in the Mysteries.

In other versions it is suggested that Eumolpus was the son of Chione by Poseidon, and was thrown into the sea and eventually given to his father's half-sister, Benthesicyme, to be raised. This Eumolpus grew up and was married to one of Benthesicyme's daughters. Unfortunately, he fell in love with another of her daughters, for which he was banished to Thrace. There, King Tegyrius also banished him for plotting his overthrow.

In Eleusis, Eumolpus mended his ways, and instructed Heracles in the worship of Demeter and Persephone. He also instructed Heracles in the arts of singing and lyre playing. Eumolpus was eventually killed by Erechtheus while fighting with the forces of Eleusis. Eumolpus was succeeded as High Priest of the Eleusian Mysteries by his son, Ceryx.

Euneus

One of three brothers who accompanied Theseus to the land of the Amazons, Euneus told Antiope of his brother Soloön's love for her. Antiope rejected this love, however, and Soloön drowned himself. Theseus eventually left Euneus and his other brother, Thoas, to oversee Pythopolis, while Theseus continued his travels.

There was also a son named Euneus born to Jason and Hypsipyle during the *Argo*'s stopover at Lemnos. This Euneus was the twin of Nebrophonus, and it was he who eventually became the King of Lemnos when he purified the Lemnian Women of their blood guilt after they killed the island's male inhabitants.

Euphemus

An Argonaut from Taenarum, Euphemus was an excellent swimmer. At Phineus' suggestion, Euphemus released a dove as the *Argo* approached the Crashing Rocks at the entrance to the Black Sea. By following close behind the dove, the *Argo* managed to just barely pass through the hazardous waterway.

When the *Argo*'s navigator, Tiphys, died, Euphemus was one of those who offered to take his place. Euphemus helped save all of the Argonauts when they were lost inland in Libya and Triton visited them. Euphemus prevented Triton from simply snatching up Jason's offer-

The Rape of Europe, Titian, 1559–1562.

ing to him, and convinced him to direct them toward the Mediterranean; he then convinced Triton to tow the ship there. During the course of their conversation, Triton gave Euphemus a clump of soil that gave his residents sovereignty over all of Libya.

Europe

The only daughter of Agenor and Telephassa, Europe was one object of Zeus' affections. Hermes, acting on the orders of Zeus, led Europe to the Phoenician waterside where Zeus, in the form of a cow, lured her onto his back and swam away with her to Cretan Gortyna. There, Zeus took the form of an eagle and ravished Europe, and she eventually bore him Minos, Rhadamanthys, and Sarpedon.

Meanwhile Agenor dispatched Europe's five brothers to find her, an effort that was entirely fruitless. One of the brothers, Cadmus, consulted an oracle which told him to give up the search as he would never find her. Europe eventually married Asterius, and when the two remained childless, Asterius adopted her three sons by Zeus.

Euryanassa

The daughter of the river god Pactolus. As the mother of Niobe, Broteas, and Pelops, Euryanassa went looking for Pelops after Tantalus butchered him and served him to the gods. Euryanassa never learned that Pelops had been resurrected by the gods and taken to live on Olympus; she was instead led to believe that the gods had eaten every last morsel of him.

Eurycleia

A woman who had served as Odysseus' nurse when he was a small child, Eurycleia remained in Odysseus' palace while he spent ten years fighting in the Trojan War and ten more struggling to get home. When Odysseus finally returned home in disguise and assured his wife, Penelope, that her husband would soon be home, Penelope instructed Eurycleia to bathe the feet of this messenger. When Eurycleia did so, she recognized Odysseus by a scar he had received as a youth. She cried out in delight and Odysseus gripped her by the throat and demanded her silence. In the meantime, Athene distracted Penelope from hearing Eurycleia's cries of recognition.

Orpheus and Eurydice, Nicolas Poussin, c. 1650.

After Odysseus slaughtered Penelope's suitors, he asked Eurycleia to point out those servants who had remained true to him. The twelve maids that Eurycleia reported as having disgraced themselves were made to clean the blood and gore that resulted from the slaughter of the suitors. Once they had finished this task, they were all simultaneously hanged.

Eurydice

The most famed Eurydice married Orpheus following his return from Colchis with the Argonauts. When Aristaeus tried to molest her, Eurydice ran from him alongside the river Peneius, where she was bitten by a serpent and died. Orpheus, a famed poet and musician, gained entrance to the underworld by mesmerizing Charon and Cerberus with beautiful music. After much discussion, Hades decided to allow Eurydice to leave Tartarus under the condition that the musician not look back at his wife until they reached the land of the living. During the journey, Orpheus made the mistake of glancing back to check Eurydice's progress; this resulted in her permanent return to Tartarus.

Eurylochus

A close companion of Odysseus, Eurylochus accompanied the wanderer throughout much of his decade-long travels following the fall of Troy. When Odysseus' sole remaining ship landed on the island of Aeaea, Eurylochus was chosen to lead a shore party of twenty-two men sent to

Orpheus and Eurydice, Roman copy after Phidias, c. 425–420 B.C.

explore the island. After Circe drugged the visitors and transformed them all into hogs, Eurylochus fled to report these developments to Odysseus. With help from Hermes, Odysseus managed to outsmart Circe and rescue his men.

Later, when the crew became stuck in Sicily and supplies began to run short, Eurylochus suggested that they slaughter some of Hyperion's divine cattle, which were grazing nearby, and repay their owner by building a temple in Ithaca upon their return. Odysseus opposed this plan, but the ravenously hungry men waited until their leader had fallen asleep and slaughtered many of the beasts. Odysseus awoke and insisted that they sail immediately. In the meantime, Hyperion complained to Zeus, protesting the slaughter of his cattle. Zeus brewed up a storm that seized Odysseus' ship and destroyed it, killing all aboard except Odysseus.

Eurynome

Known in the beginning as the Goddess of All Things, Eurynome rose naked out of Chaos and separated the sea from the sky, dancing upon the waves as she went. She rubbed the North Wind between her hands to create the serpent Ophion, by whom she later became pregnant. Eurynome assumed the form of a dove and delivered the Universal Egg, which produced all things that exist. Eurynome and Ophion took up residence on Mount Olympus, where Ophion began to take credit for producing the Universal Egg. Eurynome grew angry and thrashed the serpent soundly, knocking out his teeth and banishing him to the dark caves below the earth (this is paralleled in the falls from grace recounted in other religions). Eurynome later created the seven Planetary Powers.

As control of Peloponnesus fell into the hands of patriarchal societies, their mythological tales presented Eurynome as a far less influential figure: one of three daughters of Oceanus and Tethys, the subject of Zeus' affections, and the mother by him of the Graces and numerous other daughters. Eurynome was given minor roles in the stories of other deities, but never regained the position of prominence she once held.

Eurypylus

The name given to several prominent characters, one of whom was a son of Eurystheus who was one of three killed by Heracles when Eurystheus insulted the warrior with an insufficient portion of a sacrifice at the end of his labors. Another Eurypylus, a son of Poseidon and Astypalaea, was the father of Chalciope.

The best known of the characters named Eurypylus was the son of Telephus and Astyoche who became famous for his participation in the Trojan War. Eurypylus fought alongside the men of Troy and was wounded during the battle that revolved around Hector's temporary breaching of the Greek lines.

Eurypylus slew many Greeks, including Machaon, and defended Troy well until he was slain by Achilles' son, Neoptolemus.

Eurystheus

The son of Archippe, and the grandson of Pelops and Hippodameia, Eurystheus was also the brother of Alcyone and the nephew of Atreus. In some versions Eurystheus is described as the son of Sthenelus and Nicippe, and it is stated his delivery was accelerated by Hera so that Eurystheus, and not Heracles, would be the beneficiary of promises Zeus had made regarding the next royal birth. Since Heracles was Zeus' son out of wedlock, and Hera was jealous of her husband's infidelities, Eurystheus became the beneficiary of Hera's antipathy toward Heracles.

When Heracles was assigned his labors, it was Eurystheus who assigned the individual tasks. (There are even some versions in which it is suggested that Eurystheus and Heracles were lovers, and that it was for Eurystheus' love that the labors were undertaken.) When Heracles returned from his first task with the Nemean Lion's imposing pelt, Eurystheus hid inside a brazen vessel and sent his herald Copreus to relay messages. Scared of Heracles' powers, Eurystheus instructed Heracles to stop at the Mycenaean gates at the edge of the city and leave the fruits of his remaining labors there. Despite this, Eurystheus continued to hide from Heracles whenever he returned from one of his tasks.

Eventually Heracles undertook twelve tasks, ten of which were accepted by Eurystheus. After Heracles' apotheosis, Eurystheus expelled all of Heracles' sons and allies, afraid that they might look to avenge his role in Heracles' long and arduous labors. The Heraclids allied with Theseus, whose Athenian troops joined them in their battle against Eurystheus and his Peloponnesian forces.

Eurystheus named his uncle Atreus as his regent when he went off to fight Theseus and the Heraclids. During the course of this battle, Eurystheus' sons were killed, and Eurystheus himself was either killed or captured.

Eurytion

The adoptive son of Actor, Eurytion purified Peleus after the latter fled to his father's court following the death of his stepbrother Phocus. This Eurytion went on to participate in the hunt for the Calydonian Boar, during which he was accidentally killed by Peleus' errant spear.

Eurytion was also another name for the Centaur Eurytus. Another Eurytion, a son of Ares, served as herdsman over Geryon's cattle,

Heracles and Eurytion, from sarcophagus, Hellenistic period.

which were the subject of Heracles' tenth labor. This Eurytion was assisted by the two-headed hound Orthrus, but both were clubbed to death by Heracles, who took the cattle and then killed Geryon and others in the ensuing battle.

Eurytus

There are several well-known characters named Eurytus, the most prominent of whom was the son of King Melaneus. This Eurytus, credited with having taught Heracles the finer points of archery, challenged each of the suitors who wished to marry his daughter, Iole, to first defeat himself and his sons in an archery contest. It was said that Eurytus had been personally instructed in the art of the bow by Apollo.

When Heracles came to challenge Eurytus and his sons for the right to marry Iole, Heracles won, but Eurytus refused to acknowledge the victory. Initially, Eurytus' son Iphitus supported Heracles' claims, but was eventually tricked into suspecting Heracles of stealing his father's cattle. Heracles, innocent of the charges, responded by hurling Iphitus to his death. To purify himself for Iphitus' murder, Heracles sold himself into slavery for a year and offered the money to Iphitus' orphans. Eurytus insisted that they refuse the money.

Another Eurytus, the son of Actor and Molione, served as a general in Augeias' Elian army. When Heracles attacked Augeias' forces, Eurytus, along with his brother Cteatus and the Moliones, successfully led the defense. Heracles' army was soundly repelled the first time, but a second force was assembled years later; this army overran Oechalia, and Eurytus and all of his sons were riddled with arrows.

Eurytus is also the name of one of the giants who fought the Olympians, and of the Centaur, also known as Eurytion, who led the drunken assault on Hippodameia at her wedding to Peirithous, inciting a war between the Lapiths and the Centaurs.

Evadne

A daughter of King Pelias, Evadne was the sister of Amphinome and Alcestis. When Medea tricked Phylacus into thinking she was a priestess, she convinced Evadne and Amphinome to cut their father to pieces so that Medea might rejuvenate him and make him younger and stronger. (Phylacus had killed Jason's parents, which is why Medea, Jason's wife, contrived this murder.) Alcestis refused to help her sisters, both of whom were banished to Mantinae after they had butchered their father. Evadne and Amphinome were eventually purified and honorably married.

Another Evadne, the daughter of Phylacus, married Capaneus, who died at Thebes when he was struck by one of Zeus' lightning bolts during a battle. Because Capaneus was buried, rather than burned (as was the custom with such fatalities), Evadne threw herself onto the group funeral pyre and was consumed by flames.

Evander

The son of the nymph Nicostrate, Evander was the stepson of Echenus. Evander, whose real father was Hermes, was convinced by Nicostrate to kill Echenus. Mother and son were banished from Arcadia for their crime, and went to what is now known as Italy, where Evander eventually became one of the most powerful rulers in that country. Evander and his mother are best remembered for having brought the Pelasgian alphabet to Italy, where they customized it to local needs.

Later, Heracles encountered Evander on his way home from his tenth labor. Evander aided Heracles' efforts to build temples to Zeus after he killed Cacus. Evander then helped Heracles prepare for the final portion of his journey back to Mycenae.

Fates Three sisters conceived by Erebus upon Night, his sister, the Fates control the destinies of all mortals. Clotho, Lachesis, and Atropos were given the respective responsibilities of spinning, measuring, and cutting the threads of life. As Zeus' status in the pantheon became greater, he was credited with weighing the lives of each mortal and informing the Fates of his decisions, and even with having fathered the sisters on Themis during the sexual rampage that followed his fight with his

Ganymede on the Eagle, Benvenuto Cellini, 1546–1547.

mother, Rhea. In some drastically abbreviated appearances, the Fates were reduced to two in number, representing birth and death, with Zeus alone responsible for determining the amount of time between the two events. In some versions, however, Zeus' preeminence is acknowledged but it is suggested that even he may have been subject to the decisions of the Fates, with which none of the gods could contend.

The Fates were assisted by Hermes in the composition of the first basic Pelasgian alphabet. More importantly, the Fates aided Zeus in two major battles: they smashed the heads of Agrius and Thoas with brazen pestles during the giants' unsuccessful attack on Olympus and gave Typhon the poisonous fruits that helped turn the tide in his battle against Zeus. Also, the Fates supported Hades' protests to Zeus when Asclepius revived Hippolytus, insisting that Asclepius be punished since he was negating their powers.

Furies The Latin name given to the Erinnyes.

Gaea The name by which Mother Earth is more properly known.

Galanthis A faithful, yellow-haired maiden, Galanthis helped deceive Eileithyia, the goddess of childbirth, during Heracles' birth. When Galanthis mocked the goddess afterward, Eileithyia turned her into a weasel; she was further punished by Hera by being condemned to bring forth her young through her mouth. (This is derived from the ancient interpretation of the way such animals carried their young in their mouths.)

In other versions that connect Galanthis to Heracles' birth, she was a harlot who was punished by Hecate and who frightened Alcmene into labor. Galanthis is also known as Galen or Galanthias.

Galatea Originally an ivory statue of Aphrodite created by Pygmalion because of his desire for the goddess, Galatea was brought to life when Aphrodite took pity on the sculptor. Galatea subsequently conceived Paphus and Metharme with Pygmalion.

Ganymede The son of King Tros, Ganymede was said to have been the most beautiful youth alive. Initially, Ganymede was abducted and seduced by Tantalus and taken to Paphlagonia. When word of his beauty reached Mount Olympus, Zeus himself desired Ganymede and abducted him. He brought Ganymede to Olympus, where he served as Zeus' cup-bearer. To compensate King Tros, Zeus sent Hermes to deliver some of Hephaestus' golden handiwork and two divine horses. Zeus also made sure Hermes told King Tros that Ganymede was now immortal and in the company of the Father of Heaven. Zeus' affair with the young boy was cited by many Greeks and Romans, including some prominent philosophers, as an ideal relationship.

Geryon The son of Chrysaor and Callirrhoë, Geryon became the King of Tartessus on the Iberian peninsula beyond the Pillars of Heracles. Geryon was known as one of the strongest men alive, and in some versions is described as having three heads, six hands, and three bodies joined at the waist.

Geryon figured in the tale of Heracles' tenth labor, the capture of Geryon's cattle, which were said to have been extraordinarily beautiful. Geryon was killed when Heracles let loose either three arrows at once or just one well-placed arrow that entered Geryon's side and passed through each of his three torsos.

Giants Tall, terrible beings with long beards and serpent tails for feet. There were twenty-four giants, the most prominent of whom was Alcyoneus, born to Mother Earth at Phlegra. Said to have been born of the blood from Uranus' severed genitals, the giants were half-brothers to the Titans, whom Zeus had imprisoned in Tartarus. Mother Earth con-

The Triumph of Galatea, Raphael, 1511.

spired to convince the giants to make war against Zeus and the Olympians, at which time Hera prophesied that the gods would be able to defeat the giants only if a specific herb, which gave its possessor invulnerability, were found and if a lion-skinned mortal fought alongside the Olympians. The herb was eventually found, and Heracles, wearing the invulnerable pelt of the Nemean Lion, fought against the giants. The gods could only stun the giants, and it was Heracles who provided the finishing blows.

The giants were wounded and killed by Heracles and the gods in a number of ways, some particularly gruesome. In addition to Alcyoneus, the giants included Porphyrion, Ephialtes, Eurytus, Clytius, Mimas, Pallas, Enceladus, Polybutes, Hippolytus, Gration, Agrius, and Thoas.

Glauce

The daughter of King Creon to whom Jason was engaged to marry as soon as he divorced Medea. When Medea found out about Jason's plan, she became enraged and sent Glauce (also called Creüsa) a golden robe and crown. The presents, it turned out, were poisoned. When they began to burn Glauce, Creon went to her assistance and he too was killed.

Glaucia

The mistress of Deimachus, an ally of Heracles, Glaucia had already become pregnant with Deimachus' child when he was killed during a war against Laomedon. Heracles protected her well, and Glaucia eventually gave birth to Scamander, whom she named after the river that had fathered her.

Glaucus

A son of Minos and Pasiphaë, Glaucus became lost in the Labyrinth his father had built on Cnossus. Minos sent Polyeidus, a seer, to search for the boy, who was found dead. Minos then locked Polyeidus up with his dead son with instructions that he be brought back to life. Polyeidus watched as a snake brought its mate back to life with a certain herb, and then gave that same herb to Glaucus. The child was revived, and Minos rewarded Polyeidus extravagantly. Minos then insisted that Polyeidus teach Glaucus the art of prophesy, but Polyeidus caused Glaucus to lose that knowledge just before his departure.

Another Glaucus was the son of Sisyphus and Merope. This Glaucus scorned Aphrodite and refused to let his mares breed, thinking it would make the beasts tougher and faster. Aphrodite punished Glaucus by causing the horses to become wild and drag their master to his death, then eat him. It is said that Glaucus'

ghost, known as Taraxippus, haunts Corinth and scares passing horses, often causing the deaths of their riders.

Another Glaucus, a son of Hippolochus who fought in the Trojan War, was co-king of Lycia with Sarpedon (both of whom went to Troy to help defend it against the Greek alliance). This appears to have been the Glaucus who was beloved by Circe.

> . . . Hippolochos begot me, and I claim that he is my father; he sent me to Troy, and urged upon me repeated injunctions, to be always among the bravest, and hold my head above others, not shaming the generation of my fathers. . . . Such is my generation and the blood I claim to be born from.
> —Glaucus, The Iliad, Homer

Gordius

A poor, humble countryman, Gordius received prophesies that eventually led him to marry the prophetess and become King of Phrygia. Gordius remained childless, but adopted Midas as his son and was succeeded by him.

When Gordius first arrived in the market of Telmissus, he knotted the yoke of his cart to a pole in a manner that inspired the prophesy for his succession. It was said that whoever could untie the knot would replace Gordius and his line. The so-called Gordian Knot remained until Alexander of Macedon cut it with his sword, signifying a transition of power from the realm of religious mystery to that of military might.

Gorgons

Three of Ceto and Phorcys' daughters, the Gorgons were Stheino, Euryale, and Medusa, all of whom were once quite beautiful. Medusa was the youngest and most beautiful of the three, and eventually met her end at the hands of Perseus.

Medusa was turned hideous by Athene after Medusa had lain with Poseidon in one of Athene's temples. Why and when Stheino and Euryale were transformed is not entirely clear, although in some versions it is suggested that they might have been born ugly. The Gorgons are usually depicted as hideous old women.

Gorgophone

The daughter of Perseus, Gorgophone became notorious for being the first widow ever to remarry, breaking a tradition of wives taking their own lives when their husbands died.

Graces

Daughters fathered upon Eurynome by Zeus—other possible parents include Helius and Aegle and either Zeus or Dionysus with

Aphrodite—the three Graces are also referred to as the Charites. The Graces were attendants to Aphrodite, and were described as beautiful young personifications of grace. The names of the Graces are most often given as Aglaia, Euphrosyne, and Thalia.

Graeae

Three fair-faced, swanlike sisters, the Graeae were members of the Phorcids. The three Graeae—Enyo, Pemphredo, and Deino—had gray hair since birth and shared one tooth and one eye among them.

Hades

One of the children of Cronus and Rhea, Hades was swallowed at birth by his father because Cronus feared a prophesy that warned that one of his offspring would usurp his throne. When Zeus tricked Cronus into vomiting up his brothers and sisters, the siblings allied under Zeus' command to overthrow their father. Hades was given a helmet of darkness that permitted him to see at night and that he used to help Zeus and Poseidon kill Cronus. In the separation of powers that followed Cronus' downfall and Zeus' ascension, Hades was placed in charge of the underworld and the spirits of the dead.

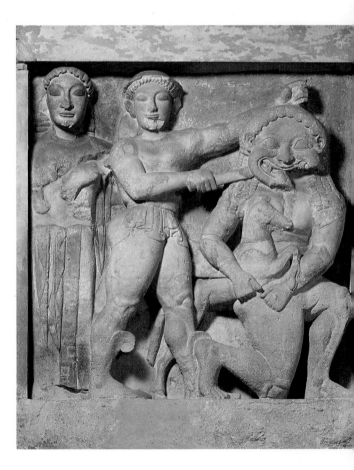

Perseus and Medusa, relief from sarcophagus, early 6th century B.C.

Because of Hades' responsibilities regarding the dead, he was never allowed to sit among the ruling Olympians, which put him alongside such deities as his wife, Persephone, Hecate, Mother Earth, and Pan. Hecate, Hades, and his wife were not even allowed to visit Olympus. Among this threesome, Hecate and Persephone symbolized aspects of reincarnation, while Hades represented the finality of death. For this reason, Hades was paid little attention by the living. His name was rarely used, and many euphemisms were coined for him; the most popular of these was Pluto or Pluton, which meant "the rich one" and harkened back to Hades' earliest role as a chthonic deity.

The single episode for which Hades is best known is the abduction of Demeter's daughter, Core, whom Hades hoped to make his wife. After Demeter discovered Core's whereabouts, she brought her grievance to Zeus, who devised a compromise in which Core spent nine months of the year with Demeter and the remaining three as Persephone, the wife of Hades and the Queen of Tartarus.

Persephone, who is present in most of the stories in which Hades plays a part, eventually came to be an omnipresent figure in Tartarus.

Hades was one of those tricked by Sisyphus when Zeus sought to punish him, and he had frequent dealings with Hermes, who was engaged to bring the dead calmly and quietly into the underworld. Most of Hades' more prominent appearances, however, involved the few mortals who managed to escape the underworld after having gone there on some quest.

Haemon

The son of Creon, Haemon, despite being engaged to Antigone, was sent by his father to bury her alive when she defied Creon's orders denying proper burial to her brother. Instead of obeying his father's command, Haemon secretly married Antigone, and the two conceived a child. When their son came of age, Creon recognized him by a birthmark and killed him. Most versions of this story end with Haemon subsequently killing Antigone and himself. (In the story of Oedipus, however, Haemon is specified as one of the victims of the Sphinx, whose riddle he was unable to answer.)

Sophocles portrayed Haemon's self-inflicted death as taking place in response to his father's commands regarding Antigone's live burial. When Creon failed to heed his son's pleas, Haemon took his own life, either after Antigone committed suicide, or in the homicide-suicide fashion described in the other version as taking place years later.

Priam Before Hector's Tomb in the Temple of Apollo, **from the studio of Colombe, c. 1500.**

Corpse enfolding corpse he lies. He has won his nuptial rites, poor youth, not here but in the halls of Death. And he has witnessed to mankind that of all curses which cleave to man ill counsel is the sovereign curse.
—Messenger, Antigone, Sophocles

Halia

A nymph upon whom Poseidon begot six sons and one daughter, Rhode. After the sons became the Eastern Demons, Halia threw herself into the sea—probably as an act of cleansing—and was deified as Leucothea.

Hamadryads

Tree nymphs and partners in merriment with the likes of Apollo, Hermes, Pan, and the Satyrs, the Hamadryads were also companions of Dryope, with whom they were cavorting when Apollo frightened them off so that he could lie with Dryope. Eventually the Hamadryads returned and rescued Dryope, leaving a poplar tree in her place.

Harmonia

The product of Aphrodite's affair with Ares during her marriage to Hephaestus, Harmonia was eventually married to Cadmus, and their wedding was the first between mortals to have Olympians in atten-

dance. From her mother Harmonia received the golden necklace Hephaestus had crafted for Zeus to give Europe, and from Athene she received a golden robe. (Each of these gifts was said to make its wearer irresistibly beautiful.) Harmonia also received wedding gifts from Hermes and Cadmus, and was initiated into the rites of the Great Goddess (who is sometimes identified as Mother Earth, sometimes as Rhea) by Electra. Demeter assured the newlyweds prosperous harvests, and Apollo serenaded them with his lyre.

The parents of Illyrius and Agave, Harmonia and Cadmus eventually retired to the land of the Encheleans, and, fulfilling a prophesy made by Dionysus, were transformed into blue-spotted black serpents and were sent to the Islands of the Blessed in Tartarus.

Harpies

Monstrous, vulturelike female creatures who were usually thought to be the daughters of Thaumus and Electra, the Harpies were fierce, filthy creatures who were said to be responsible for all lost items never found. They often served the Erinnyes or Hera in capturing or tormenting those who had fallen into their disfavor. It is sometimes suggested that the Harpies are closely related to the Sirens (as both are depicted as birdlike females).

Hecabe

The second wife of Priam, Hecabe was Queen of Troy before its fall to the Greeks. Hecabe bore nineteen of the fifty sons Priam sired, and was pregnant with one of them when a dream of hers led Priam's son Aesacus, a seer, to predict that an impending noble birth would lead to the downfall of Troy. This prophesy led to the murder of Priam's nephew Munippus and the abandonment of his son Paris.

While Hecabe is considered important mostly because she is the mother of several of the Trojan War's principals, her most active role took place during the fall of Troy. When Odysseus managed to sneak inside Troy's walls, he was harbored by Helen, who told only Hecabe of his arrival. Hecabe confronted Odysseus, who begged that she not denounce him; she agreed on the condition that she and those residents of Troy who put up no resistance be spared. (The pillage of Troy nevertheless bordered on a wholesale massacre.)

The death of Polydorus was depicted as the last straw for Hecabe in Euripides' *Hecabe*, and resulted in her attack on Polymnestor and his sons. Polymnestor did not know that Hecabe was aware of his part in the murder of Polydorus. Hecabe lured Polymnestor into a trap where she murdered his sons and then gouged out his eyes. Agamemnon ruled that Hecabe's crimes were justifiable because Polymnestor had killed Polydorus and abused Priam's trust.

Hecabe was later claimed by Odysseus as a spoil of war, and it is said that she was eventually murdered somewhere near Chersonese for hurling hideous invectives upon her captors. It is more likely, however, that Odysseus realized that it would not be to his advantage for Hecabe to live to be able to tell of the assistance she had given him in obtaining the Palladium. After Hecabe was slain, her spirit rose up and took the form of the fearful black bitches that were known to follow Hecate about. Her tomb became known forever after as the Bitch's Tomb.

Hecate

Credited with far-reaching powers in early incarnations, Hecate was eventually reduced to the role of overseer of the world of the dead. She also became associated with magic and witches, and was said to have the power to bestow on or withhold from mortals any gifts she chose.

Because of her connection with the underworld, Hecate is often portrayed as possessing traits similar to those of Persephone, and it was Hecate who originally offered to make sure that Zeus' ruling regarding the division of Core's time was being obeyed. Like Persephone and Hades (as well as Mother Earth and Pan), Hecate was never allowed to sit as a member on the council of Olympians. She nonetheless sided with the Olympians in their battle against the giants.

Priam Begs Achilles for the Body of His Slain Son Hector, **red-figured vase, 5th century** B.C.

Aeneas and His Companions Fighting the Harpies, **Francois Perrier, early 17th century.**

Hecate is often described as possessing three monsterlike heads, and is said to have given birth to the Empusae.

Hector

The greatest of all of Troy's defenders, Hector is in many ways the most likable and respectable of all the participants in the Trojan War. The Greeks acknowledged Hector's prowess on the battlefield and credited him with fighting honorably to protect his homeland. As was the case for all such noble opponents, however, Hector was destined to fall to the Greeks—survival would have meant submission, a fate unworthy of such a valiant warrior.

Hector was the favorite of Priam and Hecabe's many children and probably one of the most popular figures in all of Troy. In some versions it is suggested that Apollo actually fathered Hector upon Hecabe. This variation probably had something to do with the notion that such a respectable figure must have been the product of a deity rather than a feeble old king whose other son had been responsible for the whole sordid affair.

Hector was married to Andromache, the daughter of the Cilician King Eëtion. They were the parents of Astyanax, whose birth probably occurred late in the course of the Trojan War. Before that time Hector had done a superb job of holding off the Greeks.

When Achilles asked permission to marry Hector's sister Polyxena, Hector informed him that he would be allowed to do so only if he betrayed the Greeks or at least killed Great Ajax. When Achilles refused, Hector eventually challenged him to combat, but by that time Achilles had withdrawn from the battle. Achilles refused to fight Hector, and Great Ajax accepted in his place. Hector and Ajax met in an epic battle that ended in a draw. The two withdrew with great respect for one another, and exchanged presents that would later be involved with their deaths.

When Hector breached the Greek lines and pushed the battle perilously close to their ships, Poseidon aided the Greeks by allowing Ajax to nearly kill Hector by throwing an enormous stone at him. Zeus then intervened in the squabble between Apollo and Poseidon, who were fighting through their respective champions, and revived Hector, whose injuries forced him to retreat once Patroclus organized the Greek defense and pushed the Trojan forces back within their city's walls. Eventually, Apollo intervened once again, wounding Patroclus grievously. Hector, having just recently returned to battle, finished Patroclus off.

Achilles then sought out Hector for combat, and Hector made the mistake of trying to tire out his swift opponent by running around the perimeter of Troy's walls. On the third lap Achilles caught up with Hector and killed him with a single stroke of his sword. The dying Hector pleaded with Achilles to let his body be ransomed for a proper burial, but Achilles refused and dragged Hector's corpse behind his chariot.

Tall Hektor of the shining helm was leader of the Trojans, Priam's son; and with him far the best and bravest fighting men were armed and eager to fight with the spear's edge.

—The Iliad, *Homer*

Straightway in all his armour he sprang to the ground from his chariot and shaking two sharp spears ranged everywhere through the army stirring men up to fight and waking the hateful warfare; and these pulled themselves about and stood to face the Achaians, while the Argives held in their close order and would not be broken.

—The Iliad, *Homer*

Helen When Zeus and Nemesis coupled in the form of swans, the result was an egg that was entrusted to Leda, the wife of Spartan King Tyndareus. In some versions Leda simply waited for the egg to hatch, and in others she internalized it and delivered Helen herself.

Helen was the sister of Polydeuces and the stepsister of Castor and Clytaemnestra. The most beautiful of all mortal women, she was abducted at a young age by Theseus and Peirithous, who drew lots to see which one would marry her when she reached womanhood. Theseus won, and entrusted her to his friend Aphidnus and Theseus' mother, Aethra. When Helen became old enough to marry, Peirithous demanded that Theseus uphold his promise to find him a wife of equal status. Peirithous chose Persephone.

During Theseus' absence, Helen was rescued by her brother and stepbrother, the Dioscuri. They brought Helen, along with Aethra and one of Peirithous' sisters, back to Sparta. Shortly after this happened,

The Abduction of Helen, **Guido Reni, 1631.**

Agamemnon killed Tantalus and claimed Clytaemnestra as his wife. In some versions the Dioscuri are then killed in an attempt to defend Clytaemnestra and Helen is quickly married off to Agamemnon's brother Menelaus. In more elaborate versions, Helen is the subject of a great contest in which suitors from all around Greece come to vie for Tyndareus' permission to marry her.

Helen's suitors included, among others, Odysseus, who soon realized that he had little chance to be selected by Tyndareus and advised Helen's father to make the suitors swear to promise to defend the honor of whoever was chosen. Once all had vowed to do so Tyndareus announced his choice: Menelaus. The oath that the remaining suitors swore would eventually demand their participation in the Trojan War.

Unfortunately, Tyndareus had angered Aphrodite some time earlier, and Aphrodite had sworn to make each of his three daughters an adulteress. In Helen's case, Aphrodite arranged this by promising Paris of Troy that she would make Helen fall in love with him.

When Paris later came to Sparta, about the only person who did not realize Paris was wooing Helen was Menelaus, who foolishly left the two alone when he sailed away for a previous engagement. Helen and Paris ran off together that night, and while some Greeks tried to suggest that Paris had kidnapped Helen, it is usually agreed that she was a willing participant. At Cranaë, their first port of call, the couple consummated their affair. While they were still on the way to Troy the Greeks paid a call on Paris' father, Priam, and demanded Helen's return. Priam announced, truthfully, that he knew nothing about the Paris and Helen incident.

When Helen arrived in Troy, she was received warmly, and Priam promised to give her protection from Menelaus and the Greeks. The Trojan War began shortly thereafter.

The Trojans chose to continue protecting Helen even after Paris was killed in battle. At that point, Paris' brothers Helenus and Deiphobus argued over who would lay claim to their brother's wife, and Priam eventually supported Deiphobus. Helen responded by making her first attempt to escape, but was caught in the process. She was then forced into marrying Deiphobus, much to her disgust (and that of many Trojans who believed the marriage improper).

Helen harbored Odysseus when he sneaked into Troy in an attempt to steal Athene's Palladium, and even paved the way for Hecabe to assist him. Later, when the Trojan Horse was brought within the city's walls, Helen went with Deiphobus to see it. Suspecting the offering's true nature, Helen proceeded to mock the wives of each of the men hidden inside, nearly causing a handful of them to break their silence.

Once the Greeks emerged from the Trojan Horse, Menelaus headed straight for Helen's quarters. Intending to kill her outright, he was distracted from his mission by an incredibly bloody battle with Deiphobus. In some versions, Helen is credited with stabbing her newest husband in the back while Menelaus had him engaged. This, in combination with the sight of Helen's bared breasts, weakened Menelaus' resolve to kill Helen and led him instead to bring her safely to his ships.

Menelaus and Helen's journey home was a lengthy one as conditions forced them to travel along the southern coast of the Mediterranean. When they finally reached Greece, Menelaus sent Helen ahead to see what reception might await them. Helen learned that her sister Clytaemnestra had been killed that very day by Orestes.

Helen would have preferred to have mourned for her sister in public, but feared to do so since she herself had been the cause of so much bloodshed. Instead, she asked Electra to make an offering on Clytaemnestra's grave. Helen cut off the very tips of her hair (she was prevented by her vanity from cutting off any more); this disgusted Electra and caused her to decline Helen's request.

There are some versions in which Helen and Menelaus' return to Sparta took place on the day of Orestes' trial for the murders of Aegisthus and Clytaemnestra rather than on the day of the murders. In either case, Orestes chose to extend his wrath to Helen for having brought about the situation that led to his parents' deaths. Sentenced to commit suicide, Orestes decided to first kill Helen. Zeus sent Apollo down to wrap Helen in a cloud and take her back up to Olympus, where she would join her brothers, the Dioscuri, as guardians of sailors in distress.

"Surely there is no blame on Trojans and strong-greaved Achaians if for a long time they suffer hardship for a woman like this one. Terrible is the likeness of her face to immortal goddesses. Still, though she be such, let her go away in the ships, lest she be left behind, a grief to us and our children."

—The Iliad, *Homer*

Helenus A son of Priam and Hecabe, Helenus and his sister Cassandra received the power of prophesy when their parents left them behind in a temple and two snakes licked their ears. Priam and Hecabe returned in time to save the children's lives, but the twins retained the ability to predict the future.

After Paris was killed, Helenus quarreled with Deiphobus over which of them might marry Helen. Priam ruled in Deiphobus' favor, in response to which Helenus abandoned Troy and went to live with Arisbe on Mount Ida or took refuge as Chryses' guest in an Apollonian temple.

The Greek seer Calchas told Agamemnon that only Helenus could reveal the oracular secrets that were protecting Troy, and Odysseus was dispatched to bring Helenus, who was then staying with Chryses, to the Greek camp. Odysseus found Helenus willing to disclose the necessary information on the condition that he be promised safe haven. Helenus explained that he was deserting Troy because it was impossible to support Paris' sacrilegious murder of Achilles in Apollo's temple and because no attempts had been made to assuage the gods for his actions. Helenus went on to tell the Greeks that Troy would fall that very summer as long as they were able to retrieve a bone of Pelops, bring Neoptolemus to the field of battle, and ensure the removal of Athene's Palladium from the citadel.

Helius The son of Hyperion and either Theia or Euryphaessa, and the brother of Selene and Eos. It would make the most sense that Helius' parents were Hyperion and Theia, since they were the Titan and Titaness who oversaw the sun and Helius is best known for his responsibility of riding Hephaestus' divine chariot across the sky each day, trailing the sun behind. Each morning Eos announces his arrival as he is roused by the crowing of the cock, the bird most sacred to Helius. After driving his chariot across the sky during the course of the day, Helius set down amongst the Islands of the Blessed, where the horses were left to pasture until the next morning when the cycle was repeated.

When Zeus realized that Helius, busy fer-

The Love of Paris and Helen, David, 1788.

rying the sun across the sky, had been left out of the parceling of mortal lands, he gave him the island of Rhodes and gave him Rhode herself in marriage. Together they conceived seven sons, among them Aloeus and Aeëtes, and a daughter. Helius was also said to have owned hundreds of head of cattle, most of which were tended in Sicily by a pair of daughters, Phaetusa and Lampetia.

Helius was a model of consistency on his job, although his rare lapses were always monumental events. When Helius allowed another of his sons, Phaëthon, to drive his chariot one day, Phaëthon lost control and burned much of the earth; as a result, Zeus struck the boy dead. Another time Zeus and Eris persuaded Helius to reverse the laws of nature by riding his chariot from the west to the east so that Atreus could wrest the throne of Mycenae away from his brother Thyestes. And when Zeus prepared to lie with Alcmena to conceive Heracles, Hermes persuaded Helius to take two days off so that night would lay over the land for three straight "days."

It is worth noting that Helius was sometimes referred to by his father's name, Hyperion. Odysseus in particular seems to have confused the two. As a result, the slaughter of Hyperion's cattle during Odysseus' wanderings may in fact have involved portions of Helius' herds that were kept on the isle of Erytheia.

Helle The daughter of Athamas and Nephele, and the sister of Phrixus and Leucon. When Phrixus escaped from Athamas, Helle joined him by grabbing hold of the golden, winged ram that carried him to safety. When they were well above the seas, Helle became giddy and lost her hold; she plummeted into the straits between the Mediterranean and Black seas, and the Hellespont was named in her honor.

In some versions, Ixion is named as her father, and Helle and Phrixus are described as taking a ride on the ram after Nephele found them cavorting in a Dionysian frenzy.

Hemera The name given to Eos as she rides with her brother Helius before being transformed into Hespera.

Hephaestus The son of Hera whose father is said to have been Zeus or Talos, Hephaestus was told by Hera that his conception had been parthenogenetic. Hephaestus did not believe his mother, and once imprisoned and tortured her to discern the truth, but even under such circumstances she maintained that what she had told him had been the truth.

Thetis in Hephaestus' Forge, **Roman wallpainting,** A.D. **1st century.**

Hera was initially disgusted by the sickly child she had delivered, and threw him from the heights of Olympus. The infant fell into the sea and was rescued by Thetis and Eurynome, who raised him and gave him his first smithy, where he became a master craftsman. One day Hera admired a brooch that Thetis was wearing, and in the course of learning about its creator recognized Hephaestus as her son. Hera brought him back up to Olympus, presented him with the finest equipment and materials, and arranged his marriage to Aphrodite.

Despite Hephaestus' skills as a craftsman, it is hard to imagine that Aphrodite was too pleased with Hephaestus, who is usually described as being ugly, ill-tempered, lame in the legs from one of two falls from Olympus, and heavily muscled about the shoulders and arms. Aphrodite bore three children during the time she was married to Hephaestus, but all were fathered by Ares, with whom Aphrodite maintained an ongoing affair. When Hephaestus learned what was going on, he crafted a trap for the lovers and captured them in a net. He then assembled the gods to pass judgment upon them.

The gods, however, made no judgment against the lovers, and Aphrodite's gratitude led her to sleep with Hermes and Poseidon. She bore children to both of them, and later slept with Dionysus and Anchises, a mortal.

Hephaestus, however, was madly in love with Aphrodite and suffered her behavior quietly most of the time.

As craftsman-of-the-gods, Hephaestus appears whenever a particularly intricate or beautiful piece of work figures prominently in a story. Hephaestus created the toys that the infant Zeus played with (which makes Zeus' alleged paternity of Hephaestus hard to explain), crafted countless wedding presents, and fashioned numerous temporary solutions to emergency situations. Hephaestus is usually credited with helping to breach Zeus' skull, leading to the delivery of Athene.

As the god who relied the most heavily on fire, Hephaestus had the greatest interest in Prometheus' theft of it from the gods. It was Hephaestus who eventually nailed Prometheus to the rock where Zeus inflicted his punishment. Hephaestus later crafted the form of a woman that was given to Prometheus' brother, Epimetheus. The four winds blew life into the figure, and it became Pandora.

Hephaestus usually supplied munitions in battles between various factions, such as the Olympians' attempt to overthrow Zeus. Hephaestus defended Hera, for which Zeus tossed him from the heights of Olympus, breaking both his legs and confining him to crutches forever after. When the giants attacked Olympus, Hephaestus helped fend them off. And in the Trojan war, Hephaestus sided with the Greeks since Achilles was the son of Hephaestus' adoptive mother, Thetis.

One of Hephaestus' most embarrassing incidents involved a time when he went to the aid of Athene. Hephaestus had the mistaken impression that Athene was attempting to seduce him, and attempted to violate her. Athene pulled away at the last minute, and Hephaestus' seed landed on her thigh. Athene wiped herself clean with a piece of wool and threw it down upon the ground. As a result, Mother Earth became pregnant and eventually delivered Erichthonius, a hideous half-man, half-serpent.

'There was a time once before now I was minded to help [Hera], and [Zeus] caught me by the foot and threw me from the magic threshold, and all day long I dropped helpless, and about sunset I landed on Lemnos, and there was not much life left in me. After that fall it was the Sintian men who took care of me.'

—*Hephaestus*, The Iliad, Homer

Hera The daughter of the great god Cronus and his sister (and wife) Rhea, Hera was born either on the island of Samos or in Argos.

Cronus swallowed the newborn infant immediately, because of a prophesy that warned that one of his children would overthrow him. After Zeus caused Cronus to throw up the children he had swallowed, Hera was taken to Arcadia and raised by Pelasgus' son Temenus, with the Seasons as her nurses. Zeus went on to become the King of Heaven, and he eventually decided that no one would make a better Queen than his older sister Hera.

In some versions Zeus ravished Hera, who then felt compelled to marry him. In other versions, their coming together is a glorious, divine event. Whatever the case, Zeus and Hera's wedding was a momentous occasion, complete with a slew of magical presents that would figure in countless myths as objects of desire and power. One of these gifts was the golden apple tree given by Mother Earth, which sat on Mount Atlas, guarded by Ladon, until Heracles shot Ladon dead and had Atlas steal three of the tree's fruits.

Core and Hera, **marble relief, 4th century B.C.**

Hera, **marble statue, 5th century** B.C.

Zeus and Hera honeymooned on Samos, where their wedding night was said to have lasted for three hundred years. According to some versions, Hera subsequently bathed in the spring of Canathus, near Argos, where she renewed her virginity. This points out a contradiction, however, as Hera is said to have been the mother of Ares, Hephaestus, Hebe, and Eris. In most cases, Zeus is said to be her children's father, but some versions describe parthenogenetic conception, and there are even versions in which it is suggested that Talos fathered Hephaestus.

Despite the important role Hera played in religious circles, her mythological role is usually that of a jealous wife. Zeus' numerous affairs kept Hera busy tormenting her husband's lovers and often extending her animosity toward Zeus' illegitimate children. While this often led to Hera being depicted as a petty, vindictive shrew, it should be noted how convenient her actions were to permit Zeus to move on to other affairs and father yet more semi-divine offspring.

Of all of Zeus' illegitimate children, none annoyed Hera as much as Heracles. When Zeus bragged of his unborn son, Hera tricked him into making great promises regarding the next royal birth, which Zeus assumed would be that of Heracles. Instead Hera slowed Alcmena's labor and accelerated Archippe's. As a result, Eurystheus became High King. Alcmena was so fearful of Hera's reprisals that she abandoned her infant son.

Hera was tricked into suckling an abandoned young infant who was, in fact, Heracles.

Heracles Ascending to Olympus, **red-figured bell krater, 4th century** B.C.

It is from this incident that Heracles derived his name, and some say that Hera's milk was responsible for making Heracles immortal. When she realized the identity of the child she was suckling Hera pulled away and the Milky Way was formed from the milk that continued to flow from her breast.

Once Heracles undertook his labors, Hera made every attempt possible to impede his progress. She rewarded the crab that had fought against Heracles alongside the Lernaean Hydra by placing its image among the stars, and was responsible for assigning Ladon to oversee her golden apple tree in place of the Hesperides. When Heracles killed Ladon, Hera set his image among the stars as well. And yet, when Heracles was deified and ascended to Mount Olympus, Hera kept quiet. In fact, she even gave Heracles her daughter, Hebe, in marriage.

Hera also played a frequent role in the art of prophesy, and in bestowing such abilities on others. It was Hera who foretold what the gods would need to defend themselves against the

giants, which, ironically, included the help of a mortal who turned out to be Heracles.

Hera was credited with aiding the Greeks against the Trojans, sending the serpent that bit Philoctetes, and countless other actions that ranged from the petty to the cataclysmic. Despite the mythological characterization of Hera, her role in the religion of the day was great. Her worship was extensive, and her position as the goddess of women was accepted throughout most of Greece.

Heracles

The greatest of all mythological heroes, Heracles was conceived of Zeus and a mortal mother, and was eventually made immortal and allowed to join the gods atop Olympus. Best known for the labors that were assigned to him, Heracles performed all sorts of heroic deeds, as well as a large number of unsavory acts. It is generally agreed that the name Heracles came to be applied to many figures, both historic and fictitious, and that the greatest accomplishments of each came to be credited to a single hero. The story of Heracles prob-

ably has as many variations as anyone's in Greek mythology, and many of them are quite contradictory.

When Zeus sought to father a great champion, a mortal who could ensure the Olympians' successful defense against an attack by the giants, he chose Alcmena, who was married to Amphitryon at the time, as the mother. Hera became enraged when she learned that Alcmena was carrying Zeus' child, and she forced Zeus into promising great things for the next divine birth. Hera then tricked Zeus by arranging it so that Eurystheus would be born just hours before Alcmena's son. In some cases, it is this supremacy over Heracles that later put Eurystheus in a position to assign the hero his labors.

Fearing Hera, Alcmena abandoned her child following its delivery. Either Zeus or Athene then managed to trick Hera into suckling the child, from which he derived his name, which means "Hera's glory." In some versions it is suggested that Heracles became immortal when he was suckled by Hera.

Once Hera had suckled the child, Alcmena and Amphitryon were assured that it would be safe to care for the child, who was returned to his mother. Along with his half-brother Iphicles, Heracles was raised in luxury, despite occasional attempts on his life by Hera, such as the time she sent snakes into Heracles and Iphicles' nursery. Heracles was tutored in all of the most respected fields by the best teachers in the land. Amphitryon taught his son chariot racing, and Heracles' other teachers included Castor, Autolycus, Eurytus, Eumolpus, and Linus.

After Heracles killed Linus, Amphitryon became concerned about the boy's strength and temperament, and sent him off to the safety of a cattle ranch, where Heracles remained until he reached manhood. At that time, Amphitryon and his neighbors were being plagued by the lion of Cithaeron, which Heracles subsequently slew. Heracles is often described as wearing a lion's skin, and in many versions it is suggested that this pelt was obtained from the Cithaeronian Lion. (Others connect the skin with Heracles' first labor, the slaying of the Nemean Lion.)

After Heracles defeated Pyraechmus and his Euboean army, he had Pyraechmus' body torn apart by colts, just one of several such actions for which he was responsible. For this and other acts, Hera punished Heracles by driving him insane. During the course of his madness Heracles attacked his nephew, Iolaus, and killed six of his own sons and two of his nephews, sons of Iphicles.

Heracles eventually managed to regain his sanity and end the bloodshed. He was purified by King Thestius and then traveled to the Delphic Oracle; the Pythoness instructed Heracles to go to Tiryns where Eurystheus ruled, and to serve Eurystheus for twelve years, during which time he would have to accomplish whatever labors Eurystheus assigned him. In many versions it is suggested that the Pythoness told Heracles that if he were to do this he would be ensured an eternal life.

There are many variations on the reasons for Heracles' acceptance of Eurystheus' labors. Some revolve around Amphitryon and his possible banishment from Thebes. Some suggest that Heracles had become Eurystheus' lover and performed the labors for his gratification. And in others it is said that Heracles' commitment to Eurystheus was not based on a span of time, but on the successful completion of ten tasks (in the end, Heracles performed twelve labors, because Eurystheus refused to allow two of them to count).

The first labor was to kill the Nemean Lion, which was impervious to Heracles' club, arrows, and sword. Heracles eventually wrestled with the beast and strangled it, although

Heracles and the Hydra, **probably from the workshop of Francesco I de' Medici, c. 1580.**

not before it managed to bite off one of his fingers. Heracles used the lion's own claws to remove its pelt.

Heracles' arrival outside Eurystheus' palace with the dead lion slung over his shoulder scared Eurystheus so badly that he hid inside a brazen vessel and always used an intermediary in assigning Heracles his subsequent tasks. The next labor was the destruction of the Lernaean Hydra—a dog-bodied, venombreathing creature with eight, nine, ten, or more heads, one of which was said to have been immortal. Heracles fought valiantly, cutting off many of the Hydra's heads only to see them regenerate, as well as fighting off a giant crab that had come to the Hydra's aid.

It was only with his nephew (and charioteer) Iolaus' help that Heracles eventually managed to cut off the Hydra's immortal head and slay the beast. Eurystheus, however, ruled that Iolaus' assistance nullified Heracles' accomplishment and refused to count it as one of the required ten labors. Instead Eurystheus decided that Heracles would now have to capture the Ceryneian Hind alive and bring it to Mycenae.

Heracles chased the Ceryneian Hind for one full year and eventually caught it by the river Ladon with a precise shot from his bow that pinned the animal's forelegs together without spilling a drop of blood.

The fourth of Heracles' labors also involved the live capture of a wild beast, in this case the Erymanthian Boar. Before he could track down the Boar, however, Heracles was drawn into a battle with the Centaurs, during which he wounded his old friend Cheiron. Heracles captured the Boar by driving it into the snow and leaping upon its back. He wrapped a chain around it and began carrying it back to Mycenae. When he received word about the gathering of the Argonauts, Heracles abandoned the Boar and went to enlist in the voyage to Colchis. (Considering the ease with which Eurystheus dismissed some of Heracles' other accomplishments, it is curious that this one was tallied as acceptable.)

Shortly after Heracles defeated Jason in a rowing competition, Heracles' companion Hylas disappeared by a spring near Pegae on Cios, and Heracles and Polyphemus went off in search of him. After a time, Jason decided that the *Argo* had waited long enough and that it should sail without Heracles, Polyphemus, or Hylas. Some Argonauts argued otherwise, but Jason stood firm.

When Heracles returned to Mycenae, he learned that his fifth assignment was to clean

Heracles Killing the Nemean Lion, **black-figured amphora, 6th century** B.C.

King Augeias' stables, which had not been cleaned in years, in a single day. Following the advice of Menedemus, and with the help of Iolaus, Heracles redirected the Alpheus and the Peneius rivers to flow through Augeias' stables and wash the filth away.

Augeias declared that the credit for cleaning his stables belonged to the river gods and not Heracles, refused to pay Heracles, and banished him and his own son, Phyleus, who had supported Heracles' claims. Eurystheus also ruled that the labor did not count.

The sixth labor involved the dispersing of the man-eating birds living in the Stymphalian Marsh. (In some versions it is suggested that Heracles accomplished this labor while he was still an Argonaut.) The birds had brazen claws, wings, and beaks, and were impervious to arrows. Heracles obtained brazen castanets or rattles from Hephaestus and scared off the birds, most of which were said to have flown to the Isle of Ares in the Black Sea.

Heracles' seventh labor called for the capture of the Cretan Bull, an animal that is variously described as the bull that carried Europe to Crete and the one that sired the Minotaur on Minos' wife. The bull, which belched fire, was in the process of ravaging Crete when Heracles attacked it. A long struggle ensued, at the end of which Heracles managed to bring the bull to Mycenae singlehandedly.

Eurystheus' eighth assignment involved the capture of the man-eating mares of Diomedes. Heracles captured the horses and left them with Abderus while he went off to fight Diomedes and his allies the Bistones. Heracles clubbed Diomedes to death and fed him to his horses, who had already devoured Abderus, then harnessed the mares.

Heracles then set out on his ninth labor, a quest to obtain Ares' divine girdle, which was in the possession of the Amazon Queen Hippolyte, and present it to Eurystheus' daughter, Admete. Heracles encountered the Amazons near the river Thermodon, where Hippolyte offered him her girdle as a love present. Hera, always annoyed by Heracles' successes, incited the Amazons to attack Heracles. While the subsequent chain of events varies from version to version, in the end Heracles completed this task.

The tenth labor of Heracles was the capture of King Geryon's cattle. On the way to Geryon's kingdom, Heracles established the pillars at Gibraltar while ferrying his troops north from Africa. When Heracles arrived, he quickly dispatched Geryon's guards, Eurytion and Orthrus. Heracles stole the cattle and dispatched the three-headed Geryon with one very well placed arrow.

Heracles had now undertaken ten labors, eight of which had been ruled valid. It had taken him eight years and a month to accomplish all this, and as there were still two more tasks for him to complete, Heracles moved on to his eleventh labor: the gathering of fruit from Hera's golden apple tree, which was guarded over by the serpent Ladon. Nereus warned Heracles that his mission would succeed only if he found someone else to actually gather the apples for him. Since Atlas was supporting the celestial globe nearby, Heracles agreed to relieve Atlas for a short while in order for Atlas to retrieve the fruits, which he did once Heracles shot and killed Ladon.

Hoping to escape his punishment, Atlas suggested that he deliver the golden apples to Eurystheus personally. Heracles sensed Atlas' intentions and told him he would be happy to let him bring the apples to Eurystheus as long as Atlas would relieve him for a moment. Once Atlas was tricked into reaccepting his burden, Heracles departed, leaving Atlas back where he had been all along.

On the way home, Heracles killed Antaeus, Antaeus' half-brother, Busiris, and

Busiris' son, Amphidamas. Once Heracles reached Mycenae, Eurystheus refused to accept the apples, since they had belonged to Hera and he was wary of accepting anything that had been stolen from her, and informed Heracles that his twelfth and final labor was to bring Cerberus up from Tartarus.

Heracles began preparations for his final labor by being instructed in the Eleusian Mysteries, knowledge deemed essential for safe escape from the land of the dead. While being ferried across the river Styx by Charon, Heracles was confronted by the ghosts of Meleager and Medusa. During the course of his conversation with Meleager, Heracles

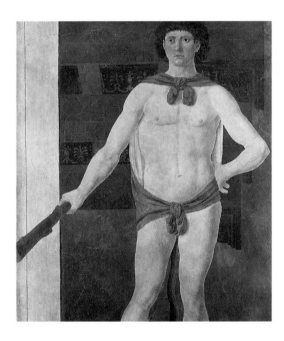

Hercules, **Piero della Francesca, c. 1465–1470.**

promised to marry Meleager's sister, Deianeira. Heracles then rescued Theseus, and possibly Peirithous, from Hades' Chairs of Forgetfulness, and Hades told Heracles that he could take Cerberus as long as he refrained from using his club or arrows.

Heracles throttled Cerberus with his bare hands until the beast yielded, and brought Cerberus to Eurystheus, who responded by grievously insulting Heracles with an insufficient portion of a sacrificial slaughter. There followed a skirmish, which resulted in the murder of three of Eurystheus' sons: Perimedes, Eurybius, and Eurypilus.

His labors complete, Heracles returned to Thebes, where he passed his wife, Megara, on to Iolaus so that he might be free to remarry.

In other versions King Lycus is on the verge of slaying Megara and Heracles' children just as Heracles returns from his labors. In these scenarios, Heracles kills Lycus, for which he is punished by Hera by being driven insane. (The similarities between this incident and a similar burst of insanity mentioned earlier are an indication of the general confusion surrounding the chronology of Heracles' adventures.) During the course of this madness, Heracles killed many, if not all, of his children, and Megara as well. He was eventually cured of his madness by Medea, who was indebted to him for the protection he had given her when she abandoned Jason.

In other versions it is suggested that Heracles simply freed himself of Megara and tried to win the hand of Eurytus' daughter, Iole, by besting Eurytus and his sons in an archery competition. Heracles won, but Eurytus denied his victory, and Autolycus complicated matters by making it appear as if Heracles had stolen some of Eurytus' cows in revenge. This led to Heracles' murder of Eurytus' son, Iphitus, for which Heracles had difficulty being purified. Eventually the Pythoness Xenoclea told Heracles that he must sell himself into slavery to Queen Omphale for a Great Year (a period that may have encompassed as many as eight years) and give the payment he received from her to Iphicles' orphans.

Heracles' next adventure involved the rescue of Laomedon's daughter, Hesione. In some versions it is suggested that these events actually took place while Heracles was on his way home after having been abandoned by the *Argo,* while in others the rescue of Hesione took place then, and the follow-up revenge did not take place until after the labors had been completed. At some point, Heracles told Laomedon that he would rescue Hesione and kill the monster in exchange for Laomedon's two divine horses, and a deal was struck. After Heracles killed the animal, Laomedon, the King of Troy, refused to uphold his end of the bargain, and a war ensued.

Heracles' forces eventually overcame the Trojans, and Heracles killed Laomedon and all of his sons except Podarces, who was later renamed Priam. Soon after, Heracles performed the service he had been sired to fulfill: helping the Olympian gods defeat the giants.

When the time came for the great battle, Heracles was on hand to dispatch each of the giants. All were wounded or stunned in some ghastly way by the deities, but only Heracles was capable of delivering the necessary coups de grâce.

Following the victory of the Olympians, Heracles went to avenge himself against Augeias for the king's earlier treatment of him. Augeias and his allies the Moliones successfully defended themselves against Heracles' armies, however, and killed Heracles' half-brother Iphicles. Heracles then retreated to Olenus, where he deflowered Meleager's sister Deianeira, promised to marry her, and departed. Eurytion the Centaur arrived shortly after Heracles' departure and attempted to marry Deianeira himself. Heracles arrived just before the marriage and killed Eurytion and his brothers, for which Eurystheus banished him from Argos. Heracles took Deianeira and went to Pheneus, where he avenged himself with an ambush upon the Moliones, and then resumed his attack on Augeias' city of Elis. The city was overrun, and in some versions it is suggested that Augeias and his sons were killed during the fighting.

Heracles then competed successfully at an Olympiad where Eurystheus determined that there should be no payment to any of the victors (since he wished to avoid giving Heracles anything). During these Olympics, Heracles engaged in an epic wrestling match with someone who appeared to be a mortal but turned out to be Zeus in disguise; the contest ended in a draw.

Later, on the way home from Sparta or perhaps on his way to battle with Augeias, Heracles visited King Aleus of Tegea and violated Aleus' daughter, Auge, a rape that resulted in the birth of Telephus. Heracles moved on to Calydon, where he defended Deianeira from Achelous and finally married her. Heracles and Deianeira moved to the city of Ephyra, where they lived until the accidental murder of one of Architeles' sons led Heracles and Deianeira, as well as a newborn son, Hyllus, to Trachis. On the way to Trachis, the Centaur Nessus tried to violate Deianeira as she crossed the river Evenus ahead of Heracles. After Heracles dealt Nessus what proved to be a mortal wound, the Centaur convinced Deianeira that his blood and semen, mixed together, would function as a love charm; it was in fact a torturous concoction that led to Heracles' apotheosis.

After Heracles finally brought his forces to avenge himself against Eurytus for the fight they had had over Iole, who was captured by Heracles during the battle, Heracles returned home to Deianeira. He left Iole in her care and predicted that if he were not back within fifteen months he would be dead, but that if he were able to return it would mean eternal tranquility for both of them.

Hercules and Omphale, François Lemoyne, 1724.

When word of Heracles' imminent return reached Deianeira, who was jealous of any designs her husband might have had on Iole, Deianeira applied the "love" potion Nessus had given her to a shirt, which she later presented to Heracles. Deianeira sent the messenger Lichas with the shirt, which Heracles put on at just about the same time Deianeira realized she had been tricked. When Heracles donned the shirt, he was driven into a tortured frenzy, killing Lichas on the spot and suffering excruciating pain.

The agony of Nessus' poison was so great that Heracles called for Hyllus, one of his sons, to carry him away so that he could die in solitude. Hyllus carried his father to the top of Mount Oeata, and built a pyre upon which he placed Heracles. Philoctetes lit the flame which began to consume Heracles alive until a great bolt of lightning came down from the sky and reduced it all to ashes. Zeus oversaw Heracles' apotheosis, and even Hera reluctantly approved of Heracles' deification, giving him her daughter, Hebe, in divine marriage.

Heracles became the porter of Olympus and waited by the gates each night for Artemis to return from her hunt. In most cases Heracles was considered an Olympian in full standing, although Homer was a conspicuous exception in that regard. Heracles went on to meddle

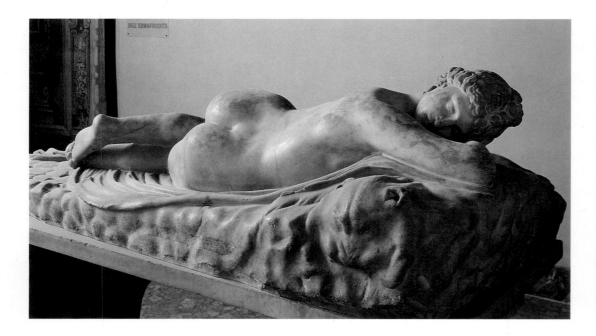

Hermaphroditus, **marble statue, c. 150–100** B.C.

Hermes, **marble statue, Hellenistic period.**

with mortals during the course of the Trojan War, but his tenure on Olympus was a relatively quiet one.

> *These toils and countless others have I proved, nor has any man wanted a triumph over my prowess. But now, with joints unhinged and with flesh torn to shreds, I have become the miserable prey of an unseen destroyer—I who am called the son of noblest mother, I whose reputed sire is Zeus, lord of the starry sky.*
> —Heracles, Trachian Women, Sophocles

> *. . . The Queen of Heaven placed fierce-eyed snakes*
> *Inside my cradle to destroy me. When I grew up*
> *And strong flesh wrapped my limbs, need I recount what labours*
> *I went through? Lions, giants with three bodies, the four-hooved Squadrons of Centaurs— all I fought and overcame.*
> *The hydra too, swarming with heads that grew again,*
> *I killed; finally, I crowned a host of other toils*
> *By invading the dark regions at Eurystheus' word*
> *To capture the three-headed watchdog of the dead*
> *And drag him up to earth.*
> —Heracles, Heracles, Euripides

Heraclids The name by which the sons (and descendants) of Heracles were collectively known, and which was occasionally used to include their allies as well. Following Heracles'

apotheosis, the Heraclids were banished by Eurystheus. Despite early successes, which included the murder of Eurystheus' sons and the subsequent capture and execution of Eurystheus himself, a drought forced the Heraclids to retreat for three years. Several generations later the Heraclids, led by Temenus, Cresphontes, and the twins Procles and Eurysthenes, reconquered Peloponnesus.

Hermaphroditus A double-sexed being born to Aphrodite after she lay with Hermes in repayment for his help during her embarrassing entanglement with Ares in Hephaestus' net. Hermaphroditus is described as a "youth with womanish breasts and long hair," and is believed to represent a transition from matriarchal theologies to patriarchal ones.

Hermes The son of Zeus and Maia, one of the daughters of Atlas, Hermes was delivered in a cave on Mount Cyllene in Arcadia, and is said to have grown astonishingly quickly, which may reflect Hermes' original, pre-Olympian role as a phallic deity. Hermes quickly left Maia's care and went out seeking adventure. He stole several head of cattle from Apollo's herds in Pieria, was caught, and confessed. Hermes sacrificed two of Apollo's cattle to the twelve ruling Olympians (including himself as one of the twelve).

In the end, Hermes escaped with a stiff warning from Zeus that he respect the property of others. Hermes then told Zeus that he wished to serve as his herald and be made

responsible for the safety of the other gods' divine properties. Zeus entrusted Hermes with a herald's staff, winged sandals, and assorted other divine accoutrements and saw that he was welcomed into the Olympian family. (In some versions Apollo gives Hermes his staff after the two make a mutually satisfactory deal to compensate Apollo for the theft of his cattle.)

While Hermes proved helpful to many of the gods (he even assisted Hades by gently summoning the dying) it was to Zeus he reported. And of all the Olympians, Hermes was invoked by those who held the widest range of special interests. In addition to serving as the god of trade, travelers, and commerce, Hermes also was the favorite of athletes, was responsible for the replenishment of the animal kingdom, was the patron saint of thieves, was a deity of wealth, and was frequently invoked for his eloquence and oratorical skills.

Some of Hermes' most memorable episodes involved saving premature or unnaturally born children. Hermes brought Hephaestus (or Prometheus) to breach Zeus' skull and deliver Athene. He cut Asclepius from Coronis' dead body and entrusted the child to its father, Apollo. And he also was responsible for sewing Semele's six-month fetus into Zeus' thigh and later delivering Dionysus.

Hermes himself is credited with fathering Echion, Autolycus, Daphnis, and Myrtilus. While the mothers of most of Hermes' children are relatively undistinguished, Hermes did have one affair with Aphrodite, who was inspired to sleep with him following his complimentary words during her and Ares' imprisonment by Hephaestus. The result of their night together was the double-sexed being Hermaphroditus. Finally, Hermes also was the father of Pan, whom he brought to Olympus to amuse the gods.

The principal beneficiary of Hermes' actions was Zeus. During Zeus' fight with Typhon, Hermes rescued Zeus' sinews from Delphyne so that the supreme deity could regain his strength and overcome Typhon. And it was in Zeus' service that Hermes dispensed unmerciful punishment upon Ixion for having tried to seduce Hera.

There are countless other myths that incorporate Hermes to varying degrees. In some he is little more than a messenger, while in others he is the enacter of Zeus' wishes. Hermes also fought alongside the Olympians during their battle with the giants.

Hermione

The only daughter born to Helen and Menelaus, Hermione was left behind with her aunt, Clytaemnestra, when Helen ran off to Troy with Paris. Hermione is said to have married two different men following the Trojan War. She first married Neoptolemus, who claimed that Menelaus had given his consent before the Trojan War. In this marriage, Hermione was said to have been barren.

This is at odds with versions in which Hermione made offerings at Clytaemnestra's grave following Orestes' murder of Clytaemnestra and Aegisthus. Orestes attempted to kill Helen, who was making offerings with Hermione, until Apollo intervened. He told Menelaus that Hermione should be married to Orestes, and the result of their union was Tisamenus, Orestes' heir and successor.

Hesione

The daughter of Laomedon and either Oceanus or Styrmo. When Laomedon failed to make the proper sacrificial offerings to Apollo and Poseidon, they sent a drought and a sea monster, which an oracle said could be appeased only by the sacrifice of one of Laomedon's daughters.

Laomedon tied Hesione to a rock as an offering to the monster at which point Heracles passed through, rescued Hermione, and made the offer to slay the monster in exchange for two of Laomedon's divine horses. When Laomedon reneged on the deal, Heracles killed Laomedon and all of his sons except Podarces. Hesione was given to Telamon as a spoil of this victory, and Telamon allowed her to ransom Podarces (who was subsequently renamed Priam).

Hesione went on to bear two children by Telamon, Teucer and Trambelus, the latter born after she had deserted Telamon. Meanwhile Priam rose to power as the leader of Troy and pressed the Greeks for his sister's return. It was Hesione's return that Priam had in mind when he sent Paris to Greece, a move that resulted in Paris' abduction of Helen.

Eventually Hesione ended up under the protection of King Arion, who raised Trambelus as his own. Hesione is sometimes credited with being the mother of Great Ajax.

Hespera

The sister of Eos or another manifestation of her, Hespera was the personification of Dusk, and was responsible for marking the end of each day by announcing Helius' safe arrival on the western shores of Ocean.

Hesperides

Three nymphs described alternatively as the daughters of Atlas and Hesperis, Ceto and Phorcys, or Night. The Hesperides, whose individual names were Hespere, Aegle, and Erytheis, were made guardians over the golden apple tree that Mother Earth had given Hera as a wedding present. Eventually, when Hera learned that the sisters had been stealing some of her divine fruits, Hera replaced the Hesperides with a dragon, Ladon. (In some versions it is suggested that Ladon did not actually replace the Hesperides, but simply joined them.)

Hestia

The goddess of the domestic hearth, Hestia represented personal security and the sacred duty of hospitality. She had the reputation of being the mildest, most upright, and most charitable of all the Olympians. As a result, she never took part in any wars or disputes and always resisted the amorous advances of males, including those of Poseidon, Apollo, and Priapus. Because of her role in preserving the peace at Olympus, Zeus always awarded her the first victim of every public sacrifice.

Hippasus

The son of Leucippe and the brother of Alcithoë and Arsippe, Hippasus was torn to pieces by his mother and sisters after they were driven crazy by Dionysus. His murder was atoned for annually at Orchomenus,

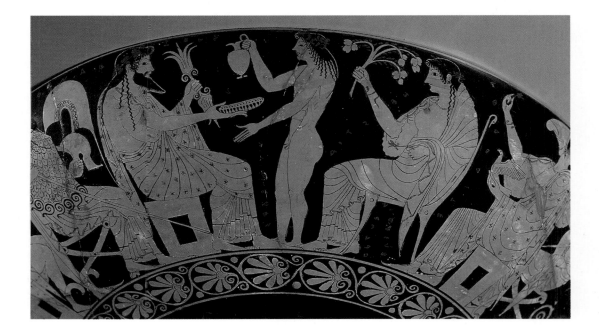

Reunion of the Gods (Zeus served by Ganymede, with Hestia and Aphrodite), Greek kylix, 4th century B.C.

Hercules and the Centaurs at the Wedding of Hippodameia, Girolamo Macchietti, 16th century.

where he was referred to as Agrionia, meaning "provocation to savagery."

Hippodameia

Oenomaus, King of Arcadia, was reluctant to see his daughter Hippodameia married, either because he himself was in love with her or because of a prophesy that suggested his son-in-law would take his life. As a result, Oenomaus challenged each of his daughter's suitors to a chariot race, in which the loser would forfeit his life. After many men lost their lives, Pelops challenged and defeated Oenomaus.

Pelops had also bribed Oenomaus' charioteer, Myrtilus, to help him win, with the promise that Myrtilus could spend the first night with Hippodameia. But when Myrtilus attempted to ravish Hippodameia, who was unaware of Pelops' promise to the charioteer, she accused him of attacking her and Pelops pushed him to his death from their winged chariot as the three flew off. In gratitude to Hera for her hand in Hippodameia's being able to marry Pelops, the princess assembled the Sixteen Matrons.

Once Pelops and Hippodameia settled down they had many children: Pittheus, Atreus and Thyestes, Alcathous, Hippalcus, Copreus, Sciron, Epidaurus, Pleisthenes, Dias, Cybosurus, Corinthius, Hippasus, Cleon, Argeius, Aelinus, Astydameia, Lysidice, Eurydice, Nicippe, Antibia, Archippe, and Chrysippus (who was actually the result of an affair Pelops had with Astyoche).

Chrysippus was later abducted, and in the versions in which he is rescued, Hippodameia grows jealous that Pelops is favoring him above the sons she herself bore, and attempts to convince Atreus and Thyestes to kill Chrysippus. When they refuse, she commits the murder herself. In his dying breaths, Chrysippus names his stepmother as the culprit. Hippodameia then flees to Argolis, where she eventually takes her own life.

There was also another character named Hippodameia, whose father, Adrastus (or possibly Butes), married her to Peirithous. It was at their wedding ceremony that Ares and Eris, slighted by not having been invited, caused the Centaurs to get drunk and begin a brawl that led to a war.

Hippolyte

An Amazonian Queen whose golden girdle (which originally belonged to Ares) was the subject of Heracles' ninth labor, Hippolyte led many successful campaigns to help establish the cunning and ferocity of the Amazon forces.

In some versions Heracles kills Hippolyte when he comes to get the girdle, while in others she escapes. In those versions in which Hippolyte survives her encounter with Heracles, she is said to have been accidentally shot by her sister, Penthesileia, while hunting or during the fighting that broke out at the wedding of Theseus and Phaedra.

Hippolytus

The son of Theseus and Antiope. When Theseus attempted to replace Antiope with a new wife, Phaedra, Hippolytus' mother was not so willing to be cast out. She stormed the wedding between Theseus and Phaedra and was killed by her own husband. Hippolytus continued to live with his father and to show great allegiance to Artemis. The boy's continued loyalty to Artemis angered Aphrodite, who repaid his indifference toward her by making his stepmother, Phaedra, fall in love with him.

When Hippolytus failed to reciprocate Phaedra's feelings, and rebuked her for having even entertained them, Phaedra hanged herself and left a note accusing Hippolytus of having violated her. Theseus responded by banishing his son and praying that he might die that very same day. On his way out of town, Hippolytus' chariot went out of control and broke to pieces. Hippolytus was dragged to his death by his team of frenzied horses.

Artemis, upset with the entire chain of events, then had Asclepius revive Hippolytus. Artemis disguised the reborn Hippolytus and married him to a nymph named Egerhia, with whom he lived under the name Virbius, meaning "twice a man." In some versions it is suggested that Theseus was most eager to have Hippolytus join him in Athens, but the latter refused. It is also said that Hippolytus lived in an adulterous situation with Aegialeia, although in some versions his partner's name is given as Cometes.

Hope

A female entity sealed inside Pandora's jar by Prometheus, Hope remained trapped inside the jar when the evils were released. Though Hope is more a concept than a character, she is occasionally personified.

Hundred-handed Ones

In the Olympian creation myth, the Hundred-handed Ones were the children of Mother Earth, and were considered the first semihumans. Initially confined to Tartarus when Cronus came to power, the three hundred-handed giants—Gyges, Briareus (also called Aegaeon), and Cottus—were rescued by Zeus and the Cyclopes during the course of their overthrow of Cronus and were later asked to guard the Titans who had supported Cronus. The brothers are thought to have been described as having one hundred hands either because of priests that were organized in bands of fifty, or for war bands, such as those employed by the early Romans, that consisted of one hundred soldiers.

Hyacinthus

A beautiful Spartan prince who was the first to be propositioned by both a mortal and a deity of the same sex. Apollo quickly dispatched his mortal competitor, but the West Wind then became jealous. When Apollo was teaching Hyacinthus to throw the discus, the West Wind blew the projectile back into Hyacinthus' skull, killing him. The flowers that bear his name sprang from the ground where drops of his blood had fallen.

Hylas

The son of Theiodamas and Menodice. When Heracles slew Theiodamas in battle, he took the infant Hylas as a spoil of war. Hylas grew to become Heracles' squire, and is described as having been his "minion and darling." Hylas accompanied Heracles aboard the *Argo* but never made it to Colchis.

When the ship stopped to fetch water at a pool near Pegae on Cios, Hylas was enticed by Dryope and her sister nymphs to live with them in an underwater grotto. Heracles and Polyphemus searched all over for Hylas, but were unable to find him.

Hyllus The son of Deianeira and Heracles, Hyllus went with his parents when they moved to Trachis. When Hyllus was grown and Deineira accidentally poisoned her husband, Heracles summoned his son to carry him to the summit of Mount Oeta, where Hyllus constructed a pyre upon which Heracles was placed while still alive. Heracles' final wish was that Hyllus should marry Iole, whose arrival had led to his apotheosis.

Hyllus married Iole as his father wished, and was adopted by Aegimius. Hyllus later played a major role in the Heraclids' alliance with Theseus and his Athenian forces against Eurystheus and the Peloponnesian armies. Hyllus settled at the Electran Gate at Thebes and successfully conquered the Peloponnese. But a drought followed, and an oracle suggested a three-year retreat. When Hyllus returned he challenged anyone to single combat and ended up fighting Echemus, the King of Tegea. Echemus killed Hyllus, who was subsequently buried in Megara.

Hyperion According to the Pelasgian creation myths, Hyperion was a Titan created by Eurynome to oversee the Sun along with Theia. Together they were the parents of Eos, Helius, and Selene, although Euryphaessa is described as the mother of some or all of Hyperion's children. Over the course of time, however, Hyperion became increasingly confused with his son, Helius, who was responsible for steering the sun across the sky each day.

This confusion peaks in the story of Odysseus' wanderings. When Odysseus' hungry crew slaughtered cattle that were said to belong to Hyperion's herd they paid for the transgression with their lives. Hyperion was informed of the crime by his daughter Lampetia, who served as his chief herds-herdswoman. As Lampetia is also described as Helius' daughter, and as Helius also was known to have had extensive herds in the region, it seems likely that the entire tale was actually about Helius.

Hypermnestra A daughter of Danaus, Hypermnestra was one of the fifty Danaids, who sought to avoid marriage to their cousins, Aegyptus' sons. When the marriage was forced upon them and the Danaids agreed to kill their

Hope, **George Frederic Watts, 1886.**

husbands on the wedding night, Hypermnestra alone spared her husband, Lynceus, in gratitude for his having spared her virginity. Danaus was furious with Hypermnestra and argued for her death. The Argive judges absolved her, and reunited her with Lynceus.

Hypsipyle

A princess who was the daughter of the Lemnian King Thoas. When the women of Lemnos agreed to murder all of the men in the land for having taken lovers, Hypsipyle secretly spared her father and allowed him to escape. She later became a leader of the Lemnian Women, and represented them when the *Argo* arrived in their port. Following the advice of her aged nurse, Polyxo, Hypsipyle convinced the Lemnian Women to welcome the Argonauts to their beds so as to repopulate their kingdom. Hypsipyle herself bedded Jason, by whom she had twin sons, Euneus and Nebrophonus. Hoping to entice the Argonauts to stay, Hypsipyle invited Jason to serve as the Lemnian King, but the crew was eventually reminded of their quest by Heracles, who herded them back to the *Argo*.

After the *Argo* departed, the Lemnian Women learned that Hypsipyle had spared her father and sold her into slavery to the Nemean King Lycurgus. Hypsipyle later became nursemaid to Lycurgus' son Opheltes.

Iasius

One of the Dactyls, Iasius (also known as Iasion) became Demeter's lover during the wedding of Cadmus and Harmonia. After Iasius and Demeter slipped outside and coupled in a plowed field, they returned to the banquet, where Zeus observed the mud on their bodies and the way they were acting toward each other, and deduced what had happened; he then became angry and struck Iasius dead with a thunderbolt. Later, Demeter gave birth to Plutus.

In some versions it is said that Iasius was killed by his brother Dardanus or was torn to pieces by his own horses. It is sometimes said that Iasius was the son of Electra.

Iasus

The son of Phoronus and Cerdo, Iasus shared control of Peloponnesus with his two brothers Pelasgus and Agenor. When Iasus' wife, Clymene, delivered a daughter, Iasus, who was intent upon having a son, abandoned the newborn on a mountain, where she was suckled by a bear and raised by hunters. This daughter, Atalanta, became a formidable hunter, and was greatly successful in the hunt for the Calydonian Boar. After this, Iasus finally recognized her as his daughter, but insisted that she take a husband.

Icarus, Sidney Meteyard, c. 1900.

Icarius

The son of Gorgophone and Oebalus, Icarius was the brother of Tyndareus, with whom he became co-ruler of Sparta following their father's death. Tyndareus and Icarius were eventually unseated by Hippocoön and his sons, and in some versions it is suggested that Icarius might even have sided with Hippocoön.

Icarius was the father of Perilaus, who lobbied the Athenians against Orestes for his murder of Perilaus' cousin, Clytaemnestra. Icarius was also the father of a daughter named Arnaea by the Naiad Periboea.

Icarius was also known as the first man to make wine, and for the fact that he did not mix it with water. When Icarius gave his concoction to local shepherds, who became so drunk that they thought they had been bewitched, they killed Icarius and left his body in the woods.

Icarus

The son of Daedalus and Naucrate, Icarus was imprisoned inside Minos' Labyrinth along with his father when Minos became angry at Daedalus for having helped Pasiphaë fulfill her unnatural lust for a bull. As Daedalus and Icarus were unable to escape by sea since Minos controlled the waterways, Daedalus

fashioned wings for Icarus and himself, and warned his son not to fly too high. Once airborne, Icarus ignored his father's advice. The sun melted the wax that held Icarus' wings in place, and he plummeted into the sea and died. (In some versions it is suggested that Icarus drowned as the two attempted to swim to freedom.)

Idas

A son of Poseidon born to Arene while she was married to Aphareus. Idas and his half-brother, Lynceus, were involved in a number of oft-recounted exploits, including the hunt for the Calydonian Boar and the voyage of the *Argo*. The brothers were initially engaged to their cousins, the Leucippides, who were abducted by the Dioscuri. After the abduction, Idas fell in love with Marpessa, whose father, Evenus, challenged each of her suitors to a chariot race in which the winner could marry Marpessa, while the loser would be killed.

Idas enlisted Poseidon's help for his race, and used one of the god's divine chariots to help him defeat Evenus, who killed his horses and took his own life immediately thereafter. Idas prepared to marry Marpessa, but Apollo, also attracted to her, attempted to steal her from Idas. Eventually Zeus intervened and told

I O

Marpessa that she must choose between the two of them. Marpessa picked Idas because of Apollo's habit of abandoning his brides as they aged and replacing them with younger women (something he was planning to do with her).

Idas and Lynceus made peace with the Dioscuri despite the abduction of the Leucippides. They allied to attack other kingdoms, but quarreled while dividing the spoils of their successes. The Dioscuri took more than their share of the booty, leading Idas to throw a spear at one of the brothers, Castor. Idas gravely wounded Polydeuces, who had killed Lynceus, and was then struck dead by a thunderbolt thrown by Zeus. The chain of events differs in some versions but the end result is the same throughout.

Idmon The second son of Apollo born to Cyrene, Idmon was a seer and the brother of Aristaeus. As a crewmember on the *Argo*, Idmon served valiantly until a stop at Mariandyne, where he was attacked and killed by a wild boar. The Argonauts mourned Idmon's death for three days before resuming their journey.

Idmon is said to have been the father of Thestor, who was imprisoned by King Icarus.

In the water-meadow by a reedy stream there lay a white-tusked boar cooling his flanks and huge belly in the mud. This evil brute . . . lived all alone in the wide fen, and no one was the wiser. But now, as Idmon made his way along the dykes of the muddy river, the boar leapt out of some hidden lair in the reeds, charged at him and gashed his thigh, severing the sinews and the bone itself. Idmon fell to the ground with a sharp cry.
—The Voyage of Argo, *Apollonius of Rhodes*

Idomeneus A rich and powerful Cretan King who was said to have been descended from Helius, Idomeneus became a prominent member of the Greek alliance and promised the Greeks one hundred ships as long as he was allowed to share command of the alliance with Agamemnon.

Idomeneus was the husband of Meda, one of several Greek wives whom Nauplius coerced into adulterous relationships. Meda took up with Leucus, who eventually killed Meda and her daughter, Cleisithyra, and assumed control of Crete. Meanwhile, when Idomeneus' return from Troy was delayed by storms, Idomeneus swore to make an offering to Poseidon if he managed to reach home safely. That offering was the sacrifice of the first person Idomeneus encountered upon his return, which turned out to be his son. (In some versions, it is a daughter.)

Idomeneus, willing to fulfill his promise, prepared to sacrifice the child. At this point a pestilence fell upon the land and interrupted the sacrifice. Leucus used this chain of events to banish Idomeneus and maintain control of Crete. Idomeneus emigrated to Calabria, where he seems to have lived peacefully until the time of his death.

Iliona A sister of Priam, Iliona married Polymnestor, King of the Thracian Chersonese. When the Trojan War began, Priam sent his son Polydorus to Iliona for safekeeping, along with a good deal of gold, sent with the boy to pay for his care, to be hidden from the Greeks, or both.

Iliona treated Polydorus as well as she treated her own son, Deiphilus. This became a problem when the Greeks either demanded that Polymnestor kill Polydorus or bribed him to do so. In some versions, Polymnestor tricked the Greeks by killing Deiphilus and causing them to believe he had killed Priam's son. This led to a falling-out between Iliona and her husband.

Ilus The brother of Erichthonius and Idaeus, Ilus went to Phrygia to compete in athletic games. For winning all of his wrestling matches, Ilus was awarded fifty youths, an equal number of maidens, and a cow, which he was told to follow until it lay down. On that spot Ilus was instructed to build a city, which he named Ilium.

The city of Ilium was one of the settlements that were later merged to form the city of Troy. After founding Ilium, Ilus discovered the Palladium, a statue of Pallas that Athene had thrown down to the earth when Zeus violated Ilus' great-grandmother Electra. Apollo, who is credited in some versions with directing Ilus to his destiny, told Ilus that as long as he took proper care of the statue he would rule successfully.

Ino A daughter of Cadmus, Ino eventually married King Athamas. While still married to Nephele, Athamas fell in love with Ino and fathered two sons—Learchus and Melicertes—on her. Nephele schemed against the brothers, and enlisted Hera's help to avenge Athamas' desertion of her. In the meantime, Zeus entrusted Ino and Athamas with young Dionysus, whose existence he wished to keep secret from Hera. Ino plotted to outwit her predecessor, and eventually gained the upper hand and tricked Athamas into attempting to sacrifice Phrixus, his son by Nephele. The child was saved, and Ino's role in the proceedings was eventually revealed. Hera punished them by driving Athamas mad and causing him to kill Learchus. Fearing Athamas' insane fury, Ino leapt into the sea from the Molurian Rock with Melicertes. (In some versions Ino is depicted leaping alone, after murdering her sons.) Zeus, still grateful to Ino for her care of Dionysus, deified her as Leucothea and young Melicertes as Palaemon.

Io A daughter of the river god Inachus, the first King of Argos, Io was a priestess in one of her father's temples to Hera, where she was spotted by Zeus, who fell in love with her because of a spell cast upon him by Iynx. Io wished to keep her virginity, but the oracles made it clear to Inachus that Zeus would wreak havoc on his kingdom if Io were not expelled from her home. Io was cast out, and was transformed by Hera into a white, horned cow. Hera made Argus the herdsman over Io, and Zeus sent Hermes to kill Argus. Hera responded by sending a gadfly to torment Io endlessly.

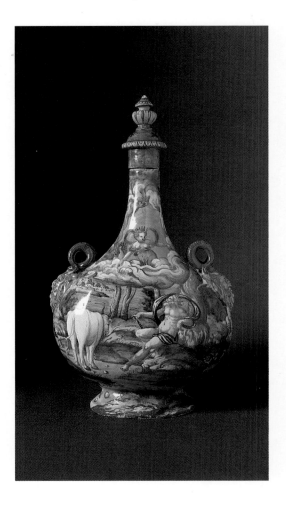

Io and Juno, **flask from the region of Urbino, mid-16th century.**

Jupiter and Io, **Correggio, 1530.**

When Io encountered Prometheus during his confinement, Prometheus prophesied that Io's peace would be restored when she reached Canopus on the Nile delta. When Io finally reached Canopus, Zeus restored her mind and came upon her "with a gentle touch." The result of this touch was Epaphus (whose name means "child of a touch").

In some versions Io dies after giving birth to Epaphus, while in others she bears Zeus another child, Libya, then flees to Mount Silpium, where she dies of grief.

Iobates

The King of Lycia, Iobates gave his daughter, Stheneboea (who may also have been named Anteia) to Proetus in marriage.

After Stheneboea accused Bellerophon of having tried to seduce her, and demanded that her husband kill him, Proetus sent Bellerophon to Iobates, requesting that Iobates kill his daughter's attacker. Iobates then sent Bellerophon to kill the fire-breathing Chimaera.

When Bellerophon returned, having killed the beast, Iobates was shocked and suggested that he battle the Solymians and their allies the Amazons. This Bellerophon also accomplished successfully. Later, when Bellerophon advanced across the Xanthian Plain, bringing with him a flood caused by Poseidon, the Xanthian women offered themselves to Bellerophon en masse in the hope of getting him to stop his destruction of their homeland. Bellerophon then ran away, taking the flood with him.

Taking Bellerophon's response to the Xanthian women into consideration, Iobates eventually realized that his daughter's claims against him were not true. As a result, he gave him Philonoë, another of his daughters, in marriage, and established him as the heir to the Lycian throne.

Iocaste

Because of the popularity of Oedipus' tale in Greek theater and her role in his story, Iocaste is one of the better-known figures in mythology.

When it was prophesied that any child of Laius would grow up to take its father's life, Laius decided not to tell his wife, Iocaste, about the prophesy. Misunderstanding his reasons for keeping shy of her, Iocaste got him drunk so that he would lie with her. When a son resulted from this union, Laius pinned the infant's feet together and abandoned him to die on Mount Cithaeron.

Years later, when the Sphinx was plaguing Thebes in response to Laius' abduction of Chryssipus, Iocaste's husband was killed en route to consult with an oracle on how to rid his land of its plight. Shortly after Laius' death, a newcomer, Oedipus, answered the Sphinx's riddle and saved Cadmus. Oedipus was then made king, and married Iocaste, with whom he had four children: Polyneices, Eteocles, Antigone, and Ismene.

During a plague many years later, Iocaste's father, Menoeceus, leapt to his death when an oracle suggested that his doing so might placate the gods. While this sacrifice improved the situation slightly, it was eventually revealed that Iocaste's husband Oedipus was also her long-lost son. The implications of this revelation were so great that Iocaste immediately retired to her chambers and hanged herself.

Iolaus

The son of Iphicles and Automedusa, Iolaus was the nephew of Heracles, who nearly killed him when Hera drove Heracles mad. Iolaus escaped from Heracles, and later became his uncle's charioteer and shieldbearer, accompanying him on many of his labors.

When Iolaus returned home with his uncle, Heracles gave his wife, Megara, to Iolaus to marry in his place (despite Iolaus being half her age), so that Heracles could pursue his passion for Iole. Iolaus accompanied Heracles in battles against Troy, went to Pheneus with him when Heracles was banished from Argolis, and led Calydonian forces under Heracles' direction against Sardinian troops. Iolaus oversaw the occupation of Sardinia, founding the city of Olbia in the process. In some versions Iolaus subsequently returned to Greece.

After Heracles' apotheosis, Iolaus returned to Trachis, but was eventually expelled by Eurystheus along with Heracles' children and his allies. The exiles were given refuge in Athens by Theseus, and Iolaus eventually led the combined forces of Athenians and Heraclids against Eurystheus.

It is said that Iolaus eventually died in Sardinia, and was awarded a hero's shrine in Thebes. Iolaus was also the name by which Protesilaus was originally known.

Iole

The daughter of Eurytus, who announced that in order to marry Iole, a suitor would have to defeat him and his sons in an archery contest. Heracles was attracted to Iole and accepted the challenge. When Heracles won the contest, Eurytus claimed that he had not won fairly and refused to turn over Iole.

Many years later, Heracles decided to avenge himself upon Eurytus, which he did by killing Eurytus and his sons in front of Iole, who responded by leaping from the height of the city's walls. Miraculously, Iole survived— her billowy dress was credited with slowing her fall like a parachute. Heracles sent Iole home to his wife, Deianeira, and it was her jealousy of this new object of his affections that led to Deianeira accidentally poisoning her husband.

Iphianassa

A popular name (or variation on a name) for several well-known mythological characters. One Iphianassa was the daughter of Agamemnon and Clytaemnestra who was more commonly known as Iphigeneia. Another Iphianassa (also known as Cyrianassa) was one of the three daughters of Proetus and Sthenoboea who were driven mad for showing disrespect toward either Dionysus or Hera. This Iphianassa was rescued by

The Sacrifice of Iphigeneia, **Giambattista Tiepolo, 18th century.**

Melampus and married to his brother, Bias. The last Iphianassa was the wife of Endymion.

Iphicles

Heracles' twin brother by a different father. While Heracles' conception was divine, Iphicles' was credited to his mortal parents, Amphitryon and Alcmene. When the two were still toddlers, it was Iphicles' cries that alerted Heracles to the snakes that Hera had sent to kill him. Later on, Iphicles participated in the hunt for the Calydonian Boar, and grazed its shoulder on the first charge, drawing the first blood.

Iphiclus

The beloved son of King Phylacus, Iphiclus was scared into impotence when he saw his father gelding rams and believed that a similar fate was about to befall him. Phylacus convinced Melampus to use his prophetic skills to derive a cure for Iphiclus, who soon fathered

Podarces and Protesilaus (also known as Iolaus).

Iphigeneia

The child of Agamemnon and Clytaemnestra, Iphigeneia was said to have been Agamemnon's most beautiful daughter. When Calchas prophesied that the Greek forces would not be able to defeat the Trojans unless Iphigeneia were sacrificed, Agamemnon sent some of his allies back to Greece, where they tricked Clytaemnestra into entrusting them with Iphigeneia.

In most versions it is suggested that Agamemnon's sacrifice of Iphigeneia (also known as Iphianassa) was completed, but in some she is rescued by Artemis, who subsequently made Iphigeneia the chief priestess responsible for a sacred image of Artemis that was kept among the Taurians. Years later Iphigeneia helped her brother steal this icon.

Most versions end with Electra and Pylades getting married, and in some it is suggested that Iphigeneia goes on to marry Achilles in place of Deidameia, which would make her the mother of Neoptolemus. It is said that Iphigeneia eventually died in Brauron or Megara, and that Artemis made her immortal to repay her faithful service.

So Agamemnon, rather than retreat,
Endured to offer up his daughter's life
To help a war fought for a faithless wife
And pay the ransom for a storm-bound fleet.
　　—*Chorus, Agamemnon, Aeschylus*

Iphimedeia

After falling in love with Poseidon, Iphimedeia crouched down by the seashore and scooped water into her lap. She became pregnant by this act, and eventually gave birth to Ephialtes and Otus. Iphimedeia went on to marry Aloeus, from whom her sons derived their collective name, the Aloeides. With Aloeus, Iphimedeia conceived a daughter, Triops.

Iphinoë

The daughter of Proetus and Stheneboea, Iphinoë was driven mad along with her sisters Lysippe and Iphianassa for having been disrespectful to Dionysus (or Hera). The three sisters were rescued by Melampus, but Iphinoë (who was also known as Hipponoë) died on the way to Lusi, where the other two were purified.

Iphitus

One of Eurytus' sons, Iphitus supported Heracles' claims on his sister, Iole, after Heracles had beaten Eurytus and his sons in an archery contest. Iphitus later gave the young Odysseus the huge bow that figured prominently in the events subsequent to Odysseus' return to Ithaca. Iphitus also served aboard the *Argo* and is said to have been the only Argonaut killed in Colchis in the struggle that followed the taking of the Golden Fleece (this contradicts some versions wherein he is killed by Heracles despite his earlier support of the hero).

Irus

An Ithacan beggar, Irus was given his nickname as a masculinized version of Iris, the goddess of the rainbow who was a messenger of Zeus. Irus served a similar function for Penelope's suitors. It was Irus who told Odysseus, who was disguised as a beggar, that he would not be admitted to see Penelope, and who then challenged the unknown beggar to a boxing match. When Odysseus prepared for the competition Irus saw his opponent's strong physique and tried to talk his way out of the contest. The suitors heaped a great deal of abuse on Irus and Odysseus struck him down with a single blow, making sure not to reveal too much of his strength lest he be recognized.

Ismene

The daughter of Oedipus and Iocaste and the sister of Antigone, Eteocles, and Polyneices.

Ixion

A rowdy sort who married Dia, Ixion tricked his father-in-law, Dioneus, into a trap and burned him to death. The gods felt Ixion deserved retribution, but Zeus was forced to admit he had committed worse acts, and invited Ixion to his table. When Zeus became aware of Ixion's intentions to seduce Hera, the god shaped a cloud to resemble his wife. Ixion coupled with this cloud; Zeus accosted him in the act, and had Hermes torment him mercilessly until Ixion agreed that benefactors

Jason Before Pelias, **Roman wallpainting,** A.D. **1st century.**

deserved much better treatment. Ixion was subsequently bound to a fiery wheel which rolls eternally through the sky.

The cloud that Zeus had shaped to resemble Hera became known as Nephele, and gave birth to Centaurus. In some versions, Ixion is also credited with fathering Phrixus and Helle on Nephele, as well as Peirithous on Dia.

Jason

The son of Aeson and Polymele, Jason was originally named Diomedes. Aeson had been the heir to his father's throne on Iolcus, but had been unseated by Pelias, who was warned that a son of Aeson would kill him. Because of the prophesy, Polymele pretended that her child had been stillborn, and

secretly entrusted the infant Diomedes to Cheiron the Centaur. (Later, another oracle warned Pelias that his successor would appear wearing only one sandal.) Cheiron raised Aeson's son to manhood under the name Jason, by which he would become famous. (Other accounts state that Jason was raised by a fisherman.)

When he came of age, Jason set out, directed by Hera, who was angry with Pelias, to return to Iolcus. When Hera disguised herself as a feeble old woman, she tricked Jason into carrying her across the river Anaurus, in whose muddy banks he lost one of his sandals. In this condition, Jason encountered Pelias, who recognized the threat that Jason represented, but of which Jason was unaware. Pelias asked Jason what he would do in such a "hypothetical" situation, and Hera caused Jason to suggest that such a threat should be sent to retrieve the Golden Fleece of the divine ram that had carried Phrixus to Colchis from Greece. Since Colchis was at the far end of the Black Sea, and represented the farthest regions of the known world, it was a destination that seemed virtually unreachable.

When Pelias revealed to Jason the truth of his lineage and the threat that he posed to Pelias, Jason, backed by his allies Pheres and Amathaon, laid claim to the throne. Pelias then said that he would relinquish the throne peacefully only if Jason removed the curse that had been placed over Iolcus by Phrixus' ghost, who wanted Phrixus' remains and the Golden Fleece brought back from Colchis. Jason accepted the challenge and sent word throughout all of Greece for the bravest and strongest volunteers.

First a ship was constructed, using the finest materials, and it was named the *Argo*. Then Jason assembled its crew, consisting of an all-star assemblage of mythological heroes.

***Jason and Medea,* Gustave Moreau, 1865.**

This group initially wanted to name Heracles their captain, but he deferred to Jason.

The story of the voyage of the *Argo* is a long and eventful tale that has somehow been given status beneath the tales of Homer and those of the Greek dramatists. The Argonauts, as the ship's crew became known, were first welcomed by the women of Lemnos, who had killed their men some time earlier, and now wished to take the Argonauts into their beds. Jason himself lay with the Lemnian leader, Hypsipyle, and fathered Euneus and Nebrophonus before Heracles finally reminded the crew of their primary mission.

Upon arriving in Colchis, Jason, Cytisorus, and a small contingent approached Aeëtes and peacefully requested the Fleece and Phrixus' remains. Aeëtes denied their request, and threatened mutilation of Jason and his men if they did not leave. When Aeëtes realized he had been a bit harsh with Jason, Aeëtes told him that he would comply with the requests if Jason accomplished a number of seemingly impossible tasks.

When Aeëtes did not know was that Hera had caused his daughter, Medea, to fall in love with Jason, and that Medea had told Jason that she would help him if he promised to marry her and take her back to Greece with him. With her help, Jason yoked the fire-breathing bulls and plowed the enormous Fields of Ares with them, then sowed dragon's teeth in the fields as Cadmus had once done. These teeth grew into earth giants whom Jason then fought and killed. Still unaware of his daughter's infatuation with Jason, Aeëtes revealed to Medea his plan to ambush the Argonauts that night. Medea warned Jason, and then helped him obtain the Golden Fleece by drugging the dragon that stood guard over it. Following a brief skirmish with the Colchians, the Argonauts left Colchis having suffered only a single fatality.

After Jason and Medea stopped at Medea's aunt Circe's to be purified for their blood sins, among them the brutal murder of Apsyrtus, the *Argo* stopped on the islet of Macris, where a Colchian fleet caught up with them and asked the local king, Alcinous, to rule that Medea and the Fleece be returned. Alcinous told his wife, Queen Arete, that he would rule that Medea could continue on with Jason only if she were no longer a virgin. Arete alerted Jason to this decision, and Jason and Medea were married that night.

When the *Argo* had nearly reached home, an enormous wave sent the ship nearly a mile inland into Libya. The Argonauts eventually made their way back to the Mediterranean, but not without the help of Triton, whom Euphemus, one of the Argonauts, had coerced into helping them.

Upon his return to Iolcus, Jason learned that Pelias, hearing rumors that the Argonauts had been lost at sea, had killed Jason's parents, Aeson and Polymele, as well as Promachus, a son of Jason who had been born after his departure. Medea tricked two of the daughters of Pelias into killing their father, and the throne was left open. Jason was banished for his part in Pelias' death; this was not a problem for Jason, however, as he had designs on the throne of Corinth, to which Medea could lay claim as Aeëtes' only surviving child.

Jason ruled Corinth for ten prosperous years, until he decided to divorce Medea and marry King Creon's daughter Glauce. Jason claimed to have recently discovered that Medea had poisoned his predecessor a decade earlier, and used this knowledge as an excuse to divorce her. Medea became enraged and sent to Glauce a poisoned robe and crown that killed her and Creon. In some versions, Medea then killed all or most of the children she had conceived with Jason, or sacrificed them to Hera, who had promised to make them immortal. Jason was left without a wife, and with few (if any) children, although it is generally agreed that his sons Thessaly and Pheres survived and grew to rule elsewhere.

Jason himself lost favor with the gods for having broken his vows to Medea, and wandered homeless for many years, despised by gods and mortals alike. He returned to Corinth in his old age, and while contemplating hanging himself from the prow of the *Argo*, he was struck by a piece of the ship's crumbling frame and killed.

Remember, we hold the future of our children, our dear country, and our aged parents in our hands. Hellas depends on us. We can plunge her in grief; we can bring her glory.
—Jason, The Voyage of Argo,
Apollonius of Rhodes

You, as you deserve,
Shall die an unheroic death, your head shattered
By a timber from the Argo's hull. Thus
    wretchedly
Your fate shall end the story of your love for me.
—Medea, Medea, Euripides

Lachesis One of the three Fates, Lachesis was responsible for measuring the thread of life. Lachesis was also called upon by Zeus to witness his making a present of Rhodes to Helius.

Ladon A serpent that was capable of human speech (in many tongues), Ladon was one of the Phorcids. Ladon is also depicted as the hundred-headed dragon that Atlas made guardian over Hera's golden apple tree. (As Ladon is depicted as being increasingly more monstrous, his parentage is often credited to Typhon and Echidne, or even to Mother Earth, who conceived him parthenogenetically.) Heracles shot Ladon with an arrow, allowing Atlas to steal three golden apples while Heracles temporarily assumed Atlas' burden of holding up the sky.

Laelaps A magical hound who was destined to catch every quarry he ever chased, Laelaps was first given by Minos to Procris, who later gave him to her husband, Cephalus. Laelaps was instrumental in the hunting "accident" that resulted in Cephalus' murder of Procris.

Some time after Procris' death, Cephalus lent Laelaps to Amphitryon, who was trying to hunt down the Teumessian Vixen, an animal that was fated never to be caught. Zeus eventually settled the paradox that arose from Laelaps being sent to hunt the Vixen by turning both beasts to stone.

Laertes The son of Acrisius, Laertes was an Argonaut who married Anticleia. Laertes' wife gave birth to Odysseus, whose actual father was Sisyphus.

Laertes, **detail from terra-cotta relief, 5th century** B.C.

After Odysseus finally returned home and killed Penelope's suitors, he was reunited with Penelope and Laertes. While he was filling them in on two decades worth of adventure, the allies and relatives of the dead suitors attacked. Laertes, despite his advanced years, fought valiantly at Odysseus' side and helped him gain an advantage until Athene put an end to the fighting.

Laius The son of Labdacus, Laius married Iocaste, but remained childless. When he consulted an oracle, he was told that his failure to sire an heir was to his benefit, since it was fated that any son of his would kill him. After hearing this prophesy, Laius imprisoned Iocaste without telling her why. She then got Laius drunk and tempted him to her bed, which led to the conception of a son. When the child was born, Laius pinned his feet together and abandoned him to die on Mount Cithaeron, where he was subsequently discovered and rescued.

Many years later, while staying with Pelops in Pisa, Laius was introduced to his host's young bastard son, Chrysippus, whom he kidnapped and brought back to Thebes. In most versions sexual motives are ascribed to Laius' actions, and he is sometimes described as one of the first pederasts.

In punishment for Laius' abduction of Chrysippus, Hera sent the Sphinx to plague Thebes. Unable to rid his kingdom of the monster on his own, Laius set out to consult an oracle and was killed by Oedipus.

Lamia A beautiful daughter of the Libyan King Belus, Lamia caught the attention of Zeus, who bestowed upon her the singular power of removing and replacing her eyes, so that she could, if necessary, leave them places and later "see" what happened in her absence.

Lamia bore Zeus many children, of whom all but Scylla were killed by Hera in a fit of jealousy. Lamia, her face turned into a nightmarish mask, took revenge for Hera's acts by destroying the children of others. Lamia later joined the deadly Empusae.

Laocoön The son of Antenor, Laocoön was a seer and a priest of Thymbraean Apollo in Troy. When the Greeks left their giant wooden horse behind as an offering, Laocoön was one of the most vocal of those who insisted that the "gift" be burned.

To illustrate his suspicions of the horse, Laocoön threw his spear into its flank, which caused the weapons and armor of the Greeks inside to clash together when they recoiled

from the thrust. Most Trojans heard the noise and agreed that the horse should be burned, but Priam and his supporters claimed to have heard nothing and believed the offering to be sacred. When it became clear that Priam would bring the offering into the city, Laocoön went off to sacrifice a bull to Poseidon.

By now Apollo had become irritated with Laocoön for a number of reasons, among them his breaking of his celibacy vow by being married to and having children with Antiope. (It was suggested that Laocoön and Antiope may have broken this vow in the presence of one of Apollo's statues.) While Laocoön was preparing the bull for sacrifice, Apollo sent one or two serpents to Troy to seek out the priest's twin sons, Antiphas and Thymbraeus, and crush them to death. Laocoön went to his sons' rescue and was also killed by the snakes.

Laocoön's death was interpreted by Priam as a sign of punishment for having thrown the spear at the Trojan Horse and was used by the king to justify his misguided decision to bring the offering inside Troy's walls.

Laodameia A name given to several prominent characters, the best known of whom was the daughter of Acastus who married Protesilaus. When Protesilaus went off to join the Greeks in the Trojan War, Laodameia, who sometimes is referred to as Polydora, missed her husband so much she made a statue of him and slept with it. When word of Protesilaus' death in Troy reached Laodameia, she prayed to Zeus that she be allowed to sleep with the ghost of her husband. Zeus granted them three hours together, at the end of which Laodameia killed herself so that she might join Protesilaus in the afterlife.

There are some versions in which it is suggested that Acastus made Laodameia remarry following Protesilaus' death. Laodameia kept sleeping with the statue, and when Acastas discovered it and set it afire, Laodameia took her own life by throwing herself upon the statue's pyre.

Another Laodameia, a daughter of Bellerophon, became the mother of Sarpedon by Zeus.

Laodice A name used alternatively with several others for a confusing assortment of mythological characters. Laodice is said to have been another name for Electra, one of Clytaemnestra and Agamemnon's daughters. Priam and Hecabe are said to have had a daughter named Laodice, who is occasionally described as having married Heracles' son Telephus. And there was a character named

Laocoön, A.D. 1st century.

fer a drought. An oracle told Laomedon that he would need to sacrifice a daughter to appease the gods; the king eventually chose Hesione and chained her to a rock as an offering. The sea monster was on the verge of devouring her when Heracles, who was traveling with Telamon, came to the rescue. Heracles agreed to kill the monster in exchange for Laomedon's two divine, man-eating horses. (These were the mares Zeus had given to Tros, the first King of Troy, as compensation for his abduction of Tros' son Ganymede.)

Once the monster was dead and Heracles had given Hesione to Telamon, Laomedon again refused to uphold his end of a bargain, which caused Heracles to lead an assault on Troy. Once inside the city, Heracles killed Laomedon and all of his sons except Podarces, who had sided with Heracles when his father refused to hand over the mares.

Leda

The daughter of King Thestius of Aetolia, who gave refuge to Tyndareus, Leda married Tyndareus, who later became King of Sparta. In Sparta, Leda somehow came into possession of the egg Nemesis produced after coupling with Zeus, and from which Helen of Troy was hatched. In some versions Leda simply finds the egg, while in others it is thrown or placed inside Leda, who then delivers Helen "normally."

Leda and the Swan, terra-cotta plate, c. 1580.

Laodice who married Helicaon (this may be the same Laodice who was Priam's daughter). This Laodice lay with Acamas out of wedlock and bore Munitus. At the fall of Troy, she was swallowed by the earth in a sanctuary at Tros.

Laomedon

An early King of Troy, Laomedon kept watch over the Hellespont to prevent any Greeks from entering into the Black Sea. (Laomedon is mentioned by name in the *Argonautica* as the overseer the *Argo* slipped past in the dark of the night.) Laomedon had had Apollo and Poseidon's help in building Troy's walls—the two had been given to the king as bond servants—but they argued over payment when the task was completed. Laomedon and his wife, Strymo, had many children, including the daughters Hesione, Cilla, and Astyoche and the sons Tithonus, Lampus, Clytius, Hicetaon, and Podarces. Laomedon also fathered bastard twins on the nymph Calybe. Laomedon is also said to have been the father of Procleia, who was the mother of one of the many characters named Cycnus.

When Laomedon fell out of favor with Apollo and Poseidon, the two sent a sea monster to ravage Troy and caused the land to suf-

The Rape of the Daughters of Leucippus (The Leucippides), Rubens, c. 1618.

eight or nine snakelike heads, one of which was immortal. (Some versions credit the Hydra with possessing fifty, a hundred, or even ten thousand serpentine heads.) The Hydra was so venomous that its breath, or even the mere smell of its tracks, could kill anyone in its presence. Its name was derived from the fact that it lived by the Lernaean Lake.

The Hydra was the subject of Heracles' second labor, and may have been raised by Hera in preparation for its encounter with the warrior. Heracles eventually cut off the Hydra's immortal head and, before burning the rest of its body, dipped his arrows in the Hydra's innards, thus making the arrows poisonous.

Lethe The daughter of Eris, Lethe was the personification of Oblivion. The river of Oblivion in Tartarus was named for her.

Leto The daughter of the Titans Coeus and Phoebe. When Leto coupled with Zeus out of wedlock, both of them in the form of quails, Hera became jealous and had Leto pursued all over the world, vowing that she would not deliver Zeus' children in the light of day. Leto eventually bore Artemis in a cave at Ortygia, and then, nine days later, delivered Apollo in a cave on Mount Cynthus.

Leto is best known for giving birth to these two divines and for the revenge they often exacted on her behalf. When Tityus, a giant, attacked her in a sacred grove at Delphi, Apollo and Artemis struck him dead and sent him to Tartarus for eternal punishment. And when Niobe belittled Leto for having given birth to only two children, as compared to Niobe's fourteen, Apollo and Artemis struck down nearly all of Niobe's sons and daughters.

Leto was also the mother of Britomartis.

Leuce A beautiful nymph whom Hades tried to violate, Leuce was transformed by Persephone into a white poplar before Hades could consummate his desires. In some versions Leuce is portrayed as a willing mistress of Hades whom Persephone transformed as a way of punishing the lovers.

Leucippe A common name, Leucippe is used for a number of characters who had problematic dealings with the gods. There was a daughter of Minyas named Leucippe who, with her sisters, Arsippe and Alcithoë, refused to revel with Dionysus. The god drove Minyas' three daughters mad, during the course of which Leucippe offered up her son, Hippasus, as a sacrifice to cure herself and her sisters (often called the Minyads). After they tore the

Leda is considered, in various combinations, the mother of Castor, Polydeuces, Clytaemnestra, and/or Helen. It is unclear which were Tyndareus' children and which were conceived with Zeus.

Lemnian Women The women of the island Lemnos who murdered all of their men for having taken lovers during their defeat of Athens. The women killed the men and the children they had fathered upon the Athenians, and soon realized that they were

unable to repopulate their island. When Jason and his Argonauts stopped on Lemnos en route to Colchis, the women welcomed the Argonauts into their beds. The Argonauts enjoyed this hospitality for some time, long enough for Jason to father twins on Hypsipyle, the Lemnian Queen, but departed when Heracles reminded them of their quest.

Lernaean Hydra A hideous monster born to Typhon and Echidne, the Lernaean Hydra had an enormous, doglike body capped by child to pieces the sisters went from mountain to mountain in a frenzy until Hermes took pity on them and changed them into birds. In alternate versions Dionysus himself turns Leucippe and her sisters into bats.

Leucippe is also described as the mother of Teuthras. A third Leucippe, the daughter of Thestor and the sister of Theonoë, was instrumental in freeing her sister and father from King Icarus.

Leucippides

The name given to Leucippus' daughters, Hilaeira and Phoebe. The Leucippides were betrothed to their cousins, Idas and Lynceus, but were carried off by the Dioscuri, by whom they became pregnant.

Leucippus

The son of Oenomaus and a rival of Apollo for Daphne's affections. When Apollo learned that Leucippus had disguised himself as a girl in order to revel with Daphne and her nymphs, the god arranged it so that Leucippus' presence would be revealed to them. Discovering a male amongst their midst, the nymphs tore Leucippus to pieces.

Another Leucippus, the son of Gorgophone and Perieres, served as co-ruler with his brother, Aphareus, and was also the father of Phoebe and Hilaeira, the Leucippides.

Leucothea

A name meaning "the white goddess" that was given to two different suicides: Halia and Ino.

Leucus

At the instigation of Nauplius, Leucus had an affair with Meda while Meda's husband, Idomeneus, was off fighting in the Trojan War. Once he had established himself in Idomeneus' court, Leucus drove Meda and her daughter Cleisithyra away and later murdered them. He gained control of ten cities and usurped Idomeneus' throne. Leucus developed such a strong base of power that once Idomeneus returned from the war he was banished on the most tenuous of pretexts.

Lichas

A prominent Spartan who, following the instructions of the Delphic Oracle, went to Tegea to recover Orestes' bones. Lichas brought them back to Sparta, where their presence ensured that Sparta would always be victorious over Tegea.

It was Lichas who brought to Heracles the poisoned shirt that Deianeira had sent him, thinking it had been treated with a love potion. The shirt caused Heracles insufferable pain and sent him on a rampage. Lichas was thrown into the Euboean Sea and transformed into a rock that retained a human form, and that sailors knew to avoid thereafter.

Licymnius

The illegitimate son of Amphitryon and a Phrygian woman named Midea, Licymnius went with his father when Amphitryon was banished to Thebes, where King Creon gave his sister, Perimede, to Licymnius in marriage. One of the couple's sons was Oeonus, a good friend of Heracles. When Oeonus was beaten to death by Hippocoön's son, a war ensued. Licymnius' sons Argeius and Melas died while fighting alongside Heracles, who eventually led the Thebans to victory over Hippocoön, his sons, and their Spartan allies.

After Heracles' mortal life ended and he joined the Olympians, Eurystheus expelled Licymnius and his entire family from Greece. Allying with the Heraclids, who brought with them Theseus and his forces, Licymnius never left Peloponnesus and lived to see Eurystheus killed. In his old age, Licymnius was accidentally killed by Heracles' son (and his own grand-nephew) Tlepolemus.

Linus

A popular name given to at least three mythological figures. The first Linus, the son of the river god Ismenius, taught Heracles literature. When Heracles' lyre teacher, Eumolpus, missed a class, Linus took his place, and abused Heracles for refusing to learn a different approach to the instrument. Heracles responded by striking Linus dead.

Another Linus was the son of Apollo and Psamathe who was exposed on a mountainside in Argos. Linus was reared by shepherds before being torn to bits by hounds belonging to his grandfather Crotopus, who feared his daughter's progeny.

The final Linus was a poet who was said to have been the son of Oeagrus and Calliope and the brother of Orpheus. (Other potential parents include Apollo and Urania or Arethusa, Hermes or Amphimarus and Urania, and Magnes and Clio) Linus was considered the greatest musician of all, an honor for which he was killed by Apollo in a fit of jealousy. Linus was credited with having taught music to both Thamyris and Orpheus.

Lycaon

The son of Pelasgus, Lycaon angered Zeus by sacrificing a young boy during the settlement of Arcadia. Zeus, strongly opposed to human sacrifices, transformed Lycaon into a wolf and struck his house down with a bolt of lightning.

Lycaon's many sons failed to learn a lesson from their father's fate. When Zeus made a dis-

Hercules and Lichas, Antonio Canova, **early 19th century.**

guised visit to Lycaon's sons they served him a stew that included portions of their brother Nyctimus. Zeus then turned all of them into wolves, and resurrected Nyctimus. This incident is often cited as one of the events leading to Zeus' decision to create the Deucalionian Flood.

Lycaon was also the father of Dia, by whom Apollo became the father of Dryops. Another Lycaon, a son of Priam, was captured by Achilles during the course of the Trojan War and sold in Lemnos to King Euneus. This Lycaon was eventually ransomed by Eëtion so that he could return to Troy, where he was killed in battle twelve days later by Achilles.

Lycomedes

The King of Scyros to whom Thetis entrusted the young Achilles, disguised as a girl. Lycomedes raised Achilles in secret until the young man was enlisted in the Greek forces headed for Troy. Before leaving, Achilles lay with Lycomedes' daughter Deidameia, who consequently became pregnant with Neoptolemus. When it was determined that the twelve-year-old Neoptolemus was needed in Troy in order for the Greeks to prevail, Odysseus, Phoenix, and Diomedes went to Lycomedes and persuaded him to permit the child to go.

Later, when Theseus came to Scyros, Lycomedes treated Theseus well until the latter asked for an estate of which Lycomedes had taken control. Lycomedes pretended to go along with Theseus' request and tricked him into looking over a high cliff nearby. Lycomedes then pushed Theseus to his death and claimed that it was an accident caused by Theseus being drunk.

Lycurgus The King of the Edonians in Nemea, Lycurgus allowed Adrastus and his champions to resupply on the way to Thebes. During their visit, Lycurgus' young son, Opheltes, was fatally bitten by a serpent. It was in his honor that Adrastus and his men instituted the Nemean Games. The Argives took to referring to the dead boy as Archemorus, meaning "the beginner of doom."

Lycurgus was not nearly as hospitable to Dionysus, whose troops he captured during battle while the god himself managed to escape. The Olympians were not pleased with Lycurgus' success, so Rhea helped the prisoners escape and drove Lycurgus mad. In the course of his insanity, Lycurgus killed and mutilated his own son, a crime so terrible that all of Thrace grew barren in horror. Dionysus then promised to rectify the situation if the people

Achilles Recognized at the Court of Lycomedes, Simon Vouet, 17th century.

put Lycurgus to death. He was subsequently led to Mount Pangaeum, where he was pulled to pieces by wild horses.

Lycurgus, the son of Aleus and Neaera, is one of the people thought to have been raised from the dead by Asclepius. When the Lemnian Women sold Hypsipyle into slavery for failing to fulfill her oath, it was Lycurgus who bought her.

Lycus A very popular name given to several characters who appear in various minor roles. There are two who are most worth mentioning. One Lycus, the uncle of Antiope, "rescued" his niece from the King of Sicyon and exposed her twins on Mount Cithaeron. Lycus' wife, Dirce, was eventually killed by the abandoned twins, who grew to be known as Amphion and Zethus.

Another Lycus, a descendant (possibly a son) of Dirce, ruled over Euboea and overran Thebes and killed Creon while the Thebans fought amongst themselves. This Lycus' victory coincided with Heracles' visit to the underworld to complete his final labor. Lycus captured Heracles' family and, when he came to believe that Heracles had perished, pressed himself upon Heracles' wife, Megara, who resisted valiantly. When it became clear that

Megara would not reciprocate, Lycus made ready to kill her and her children, but was prevented when Heracles finally returned. Heracles struck Lycus dead, but was driven mad for doing so by Hera, who was partial to Lycus for having always worshiped her above all others.

Lynceus One of Aegyptus' fifty sons, all of whom were engaged to their cousins, the Danaids. When the Danaids were finally forced to marry their cousins, all but one of them murdered their husbands on their wedding night. Hypermnestra spared Lynceus since he had spared her virginity.

Danaus was outraged, and sought to have Hypermnestra tried and executed, but the Argive judges acquitted her, and she and Lynceus were reunited. Lynceus eventually killed Danaus, and ruled all of Argos.

Another Lynceus, the son of Arene and Aphareus and the half-brother of Idas, had remarkable eyesight, which allowed him to see in the dark and to find buried treasures. For this reason, he was one of those invited to hunt the Calydonian Boar. He was also the lookout man on the *Argo*.

Lynceus and Idas were engaged to the Leucippides, who were abducted by the

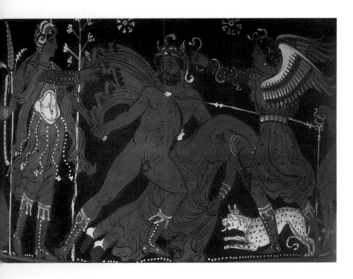

The Madness of Lycurgus and Dionysus, **Greek vase, 4th century** B.C.

Dioscuri. In revenge, Lynceus and Idas kidnapped Castor and Polydeuces' younger sister, Helen. Despite these initial dealings, Lynceus and Idas eventually became allied with the Dioscuri, but were slain when the two pairs became embroiled in argument while dividing the spoils of battle.

Lysippe The name given to at least two mythological characters. The first Lysippe, a daughter of Proetus and Stheneboea, was one of three sisters who were driven mad for offending either Dionysus or Hera. Lysippe was eventually saved by Melampus, to whom she became married.

The second Lysippe was an Amazonian Queen who is credited with having built the city of Themiscyra. This Lysippe was the mother of Tanais, who angered Aphrodite. As punishment, Aphrodite caused Tanais to fall in love with his mother. Tanais killed himself rather than commit incest. Lysippe responded by leading a group of Amazonians around the Black Sea to the river Thermodon, where they split into three tribes and established three cities.

Macareus One of six sons born to Aeolus and Enarete. With the family growing up in virtual isolation on Lipara, Macareus had an incestuous relationship with his sister, Canache (the two were unaware of the taboos involved). Some say that the fruit of their relationship was subsequently fed to the dogs, while others suggest that the result of their love was Amphissa, who was much beloved by Apollo.

Macaria The only daughter born to Heracles. After Heracles' apotheosis, an oracle told the Heraclids and their Athenian allies that the only way they would be able to overcome Eurystheus and his Peloponnesian army was if one of Heracles' children died. Macaria took matters into her own hands and committed suicide in the city of Marathon.

Machaon The son of Asclepius, Machaon was instructed in the art of surgery by his father. Along with his brother Podaleirius, Machaon accompanied the Greeks to Troy, where he tended to the men who were wounded during the course of the Trojan War. Machaon himself was wounded when Hector temporarily breached the Greek line.

Machaon's most famous patient was Philoctetes, whose wound received on the way to Troy caused the Greeks to abandon him. After nine years, Philoctetes came to Troy, and Machaon operated on his wound; he cut away the decayed flesh, poured wine upon it, and applied healing herbs and a serpentine stone. Philoctetes recovered quickly and later slew Paris.

Machaon was killed in battle near the conclusion of the Trojan War. The Amazon Queen Penthesileia is often said to have killed him, though Eurypylus is credited with the deed in some versions. Machaon's bones were taken by Pylus and Nestor to a sanctuary at Geraneia that became known for the healing powers vested in it and its priests.

Madness Described in Euripides' *Heracles* as the daughter of Heaven and Night, Madness was sent by Hera to drive the title character insane.

> *Madness has mounted her chariot;*
> *Groans and tears accompany her.*
> *She plies the lash, hell-bent for murder,*
> *Rage gleaming from her eyes,*
> *A Gorgon of the Night, and around her*
> *Bristle the hissing heads of a hundred snakes.*
> —Chorus, Heracles, *Euripides*

Maenads A group of Dionysus' female followers, the Maenads accompanied him on his worldwide adventures. (Pan, a first-class reveler in his own right, claimed to have slept with all of the Maenads.) In Thebes, Dionysus, the Maenads, and the Satyrs were all arrested by Pentheus. This act was avenged by Dionysus when he created a situation in which Pentheus' mother, Agave, led the Maenads in an attack on Pentheus in which he was ripped to pieces. The Maenads were also said to have killed Orpheus (in the same way) and thrown his head into the river Hebrus. It is likely that this favored mode of murder for the Maenads is a reference to the use of sacred mushroom heads.

The Maenads' husbands tattooed them in punishment for what they had done to Orpheus, while the Olympians, who felt that more severe retribution was required for this horrible crime, had Dionysus turn them all into oak trees.

Maera The name by which Priam's widow, Hecabe, became known when she was transformed into a wild bitch that howled so dismally that the Thracians who had attacked the woman were driven off. Maera was also the name of the hound that led Icarius' daughter Erigone to her father's corpse. This beast is said to have been set among the heavens as the lesser dog star.

Manto A daughter of the seer Teiresias, Manto was captured by the Epigoni when they conquered Thebes. In some versions, Manto was sent directly to Apollo and became his

The Maenads in Orgy, **marble relief, Roman copy after Greek original, 5th century** B.C.

Pythoness. In other versions, however, Alcmaeon, leader of the Epigoni, lay with Manto and conceived Amphilochus and Tisiphone with her before sending her to Apollo. Her children were entrusted to Creon, the King of Corinth, whose wife was so jealous of Tisiphone's beauty that she sold her as a slave to Alcmaeon himself.

Eventually, Apollo sent Manto to Colophon, where she married King Rhacius of Caria and bore Mopsus, who became a famous soothsayer like his grandfather. In some versions of Mopsus' adventures, his father is said to be Apollo, so it is unclear whether Manto became pregnant before or after she was sent to Ionia.

Marathon

The father of Corinthus, Marathon may also have been the father of Sicyon. Corinthus usurped the throne of the kingdom that would eventually bear his name, Corinth, from the regent Bunus, and was in turn poisoned by Medea so that Jason could take possession of the kingdom.

It is generally believed that the city of Marathon was named for this character, although some suggest that Marathus, a leader of a group of Arcadians in alliance with the Dioscuri, was the true namesake.

Marpessa

The daughter of Evenus and Alcippe. Marpessa's father proclaimed that she would marry only the man who could beat him in a chariot race. When Idas, with the help of his father, Poseidon, won the race, Apollo, who also desired Marpessa, challenged Idas to a duel. Zeus eventually intervened, and asked Marpessa to choose the one she would rather marry. Aware of Apollo's proclivity for soon growing tired of his mates, she chose Idas. Years later, upon Idas' death, Marpessa, following tradition, took her own life.

Marsyas

A Satyr who found a charmed flute that had once belonged to Athene. When Marsyas' skill on the magic instrument became widely touted (and Marsyas was not humble enough to declaim his admirers' proclamations), Apollo challenged him to a contest. (The judges of this contest included Tmolus, who favored Apollo, and Midas.) Although their skills were considered even, Apollo eventually defeated Marsyas by playing his lyre in a way that could not be duplicated on a flute. As the winner, Apollo was allowed to inflict whatever punishment he desired upon the loser; the god flayed Marsyas alive and nailed his skin to a tree alongside the river that now bears his name.

The Punishment of Marsyas, Roman copy after Greek marble figure, 3rd century B.C.

Medea and the Daughters of Pelias, **Roman copy after Greek marble relief, 2nd century** B.C.

Meda

The daughter of Phylas, Meda was impregnated by Heracles after he had killed her father and conquered Phylas' Dryopian kingdom. Meda gave birth to Antilochus while Heracles was expelling her relatives and installing new rulers upon Phylas' throne.

Meda later married Idomeneus, who departed soon after for the Trojan War. During Idomeneus' absence, Meda was introduced to Leucus by Nauplius. Once Leucus established a base of support, he banished Meda and her daughter by Idomeneus, Cleisithyra, and then killed them where they took sanctuary.

Medea

The daughter of Asterodeia and King Aeëtes of Colchis, the city on the far side of the Black Sea where the Golden Fleece was kept. When Jason and the Argonauts arrived in Colchis on their quest to obtain the Fleece, the Olympian gods, favoring Jason, caused Eros to make Medea fall in love with him. She first secretly helped Jason accomplish the seemingly impossible tasks assigned him by Aeëtes, then warned Jason of Aeëtes' plans to ambush the Argonauts. This warning saved Jason and his men, and Medea then used a potion to put to sleep the dragon that kept watch over the Golden Fleece, allowing Jason to take his prize.

In most versions of the story of the *Argo* it is suggested that Medea brought her half-brother Apsyrtus along with her and killed him while the ship was being chased by Aeëtes' fleet. Medea butchered Apsyrtus and threw the pieces, one at a time, into the sea to delay Aeëtes, who felt obliged to retrieve and bury each of them. In other versions, however, Apsyrtus commands a ship that traps the *Argo* and asks the local Brygians to support his claims on Medea and the Fleece. The Brygians call a truce to make a decision, during which Medea tricks Apsyrtus into breaking the truce, causing Jason to kill him.

In those versions in which Apsyrtus is slaughtered on board the *Argo*, a truce between the Argonauts and the Colchians is arranged by King Alcinous. The king tells his wife, Arete, that he will rule in favor of returning Medea and the Fleece to Colchis only if she is still a virgin. Arete, partial to the Argonauts' cause, sends word to Jason, who marries Medea and consummates their marriage that night.

When the *Argo* had nearly reached home, the ship was assaulted by Talos, a bronze sentinel who stood guard over the southern shores of Crete. Medea promised him immortality with one of her magic potions, but instead gave him an elixir that made him sleep. Medea then pulled out the stopper in his ankle that contained his life fluids. Talos "bled" to death, and the *Argo* continued on its way.

After Jason returned home and learned that Pelias had forced the suicides of Jason's parents and killed a son of Jason who was born after his departure, Medea devised a plan in which she and her ladies-in-waiting would disguise themselves as priestesses of Artemis and infiltrate Pelias' palace. There Medea

tricked two of Pelias' three daughters into cutting their father to pieces (by telling them that she would then revive him as a younger, more powerful man). With Pelias dead, the throne became available.

Jason and Medea were banished from Iolcus for the murder of Pelias, and Medea, as Aeëtes' sole surviving child, laid claim to the throne of Corinth. After ten years of prosperous rule, Jason announced that he wished to divorce Medea, claiming that he had only recently discovered that Medea was responsible for having poisoned his predecessor, Corinthus, in order for Jason to lay claim to the throne. Jason's plan to marry Glauce, the daughter of the powerful King Creon of Thebes, suggests that his motives were not as pure as he claimed. Medea was outraged by her husband's actions and, pretending to accept his decision, sent Glauce a robe and crown as a wedding present, both of which were laced with a poison that burned her skin and killed her. When Creon came to his daughter's aid, he too was slain.

Following this, most of Medea's children were slain, and Medea fled in the winged chariot of her grandfather Helius, bequeathing her claim on Corinth to Sisyphus. First Medea went to stay with Heracles in Thebes, where she cured him of the madness that had caused him to kill his wife and children.

Despite the support of Heracles, the Thebans insisted that Medea leave, since Creon had been the King of Thebes. Medea then traveled to Athens, where she married King Aegeus. They had a son, Medus, and Medea became jealous when Theseus, Aegeus' son from a previous marriage, returned to Athens. Medea attempted to poison Theseus, but Aegeus prevented it at the last moment. Fearing Theseus' revenge, Medea eventually fled Athens with Medus.

Eventually, Medea and Medeius, the son Medea had conceived with an Asian King, returned to Colchis to challenge her uncle Perses' attempt to usurp Aeëtes' throne. Medeius killed Perses and restored Aeëtes to his throne.

> Let no one think of me
> As humble or weak or passive; let them
>   understand
> I am of a different kind: dangerous to my
>   enemies,
> Loyal to my friends. To such a life glory
>   belongs.
> —Medea, Medea, Euripides

Medea Premeditating the Murder of Her Children, Roman wallpainting, A.D. 1st century.

Poor Medea! Scorned and shamed,
She raves, invoking every vow and solemn
pledge
That Jason made her, and calls the gods as wit-
nesses
What thank she has received for her fidelity. . .
—Nurse, Medea, Euripides

Medusa One of the Gorgons, Medusa was originally very beautiful, which led Poseidon to be attracted to her and lie with her in one of Athene's temples. Athene was outraged by the sacrilege and transformed Medusa into a winged monster with grotesque features, brazen claws, and serpentine hair whose gaze turned men to stone.

For reasons that had nothing to do with Medusa personally, Perseus was sent to decapitate her; with Athene's help, he succeeded. From her headless body sprang the mythic creatures Chrysaor and Pegasus. Medusa's blood was shared by Athene and Asclepius, who were able to use it to either raise the dead or kill the living.

***Medusa**, Caravaggio, 1596–1598.*

Megapenthes The son of Proetus, Megapenthes eventually assumed his father's throne. When Perseus accidentally killed Acrisius, he and Megapenthes exchanged portions of the kingdom of Argolis that Acrisius had originally split with his brother Proetus; Perseus assumed control of Argos, while Megapenthes became the ruler of Tiryns, which was on the other side of the Inachus River.

Megara A daughter of Creon, the King of Thebes, Megara was given to Heracles in marriage when Heracles helped her father defend his kingdom against the Minyans. Megara and Heracles had several children.

In some versions, Heracles returns from a ten-year absence while performing his mighty labors and marries Megara off to his nephew Iolaus. In other versions, however, Megara and her three sons by Heracles are captured by Lycus, who had killed Creon and taken control of Thebes. When Megara refused Lycus' offer to become his wife, Lycus made ready to kill her and the children, but was stopped when Heracles finally returned. Heracles killed Lycus, but was then driven mad by Hera, who had been well disposed toward Lycus. In the frenzy that followed, Heracles killed Megara and her children before he could regain his sanity.

Megareus The son of Oenope and Hippomenes, Megareus entered Nisa after Minos had finished sacking it, and became Nisus' successor. Megareus renamed the city Megara in his own honor, and married Nisus' daughter, Iphinoë.

The Megareans attempted to soften the story of Megareus' ascension to power, and suggested that he was a peaceful successor. In their version, Megareus later offered his daughter, Euachme, in marriage to whoever would avenge the death of his youngest son, Euippus. Alcathous is credited with this noble deed, and would therefore have become Megareus' son-in-law and heir, though it is more likely that the transfer of power was not quite so amicable.

Melampus The twin brother of Bias, Melampus, the first mortal to be granted prophetic powers by Apollo, was also the first physician and is frequently credited with being the first man to temper wine with water. Melampus also had the ability to understand the language of birds and animals.

When Bias fell in love with his cousin, Pero, his uncle Neleus said that he could marry Pero only if he drove King Phylacus' cattle out of Neleus' kingdom. To help his brother, Melampus allowed Phylacus to capture him and then used his prophetic skills to impress Phylacus. The two eventually agreed that if Melampus could cure Phylacus' son Iphiclus of his impotence, Phylacus would give Melampus his freedom and throw in the cattle as well. After Melampus cured Iphiclus, Melampus moved the cattle out of Neleus' kingdom and won the right to marry Pero, which he transferred to Bias.

Later, Melampus offered to cure the daughters of the Argive King Proetus, who had been driven mad by either Hera or Dionysus, in exchange for one third of Proetus' kingdom. Proetus declined this offer, but came back to Melampus when all of the women in Argos went mad. At this point Melampus informed him that the price would now be equal to two thirds of Proetus' lands. Proetus agreed, and was instructed to sacrifice twenty red oxen to Helius, with whom Melampus had arranged a deal with Artemis, who in turn made a deal with Hera to relieve the women of Argos of their madness. Proetus' three daughters, however, remained afflicted. Melampus and Bias took them to Lusi, but one of the sisters, Iphinoë, died along the way. The two surviving sisters, Iphianassa and Lysippe, were purified; Bias then married the former (Pero had died), while Melampus wed the latter.

Melanion

A son of Amphidamas, Melanion fell in love with Atalanta. When Melanion was told that the only way the athletic Atalanta would marry him was if he beat her in a foot race, he secured three golden apples from Aphrodite, which he dropped during the race. Atalanta stopped to pick up each in turn, allowing Melanion to win.

Following their marriage, Melanion convinced Atalanta to lie with him in Zeus' sanctified grounds. This angered Zeus greatly, and he turned the two of them into lions, since it was thought at the time that lions did not mate with each other and such a transformation would prevent the lovers from ever being intimate again.

Melanippe

The foal dropped by the mare Euippe, Melanippe was renamed Arne when she was transformed into a human infant.

Melanippus

A name given to two mythological figures, the most prominent of whom was the son of Astacus who was allied with Eteocles against Adrastus' seven champions in their attack on Thebes.

The second Melanippus, the son of Oeneus, was the brother of Tydeus, whom it was prophesied that he would kill. Tydeus "accidentally" killed his brother in the course of hunting, and was banished only because most believed that he had done so to prevent the prophesy from coming true.

Melantheus

A goatherd who worked for Odysseus, Melantheus failed to recognize his disguised master upon his return to Ithaca. Melantheus mistreated Odysseus, taking him for a common beggar, and even went so far as to kick the disguised Odysseus, who refrained from immediate vengeance.

When the battle between Odysseus and his wife's suitors broke out, Melantheus allied with the suitors and ran off to secure weapons for them. He managed to arm some of them before being captured on a second visit to the armory. Melantheus was kept bound until all of the suitors were dead, after which Eumaeus and Philoetius, servants who had remained loyal to Odysseus, cut off Melantheus' nose,

Meleager Kills the Calydonian Boar, **red-figured pelike, 5th century** B.C.

ears, hands, feet, and genitalia and fed them to the dogs.

Meleager

The son of Althaea by Ares conceived while Althaea was married to Oeneus. At the time of Meleager's birth, the Fates told Althaea that he would die only when one of her fire brands was burned. Althaea hid the brand, and Meleager grew to become a bold and invulnerable warrior, reputedly the best javelin thrower in all of Greece.

When Meleager's father angered Artemis, the goddess sent a wild boar to kill Oeneus' livestock, his workers, and his crops. The hunt for the Calydonian Boar attracted many renowned hunters, among them Atalanta, whose gender caused some of the hunters to object to her participation. Meleager, despite being married to Cleopatra, was greatly attracted to Atalanta, and ruled that she be allowed to participate. Meleager delivered the final blows to the wounded Boar, sticking it with his javelin as it charged Theseus and then finishing it off with his hunting spear.

Meleager presented the Boar's pelt to Atalanta on the specious grounds that she had drawn first blood in the hunt. This greatly angered two of Meleager's uncles, who suggested that it should go to the elder of the two of them or to Iphicles, who had truly drawn first

blood. Meleager responded by killing these uncles, for which his mother Althaea put a curse on him. This curse prevented Meleager from defending himself against Althaea's other two brothers until Cleopatra convinced him to take up arms. Meleager quickly dispatched his remaining uncles, at which point the Furies reminded Althaea of the unused brand. She threw it into the fire and her son was vanquished. Althaea and Cleopatra subsequently hanged themselves out of guilt for their respective roles in the tragedy.

It is said that during his affair with Atalanta, Meleager fathered Parthenopaeus on her.

Meliae

One of several groups that are said to have risen up from the blood of Uranus' severed genitals following his overthrow by Cronus, the Meliae were ash-tree nymphs and share many traits with the Hamadryads.

Memnon

The son of Tithonus of Assyria, who was a half-brother of Priam, Memnon was sent to support his uncle in the Trojan War. Tithonus placed Memnon in command of two thousand men and two hundred chariots and sent him off. Clad in armor that had been forged by Hephaestus, Memnon fought valiantly in the war and was credited with the

Achilles and Memnon, marble frieze, 3rd or 2nd century B.C.

support that nearly enabled Hector to set the Greeks' ships on fire.

During the course of one battle, Memnon killed Antilochus, a close ally of Achilles who was withdrawn from the conflict at the time. The Greeks chose Great Ajax to battle Memnon, but when Achilles learned of Antilochus' death he pushed Ajax aside and confronted Memnon. It is said that at this point Zeus called for a set of scales with which to weigh the fates of Achilles and Memnon. The pan containing Memnon's fate sank quickly and Achilles struck Memnon dead with a single blow. Achilles completed his revenge by putting Memnon's decapitated head and his armor atop Antilochus' funeral pyre.

There are many variations on Memnon's murder and his mother's request of Zeus to immortalize her son. In some versions a group of female birds rises from Memnon's pyre; it is suggested that they emerged from his spirit. In other versions it is said that it was a group of Memnon's female companions who were transformed into birds while lamenting his death.

There are even versions in which Memnon's remains were claimed by his sister Himera, who carried them to Phalliochis.

Menelaus

The most famous of mythological cuckolds, Menelaus was the husband of Helen, who ran off with Paris and thus helped start the Trojan War. Menelaus and his illustrious brother Agamemnon are usually described as the sons of Aerope and Atreus, the King of Mycenae.

There are some versions in which Atreus died while Menelaus and his brother were still infants, after which the boys were raised by Oeneus until Tyndareus, a Spartan King, chose to support Agamemnon's claims to his father's throne. Agamemnon conquered Pisa, killed its leader, Tantalus, and abducted his widow, Tyndareus' daughter Clytaemnestra. Menelaus came to his brother's aid when the Dioscuri, Clytaemnestra's brothers, sought to save their sister. With Tyndareus' continued assistance, Menelaus and Agamemnon defeated the Dioscuri, and in some versions these

are the circumstances that led to Menelaus, Agamemnon's brother, marrying Helen.

In a considerably more elaborate version of Helen's courtship, her hand was sought by almost every eligible Greek male. When Tyndareus worried about how angry the rejected suitors might become, Odysseus advised him to pledge all the suitors to defend whomever was finally selected. Tyndareus chose Menelaus and all the suitors were sworn to defend him and the sanctity of his marriage.

Eventually, after Tyndareus died, Menelaus became the King of Sparta; before this came to be, however, Tyndareus offended Athene, who avenged herself by cursing all of Tyndareus' daughters to be plagued by adulterous marriages. Menelaus became directly involved in this curse when Paris seduced Helen and ran away with her.

When he learned of Helen's disappearance, Menelaus went to Agamemnon and insisted that an army be mustered to retrieve her. Agamemnon did not agree to this until a peaceful request proved unsuccessful.

When Agamemnon's leadership was jeopardized, Menelaus helped trick Clytaemnestra into trusting them with her daughter Iphigeneia, who was to be sacrificed to the gods so that Agamemnon might retain command. Later in the Trojan War, when Achilles withdrew from the fighting, Agamemnon proposed direct combat between Menelaus and Paris to determine the fate of Helen. Menelaus overwhelmed his opponent, and Paris would have died had Aphrodite not spirited him away. The war resumed, and Menelaus refocused his attention upon the Trojan alliance by first killing Euphorbus in repayment for his recent attack on the injured Patroclus.

Near the end of the war, Menelaus had another chance to kill Paris, who had been mortally injured by Philoctetes' arrows, but Paris managed to escape to the temporary safety of Troy. Menelaus then found himself inside the Trojan Horse. While the Greeks remained hidden inside the statue they overheard Helen's mocking remarks about Menelaus, who needed to be restrained by Odysseus lest he reveal their hiding place.

When the Greeks emerged from the Trojan Horse, Menelaus headed directly for Helen, although a bloody battle with Deiphobus took place first. It is possible that Helen helped in the slaying of Deiphobus, which might have deterred Menelaus from killing her for her betrayal. (Another possible reason for his not killing her was the sight of Helen's bare breasts, which moved Menelaus to embrace his estranged wife and bring her to the safety of his ship.)

When Agamemnon announced that the Greeks needed to make a sacrifice to Athene before they left, Menelaus, who felt that her role in their victory had been negligible, became annoyed. The brothers argued with one another and departed on bad terms. On the way back to Argos, Menelaus' fleet was caught in a series of storms. Only five ships survived these storms, and all of them were blown to Crete, from which they proceeded to Egypt and remained stuck in southern waters.

Menelaus was welcomed by the royalty at the ports at which he came to call and was presented with numerous gifts. When he arrived in Pharos, he was aided by the nymph Eidothea, who directed him to coerce her prophetic father, Proteus, to tell them how they might return safely to the north. After Menelaus was told that Agamemnon had been murdered, Menelaus raised a cenotaph to Agamemnon in Egypt and was finally able to sail north.

On the day that Menelaus arrived in Sparta, accompanied by Helen, Orestes was avenging Agamemnon's murder by killing Clytaemnestra and Aegisthus. Tyndareus, the father of Helen and Clytaemnestra, lobbied Menelaus to have Orestes and his conspiring sister, Electra, stoned to death. Menelaus tempered the judgment against Orestes and Electra by commuting their sentence to forced suicide. When Orestes attempted to end Helen's life before he took his own, Zeus intervened and had Apollo bring Helen up to Olympus. A standoff followed, with Priam's sister Hesione being held hostage, and Apollo eventually told Menelaus to take a new wife and to betroth Hermione to Orestes. Menelaus resumed control of Sparta and ruled until he died a natural death and was succeeded by Orestes.

Menestheus

The son of Peteos, who was the grandson of Erechtheus. After Peteos was banished from Athens by Aegeus, the Dioscuri repaid this slight by making Menestheus the regent of Athens after they had defeated the Athenians in battle. Despite the initial resentment of the people of Athens, Menestheus became a demagogue when he began to question the federation Theseus had created while being held hostage in Tartarus.

Theseus eventually returned to Athens, but left shortly thereafter, leaving Menestheus in uncontested control of the city. In this role Menestheus became one of the suitors for Helen's hand. He even had the support of his old allies, the Dioscuri (Helen's brothers).

Menestheus also was part of the Greek alliance against Troy, and was said to have been an excellent tactician whose skills in commanding cavalry and infantry were second only to those of Nestor. In some versions, these skills were not enough to prevent Menestheus from being killed in battle, while in other versions he survived. He supported Acamas and Demophon's request to repatriate their grandmother, Aethra, and then left Troy. Instead of returning to Athens, Menestheus assumed the vacant throne of Melos. It is possible that his failure to return to Athens led to the assumption that he had died. His original throne was eventually regained by Theseus or his sons.

Merope

The name of a handful of different characters important throughout the mythological canon.

As the daughter of Oenopion, Merope was the subject of Orion's attentions. Oenopion, himself attracted to Merope, assigned Orion the seemingly impossible task of killing all of the dangerous beasts on Chios. When

Helen and Menelaus, reverse side of **Etruscan mirror, 4th century** B.C.

Oenopion continued to create delays to the fulfillment of his promise, Orion violated Merope, for which her father blinded him.

Another Merope, the daughter of Atlas, was a Pleiad who married Sisyphus and conceived three sons with him: Glaucus, Ornytion, and Sinon. Once Sisyphus' disgrace and eternal punishment in Tartarus became known, Merope disappeared from the night sky (she is commonly referred to as the lost Pleiad) and was never seen again.

A third Merope was one of Pandareus' three daughters who were initially favored by a number of gods, but eventually given over to the Erinnyes at Zeus' direction and made to suffer for the sins of their father, who had stolen Zeus' golden mastiff.

Metapontus

A King of Icaria, Metapontus grew suspicious that his wife, Theano, might be barren. She produced Arne's twins, Aeolus and Boeotus, to satisfy him, but later gave birth to twins of her own. Metapontus was unaware that the first set of twins were not his own, and Theano grew jealous when he remained partial to them. When Theano's intriguing led to her twins' deaths and her own suicide, Metapontus took Arne for his wife and adopted her sons as his own. Years later, Metapontus decided that he wanted to be rid of Arne, and took Autolyte on in her place. In the struggle that ensued between Metapontus and the twins, Aeolus and Boeotus, Autolyte was accidentally killed.

Metion

One of the four sons of Erechtheus who fought over the succession to their father's throne. Metion and his brother Orneus disputed Cecrops' selection as heir by their brother-in-law Xuthus and eventually ran them both out of Athens. Metion's fight for control of Athens passed on to the next generation, with his three sons eventually expelling Cecrops' son, Pandion, from the city.

Metis

A Titaness created by Eurynome to serve as one of the Planetary Powers, Metis oversaw Mercury along with Coeus. In some creation myths it is said that Metis was born from a union between Mother Earth and Air. Whatever her origins, Metis was widely pursued by Zeus. She kept changing form in order to avoid him, but was finally caught and impregnated. One of Mother Earth's oracles prophesied that the child would be a girl, but that Metis' first son would grow to dethrone Zeus as the god had done to his own father, Cronus, and Cronus before him had done to his father, Uranus. To prevent her from having any sons at all, Zeus lured Metis to his couch and swallowed her. Zeus claimed that Metis continued to counsel him from within his skull, and the result of Metis' pregnancy was Athene, who eventually was delivered through a breach in Zeus' skull.

Midas

A Macedonian King, Midas was adopted by Gordius, a childless king whom he succeeded. Midas had been tutored by Orpheus, and was best known for his hedonism and his celebrated rose garden. When Silenus, a Satyr, was found drunk amongst Midas' prized roses, Midas held him for five days, during which Silenus regaled him with tall tales. Dionysus was so grateful for Midas' favorable treatment and return of Silenus that he granted him a single wish. Midas wished that anything he touched might turn to gold, a decision he quickly regretted since he was unable to eat or drink anything before it was alchemized. He went to Dionysus and expressed his desire to rescind the wish, and Dionysus told him that if he cleansed himself at the source of the river Pactolus (near Mount Tmolus) he would be freed of his plight.

Later, Midas disputed Tmolus' verdict in the musical competition between Apollo and Marsyas. For his dissenting vote in favor of Marsyas, Apollo rewarded Midas by burdening him with the ears of an ass. Midas managed to keep the ears a secret from everyone but his barber, whom he threatened with death if any-

King Midas Enthroned, Botticelli, 1497–1498.

one found out. The barber struggled to keep the secret, and eventually dug a hole by a riverbank, spoke of Midas' oddity, and filled the hole back in with dirt. But a reed grew on that spot and whispered the secret to all who passed. Midas killed the barber and then committed a most painful suicide by drinking bull's blood.

Miletus

The beautiful son of Apollo and Areia (or Aria, Deione, or Theia), Miletus was courted by the brothers Minos, Rhadamanthys, and Sarpedon. When Miletus chose Sarpedon to be his lover, he was driven off by a jealous Minos and went to Caria in Asia Minor, where he founded his own kingdom.

Minos

One of the three sons conceived when Europe was ravished by Zeus. Minos' brothers were Rhadamanthys and Sarpedon, and all three were adopted by their stepfather, Asterius. Trouble arose between the brothers when all began to vie for the attention of a pretty youth by the name of Miletus (or Atymnius). When Miletus chose Sarpedon, Minos expelled the youth from the kingdom. Once Asterius died and Minos assumed his place on the throne, he also expelled his brother Sarpedon, who was still bitter over Miletus' banishment. Minos also banished a daughter, Clymene, at this time because he feared a prophesy that suggested a child of hers would kill him.

To prove that the gods favored his ascension to Asterius' throne, Minos conjured a white bull to emerge from the sea, which angered Poseidon. (In some versions it is suggested that Minos simply withheld the bull from his sacrifices to Poseidon.) Minos married Pasiphaë shortly thereafter, and Poseidon avenged himself by causing Minos' new wife to fall in love with the bull. Pasiphaë convinced Daedalus to create a device that would allow her to consummate her desire for the bull, which resulted in the birth of the Minotaur.

Minos was embarassed by the events, and hid his shame by having Daedalus build the Labyrinth, a maze on Cnossus that none could escape. At its center Minos established a dwelling for both Pasiphaë and the Minotaur.

Minos was also the father of Glaucus, who got lost in the Labyrinth when he was quite young. Polyeidus was enlisted to find the child, which he did, but by this time Glaucus was dead. Polyeidus eventually revived the boy and was rewarded with many gifts.

Minos was the first king to control the Mediterranean, but he eventually realized that he would not be able to conquer Athens.

Instead he prayed to Zeus to avenge the murder of his son Androgeus, which Zeus did by causing earthquakes and fire throughout the Greek peninsula. The Aegean King Aeacus offered up prayers, and the daughters of Hyacinthus were sacrificed to stop the destruction, but it was not until Minos was given whatever satisfaction he wanted that the trouble ended. In the end, that satisfaction consisted of a tribute of seven youths and seven maidens to be brought annually for nine years as prey for the Minotaur.

After being banished by the Areiopagus, Daedalus sought refuge with Minos, despite his role in aiding Pasiphaë's unnatural desires for the bull. When Minos finally learned of Daedalus' contributions to the ignoble endeavor, he trapped him and his son, Icarus, inside the Labyrinth as well.

After Daedalus escaped, Minos tracked him down in Sicily, where he was hiding in the court of Cocalus. Minos would probably have been able to recapture Daedalus were it not for Cocalus' daughters, who were thrilled to have such a talented craftsman making them toys. In some versions, they help Daedalus kill Minos, while in others it is suggested that Minos was lost at sea when his warships set out to pursue Daedalus.

In some versions Minos' son Deucalion loses his Cretan kingdom to Theseus, while in others Theseus' defeat of the Minotaur takes place during Minos' lifetime. After Minos died, he became one of the three judges for the newly dead in Tartarus. Along with his brother Rhadamanthys and his former adversary Aeacus, Minos was responsible for evaluating the merits of each new arrival to the underworld. It is Minos to whom the other two referred their most difficult cases.

Minotaur

A monstrous creature with the head of a bull and the body of a human, the Minotaur was conceived by Minos' wife, Pasiphaë, and a white bull that Poseidon, because he was angry with Minos, had caused her to lust after. Minos was dreadfully embarrassed by this creature, and commissioned a complex maze on Cnossus that became known as the Labyrinth. He kept Pasiphaë and the Minotaur at its center, so that they could never escape and so that no one from the outside would ever be able to find them.

After the Athenians murdered Androgeus, one of the Minotaur's half-brothers, Minos demanded compensation that consisted of fourteen youngsters each year to be prey for the Minotaur. Theseus led the third group of sacrifices with the promise that he would conquer

Minotaur, Picasso, 1958.

the beast with his bare hands and end the killings. The Minotaur's half-sister, Ariadne, fell in love with Theseus, and provided him with a magic thread that allowed him to find his way through the Labyrinth to kill the Minotaur and then find his way back out. The Minotaur is occasionally referred to by the names Asterius and Asterion. In some versions it is suggested that the white bull that sired the Minotaur on Pasiphaë may also have been the Cretan Bull that Heracles captured during the course of his seventh labor.

Moliones

The name given to the sons of Actor and Molione, Eurytus and Cteatus. Both served as generals in the army of their uncle, Augeias, the King of Elis. The Moliones (or Molionides, as they were also known) successfully defended themselves against Heracles when the latter attempted to avenge himself on Augeias for Augeias' treatment of him during the course of his fifth labor.

The Moliones later married the twin daughters of Dexamenus the Centaur, and fathered several sons on them. Heracles ambushed the Moliones on their way to an Isthmian festival, and killed them both. Their orphaned sons also became known as the Moliones. These Moliones managed to escape Nestor's rampage through Elis and eventually ruled there peacefully.

Mopsus

The name of two famous seers. The lineage of one of these soothsayers, a Lapith who accompanied the Argonauts on their quest, is unclear, although his father is sometimes said to have been Ampycus. This Mopsus warned the Argonauts that they needed to appease Rhea before they would be able to leave Arcton on their way to Colchis. He survived the escape from Colchis, but met his end in the Libyan desert after the *Argo* had been washed ashore. Just days after Canthus had died, Mopsus was bitten on the heel by a serpent near the shore of Lake Tritonis; Mopsus died an agonizing death before being given a hero's burial by the Argonauts.

The second Mopsus, who was said to have been the greatest of all prophets, was the son of Rhacius, a King of Caria, and Manto, a daughter of Teiresias. (It is sometimes suggested that Mopsus' real father was Apollo.) This Mopsus was living in Colophon when Calchas passed through on his way home. Calchas challenged Mopsus' skills with an extremely difficult test of prophetic ability. Mopsus responded with astonishing accuracy, and then came up with a much simpler challenge for Calchas. When Calchas offered his prophesy, Mopsus countered with an answer that was much different. Mopsus again was correct, and Calchas died, his heart broken by this encounter with a seer far greater than himself, an event that had been prophesied some time earlier.

Mopsus went on to found the city of Mallus in Cilicia with one of Calchas' companions, Amphilochus. After some time Amphilochus went off to found another city, but returned a year later when he grew dissatisfied. Amphilochus assumed that Mopsus would again share control of Mallus, but the seer was not willing to relinquish even a portion of his throne. The two argued until the embarrassed Mallians suggested a combat to the death to determine who should rule their kingdom.

In the fight that followed, both Amphilochus and Mopsus received mortal wounds. Their corpses were burned separately, but the smoke from their pyres mingled as it rose skyward. As a result, the ghosts of the two were said to have become friendly once again, and a common oracle was established in both of their names. This oracle supposedly had a higher reputation for truth than any other, including Apollo's Delphic temple.

Mother Earth

One the most prominent figures in the earliest mythological stories, Mother Earth suffered a diminished status with the transfer of power to patriarchal societies. According to the Olympians, Mother Earth emerged out of Chaos and gave birth to Uranus in her sleep. She drifts between being an individual figure and a personified conceptual entity representing the original life force of the earth. She is said to have given birth to the grass, flowers, trees, rivers, lakes and seas, and the beasts and birds that were proper to each. Mother Earth is frequently referred to as Gaea or Gaia, a name that is an oversimplified translation of the Greek. While much Greek literature uses this original name, the modern reader will probably be most familiar with the name Mother Earth.

Mother Earth produced a series of offspring, the first of whom met with limited success. First were the semihuman Hundred-handed Ones. Although they reappear through-

Gaia, **relief from temple of Artemis, Corfu, 7th century** B.C.

Three Muses **(Melpomene, Erato, and Poyhymnia), Eustache Le Sueur, c. 1640.**

out the earlier myths, these giants were never able to establish their own civilization. The same is true of Mother Earth's second set of children, the one-eyed Cyclopes.

Mother Earth is also said to have had an important role in keeping young Zeus safe from Cronus, and later abetting him when he ousted his father from his throne. Mother Earth even proved helpful when Zeus fought Atlas and the Titans shortly after taking power.

Mother Earth and Zeus eventually parted ways when her twenty-four sons—the giants—attacked Olympus. Perhaps this battle represented the last attempt to reassert female leadership over the heavens or symbolized the war fought between proponents of patriarchal philosophies and those of matriarchal ones. The giants waged a strong assault, but were finally defeated by Zeus and his Olympian allies. To avenge her sons' deaths, Mother Earth lay with Tartarus and conceived Typhon, the largest monster on the face of the earth.

While Mother Earth appeared in minor roles in a handful of later myths, the shift to Zeus' rule saw a steady diversion of responsibilities and accomplishments away from her. Like Echo, who was eventually reduced to a voice that could only mimic others, Mother Earth gradually came to be perceived as more of a concept or metaphysical notion than an active goddess. She is sometimes referred to as the Mother Goddess, or the Goddess of All Things, but in most cases the lists of major deities skip Mother Earth and begin with the core Olympians. Even when Mother Earth is included among the Olympians, it is pointed out that she was never part of the Olympians' council of twelve because she was too old and set in her ways to be able to consider the needs and concerns of the divine community. (This suggests the extent to which Mother Earth's original depiction came to be minimized as much as possible with the ascent of the Olympian deities.)

Muses
Nine female entities who were originally said to have been the daughters of Mother Earth and Air before Zeus' ascendancy led to his being described as the father of these lesser deities. It was said that Zeus conceived the Muses on Mnemosyne during the orgiastic frenzy that followed his violation of his mother, Rhea. The Muses were a wild lot until they were reformed by Apollo, who tamed them and taught them formal and decorous dances through which they might express themselves.

The Muses taught the Sphinx her riddle and also defeated the Sirens in a musical con-

The Muses Leaving Apollo to Enlighten the World, Gustave Moreau, 1868.

test, claiming the Sirens' wing feathers as their prize. The Muses were often described as the queens of song, and no Olympian banquet was complete without them.

Initially without individual personalities, the Muses were eventually assigned names and specific traits. Clio was the Muse of history, Urania of astronomy, Melpomene of tragedy, Thalia of comedy, Terpsichore of dance, Calliope of epic poetry, Erato of love poetry, Polyhymnia of songs to the gods, and Euterpe of lyric poetry. As patrons of the fine arts, the Muses were often perceived as promoters of the more civilized aspects of mortal existence. For these reasons, the Muses were frequently invoked in several millennia of artistic expression, and remain reference points for painters and poets alike.

Myrmidons
The men who sprang up from ants on the fields of Oenone in answer to Aeacus' prayers, the Myrmidons later accompanied Peleus into exile and fought beside Achilles and Patroclus at Troy.

It is sometimes said that the Myrmidons were named for King Myrmidon, father of Eurymedusa, who was seduced by Zeus in the form of an ant. It is also suggested that the name was derived from Myrmex, who had been turned into an ant by Athene for claiming credit for inventing the plow.

Sarcophagus of the Muses, c. A.D. 160.

Hylas and the Nymphs, **John William Waterhouse, 1896.**

Myrtilus Oenomaus' charioteer, Myrtilus guided his master's divinely conceived horses in marriage-or-death races against suitors of Oenomaus' daughter, Hippodameia. After many victories, Myrtilus was bribed by Pelops with the promise that if Pelops won, Myrtilus could have the first night with Hippodameia.

Following Pelops' victory, Oenomaus cursed Myrtilus for his treachery and prophesied that he would die at Pelops' hand. Myrtilus, Pelops, and Hippodameia left together following their victory, and when Myrtilus attempted to "collect" his spoils, Hippodameia, unaware of the deal her new husband had made, complained that Myrtilus had tried to ravish her. The three got back into Pelops' winged chariot, and as they flew over the sea, Pelops killed Myrtilus by kicking him from the chariot. As he fell, Myrtilus cursed Pelops

and his home. Myrtilus' ghost was said to haunt the stadium in Olympia, where charioteers would offer sacrifices to him in the hope of a safe race.

Myrtilus' parentage is quite uncertain, but it seems most likely that his father was Hermes, since it was that god who avenged Myrtilus' death on Pelops' sons and all of Peloponnesus.

Naiads Water nymphs of various origin, usually divine, the Naiads were often said to be the daughters of Zeus. The Naiads presided over lakes, rivers, springs, and fountains, aiding those whose intentions they liked or to whom they might be related.

Narcissus The son of the blue nymph Leiriope, Narcissus was conceived when the

river god Cephissus raped his mother. The seer Teiresias prophesied that Narcissus would live to an old age as long as he never came to know himself. Narcissus was a beautiful child who heartlessly rejected scores of admirers (including Echo), many of whom took their own lives as a result. Narcissus was stubborn and took great pride in his attractiveness. When Ameinius, one of his most persistent admirers, continued to court him, Narcissus sent him a sword, which the would-be lover used to kill himself on Narcissus' threshold while calling out to the gods to avenge his death. Artemis caused Narcissus to catch a glimpse of his own reflection in a pristine pool of water and fall in love with himself; this made it impossible for him to ever consummate his love or possess his beloved (just like those suitors he had callously turned away). Eventually Narcissus' grief became so great that he plunged a dagger into his breast and took his own life. The blood that fell to the ground sprouted flowers that were given his name.

Nauplius

The son of Poseidon and Amymone who was conceived after the god rescued her from a satyr's attack, Nauplius became a famous navigator who discovered the art of steering ships by the constellation of the Great Bear. He served aboard the *Argo* before founding a city that he named after himself.

When King Catreus decided to kill his daughter Aerope for having had a lover, Nauplius persuaded the king to instead sell him Aerope and her sister Clymene as slaves, with the promise that they never return to Crete. (Nauplius played a similar role in saving the life of Aleus' daughter Auge.) Aerope later married Atreus, and Nauplius made Clymene his own wife, and with her conceived Oeax and Palamedes.

In response to Palamedes' death by stoning, which was brought about by Odysseus, Nauplius is said to have plotted against the Greek leaders, though there is some confusion as to whether Nauplius went to Troy at all. In some versions, Nauplius stayed in Greece to seek his revenge, while in others he petitioned Agamemnon to receive satisfaction for Odysseus' treachery, and after Agamemnon refused to punish Odysseus, Nauplius sailed for Greece.

The nature of Nauplius' revenge was to convince the wives the Greeks had left behind that their husbands were not only being unfaithful to them, but that they would be returning with gorgeous Trojan princesses. (The idea that he might have this knowledge would support the versions in which Nauplius spent some time with the Greek army on the outskirts of Troy.) Some wives committed suicide upon hearing these rumors, while others used the reports as excuses to engage in affairs of their own. Nauplius was said to have been instrumental in bringing Aegisthus and Clytaemnestra together, as well as encouraging affairs between Diomedes' wife, Aegialeia, and Cometes, and Idomeneus' wife, Meda, and Leucus.

In addition to all of his scheming, Nauplius lit a fire on Mount Caphareus, tricking many Greek ships into believing it was the beacon that signaled the entrance to the shelter of the Pagasaean Gulf. Many ships were wrecked upon the rocks of the Euboean coast and many people died, though no prominent leaders are thought to have been among the fatalities. When Zeus learned of Nauplius'

crime, he saw to it that Nauplius would meet a similar fate a few years later.

Neleus

A son of Tyro and Poseidon and the twin brother of Pelias. Neleus and Pelias were abandoned by Tyro, but were found by a horse-herd and later reunited with their mother. When Tyro married Cretheus, he adopted the twins. When Cretheus died, Pelias became king and exiled Neleus, and sent Cretheus' grandsons Melampus and Bias with him. Neleus went to Messene, where he took over the city of Pylus and married Chloris, with whom he had twelve children.

One of those children was a daughter named Pero, a beautiful woman who was widely courted. Neleus proclaimed that he would allow her to marry only the man who could drive King Phylacus' cattle off his land. Through the assistance of Melampus, Pero was eventually married to Bias.

Some time later, Neleus refused to purify Heracles for having killed Eurytus' son Iphitus, because Eurytus had been an ally of Neleus. Nestor helped Heracles get purified, and when Heracles later attacked Pylus for having allied with Elis against him, he killed all of Neleus' children except Nestor. Neleus himself escaped, and later fought Augeias and the Eleans.

Nemean Lion

An enormous, vicious beast whose pelt was invulnerable to iron, bronze, and stone weapons, and whose claws were sharp as razors. In most versions it is said that the Nemean Lion was conceived by Echidne and her son Orthrus, although fantastic creatures such as Typhon, the Chimaera, or Selene may also have been its parents. Selene is credited with setting the beast upon the Bambinaeans, who had failed to fulfill a promised sacrifice in her name. It was in the course of depopulating Nemea that the beast was given its name. The Nemean Lion was the subject of Heracles' first labor.

Nemesis

The daughter of Oceanus, Nemesis was responsible for punishing those who accepted Tyche's good fortune without honoring the gods or sharing their luck with their fellow citizens. She punished them with humiliation, and was said to have beauty comparable to that of Aphrodite.

Because of her beauty, Nemesis was violated by Zeus in the shape of a swan. Leda, the wife of King Tyndareus, cared for the egg that Nemesis delivered, and some versions of the story had Leda bearing the egg. Helen of Troy was born from this egg.

Narcissus, Caravaggio, c. 1594–1596.

Neoptolemus

Originally named Pyrrhus, Neoptolemus was the son of Achilles and Deidameia (or Iphigeneia). The boy was reared by Deidameia's father, Lycomedes. When the Greeks came looking for him because of a prophesy that one of the conditions that needed to be met in order for Troy to fall was the presence of Neoptolemus on the battlefield, Lycomedes was wary of letting his grandson go since he was still quite young (perhaps as young as twelve at that time).

Neoptolemus didn't reach Troy until his father had already been killed. Achilles' ghost appeared before Neoptolemus on his way there, and once the boy arrived Odysseus gave him some of the armor that had belonged to his father. Neoptolemus quickly distinguished himself in council as well as in battle. Neoptolemus was one of the Greeks who hid inside the Trojan Horse, and was said to have been the only one not to show any fear while inside the statue, even when Laocoön's spear pierced the planks perilously close to his head.

While inside the horse, Neoptolemus continuously urged Odysseus to order the assault and maintained a menacing grip on his lance and sword. Once the Greeks emerged, Neoptolemus led a group who went on to chase Priam's son Polites. After Priam was killed, Neoptolemus fulfilled his duty to his father by dragging the king's corpse to sit atop Achilles' tomb and leaving it to rot, headless and unburied.

As the Greeks were preparing to depart, Achilles appeared to Neoptolemus to remind his son of his desire that Priam's daughter Polyxena be sacrificed upon his tomb. Neoptolemus was instrumental in convincing Agamemnon that Achilles' wishes had to be honored, and Neoptolemus then performed the sacrifice.

Finally the time came for Neoptolemus to sail for home, although he willingly delayed his departure to make the sacrifices to Athene that Agamemnon deemed proper but that others chose to eschew. Following the advice of Helenus, Neoptolemus made for Molossia, where he killed its king, Phoenix, and made Helenus its new ruler. From there Neoptolemus reached Iolcus and reclaimed his grandfather Peleus' throne, which the sons of Acastus had usurped.

While seeking satisfaction for Achilles' death at the hands (or direction) of Apollo, Neoptolemus arrived at the Delphic Oracle. The Pythoness denied all requests, which led Neoptolemus to plunder the shrine and set it afire. From there, Neoptolemus proceeded to Sparta, where he claimed to have been promised Hermione in marriage before the Trojan War had begun. In the interim, how-

ever, her grandfather Tyndareus had given her to Orestes, and Neoptolemus claimed that Orestes did not deserve her as he was currently being pursued by the Erinnyes.

It was ruled that Hermione should be given to Neoptolemus as was originally promised, but it turned out that she was barren. Neoptolemus traveled to the Delphic Oracle, which had been partially rebuilt, where he was instructed to make placatory offerings. While there he encountered Orestes, who would have killed Neoptolemus on the spot had Apollo not intervened,

Apollo's rescue of Neoptolemus was short-lived. That same day Neoptolemus took offense at the flesh sacrifices being made to the Delphic Oracle and attempted to prevent the carcasses of oxen from being hauled away. The Pythoness had had enough of Neoptolemus' interference at this point and proclaimed that it was time to be rid of him. At this point a Phocian named Machaereus slew Neoptolemus with his sacrificial knife. The Pythoness ordered that his body be buried beneath the threshold of the new sanctuary so that his ghost could guard it against attack, and promised that if Neoptolemus' ghost were to repent it would be allowed to preside over sacrifices made to heroes such as himself.

> *You have shown the race, my son, from which you spring; no child, you, of Sisyphus but of Achilles, whose fame was fairest when he was with the living, as it is now among the dead.*
> —*Philoctetes*, Philoctetes, *Sophocles*

Nephele The name given to the cloud created by Zeus to resemble Hera and entrap Ixion, who sought to seduce the goddess. When Ixion coupled with Nephele, the result was Centaurus.

Nereids Nymphs who sprang from the union between the Sea and its Rivers in creation myths such as Hesiod's, the Nereids were mermaids, and were sometimes described as the daughters of the nymph Doris by Nereus, making them cousins of the Phorcids. They were fifty in number, and served as attendants to Thetis.

When Cassiopeia bragged that she and her daughter, Andromeda, were more beautiful than they, the Nereids pleaded their case to Poseidon, who sent a sea monster to terrorize Philistia. Cassiopeia and her husband, Cepheus, were eventually turned to stone as a result. The Nereids also are credited with smoothing the *Argo*'s way during its famous voyage.

> *. . . the Nereids, passing the ship from hand to hand and side to side, kept her scudding through the air on top of the waves. It was like the game that young girls play beside a sandy beach, when they roll their skirts up to their waists on either side and toss a ball round to one another, throwing it high in the air so that it never touches the ground. Thus, though the water swirled and seethed around them, these sea-nymphs kept* Argo *from the Rocks.*
> —The Voyage of Argo, *Apollonius of Rhodes*

Nereus A sea god born to Pontus and Mother Earth, Nereus made his home in the river Po. Nereus had the power to change shape, and fathered the Nereids on Doris.

Nereus was forced by Heracles to reveal how he could obtain the golden apples from Hera's divine tree. Nereus told Heracles that he would need to get someone else to get the apples for him. In the end, Nereus was killed by his own nephew, Telephus.

Nessus One of the Centaurs who fled following the battle with Heracles, Nessus escaped to the river Evenus, where he attempted to violate Heracles' wife, Deianeira, while Heracles was in transit across the river. From a half mile away, Heracles pierced Nessus with an arrow. As he died, the Centaur told Deianeira that if she mixed his seed and his blood together it would make Heracles eternally faithful to her. In reality, the potion, which was applied to a shirt, was torturously painful, and Heracles' donning of the shirt led to his apotheosis.

Nestor The youngest son born to Chloris and Neleus, the King of Pylus, Nestor was a participant in the hunt for the Calydonian Boar, in which his sole noteworthy action was being driven up a tree during one of the Boar's charges. Nestor was also present at the wedding of Peirithous and Hippodameia.

When Neleus argued with Augeias, Nestor was put in command of Neleus' forces. In an initial raid, Nestor obtained hundreds of head of livestock, the majority of which were given to Neleus and the remainder of which were divided among the troops. Augeias' Eleans mounted an attack a few days later, but Nestor and the Pylians pushed them back. Nestor personally killed the Elean commander, Amarynceus, and as many as one hundred others as he and his troops routed Augeias' men. At the funeral games held in Amarynceus' honor, Nestor won all the events except the chariot race, which was won by the second generation of Moliones.

A Nereid Riding a Seahorse, **marble statue, 4th century** B.C.

Nestor helped Heracles get purified for killing Eurytus' son Iphitus when Neleus refused. This apparently was the reason Nestor was the only one of Neleus and Chloris' children to be spared by Heracles when he laid waste to Pylus. (Nestor also was out of town during the attack.) Heracles made Nestor the King of Messenia and the two became allies.

Nestor became well known for his wisdom and tactical skills, both of which were greatly valued by Agamemnon. Although Nestor was an old man by the time the Trojan War began, he became Agamemnon's most trusted advisor. Although Nestor was too old to fight as well as he once had, it was said that he was the best tactician of all (better even than Menestheus).

Nestor had a son named Antilochus who was slain by Memnon, an Ethiopian.

Despite the death of his son, Nestor continued to provide sage advice to Agamemnon. Once Troy had fallen, Nestor supported Agamemnon's desire to make sacrifices to Athene before departing; as a result, he was one of the few Greeks to enjoy a prosperous journey home. Of all the Greek leaders only Nestor, who had always been respectful of the gods, prudent, and just, was able to live a long, happy, and untroubled life after Troy. Despite his great age, Nestor outlived all of them; it is said that his longevity (he is said to have lived as long as three centuries) had been decreed by Apollo to make up for the years taken from his maternal uncles, sons of Amphion and Niobe who had been shot down by Apollo and Artemis.

. . . Nestor the fair-spoken rose up, the lucid
*   speaker of Pylos,*
from whose lips the streams of words ran sweeter
*   than honey.*
In his time two generations of mortal men had
*   perished,*
those who had grown up with him and they who
*   had been born to*
these in sacred Pylos. . .

—The Iliad, Homer

"Aged sir, if only, as the spirit is in your bosom,
so might your knees be also and the strength stay
*   steady within you;*
but age weakens you which comes to all; if only
*   some other*
of the fighters had your age and you were one of
*   the young men!"*

—Agamemnon, The Iliad, Homer

Nicippe One of Pelops and Hippodameia's many children, Nicippe married King Sthenelus. Nicippe was the mother of

Niobe and Four of Her Daughters Playing Dice, **Alexander Ateniese, 16th century.**

Eurystheus, whose birth was accelerated by Hera, who wished to thwart Zeus.

Nicostrate The daughter of the river Ladon, Nicostrate was also known as Carmenta. Nicostrate was the wife of Echenus, but the mother of Evander by Hermes. After Nicostrate convinced Evander to kill Echenus, both were banished from Arcadia and went to Italy. Nicostrate is best known for having adapted the thirteen-consonant Pelasgian alphabet from a more primitive one.

Niobe An arrogant woman whose disrespect toward Leto resulted in her downfall, Niobe was the daughter of Tantalus and Euryanassa,

Eurythemista, Clytia, or Dione. It is commonly agreed that her brothers were Broteas and Pelops.

Niobe married Amphion, and bore him fourteen children, seven males and seven females. Unduly proud, she mocked a ceremony in honor of Leto, who had managed to produce only two children. When Manto, a daughter of Teiresias and a prophet herself, instructed the women of Thebes to apologize for their queen's remarks, Niobe compounded her earlier insults with more vicious taunts. As a result, Leto's children, Apollo and Artemis, struck down all but two of Niobe's children. When Amphion went to avenge his children's slaughter (Amyclas, a son, and Meliboëa, a daughter, were spared when they offered apologetic prayers to Leto), he too was killed by Apollo.

With most of her family dead and no one around to bury them—Zeus had turned all Thebans to stone—Niobe roamed aimlessly for nine days and nine nights before the Olympians consented to bury her children. Niobe fled to her father's home on Mount Sipylus, where Zeus took pity on her and turned her to stone. Every summer, her statue is said to weep in memory of her losses.

Niobe was the first mortal lover Zeus took with the intention of siring a child who could protect both the gods and mortals from destruction.

> *I have heard in other days how dread a doom*
> *befell our Phrygian guest, the daughter of*
> *Tantalus, on the Sipylian heights; how, like*
> *clinging ivy, the growth of stone subdued her;*
> *and the rains fail not, as men tell, from her*
> *wasting form, nor fails the snow, while beneath*
> *her weeping lids the tears bedew her bosom.*
> —Antigone, Antigone, *Sophocles*

Nisus
The son of Pandion and Pylia, Nisus controlled a quarter of his father's kingdom, which was evenly divided among him and his brothers Aegeus, Pallas, and Lycus. Nisus was challenged for the rule of Megara by a brother-in-law, Sciron, who ended up with control of the armies, while Nisus retained the throne.

Nisus was eventually brought down by Minos, who laid siege to Nisa in payment for the murder of his son Androgeus, perhaps at the hands of Aegeus. When Nisus' daughter, Scylla, fell in love with his enemy, she abetted Minos by snipping a lock of her father's hair that somehow contained his invulnerability. Minos won the battle, and Nisus' soul took the form of a sea eagle. When his daughter, Scylla, was left behind by Minos, who wanted nothing to do with a patricide, she attempted to cling to Minos' ship as he sailed homeward. Nisus, in eagle form, swooped down and separated Scylla from the ship, causing her to drown.

Oceanus
One of the Planetary Powers created by Eurynome, Oceanus was a Titan who oversaw Venus with Tethys. In several different creation myths, Oceanus is described as assuming the form of some stream or river that girdles a female entity, usually Tethys, and from which all living creatures originate. Some creation myths describe Oceanus as being created from a union between Air and Mother Earth, while other versions credit Oceanus with being the father of Athene. Among the other children Oceanus is occasionally said to have fathered are Asopus, Pluto, and Callirrhoë. As a sea-based deity, Oceanus was often blamed for or credited with interfering with the passage of various ships, including the one Heracles rode out of the Mediterranean into the great unknown ocean.

Odysseus
Possibly the most famous of all mythological characters, Odysseus became the subject of one of the most famous epics in history, a tale that is considered by many to be the very first classic of Western literature. Homer immortalized Odysseus, obscuring much of what he had done during the rest of his life by paying so much attention to the decade he spent at war and the decade it took him to return home.

The son of Anticleia, the daughter of Autolycus, Odysseus was conceived when Sisyphus lay with Anticleia to avenge Autolycus' thievery. Upon his birth, Anticleia asked Autolycus to name the child, whose name means "the angry one." It is possible that this name was derived from Odysseus' red hair, but in some versions it is suggested that Autolycus foresaw that his grandson would be made to pay for the crimes committed by his grandfather.

Odysseus Recognized by Eurycleia, **red-figured krater, 4th century** B.C.

When Odysseus came of age he went to Mount Parnassus, where Autolycus had promised to leave valuable gifts. Odysseus was gashed in the thigh by a boar and barely survived. He returned home and eventually became one of Helen's suitors. Odysseus realized that he had little chance against some of Greece's most powerful figures and hoped instead to marry Tyndareus' niece, Penelope. Odysseus then promised to tell Tyndareus, Helen's father, of a way to prevent Helen's suitors from becoming violent once Tyndareus made his choice; in exchange, Tyndareus would assist Odysseus' efforts with Penelope, whom he later married.

Penelope's father, Icarius, assumed that they would stay with him in Sparta, but Odysseus announced that he and Penelope would go to live in Argos. This signaled a change from the matrilocal rule that had been recognized up to that point in time. (It is also worth noting that Odysseus was the first mythological character to be given irrelevant physical attributes. Whereas previous figures had always used their abnormalities to some mythological advantage, Odysseus' exceptionally short legs were never to figure in any of his accomplishments. They merely helped paint a picture of a man who was said to have appeared much nobler sitting than standing.)

When Helen's marriage to Menelaus led to the organization of the Greek alliance against Troy, Odysseus realized that he too

Odysseus Receiving Wine to Intoxicate Polyphemus, **red-figured krater, 4th century** B.C.

The Laestrygones Attacking the Ships of Odysseus, **wallpainting, 1st century** B.C.

would have to join up. When he was warned by an oracle that if he were to go to Troy it would be twenty years before he would return home, and that when that time finally came he would be penniless and alone, Odysseus feigned insanity. When Agamemnon, Palamedes, and Menelaus came to enlist his aid, they became suspicious of Odysseus' sudden condition, and Palamedes endangered the life of Odysseus' son Telemachus. Odysseus quickly rescued his son, revealing his sanity in the process. He now had no excuse not to join the Greek alliance, and became one of Agamemnon's lieutenants.

The specific incidents in which Odysseus figures are too numerous to include in their entirety. There were wrestling matches and abductions, diplomatic missions, feats of strength, and much consultation with Agamemnon and his immediate circle. One incident worth noting involved Agamemnon

sending Odysseus on a foraging mission, from which he returned empty-handed. When Palamedes mocked Odysseus' failure, Odysseus engineered his execution.

Odysseus was a constant presence among the Greek forces. Following the death of Achilles, Odysseus was called upon for a number of important missions. He went to get Philoctetes, who was in possession of Heracles' bow and arrow, and then went to bring Helenus back from the temple of Thymbraean Apollo. This led to a journey to Scyros to convince Lycomedes to let Achilles' son Neoptolemus come to Troy, at which time Odysseus gave the boy the armor that had belonged to his father.

One of Odysseus' most important, and most confused, assignments was the retrieval of Athene's Palladium, which was kept in the center of Troy. In some versions of this quest Odysseus is described slipping into the city dis-

guised as a beggar and being recognized by Helen; in these versions Helen assures Odysseus that her allegiance is to the Greeks and helps him by bringing Priam's wife Hecabe to his aid. Odysseus is said to have groveled in fear when Hecabe appeared, and then shown great relief when she turned the Palladium over to him and gave him all the information he would need for a safe escape from the city. Odysseus then returned to the Greek camp with the Palladium and concocted a self-aggrandizing tale of how he had single-handedly accomplished the task.

There are also versions in which both Odysseus and Diomedes sneak into the city with the help of Athene's priestess Theano. In the most commonly agreed-upon version of this incident it is said that Odysseus and Diomedes climbed a ladder against the city's walls and found it to be too short. Diomedes climbed upon Odysseus' shoulders and entered

Odysseus Recognized by Eurycleia, relief, Hellenistic period.

Troy alone. He eventually gained hold of the Palladium, and emerged from the city safely. As the two walked back toward the Greek camp, Odysseus, who wished to claim the glory for himself, fell behind Diomedes and drew his sword with the intention of killing him and taking all the credit. Diomedes saw the shadow of Odysseus' threatening form in the moonlight and quickly disarmed his alleged ally. Diomedes beat Odysseus all the way back to the ship and reported the true circumstances under which they had come to possess Athene's sacred Palladium.

Odysseus next developed the plan that led to the construction of the Trojan Horse, for which he took all the credit. Odysseus then convinced the bravest of the Greeks to join him inside the statue (this group numbered from twenty-three to fifty) and was placed in charge of this illustrious group. Odysseus was forced to restrain various warriors when Helen mocked them and their wives as she strolled around the statue.

When Antenor gave the signal, Odysseus led the Greeks out of the Trojan Horse and through the streets of Troy. Despite promises made to Helen and Hecabe about sparing the noncombatants, Odysseus and the Greeks slaughtered countless Trojans. And although most of Odysseus' actions during the sack of Troy were quite bloody, it should be noted that he did intervene and rescue Glaucus and his brother Helicaon, who had been seriously wounded.

Odysseus lobbied for the elimination of all Priam's descendants, among them the young Astyanax, so that none might live to avenge their ancestor's defeat. In many versions Odysseus tossed the child from the city's battlements while the other princes hesitated to commit such a brutal act.

Odysseus also lobbied Agamemnon to sacrifice Polyxena according to Achilles' dying wishes. Agamemnon had hoped to spare her in order to endear himself to Polyxena's sister, Cassandra, but the majority of Greeks ruled the day, and Polyxena was sacrificed.

Odysseus claimed Priam's wife Hecabe as his own, and took her with him to live among the Chersonese. Hecabe heaped so much verbal abuse upon Odysseus and all the other Greeks that they eventually felt it necessary to kill her. Her spirit was transformed into a menacing black bitch who became known as Maera.

When the time came for Odysseus to leave Troy and return home, he was told it would take a full ten years to reach Ithaca. He nevertheless made an attempt by first heading to Ismarus, where his forces were attacked by the neighboring Ciconians. Odysseus and his men suffered heavy casualties before escaping to sea.

A gale drove Odysseus' fleet across the Aegean Sea and eventually to the land of the Lotus-Eaters, where three of Odysseus' men succumbed to the lotus leaves they were offered by natives.

The next island turned out to be the home of the descendants of the Cyclopes, large one-eyed creatures who had lost their ancestor's skills as smiths. These anarchistic Cyclopes lived as far from one another as possible with no laws or governance. Odysseus and his men stumbled upon a cave where they found penned livestock, which they prepared for a feast. They were caught by Polyphemus, whose cave they were in. Polyphemus closed the entrance to his cave with an enormous rock. When Odysseus implored the Cyclops to remember his duty to the gods and entertain them properly, Polyphemus responded by seizing two of Odysseus' men and eating them.

Polyphemus fell asleep after this, safe in the knowledge that Odysseus would not kill him since he and his men would never be able to move the boulder from the mouth of the cave. The next morning, after Polyphemus awoke and ate another two members of Odysseus' crew before going out to attend to his flocks, Odysseus fashioned a sharp stick. When Polyphemus returned and ate two more sailors, Odysseus offered the Cyclops some wine, aware that Polyphemus had never before drunk wine. When Polyphemus passed out, Odysseus and his men drove the spear they had made into his eye.

In his painful frenzy, Polyphemus removed the boulder from the mouth of the cave and felt for the sailors trying to escape. Odysseus, however, had anticipated this and concocted a scheme whereby he and his men escaped by tying themselves to the underside of Polyphemus' rams. This worked because, as Odysseus had figured, the Cyclops would not think to check there.

Once Odysseus was out to sea he taunted Polyphemus, who responded by hurling a large rock to within a length of Odysseus' ship. The resulting waves nearly drove Odysseus' ship back within reach of the island. Odysseus again taunted Polyphemus, telling him his name in case anyone asked who it was that had blinded him. Polyphemus prayed to his father, Poseidon, that Odysseus be made to suffer, both on his journey home and once he had finally reached Ithaca. Polyphemus hurled another enormous boulder, but this one sped Odysseus' ship to where his companions had been waiting for him, and the entire fleet then proceeded north.

The next stop was the island of Aeolus, the Warden of the Winds. Aeolus was quite hospitable to Odysseus and his men for an entire month, at the end of which he gave Odysseus a bag that contained every wind except the one needed to blow him home.

After losing many men to the cannibalistic Laestrygones, Odysseus reached the island

Odysseus' Escape Under the Ram, black-figured lekythos, 6th century B.C.

of Aeaea, which was ruled by Circe. Odysseus sent his first mate, Eurylochus, and a party of twenty-two men, to explore the island, and they eventually came upon Circe's palace. The wolves and lions that prowled about the grounds were strangely friendly toward the visitors, as was Circe, who invited them to a feast. Eurylochus was suspicious and stayed behind. He watched as Circe drugged the men and then transformed them into pigs.

Eurylochus reported back to Odysseus, who armed himself and set out for Circe's palace. Along the way he encountered Hermes, who gave him a charm against Circe's magic. When Odysseus proved impervious to Circe's magic, she pleaded with him for mercy and offered to share control of Aeaea with him. Odysseus made Circe promise to never scheme against him again, and withheld his sexual favors from her until she returned his men to their human forms.

Odysseus remained with Circe for several years, during which time they conceived Agrius, Latinus, and Telegonus. While such dawdling may seem contradictory to Odysseus' burning desire to return home, it is worth remembering the prophesy that warned of a decade-long delay in reaching Ithaca. Most likely Odysseus decided that as long as he could not reach home for ten years, he may as well find a comfortable alternative. But eventually the time came for him to set out, at which point Circe told him that he needed to visit Tartarus and consult with the ghost of Teiresias the seer, who would tell him what he needed to know to return safely to Ithaca.

Circe instructed Odysseus to sacrifice a young ram and a black ewe to Hades and Persephone upon his arrival in the underworld. Odysseus' men had grown comfortable on Aeaea and were understandably reluctant to undertake a perilous voyage to the land of the dead. Eventually Teiresias appeared, and his warnings included the need for caution along the coast of Sicily, where Hyperion's cattle would tempt Odysseus' men. Teiresias also warned Odysseus of trouble awaiting him in Ithaca. Odysseus was assured of a prosperous old age if he followed Teiresias' instructions, but it was predicted that his death would eventually come from the sea.

Odysseus thanked Teiresias for his help and went on to speak with many of the ghosts he had known when they were still alive.

Following a quick visit back to Aeaea, Odysseus' ship passed the Island of the Sirens. Following Circe's advice, Odysseus' crew had stopped up their ears with wax and Odysseus had had himself tied to the mast so that he

Ulysses Descending into Hades, Giovanni Stradanus, c. 1523–1605.

would be able to hear the Sirens but not steer towards them. The Sirens proved even more alluring than Odysseus had imagined, and Odysseus threatened the lives of his crewmen if they did not release him. The sailors responded by lashing their leader even tighter to the mast and sailing quickly from the island. But escaping the Sirens did not bring much comfort when it brought the ship to a passage between the two cliffs that harbored Scylla on one side and Charybdis on the other.

Odysseus was more concerned about Charybdis' dangers and steered so far from her whirlpool that Scylla managed to snatch six of his men, one for each of her mouths. The men screamed to be rescued, but Odysseus, knowing that any attempts to do so would only result in further losses, forced the survivors to sail on. The ship eventually reached Sicily, where Hyperion's (or Helius') enormous herds of cattle grazed. Odysseus made his men swear to leave them alone, but a month's worth of unfavorable winds stranded them there and supplies became increasingly short. Eurylochus led the men in a plot to slaughter some of the cattle, in return for which they would erect a temple to Hyperion on their return to Ithaca. When their leader awoke and saw what they had done he insisted that they set out to sea immediately to avoid Hyperion's wrath. But Hyperion had already lodged a complaint with Zeus, who stirred up winds that snapped the mast and brought it down upon the helmsman's skull.

The tempest that followed wrecked

Odysseus' ship and killed all of his crew, leaving Odysseus alone at sea, floating atop a hastily constructed raft. The winds carried this raft back towards Charybdis' whirlpool, and Odysseus managed to catch hold of a fig tree that grew from the cliff overhead. Odysseus waited until the raft was shot back out of the vortex and paddled away as quickly as possible. After nine days at sea he drifted ashore on the island of Ogygia, where Calypso lived.

Calypso made Odysseus quite welcome, and promised him immortality and eternal youth if he stayed with her. She bore him twins, Nausithous and Nausinous. Calypso tried to make Odysseus forget about Ithaca during the time he was with her (anywhere from five to seven years), but Odysseus took to sitting despondently on the shore, staring out to sea. Zeus eventually sent Hermes to inform Calypso that the time had come to let Odysseus go home.

Soon after Odysseus left, Poseidon, who had thwarted many of Odysseus' earlier attempts to return to Ithaca, noticed Odysseus' progress and saw to it that a large wave swept the wanderer off his raft. Odysseus managed to scramble back aboard the raft, but he was once again destitute, having lost the presents Calypso had given him. The goddess Leucothea took pity on Odysseus and gave him a veil, which she promised would save him if he were again washed into the sea. For two days Odysseus was tossed about, but he eventually washed ashore on the island of Drepane, where he found shelter and fell asleep.

Odysseus was discovered by Nausicaa, the daughter of Drepane's King Alcinous. Nausicaa brought him to her father's palace, where he was shown great kindness, given many presents, and provided with a fine ship to bring him to Ithaca. The crew arrived at Phorcys and carried the sleeping Odysseus ashore.

Athene came disguised to Odysseus when he awoke and eventually revealed herself to him. She helped him stash the treasures Alcinous had given him and disguised Odysseus to look like a withered old beggar so that he might keep his return secret. When Odysseus went to the hut of Eumaeus, a faithful old servant of Odysseus, the traveler was told that Telemachus had sailed off to seek word of him and that one hundred twelve suitors were trying to convince Penelope that her husband was not returning and that she needed to choose one of them to take his place.

When Telemachus returned and Odysseus revealed his true identity to him, Odysseus swore Telemachus to keep his presence a secret. On the threshold of his palace, Odysseus was recognized by his decrepit old hound, Argus, who wagged his mangy tail and then died. Eumaeus led Odysseus into his own banquet hall, where Telemachus pretended not to recognize him and treated him with standard hospitality. The suitors, however, mistreated the newly arrived beggar, and one of them, Antinous, went so far as to throw a footstool at him.

When Penelope heard that the stranger brought news of Odysseus, she summoned him to her chambers. Before he got there, however, Odysseus was challenged to a boxing match by a beggar known as Irus. Odysseus felled Irus with a single blow, but was careful not to reveal the extent of his strength.

That night Odysseus told Penelope that her husband was sure to be home soon. Penelope was grateful for the news and ordered Odysseus' old nurse, Eurycleia, to bathe the visitor's feet. While doing so Eurycleia recognized the scar on Odysseus' thigh. Odysseus kept Eurycleia quiet and began to plot with Telemachus the revenge he would exact on Penelope's suitors.

The next day, when one of the suitors demanded that Telemachus persuade his mother to select one of them, Penelope announced that she would marry whichever of the suitors could repeat Odysseus' youthful feat of shooting an arrow through the rings of twelve axe handles with the huge bow Iphitus had given him twenty-five years earlier. None of the suitors were even able to bend or string the enormous weapon, and it was decided that the trial should be postponed until the following day.

When Odysseus, still disguised as a beggar, went to take a turn with the bow and arrow, he was soundly abused by the suitors. Telemachus sent Penelope to her room so that she might not witness what was to follow. First Odysseus strung the bow, then he sent an arrow through the twelve handles. Meanwhile Telemachus had slipped out and armed himself with sword and spear. Once Telemachus returned, Odysseus revealed his true identity and promptly shot an arrow into the throat of Antinous, the most abusive of the suitors.

The rest of the suitors rushed for their weapons but found that they had been taken into a storeroom. Some pleaded for mercy, others tried to escape. Odysseus blocked the main entrance, and Telemachus was joined by Eumaeus and another servant, Philoetius. The suitors managed to provide some resistance—Melantheus, a traitorous servant of Odysseus, found their weapons and brought out as many as he could—but in the end all of the suitors were slaughtered.

Odysseus then hanged the maids who had been disloyal and had Eumaeus and Philoetius mutilate and kill the traitorous servant Melantheus.

Odysseus was finally reunited with Penelope and with his father, Laertes, and began telling them of his many adventures. When they found themselves under attack by Ithacan rebels who had allied with the kin of Antinous and the other suitors, Laertes fought alongside his son and grandson, all of whom stood their ground despite being greatly outnumbered. Athene intervened and imposed a truce, but the attackers brought legal action against Odysseus for his slaughter of the suitors. An arbiter brought in to judge the case eventually ruled that Odysseus should be banished for ten years, during which time the heirs of the suitors should make compensation to Telemachus, who would serve as the King of Ithaca in his father's absence.

Odysseus still needed to placate Poseidon, at which point he remembered advice Teiresias had given him in Tartarus and set out on foot across the mountains of Epirus. When Odysseus reached Thesprotis he sacrificed a ram, bull, and boar to Poseidon, who finally forgave him. Odysseus then married Callidice, the queen of the Thesprotians; he led her army to victory over the Brygians and stayed for another nine years, during which time he fathered Polypoetes. When the ten years had passed, Odysseus set out for Ithaca, leaving Polypoetes to assume his throne.

Odysseus with His Bow Competing with the Suitors, red-figured skyphos, 5th century B.C.

Arriving in Ithaca, Odysseus learned that Telemachus had been banished on account of an oracle that had warned that Odysseus would be killed by one of his sons. Eventually, this prophesy and the warning Teiresias had made about Odysseus' death coming from the sea were fulfilled when Telegonus came in search of his father and raided Ithaca, mistaking it for Corcyra. In the battle that followed, Telegonus killed Odysseus with his spear. Following a year in exile, Telegonus returned and married Penelope, while Telemachus married Circe. As a result, two of Odysseus' families became closely united.

Penelope is sometimes said to have been the mother of Pan, at the sight of whom Odysseus is said to have fled in shame after sending Penelope back to her father, Icarius. There are also variations in which Hermes fathered Pan on Penelope and Odysseus responded by marrying an Aetolian princess who was the daughter of King Thoas. In these versions, Odysseus is said to have fathered Leontophonus, his final son, before dying at a venerable old age.

> *. . . that cunning, honey-tongued quibbler.*
> *That pleaser of the mob . . .*
> — *Chorus,* Hecabe, *Euripides*

> *Yes, you would call him a sullen man, and a*
> *   fool likewise.*
> *But when he let the great voice go from his*
> *   chest, and the words came*
> *drifting down like the winter snows, then no*
> *   other mortal*
> *man beside could stand up against Odysseus.*
> — *The Iliad,* Homer

Oedipus

Perhaps one of the most misunderstood figures in all of mythology, Oedipus was the son of Laius, whom it was prophesied would die at the hand of his own child. Laius kept this secret from his wife, Iocaste, and stopped being intimate with her. Unaware of the prophesy, Iocaste took her husband's snub personally, got him drunk, and enticed him to lie with her. When a child was born nine months later, Laius pinned its feet together and abandoned it to die.

The child was rescued and eventually adopted by the Corinthian King Polybus and his wife, Merope. When Oedipus became a young man and was told by an oracle that he would kill his own father, Oedipus, believing Polybus to be his true father, fled Corinth for fear of fulfilling the prophecy. During his travels, Oedipus encountered a Cadmian who treated him roughly. In the fight that ensued

Oedipus killed Laius and his charioteer, unaware that by doing so he had fulfilled the prophesy.

When Oedipus reached Cadmus in Thebes, he accepted the challenge of the Sphinx. By answering the Sphinx's riddle, Oedipus was able to defeat it; he subsequently became the King of Thebes, and was married to the widowed Queen Iocaste, with all participants unaware that she was actually his mother.

A plague settled upon Thebes, and consultations with the Delphic Oracle made it clear that the blight would lift only when the murderer of Laius was expelled. Oedipus swore to see it done, oblivious to the fact that he himself was the culprit. When his search to find the guilty party continued unsuccessfully, Oedipus consulted with the seer Teiresias, whom he finally goaded into revealing the truth of the situation. When the final pieces of the puzzle came together, and everyone became aware of Oedipus' true identity, Iocaste committed suicide and Oedipus blinded himself.

In some versions Oedipus is tormented by the Erinnyes for his patricide (however unintentional it may have been), but still maintains his power over Thebes. In other versions Creon, Iocaste's brother, expels him, but not

Oedipus and the Sphinx, **Ingres, 1808.**

Oedipus Abandoned on Mount Cithaeron by the Shepherd, **marble relief from a sarcophagus,** A.D. **3rd century.**

Oedipus Kills Laius, marble relief from a sarcophagus, A.D. **3rd century.**

before Oedipus curses his two sons by Iocaste—Eteocles and Polyneices—for showing him disrespect at a sacrifice held shortly after the revelation of his crimes. In those versions in which Oedipus leaves Thebes, he is accompanied by his daughter Antigone to Colonus, where he is eventually hounded to death by the Erinnyes and buried by Theseus.

> *What man was ever as highly honoured*
> *By gods as by fellow-townsmen in the crowded*
> *   square*
> *As they honoured Oedipus*
> *On the day when he freed our country*
> *From the Fiend that preyed on human flesh?*
> *   —Chorus, Seven Against Thebes, Aeschylus*

> *. . .you have been living in unguessed shame*
> *   with your nearest kin,*
> *and do not see to what woe you have come*
> *   —Teiresias, Oedipus the King, Sophocles*

> *I was fated to defile my mother's bed. . .*
> *and that I should be the slayer of the sire who*
> *   begot me.*
> *   —Oedipus, Oedipus the King, Sophocles*

Oeneus

The King of Calydon, Oeneus was married to Althaea, with whom he conceived Toxeus and Meleager. Oeneus is also said to be the father of Tydeus and Melanippus, whose mother might have been Eriboea.

When Oeneus omitted Artemis from his sacrifices, the goddess sent a huge boar to kill Oeneus' cattle and laborers, and to ruin all of his crops. Hoping to kill the boar, Oeneus sent messengers throughout Greece to summon the best hunters in the land. The turnout for the hunt of the Calydonian Boar is said to have included Castor, Polydeuces, Idas, Lynceus, Theseus, Peirithous, Jason, Admetus, Nestor, Peleus, Eurytion, Iphicles, Amphiaraus, Telamon, Caenes, Cephesis, and Atalanta. The Boar was killed, but fighting followed the hunt when credit for the kill was disputed by some of its participants.

Oenomaus

An ardent horseman and the King of Arcadia, Oenomaus had a daughter, Hippodameia, who was widely courted. Many of the courters' motives seemed suspect to Oenomaus, who in some versions was wary of a prophesy that a son-in-law would take his life. (In other versions Oenomaus himself is in love with Hippodameia, and wants to prevent anyone else from having her.) Oenomaus challenged all Hippodameia's suitors to a chariot race; the winner would marry his daughter, while each loser would forfeit his life. (Oenomaus had a great advantage: his chariot was drawn by two "wind-begotten" mares given to him by Ares, the god commonly considered to be his father.)

Oenomaus was eventually defeated by Pelops, who was assisted by Oenomaus' traitorous charioteer, Myrtilus. After Pelops won the race, Oenomaus either committed suicide or was killed by Pelops.

Oenone

The daughter of the river Oeneus, Oenone was a fountain nymph who took Paris as her lover. The two herded flocks together, and eventually conceived Corythus. When Paris fell in love with Helen, Oenone became jealous and convinced Corythus to guide the Greek forces to Troy.

When Paris was wounded near the end of the Trojan War, he was brought to Mount Ida, where Oenone had settled. Oenone, still jealous of Helen, refused to care for Paris, though she had warned him prior to his departure for Greece that only she would be able to heal him. After sending the dying Paris back to Troy, Oenone's love for him overcame her jealousy and she attempted to save his life after all; by the time she reached Troy, however, Paris was dead. In grief, Oenone took her own life by leaping from the city's walls, by hanging herself, or by throwing herself onto Paris' funeral pyre.

Oenopion

The son of Ariadne and Dionysus, Oenopion was also the father of Merope, with whom he was in love. When Orion came to court his daughter, Oenopion agreed that he could marry her if he killed all of the dangerous beasts in Chios. Orion accomplished the task, much to Oenopion's surprise, but instead of allowing the marriage to take place, Merope's father came up with a string of delays and excuses. Orion eventually got drunk and violated Merope. With the help of Dionysus, Oenopion avenged this deed by blinding Orion. He then had Hephaestus fashion an underground chamber for him in which he could hide from Orion. Oenopion escaped Orion's wrath, despite the latter having regained his eyesight, when Orion got sidetracked by a series of events that led to his death.

Oenopion is credited with introducing the concept of mixing wine with water, which may have been related to Orion's intoxication.

Omphale

The daughter of Jordanes and the wife of Tmolus, Omphale took over her husband's kingdom when he was killed chasing after Arrhippe.

Following Tmolus' death, Omphale ruled the kingdom of Lydia, and it was in this role that she purchased Heracles' services as a slave for a Great Year (a span of time that may equal eight years). It is generally agreed that Omphale bought Heracles' services with an emphasis on his being her lover. The sons that are said to have resulted from their union include Lamus and Agelaus, and maybe even Laomedon and Tyrrhenus.

Hercules and Omphale, **François Boucher, 1750s.**

son. Aegisthus killed the substitute and assumed he had averted the inevitable. (In some versions, the infant Orestes was sent to the court of Strophius to be raised; this helps explain Orestes' alliance with Strophius' son Pylades, who would accompany Orestes on most of his adventures.)

Between eight and twenty years later, Orestes came to Electra, prepared to kill Aegisthus. This action was easily accomplished, but Electra then insisted that Clytaemnestra must suffer the same consequences. Orestes was justifiably concerned about committing matricide and consulted the Delphic Oracle. The Oracle told Orestes that if he did not kill Clytaemnestra he would suffer greatly, but that if he did the Erinnyes were sure to torment him. Apollo gave Orestes a horn bow to protect himself from the Erinnyes, and Orestes returned to Electra.

Brother and sister hatched a plot that drew Clytaemnestra to them and resulted in her death. There are many variations in the chain of events that led to the deaths of Clytaemnestra and Aegisthus and in some versions Orestes simply captures Clytaemnestra and hands her over for public judgment.

Tyndareus, the most vocal of those calling for Orestes and Electra to be tried for murder, insisted that the two be stoned to death for their crimes, and tried to enlist the support of

When Pan saw Omphale and Heracles together he fell in love with Omphale and attempted to lie with her one night. It turned out, however, that Omphale and Heracles had switched clothes, and Heracles threw Pan out of the palace.

Ophion The great serpent that was created by Eurynome, the Goddess of All Things, who formed Ophion from the North Wind as it passed through her hands. Ophion then coupled with his mother, who punished his bragging about the act by knocking out his teeth. The Sown Men sprang from Ophion's scattered teeth.

Oreithyia The daughter of Erechtheus and Praxithea, Oreithyia was courted by Boreas. When Erechtheus kept putting him off, Boreas caught Oreithyia dancing beside the Ilissus River and ravished her on a rock. The couple

eventually had twin sons, Calais and Zetes, as well as two daughters, Chione and Cleopatra.

Oreithyia later swore vengeance on Theseus for carrying off one of her sisters, Antiope. Oreithyia led the Amazons and the Scythians against Theseus, Athens, and their Attic allies, but her cause was a losing one. Oreithyia escaped to Megara, where she died of grief and despair.

Orestes The son of Agamemnon and Clytaemnestra, Orestes is best known for avenging his father's death at the hands of his mother and her lover. Orestes was the brother of Electra, Chrysothemis, and Iphigeneia, but in most versions was reared by his grandparents, Tyndareus and Leda. When Aegisthus was warned that Agamemnon's son would live to avenge his father's death, Aegisthus went to murder young Orestes, whose nurse, Arsinoë (or Laodameia), replaced him with her own

Orestes in Delphi, **marble plaque,** A.D. **1st century.**

Menelaus, who sided with Orestes and Electra, but could only sway the judges to permit them to commit suicide rather than be publicly executed. Orestes, Electra, and Pylades agreed that if such a fate were inevitable they should also kill Helen, whom they deemed responsible for the entire chain of events that led to their predicament. Apollo took Helen up to Olympus, leaving Electra to kidnap Helen's daughter Hermione, whom Menelaus had claimed. Apollo instructed Menelaus to find a new bride, and then betrothed Hermione to Orestes.

Orestes was constantly pursued by the Erinnyes. He eventually again consulted the Delphic Oracle, which led him to engage in a series of missions, during which Orestes bit off a finger, shaved his head, traveled for an entire year, and then went to Athens, where a kinsman named Pandion consented to purify him for his blood sins. Orestes went to the temple of Athene and embraced her image, hoping to win her favor in his effort to stave off the Erinnyes. Athene asked the Areiopagus to rule on the matter; Apollo argued Orestes' case and the eldest of the Erinnyes argued against him. The court found itself deadlocked, and Athene cast the deciding vote, choosing in favor of Orestes and an honorable acquittal.

Some Erinnyes still were not satisfied, and Orestes once again returned to the Delphic Oracle. This time he was instructed to sail through the Bosphorus into the Black Sea and seize an ancient wooden image of Artemis that was in the possession of the Taurians.

When Orestes and Pylades reached the land of the Taurians, they were quickly captured by a herdsman and sent to Thoas, the Taurian leader, to be sacrificed. While being prepared for the sacrifice, Orestes encountered his sister Iphigeneia, who aided the escape of Orestes and Pylades, and joined them with the statue of Artemis as they attempted to leave Thoas behind. There was a short battle before they were able to sail, and a storm almost blew them back into the hands of the Taurians until Athene convinced Poseidon to calm the waters.

When Thoas caught up with Orestes and company on the island of Sminthos and engaged them in battle, Orestes and his half-brother Chryses killed Thoas. Orestes, Pylades, and Iphigeneia then returned to the Delphic Oracle, where they met up with Electra. As a result of having obtained the wooden statue of Artemis, Orestes was finally freed from the pursuit of the Erinnyes but now he had a new problem, which concerned Neoptolemus' claim of Hermione as his own wife. Orestes

***Orestes and Electra,* marble statue, 1st century** B.C.

spied Neoptolemus at Apollo's oracle, and was about to kill him when the god intervened. Apollo saw to it that someone else killed Neoptolemus shortly thereafter, allowing Orestes to reclaim Hermione; these two later conceived Tisamenus, who would become Orestes' heir and successor as the High King of Mycenae. Later, Orestes married Erigone, by whom he became the father of Penthilus.

When Menelaus died, the Spartans asked Orestes to become their king since they had no confidence in Menelaus' bastard sons. Orestes ruled over an enormous kingdom that included parts of Arcadia, Argos, Achaea, and Sparta. He is said to have died at the age of seventy from a snake bite at Oresteium. Orestes' bones were initially interred in Tegea, but Lichas, a prominent Spartan, brought them back to

Sparta in accordance with a prophesy that assured the Spartans that they would never lose to the Tegeans again as long as they were in possession of Orestes' bones.

> *Yet we shall not die unregarded by the gods.*
> *A third shall come to raise our cause, a son resolved*
> *To kill his mother, honouring his father's blood.*
> *A great oath, sealed in sight of gods, binds him to exact*
> *Full penance for his father's corpse stretched dead in dust.*
>
> —Cassandra, Agamemnon, *Aeschylus*

Orion The son of Poseidon and Euryale, Orion was considered by many to be the most handsome man alive. Orion fell in love with

Oenopion's daughter, Merope, and was promised her hand in marriage if he freed Chios of its dangerous beasts. Orion accomplished the task, but Oenopion was reluctant to fulfill his promise since he too was in love with Merope. Tired of Oenopion's delays, Orion finally got drunk and violated Merope.

After Orion was blinded by Oenopion, in revenge for the rape, Orion consulted an oracle who told him that he could regain his eyesight if he went eastward and turned his face toward the point in the sky where Helius rose at dawn. Orion traveled to Lemnos and abducted Cedalion to serve as his guide. Cedalion introduced Orion to Eos, with whom he fell in love. Eos later helped Orion restore his eyesight.

Orion later met up with Artemis, who shared his love of the hunt, and the two became so close that Apollo eventually grew either jealous of Orion or fearful that the hunter might endanger his sister's chastity. As a result, Apollo first convinced Mother Earth to create a monstrous scorpion to pursue Orion, then tricked Artemis into killing Orion.

When Apollo's son Asclepius attempted to revive Orion, Asclepius was thunderbolted by Zeus and Orion was returned to the land of the dead. The hunter's ghost went to the Elysian Fields in Tartarus, while Artemis, in tribute to her friend and hunting companion, set his image among the stars.

In some versions of Orion's story, he is said to be the son of Hyrieus, a poor beekeeper, conceived with the assistance of Mother Earth.

Orpheus

The son of King Oeagrus and the Muse Calliope, Orpheus was widely acclaimed as the most famous poet and the most talented musician who ever lived. Orpheus had been taught music by the great teacher Linus, and had been instructed in Rhea's mysteries by the Dactyls. He himself also taught, and is credited with tutoring the young Midas and a host of others.

As a member of the crew of the Argo, Orpheus is credited with entertaining the Argonauts and raising their spirits during their long voyage. After returning safely from the Argo's mission, Orpheus married Eurydice, who died from a serpent's bite while fleeing from Aristaeus. Stricken with grief, Orpheus journeyed down into Tartarus in the hope of bringing Eurydice back. He distracted and entertained Charon, Cerberus, and the Judges of the Dead, temporarily suspending the tortures of the damned, and was given a chance to rescue his beloved. As the two reached the border of

Orpheus, Marc Chagall, 1969.

Orpheus, Eurydice, and Hermes, **marble relief, late 5th century** B.C.

the land of the living, Orpheus looked back toward Tartarus to check his wife's progress, breaking the rules that had been set, and Eurydice was lost forever.

Orpheus returned to the living, and eventually was torn limb from limb by the Maenads. Orpheus' head was thrown into the Hebrus river, and floated all the way to the isle of Lesbos. His body was buried at the foot of Mount Olympus, and the head wound up in a cave in Antissa. The head made prophesies until Apollo, from whom Orpheus was stealing worshipers, asked him to stop doing so.

> *They say that with the music of his voice he enchanted stubborn mountain rocks and rushing streams. And testifying still to the magic of his song, there are wild oaks growing at Zone on the coast of Thrace, which he lured down from Pieria with his lyre, rank upon rank of them, like soldiers on the march.*
> —The Voyage of Argo, *Apollonius of Rhodes*

Orthrus

A two-headed hound that was usually described as a child of Echidne and Typhon, Orthrus is said to have lain with Echidne, conceiving the Sphinx and the Nemean Lion with her, although in some versions it is suggested that he fathered the Lion on his sister, the Chimaera.

Orthrus was responsible for guarding Geryon's cattle along with Eurytion. When Heracles appeared on Mount Abas in the course of his tenth labor, he quickly dispatched Orthrus with his club, and subsequently killed Eurytion.

Otus

One of the bastard sons of Iphimedeia by Poseidon (in an indirect way), Otus was the twin brother of Ephialtes. Otus and his brother eventually came to be known as the Aloeides.

Palaemon

A name given to the infant Heracles in some versions of his story.

Palamedes

The son of Nauplius and Clymene and the brother of Oeax, Palamedes was the inventor of the eleven consonants that were subsequently combined with the Fates' five vowels to form the first Pelasgian alphabet. Palamedes was renowned for his superior wisdom and his inventions, which included the first pair of dice.

Palamedes was an early and prominent ally of the leaders of the Greek forces preparing to attack Troy, and figures in many of the early organizational trips throughout Peloponnesus. Palamedes was there when Odysseus feigned insanity and was the one who placed Odysseus' son, Telemachus, in jeopardy so that Odysseus would reveal his sanity.

Before fighting began in Troy, Palamedes was admitted to Priam's court, along with Menelaus and Odysseus, to request that Helen be returned peacefully. When that mission was unsuccessful, preparations for war were begun. Odysseus was dispatched on a foraging mission, from which he returned empty-handed. Palamedes mocked Odysseus, then set out on a similar undertaking and returned with a ship full of supplies. Odysseus was greatly insulted and convinced Agamemnon that Palamedes was betraying the Greeks to the Trojans. Agamemnon then saw to it that Palamedes was court-martialed and subsequently stoned to death by the army.

There are many variations on Palamedes' death; in some of these, Agamemnon and Diomedes are included in the plot against Palamedes. In some versions Odysseus and Diomedes are described pushing Palamedes down a well and then stoning him, while in others it is suggested that Palamedes was killed by one of Paris' arrows. This last version is the least likely, since it was Palamedes' death at the hands of his Greek allies that led to his father Nauplius' instigation of numerous affairs involving the wives of Palamedes' murderers.

Pallas

A name applied to prominent mythological characters of both sexes. One Pallas was a daughter of Triton who was a friend of Athene; when Athene accidentally killed her, the goddess added Pallas' name to her own in her friend's memory.

The most prominent Pallas, however, was probably the one born to Pandion and Pylia. Entrusted with the southern portion of Attica when his father died, Pallas bred a race of giants, which is probably why this name was also given to one of the giants who fought against Zeus and the Olympians.

Pallas went on to father fifty sons who fought against King Aegeus and his Athenian troops. Pallas' sons were victorious, but were later ambushed by Theseus while they themselves were in the process of arranging to ambush him; half of them were killed. This turned the tide in the battle, and led to Theseus' emerging victorious, after which he killed the twenty-five ambush survivors.

Pan

The god of the pastures and hillsides whose connection with shepherds and their stock eventually led to Pan being depicted as having the legs of a goat and the body and head of a man, with the horns of a goat atop his human head. (Centuries later, Pan's visage would serve as the basis for visual representa-

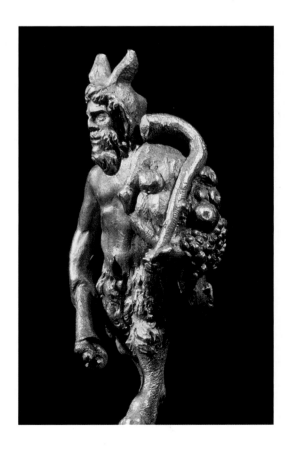

Pan, gold statuette, A.D. **2nd–4th century.**

tions of the Christian Devil.) This appearance is said to have caused his mother to abandon him, leading Hermes to have him brought to Mount Olympus for the amusement of the gods. Pan was a skilled musician who was considered to be easy-going and lazy, playful and lascivious, and prone to drunken revelry. (Pan claimed to have coupled with all of the Maenads.)

Pan's parentage is confused, with Hermes and Amaltheia the most commonly mentioned possibilities. The list of other potential parents includes Zeus and Hybris, Cronus and Rhea, and Amphinomus and Penelope. In the case of Penelope and Amphinomus, Pan's birth caused Penelope's husband, Odysseus, to flee in shame of the result of his wife's adultery.

Listed among Pan's seductions are Echo, who bore him Iynx, and Eupheme, upon whom he fathered Crotus. Pan attempted to violate a chaste nymph named Pitys, who was turned into a fir tree to prevent him from consummating his attack. Pan also chased after Syrinx, who ran to the river Ladon, where she was transformed into a reed; Pan cut several and used them to invent the pipe that now bears his name. And when Pan was aroused by Heracles' lover Omphale, he attempted to sneak up on her in the dark of the night, not knowing that Heracles and Omphale had exchanged clothes for the night. Heracles promptly kicked Pan out of the palace, and Pan avenged himself by spreading the rumor that Heracles always wore ladies' clothing.

Despite (or because of) the extent to which Pan entertained and amused the Olympians, he was never allowed to sit on the ruling council. Some of the Olympians despised Pan for his simplicity and riotous behavior, but others were grateful to him. Apollo learned the art of prophesy from Pan, and Hermes copied his musical pipes and spread their use. Even Zeus was indebted to Pan for the help he provided Hermes in rescuing Zeus' sinews from Delphyne during Zeus' epic battle with Typhon.

The concept of panic was derived from Pan's name and his traits. And Pan has continued to make his presence felt in contemporary literature and art.

Pandareus

A Cretan, Pandareus avenged Zeus' killing of Iasius by stealing the golden mastiff that Hephaestus had made to guard Zeus as a baby. Pandareus entrusted the item to Tantalus, and was rewarded by Demeter with complete resistance from hunger. Tantalus, however, quickly denied knowing anything about the entire incident, and was killed by the gods. Pandareus and his wife, Harmothoë, fled, first to Athens and then to Sicily, where they perished miserably. (In some versions Tantalus and Pandareus are switched in terms of the role played in the theft, but their respective fates remain the same.)

Pandion

The son of Metiadusa and Cecrops, Pandion returned to Athens and reclaimed the throne that rightfully belonged to Cecrops, but was eventually expelled by Metion's sons.

Pandion then went to the court of Pylas, where he married Pylia, one of his host's daughters. When Pylas killed his uncle Bias, he fled his kingdom and turned the throne over to Pandion, who ruled successfully and conceived many children with his wife. Pandion's sons Aegeus, Pallas, Nisus, and Lycus later avenged their father's expulsion from Athens by defeating Metion's sons, and split control of the Attic peninsula among themselves.

Pandion's daughters, Procne and Philomela, were not nearly so lucky. When Tereus mediated a boundary dispute for Pandion, he was rewarded with Procne, but eventually fell in love with Philomela. The murder and intrigue that resulted caused Pandion to die of grief.

Pandora

A beautiful woman created out of clay by Hephaestus. The Four Winds blew life into her form and she was then fancifully dressed by all of the Olympians. Zeus gave her to Epimetheus, who had been warned by his brother Prometheus never to accept anything from Zeus. Epimetheus either forgot Prometheus' warning or discounted it after learning the fate that his brother had suffered at Zeus' hands. He married Pandora, but proved unsuccessful in preventing her from opening a jar that held all of the Spites that would torment mortals, including Old Age, Labor, Sickness, Insanity, Vice, and Passion. As the person responsible for unleashing these terrors on humanity, Pandora became the ultimate pariah.

> . . .the woman opened up the cask,
> And scattered pains and evils among men.
> —Works and Days, Hesiod

Panopeus

A Phocian from Parnassus, an ally of Amphitryon and Cephalus, and the father of Aegle, Panopeus swore to Athene that he would not embezzle any of the Taphian spoils won by Amphitryon. Panopeus broke this vow, and Athene punished him by having his son, Epeius, be born a coward.

The Reconciliation of Helen and Paris After His Defeat by Menelaus, Richard Westall, 1805.

Paris

A son of Hecabe and Priam, Hecabe was pregnant with Paris when Priam was warned that an imminent royal birth would lead to the ruin of Troy. The day of the birth was foretold, and that morning Priam's sister Cilla delivered a son. Priam had both killed, and later that same day Hecabe delivered Paris. Priam refused to harm Hecabe in any way, and since he could not bring himself to personally injure his newborn son, he entrusted Paris to Agelaus, a herdsman, with instructions that the child be abandoned on Mount Ida.

Agelaus abandoned the infant, but it was suckled by a bear and found alive five days later, at which point Agelaus took Paris into his own home. (In some versions it is suggested that Hecabe had made a deal with Agelaus to ensure her son's safety.) Paris grew to be an impressive young man, well respected by those who knew him. The nobility of his actions during the course of a romantic affair with Oenone endeared him to the gods, which proved to be a mixed blessing.

When Hera, Aphrodite, and Athene were incited to argue over who was the most beautiful, they chose Paris as the judge. Paris wisely made all promise that the losers could not punish him for his decision, and then told them that he would have to inspect each of them nude. Each of the goddesses attempted to bribe Paris during their respective inspections, with Aphrodite promising to make Menelaus' wife,

Pasiphaë Hides in the Artificial Cow Built by Daedalus, **Giulio Romano, c. 1535.**

Helen, fall in love with Paris. Aphrodite was declared the winner and the losers, despite their vows, began to plot revenge against Paris and all of Troy.

Shortly after judging this Olympian beauty contest, Paris went to compete in the annual games held to honor Priam's "dead" son, who was in truth Paris himself. Paris excelled in the games, winning the boxing tournament and defeating his brothers in two footraces. Priam's sons became angry that an unknown competitor won all of the prizes, and eventually Hector and Deiphobus attacked him. At this point Agelaus revealed Paris' true origins.

Priam's advisors warned him not to invite this long-lost son to live with them in Troy, but Priam overruled those who objected and welcomed Paris with open arms. Paris' brothers welcomed him and pressed for him to get married, but Paris stressed a desire to lead a mission to rescue Hesione, the sister of Priam who had been taken by the Greeks when Heracles killed their father, Laomedon.

Paris promised to rescue his aunt, or at least to bring back a Greek princess of equal rank, a list which included Helen. Paris' prophetic siblings, Cassandra and Helenus, warned that the mission would lead to Troy's downfall, but Paris proceeded nonetheless.

Oenone also tried to dissuade Paris from undertaking the mission, since she did not believe Paris' motives were as pure as stated. Paris quickly reached Sparta, where he was welcomed with great hospitality by Menelaus.

Paris was surprisingly frank in his dealings with Menelaus' wife, Helen, and Menelaus seems to have been the only one ignorant of the burgeoning affair. Menelaus left the two alone together while he sailed off for a previous engagement, and that very night Paris and Helen ran off together.

When the lovers reached Troy, they were married, and Priam promised to ensure that Helen could remain in Troy forever. In the decade during which Helen and Paris were together they had a number of children, including Bunomus, Aganus, and Idaeus.

Paris was genuinely surprised when the Greeks attacked Troy in the name of Helen, since many similar incidents had taken place in the past without causing wholesale slaughter. In truth, there were two reasons for the Greeks' aggression: their oath regarding the marriage of Helen and Menelaus, and the strategic position of Troy, which overlooked the Hellespont. Paris fought well for the Trojans, and eventually found himself in a one-on-one battle with Menelaus. Were it not

for Aphrodite's intervention, Paris would certainly have succumbed; the failure of the two of them to resolve their dispute resulted in the resumption of the Trojan War.

Paris was credited with shooting the arrow that mortally wounded Achilles, although in some versions it is suggested that Apollo ensured the arrow's accuracy, while in others Apollo assumes the form of Paris and fires the arrow himself. Whatever Olympian assistance was provided, it was Paris the Greeks sought to repay for the death of Achilles. Agamemnon sent Odysseus, Diomedes, and Philoctetes to avenge Achilles' death.

The trio turned their assignment into an archery contest and Philoctetes sent three consecutive arrows into Paris' body. After one shot went wide, Philoctetes proceeded to hit Paris in his bow hand, then pierce his right eye and finally wound him mortally with a shot to the ankle. Paris survived to limp back to Troy, from which he was carried to Mount Ida in the hope of being cured by Oenone, who possessed healing skills. Oenone, still angry over his abandonment of her, refused to treat Paris and watched as he was carried back to Troy to die. Oenone eventually softened and rushed to Troy to rescue Paris, but by the time she arrived he was dead. In her grief, Oenone threw herself on Paris' funeral pyre.

So doomed, deluded, Paris came
to sit at his host's table, and seduce
Helen, his wife, and shame
The House of Atreus and the law of Zeus
　　　　　　—Chorus, Agamemnon, Aeschylus

Alexandros [Paris] the godlike leapt from the
ranks of the Trojans, as challenger wearing
across his shoulders the hide of a leopard, curved
bow and sword; while in his hands shaking two
javelins pointed with bronze, he challenged all
the best of the Argives to fight man to man
against him in bitter combat.
　　　　　　—The Iliad, Homer

Parthenopaeus The son of Atalanta, who was married to Melanion at the time she conceived Parthenopaeus with Meleager. After Atalanta abandoned Parthenopaeus on a hill that was later named in his honor, the baby was found and entrusted to King Corythus, who reared him with another foundling, Telephus. In some versions, Parthenopaeus and Telephus traveled together to Mysia, where they defeated Idas' troops. Parthenopaeus went on to fight with Adrastus, Meleager's ally, against Eteocles in the battle that is depicted in *Seven Against Thebes.*

Pasiphaë A daughter of Helius and Crete, Pasiphaë married the powerful king Minos. When Minos angered Poseidon by conjuring a white bull to emerge from the sea, Poseidon caused Pasiphaë to develop passionate feelings for the bull. (In some versions it is suggested that the bull was one that was withheld from Minos' sacrifices to Poseidon.) In order to consummate her lust, Pasiphaë enlisted the famous craftsman Daedalus to build a hollow wooden cow in which she would position herself so that the bull could mount her. Pasiphaë became pregnant by the bull and gave birth to the Minotaur, a monster with the head of a bull and body of a human.

Minos, greatly embarrassed by his wife's actions and the product of them, had an enormous Labyrinth built on Cnossus. In the center of it he housed Pasiphaë and the Minotaur so that no one could see the objects of his shame. (Pasiphaë eventually aided Daedalus' escape from Cnossus.) Meanwhile, Minos went on to have numerous affairs with other women, which made Pasiphaë angry. She cast a spell that caused Minos to ejaculate serpents, scorpions, and millipedes instead of semen; Procris, one of Minos' lovers, then helped to cure Minos, although she did not stay long

enough to enjoy the change since she feared what Pasiphaë might do to her.

In some versions it is suggested that the bull that impregnated Pasiphaë with the Minotaur may also have been the Cretan Bull caught by Heracles in the course of his seventh labor.

Patroclus One of Helen's suitors, Patroclus is best known as the cousin and constant companion of Achilles. Menoetius and Aeacus are both described as Patroclus' father, and his mother is alternately said to be Sthenele, Periopis, Polymele, and Philomele.

Patroclus fled to the court of Peleus after killing either Cleitheonymus or Aeanes in a quarrel over a game of dice, and eventually joined the Greek forces that marched on Troy. Patroclus fought valiantly throughout the conflict and was instrumental in selling Priam's son Lycaon into slavery after his capture by Achilles.

When Achilles withdrew from the war following an argument with Agamemnon, Patroclus kept fighting and was instrumental in driving the Trojans back when they were about to set fire to the entire Greek fleet. Only Protesilaus' ship caught fire before Patroclus

killed Purachmes and drove off the Trojans nearly singlehandedly. Achilles had just rejoined the battle, and Patroclus may have been successful because the Trojans mistook him for his cousin. Patroclus killed Sarpedon and drove the Trojans back inside the city's walls.

Finally, Apollo chose to intervene and repelled Patroclus' advances on the walls of Troy. A wounded Hector was unable to offer much resistance and Patroclus may well have captured Troy singlehandedly if Apollo had not come up behind him and struck him in the back between the shoulder blades. Euphorbus of Troy took advantage of this and struck Patroclus while he stumbled about dazed; Hector, recently returned to battle after having been sidelined by injury, delivered the finishing blows.

After Achilles killed many Trojans in revenge for Patroclus' death, he gave Patroclus a proper burial. When Achilles died a short time later their ashes were mixed and enshrined in the same monument on the headland of Sigaeum.

Pegasus The winged horse that was born, along with Chrysaor, from Medusa's dead body after she was decapitated by Perseus. Pegasus' father was Poseidon.

Pegasus was captured by Bellerophon with help from Athene, Poseidon, or both, and was used in Bellerophon's attack on the Chimaera. Once Bellerophon was rewarded for his accom-

Pegasus Triumphant, Odilon Redon, c. 1859–1916.

Achilles Contemplating the Body of Patroclus, Giovanni Antonio Pellegrini, c. 1675–1741.

Wedding of Thetis and Peleus, **Piero di Cosimo, after 1500.**

plishments, he became too confident and attempted to fly Pegasus up to Olympus. Zeus sent a gadfly to sting Pegasus, who reared and threw Bellerophon to earth. Zeus captured Pegasus for himself, and used him as a pack-beast for transporting his thunderbolts.

Peirithous

A son of Ixion and Dia, Peirithous took great pride in his strength and skills. Hearing a great deal of talk about Theseus' abilities, Peirithous challenged Theseus, but the two were quickly impressed with one another and became friends and allies instead.

Peirithous participated in the hunt for the Calydonian Boar and accompanied Theseus to the land of the Amazons, but he is best known for his and Hippodameia's wedding. When Peirithous invited all of the Olympians except Ares and Eris to his wedding banquet, the spurned gods incited a brawl between the Centaurs (Peirithous' cousins) and the local Lapith people. When Eurytion, one of the Centaurs, attempted to rape the bride, Peirithous cut off Eurytion's ears and nose. However, the brawl led to a battle that eventually resulted in the Centaurs' defeat of the Lapiths.

Years later, following Hippodameia's death, Peirithous convinced Theseus that they should abduct Zeus' beautiful young daughter Helen, for whom the two of them would draw lots. Theseus won, and the marriage was postponed for several years until Helen came of age. When that time came, Peirithous reminded Theseus that their initial agreement included a promise that the winner of Helen would help the loser obtain another of Zeus' daugh-

ters. An oracle suggested they try to steal Persephone from Hades.

Peirithous and Theseus were quickly captured by Hades, who imprisoned them each within a Chair of Forgetfulness, from which they could not rise without experiencing excruciating self-mutilation and in which they were ceaselessly attacked by the Furies and Hades' hound, Cerberus. After four years of this torture, they were found by Heracles, who was performing his final labor. In most versions Heracles rescues only Theseus, leaving Peirithous trapped for eternity, while in others Peirithous is also freed.

Peleus

The son of Aeacus and Endeis. When Aeacus remarried, Peleus and his brother, Telamon, conspired to kill their half-brother Phocus. Following Phocus' death, Peleus fled to the court of King Actor of Phthia, where he was purified by Actor's

adopted son, Eurytion. Actor's hospitality included the giving of his daughter, Polymela, to Peleus in marriage.

Some time after getting married, Peleus was a participant in the hunt for the Calydonian Boar. Peleus went to Telamon's aid during the hunt, and both were subsequently rescued from the charging beast by Atalanta. Toward the conclusion of the hunt, Peleus accidentally killed Eurytion with a spear that had been intended for the Boar.

Following the conclusion of the hunt, Peleus went to Iolcus, where he sought to be purified by Acastus. When Cretheis, Acastus' wife, attempted to seduce Peleus, who declined her offers, Cretheis responded by telling Polymela that Peleus was planning on replacing her with Cretheis' daughter, Sterope. Cretheis then told Acastus that Peleus had tried to violate her. Polymela responded by hanging herself, Acastus by taking Peleus out

Peleus and the Calydonian Boar, **detail from "François Vase," c. 570 B.C.**

Jason Before Pelias, **red-figured pyxis, 5th century** B.C.

on a hunt and abandoning him, unarmed, among the Centaurs, a situation that Acastus assumed would result in Peleus' death.

Cheiron convinced the Centaurs to spare Peleus, and even assisted his efforts to recover his weaponry. Peleus, now a widower, was eventually selected by Zeus to marry Thetis, of whom it had been prophesied that her child would become greater than its father. Cheiron foresaw that Thetis would resist Peleus' advances, but instructed him to catch hold of her and not let go, regardless of the various forms she might assume. Peleus prevailed, and in the end the two were locked in a passionate embrace and wedding plans were made. (It was at Peleus and Thetis' wedding that Eris created the situation that led to the "beauty contest" between Hera, Athene, and Aphrodite that Paris was made to judge.)

Later, to avenge his treatment by Cretheis, Peleus returned to Iolcus with an army of ants who were transformed by Zeus into the Myrmidons. Peleus killed Acastus, and then killed and dismembered Cretheis.

During the course of their marriage, Peleus and Thetis produced seven sons. The first six died during the course of Thetis' attempts to make them immortal. When Thetis attempted to repeat the process with her seventh son, Achilles, Peleus intervened just before Thetis had finished, and Achilles was left invulnerable except for a portion of his ankle. By the time of the Trojan War, Peleus was too old to

fight and sent Achilles in his place. When word of Achilles' death reached Iolcus, Acastus' sons were emboldened to banish Peleus. Thetis offered to take Peleus with her beneath the sea, but Peleus claimed to be concerned about his grandson, Neoptolemus, whose presence at Troy was said to be necessary in order for the Greeks to win.

To prove his concern, Peleus went out looking for Neoptolemus when his return seemed overdue. Peleus died along the way.

Pelias

The elder twin son of Tyro and Poseidon, Pelias, along with his brother, Neleus, was abandoned on a mountainside. The twins were discovered by a horseherd and were eventually passed along to King Cretheus, who raised them.

When the twins learned of the treatment their mother, Tyro, was receiving from her stepmother, Sidero, they chased Sidero into one of Hera's temples, where Pelias struck her dead. Pelias' bloodletting inside the goddess' sanctuary angered Hera, but the brothers thought the action worth her wrath since it allowed them to rescue Tyro, whom they brought back with them to Cretheus' palace. Cretheus went on to marry Tyro and adopt the twins as his own.

When Cretheus died, Pelias seized the throne, exiled his twin brother, Neleus, and imprisoned his half-brother, Aeson. Fearful of revenge, Pelias killed all of Aeson's Aeolian

allies, but spared Aeson for Tyro's sake. An oracle warned that an Aeolian would kill him in the future, and that he should be careful of a man wearing only one sandal. (Some Greek warriors battled this way, using their bare foot to secure a firmer stance.)

Hera, still angry with Pelias for his actions in her temple, contrived to bring Aeson's son Jason—who had been spirited away immediately after his birth to prevent Pelias from learning of his existence—to an encounter with Pelias. Before this encounter, Hera caused Jason to lose one of his sandals in the muddy banks of the river Anaurus. When Pelias recognized the threat Jason represented, but of which Jason was unaware, Pelias asked Jason what he would do in such a "hypothetical" situation. Jason said that he would send such a threat to recover Phrixus' remains for a proper burial and retrieve the Golden Fleece.

When the *Argo* eventually returned and Medea and Jason heard of Pelias' hand in the death of Jason's parents, Medea contrived the murder of Pelias by two of his daughters.

It was King Pelias who sent them out. He had heard an oracle which warned him of a dreadful fate—death through the machinations of the man whom he should see coming from the town with one foot bare. The prophecy was soon confirmed.

—The Voyage of Argo, *Apollonius of Rhodes*

Pelopia

The daughter of Thyestes, Pelopia became a priestess in Sicyon, where Thesprotus was king. When Thyestes was banished by his brother, Atreus, a second time, he consulted the Delphic Oracle and was instructed to beget a son on his daughter. Thyestes went to Sicyon, put on a mask, and raped his daughter. He left his sword at the scene of the crime, and fled quickly from the region.

Atreus arrived shortly thereafter, looking to finally make peace with his brother. Atreus developed the mistaken impression that Pelopia was Thesprotus' daughter, married her, and brought her back to Mycenae. When Pelopia delivered a son, she knew it to have been conceived by her unknown assailant, and attempted to abandon it. Atreus did not understand her reasoning, and rescued the infant, thinking it his own. Pelopia did not know the incestuous nature of her son's conception, but she did know that Atreus was not the father.

Years later, when Thyestes explained the entire chain of events to her, Pelopia committed suicide with the sword Thyestes had left behind when he raped her.

Pelops

Usually said to be the son of Tantalus and Euryanassa, Clytia, or Dione, Pelops is sometimes described as the son of Atlas and the nymph Linos.

When Pelops was a child, Tantalus killed and butchered him when he found himself short of food for a banquet he was preparing for the Olympians. With the exception of Demeter, who was so distracted with grief over the recent loss of her daughter that she ate a portion of the child's shoulder, the gods were quick to realize what had been done. Zeus had Hermes collect the pieces of Pelops' body, and Clotho rearticulated them. Demeter replaced the portion of the shoulder she had eaten with ivory, and Rhea breathed life into the child. Pan danced for joy at the boy's revival, and Poseidon fell in love with Pelops and made him his own personal cup-bearer and bedfellow.

Tantalus was subject to eternal punishment for this act, and Pelops was given his father's throne, which he did not retain for long, as he was soon expelled by invading barbarians. He eventually decided to marry Oenomaus' daughter Hippodameia, but first had to defeat Oenomaus in a chariot race. Twelve or thirteen suitors had given their lives in an attempt to win Hippodameia, but Pelops had help from his benefactor, Poseidon, who gave him two winged, tireless, immortal horses to pull a golden chariot that could race over the sea without getting its axle wet. In addition to this divine assistance, Pelops had another advantage: he bribed Oenomaus' charioteer, Myrtilus, by promising that Myrtilus could spend the first night with Hippodameia.

Pelops won the race, Oenomaus took his own life, and Myrtilus was eventually slain by Pelops. Pelops had himself purified by Hephaestus and succeeded Oenomaus to the throne, combining various regions of Peloponnesus. When his expansion was checked by Stymphalus, Pelops invited him over to negotiate and slaughtered him upon his arrival. A famine fell over all of Greece, and Pelops initiated the Olympic Games to atone for his actions. Pelops atoned extensively for his murder of Myrtilus and even extended honors to Hippodameia's unsuccessful suitors.

Pelops' divine shoulder became important long after his death when an oracle suggested that its presence in Troy was necessary in order for the Greeks to prevail. In some versions the piece of ivory was successfully retrieved from Pisa, while in others it is suggested that the bone was lost at sea for many years until it was eventually rediscovered by Damarmenus, a fisherman who used it to put an end to an Elean plague.

Penelope, **marble statue, Roman copy after Greek original.**

Penelope

The daughter of Icarius and Periboea, Penelope was initially named Arnaea (or Arnacia). As a child, she was thrown into the sea, but was rescued by ducks, from whom she derived her new name, Penelope, which means "with a web over her face." Icarius and Periboea took their daughter back home and raised her there until Odysseus came and married her. Icarius begged them to stay in Sparta with him, but Odysseus insisted that she return to Ithaca with him.

Odysseus soon went off to fight in the Trojan War, despite an oracular warning that it would be two decades before he would return home. As the years passed and most of the other survivors returned home from Troy, Odysseus remained absent. Although Penelope believed the oracular assurances that Odysseus would one day return, many young Ithacan princes began to court Penelope under the assumption that Odysseus was not coming back. A total of one hundred twelve suitors

Penelope Weaving, Giovanni Stradanus, c. 1523–1605.

eventually came to gather at Odysseus' palace, eating his food, abusing his servants, and depleting his riches.

Penelope eventually decided to placate the suitors by assuring them that she would choose one as soon as she had completed a shroud which she was weaving against the death of her father-in-law, Laertes. For three years Penelope wove by day and unraveled her work by night. The suitors eventually became aware of her trickery and insisted that she make a decision soon. At nearly the same time, Odysseus was disguising himself as a beggar on the far side of Ithaca.

After one day among the suitors, Odysseus came to Penelope, still disguised. He assured her that her husband would soon return home. The next day Penelope informed the suitors that she would marry any one of them that could duplicate a feat Odysseus had once accomplished of firing an arrow through the rings of twelve ax handles. The suitors were made to use the bow that Iphitus had given Odysseus twenty-five years earlier, which none of them could even bend.

When Odysseus stepped forward to fire the shot himself, the suitors abused Odysseus until he accomplished the task. A bloodbath ensued in which all the suitors were killed. At the end of it all, Odysseus, Laertes, and

Penelope were reunited, and Odysseus began to regale his wife and father with tales of his adventures. After an attack by an alliance of Ithacan rebels and relatives of the murdered suitors, Odysseus was eventually exiled for ten years.

Telemachus, the son of Odysseus and Penelope, assumed his father's throne until an oracle warned that Odysseus would be killed by his own son. The Ithacans then banished Telemachus, and Penelope came to rule in the name of Odysseus' youngest son, Poliporthis, who had been conceived upon Odysseus' return. Ten years later, Odysseus returned to Ithaca, where he ruled into a prosperous old age. At that time, Telegonus, Odysseus' son by Circe, came looking for his father. He mistakenly attacked Ithaca and killed Odysseus in the process. After an exile of one year, Telegonus returned and married Penelope. At this time, Telemachus married Circe, and two branches of Odysseus' family were united.

There are several variations on Penelope's actions during Odysseus' absence. In some she is described as taking Amphinomus of Dulichium as a lover, while in others it is suggested that she slept with each of the one hundred twelve suitors in turn. The fruit of one of these unions is said to have been Pan, although in other versions it is suggested that

his father was Hermes. In those versions where Penelope is said to be Pan's mother, Odysseus encounters the goat-man upon his return and sends Penelope back to her father in Mantinea before running away in shame.

Penthesileia
An Amazon who was pursued by the Erinnyes for having accidentally killed her sister Hippolyte, Penthesileia went to Troy, where she was purified by Priam and distinguished herself in battle fighting alongside the Trojans. Penthesileia is credited with killing Achilles or at least driving the great Greek warrior off the field of battle at one point.

In those versions in which Penthesileia is credited with killing Achilles, Zeus revives the warrior, who then kills Penthesileia. It is suggested that Achilles fell in love with Penthesileia's corpse, and may even have violated it. Diomedes threw Penthesileia's body into the river Scamander to avenge Achilles' murder of his cousin, but the corpse was eventually rescued. Either Achilles or the Trojans eventually saw to it that Penthesileia was given a proper burial.

Pentheus
The son of Agave, Pentheus was made the King of Thebes by his grandfather, Cadmus, in an attempt to placate Ares. Pentheus was unhappy with the arrival of Dionysus and his Maenads to his kingdom, and arrested them all. For this he was driven mad, resulting in his being torn to pieces by Dionysian revelers led by his mother, Agave, who decapitated her son on Mount Cithaeron.

Periander
A Corinthian tyrant who was a patron of Arion, the talented lyre player, Periander reluctantly allowed Arion to accept an invitation to compete in Taenarus. On the way home Arion was forced to jump overboard when a greedy crew planned on robbing and killing him. The musician was rescued by dolphins, who brought him back to Periander before the ship from which he jumped arrived in port. The sailors created tales of Arion's unfortunate, "accidental" death, but Periander trapped the captain and his crew in their lies and forced them to swear an oath on their lives. He then produced Arion and summarily executed the would-be murderers on the spot. Periander is based on an actual historical figure.

Periboea
The daughter of Alcathous, Periboea was the mother of Ajax by Telamon. Periboea's name is often interchanged with Eriboea's.

Periboea was also the wife of the Corinthian King Polybus and the adoptive mother of Oedipus.

A third Periboea was a Naiad who was the mother of Penelope.

Periclymenus

The eldest son of Neleus, Periclymenus was endowed by Poseidon with boundless strength and the ability to change into any shape he desired. Periclymenus is best known for a tremendous battle he had with Heracles, during which Periclymenus changed forms—from lion to serpent, from ant to eagle. Heracles is said to have pierced him with an arrow while he was in eagle form, although in some versions it is suggested that Periclymenus was able to fly to safety.

Perigune

The daughter of Sinis, who was killed by Theseus. When Theseus killed her father, Perigune watched from a hiding place and then fled, afraid that he would treat her similarly. Instead, the two fell in love and conceived Melanippus. Perigune later married Deioneus.

Periphetes

A cripple who lived on the road between Troezen and Athens, Periphetes, also known as Corunetes ("cudgelman"), clubbed wayfarers to death and robbed them. When Theseus undertook to make the passage between the two cities safe, he killed Periphetes with his own club and carried it with him forever after. It is said that once swung, the club never failed to kill.

Pero

The daughter whom Neleus said no one could marry unless they drove off the cattle of King Phylacus, Pero was eventually married to her cousin Bias.

Persephone

The name given to Demeter and Zeus' daughter, Core, after Hades kidnapped her and made her Queen of Tartarus. After Demeter found her daughter, Zeus ruled that Core could leave the underworld only if she had not eaten any of the food of the dead. Core reported that she had not eaten anything, but Ascalaphus vowed that he had seen her eat seven pomegranate seeds. An argument ensued, and Zeus finally ruled that Core could spend nine months of the year with her mother, but for the remaining three she would have to stay in Tartarus, where she became known as Persephone.

Persephone was entrusted by Aphrodite with a chest that contained the young Adonis, and the boy eventually grew to be a beautiful youth. Persephone and Aphrodite fought over

Hades and Persephone in Their Underworld Palace, **vasepainting, 4th century** B.C.

the young man's affections, and in the end, Zeus decided that Adonis' year should be split evenly between the two.

As Hades' wife, Persephone figures in many myths regarding attempts to rescue the dead from the underworld. When Dionysus was revived by Zeus, Persephone entrusted him to King Athamas to keep him hidden from Hera. Later, Dionysus bribed Persephone to let him bring his mother, Semele, out of Tartarus.

In one myth when Alcestis gave up her life in her husband's place, Persephone sent her back among the living. She also pleaded with Heracles to spare Menoetes' life during the former's visit to Tartarus.

Persephone was faithful to her husband, and had no children with him. She had, however, given birth to Zagreus by Zeus before Hades had taken her to the underworld. Along with Hades and Hecate, Pan and Mother Earth, Persephone was never established as one of the twelve ruling Olympians, and she, Hades, and Hecate were not even welcome on Olympus.

Perseus

The son of Danaë, whose father, Acrisius, had attempted to prevent her from reproducing since an oracle had warned that a grandson would kill him. Danaë was impregnated by Zeus and gave birth to Perseus.

Acrisius sealed his daughter and grandson into an ark and cast them out to sea. The ark was found by Dictys, a fisherman, who brought Danaë and Perseus to his brother, King Polydectes. Danaë and Perseus were made welcome by Polydectes, but it soon became apparent that the king was motivated at least in part by his desire for Danaë.

As Perseus grew older, he helped his mother keep her distance from their "protector." Tired of Perseus' interference, Polydectes claimed to be making plans to marry Hippodameia, and requested that Perseus bring him the head of Medusa the Gorgon as a wedding present. Since a mere glimpse of Medusa's hideous face would turn mortal viewers to stone, Polydectes assumed that he was sending Perseus to his death.

With the help of Athene and Hermes, Perseus undertook the assignment, aware that he needed items being held by the Stygian Nymphs, whose whereabouts were known only to the Graeae. Perseus went to Mount Atlas, where the Graeae lived, and stole the single eye and tooth that were shared among them until they told him where he could find the Nymphs.

Once Perseus obtained the magic wallet in which to keep Medusa's head, Hades' helmet of invisibility, and a pair of winged sandals from the Nymphs, he went to the Land of Hyperboreans, where Medusa could be found, and came upon her as she slept. Perseus then

Persephone Opening a Chest, **marble relief, Hellenistic period.**

Perseus with the Head of Medusa,
Benvenuto Cellini, 1545–1554.

Perseus and Andromeda, Rubens, 1620–1621.

took aim at Medusa's neck by looking at her reflection in Athene's shield, and decapitated the Gorgon.

On his way back to Polydectes' home in Seriphos, Perseus stopped at Atlas' home and repaid the Titan's earlier lack of hospitality by turning him into the mountain of the same name. Perseus also dropped the Graeae's tooth and eye into Lake Triton and accidentally allowed some of Medusa's Gorgon blood to spill in the desert, breeding a swarm of venomous serpents.

While passing through Joppa during his return trip, Perseus also encountered Andromeda, who had been chained naked to a rock to assuage the gods angered by her mother Cassiopeia's brash boasts. Perseus rescued Andromeda from a sea monster, which he beheaded, and promised to marry her. Andromeda insisted that the marriage take place right away, but her parents, favoring a marriage to Phineus, attempted to interfere. In the battle that ensued Perseus killed some of his opponents and turned the rest to stone by allowing them to gaze on Medusa's head.

Perseus and Andromeda returned to Seriphos to find Danaë and Dictys hiding from Polydectes, who had assumed that Perseus had been killed by Medusa. When Perseus announced the success of his mission,

Polydectes and his court mocked and abused him; Perseus removed Medusa's head from the sack that contained it and turned all in attendance to stone.

With Polydectes eliminated, Perseus gave Medusa's head to Athene for safekeeping, and gave Hermes the sandals and helmet to be returned to the Stygian Nymphs. Perseus established Dictys as king, and then led his mother, his new wife and a group of Cyclopes with whom he was allied back to Argos.

Upon hearing of Perseus' imminent return, Acrisius, still wary of the prophesy, fled to Larissa. Perseus, however, was also bound for Larissa, having been invited there for the funeral games King Teutamides was holding in honor of his father. When Perseus let his discus fly, the gods caused the wind to blow it astray and strike Acrisius, causing what proved to be a fatal wound.

Ashamed to assume the throne, Perseus exchanged kingdoms with Proetus' son Megapenthes, and reigned in Tiryns. Over the course of time, Perseus won back the parts of Proetus' original domain that had been lost over the years. He fortified Midea, and founded Mycenae.

There are some versions of Perseus' story in which the entire Medusa portion of his adventures is omitted, Polydectes and Danaë

are happily married, and Polydectes is cast in the role of peacemaker between Perseus and Acrisius. In these versions, first Proetus and then Megapenthes are the enemies, and Perseus turns the former to stone and is then killed by the latter, in revenge.

Phaedra

The daughter of Pasiphaë and Minos, and the half-sister of the Minotaur, Phaedra was married to Theseus to cement his alliance with her brother, and their wedding was made notably eventful when Theseus' first wife, Antiope, attacked them at the ceremony. Theseus killed Antiope in the fight that ensued.

Theseus had had a son named Hippolytus while married to Antiope, and that son angered Aphrodite by focusing his attentions on Artemis. Aphrodite punished him by causing Phaedra to fall in love with him. When she made her feelings known to Hippolytus he spurned her. Phaedra responded by claiming that he had ravished her, after which she hanged herself.

Phaëthon

A son of Helius, Phaëthon was allowed to drive his father's chariot one day. While showing off to his sisters Prote and Clymene, Phaëthon lost control, and Zeus thunderbolted him out of the sky to his death

The Fall of Phaëthon, Bernardino Galliari, 18th century.

one of Alcmaeon's servants let slip that Phegeus' son-in-law had, in fact, been repurified by Achelous, and had married again, Phegeus instructed his sons to kill Alcmaeon for his treachery, which they did before Arsinoë could learn of her husband's deception. Later, the sons of Alcmaeon and Callirhoë (Alcmaeon's second wife), who had become fully grown in a single day in response to Callirhoë's prayers, killed Phegeus and his sons in revenge.

Philoctetes

The son of Poeas and Demonassa, Philoctetes became famous when he was asked by his father to light Heracles' pyre. Philoctetes was subsequently awarded Heracles' bow, arrows, and quiver, which became the possessions for which he was best known. Philoctetes also was one of the first and most respected members of the original Greek expedition to the Trojan War.

The fleet Philoctetes sailed with accidentally attacked Tenedon, thinking they had reached Troy. The Greeks were victorious, and while Palamedes was giving thanks to the gods for their victory Philoctetes was bitten by a water snake.

The pain caused by this wound led Philoctetes to constantly moan and complain, and his shipmates, perhaps urged by Odysseus, eventually decided to abandon him on Lemnos. Although the island was populated, Philoctetes is usually described as living alone, his festering wound driving off any who might have been inclined to help him. Using Heracles' divine bow and arrows, Philoctetes managed to survive by shooting small game and birds. In some versions, King Actor's shepherd, Phimachus, attended to Philoctetes and dressed his wound for him.

Meanwhile, in Troy, Calchas prophesied that with Achilles dead a number of things were necessary in order for Troy to fall, among them the presence of Heracles' bow and arrows. Agamemnon sent Odysseus and Diomedes to bring back Philoctetes. There are many versions of what happened before Philoctetes agreed to return to Troy. Philoctetes is often described as blaming Odysseus for leading the call to abandon him ten years earlier and being reluctant to help out a group that had treated him so poorly. In other versions, it is suggested that Philoctetes was anxious to go to Troy and make a hero of himself. And in some versions, Philoctetes is said to have died, leaving the Greeks to obtain the bow and arrows from his heirs. Sophocles portrays a bitter Philoctetes resisting all attempts to convince him to return to Troy

in the river Po, where the sisters were turned into poplar trees along the river's banks.

> For what you ask is the one gift that I
> Would keep beyond your reach; let me attempt
> To unpersuade you of your wish, a dangerous
> one
> That asks too much, too far beyond your
> strength,
> Or any boy's. Your destiny is mortal. . . .
> —The Metamorphoses, *Ovid*

Phanes

The name by which Eros, the son of Night, is known in the Orphic creation myth. During the time that Night ruled over everything, before its sceptre was passed on to Uranus, Phanes hatched from the silver egg, and in doing so set the Universe in motion.

Phegeus

A King of Psophis, Phegeus consented to purify Alcmaeon for having killed his mother. (Phegeus was convinced of the necessity of this by Apollo.) In addition to cleansing Alcmaeon, Phegeus gave him his daughter, Arsinoë, to marry. Alcmaeon accepted her, and presented her with the divine gifts that had been endowed upon his mother.

But the Erinnyes continued to hound Alcmaeon, and turned Phegeus' kingdom barren. The son-in-law left, only to come back a year later to request the return of the wedding presents in order to propitiate the gods. When until Heracles descends from Olympus to inform him that the only way his wound will ever heal is if he agrees to go. Heracles promises him that if he does go, one of the Asclepiads or one of Hephaestus' sons, either Pylius or Pelius, will cure him.

Heracles assured Philoctetes that he would quickly be recognized as the boldest Greek fighter in action and win many prizes for his father. Heracles also informed Philoctetes that he could take Troy only if Achilles' son, Neoptolemus, fought by his side. Philoctetes

sailed to the Greek encampment outside of Troy, where he was bathed and sent to sleep in Apollo's temple. There Machaon (or his brother Podaleirius) healed Philoctetes' wound.

Once Philoctetes recovered from his surgery, he challenged Paris to archery combat. Although Philoctetes' first arrow flew wide, the second pierced Paris' bow hand, the third blinded his right eye, and the fourth mortally wounded him in his ankle. Philoctetes was cheered by his fellow Greeks and was rewarded

generously when the spoils of Troy were divided.

Philoctetes' homecoming was not nearly as successful as his arrival in Troy. He was expelled from his own Meliboean kingdom and fled to southern Italy, where he founded Petelia and Crimissa. Philoctetes prospered in Italy, allying with Aegestes to fortify Aegesta and dedicating Heracles' divine bow to Apollo in Crimissa. When Philoctetes' days came to an end he was buried overlooking the river Sybaris.

. . . here long ago I put ashore the Malian, son of Poeas (as I was bidden by my chiefs to do), his foot all ulcerous with a gnawing sore, because we could attempt neither drink-offering nor sacrifice in peace; with his fierce ill-omened cries he filled the whole camp continually, shrieking, moaning.
— Odysseus, Philoctetes, Sophocles

You suffer this sore plague by a heaven-sent doom, because you drew near Chryse's watcher, the serpent, secret warder of her home, that guards her roofless sanctuary. Know that relief from this grievous sickness can never be your portion, so long as the sun still rises in the east and the plains of Troy, where you shall meet with the sons of Asclepius, our comrades, and shall be eased of this malady; and, with this bow's aid and mine, shall achieve the capture of the Illian towers.
— Neoptolemus, Philoctetes, Sophocles

Philoetius One of the servants in Odysseus' employ who remained loyal to his master during the wanderer's prolonged absence from Ithaca and upon his return, Philoetius joined Odysseus' son Telemachus and another faithful servant, Eumaeus, against the suitors. After the battle, Odysseus allowed Eumaeus and Philoetius to avenge him against Melantheus.

Philomela The daughter of Pandion, King of Megara, and Zeuxippe. When Procne's husband, Tereus, fell in love with Philomela, he misled her into believing that Procne was dead, violated her, and cut her tongue out. Philomela eventually slipped a message to Procne letting her know that she was still alive. Philomela was freed by Procne, who murdered her son by Tereus, Itys, and served the child's remains to his unwitting father. When Tereus learned what Procne had done he chased after both sisters until the three were transformed by the gods into birds, with Philomela becoming a nightingale.

Philoctetes in Lemnos, **Etruscan cinerary urn, 2nd century** B.C.

The Phoenix, **Roman wallpainting,** A.D. **1st century.**

Phineus The son of Agenor and Telephassa, Phineus was the brother of Europe, who was abducted by Zeus. Agenor sent Phineus and his brothers out to find Europe, warning them not to return without her. Unable to locate their sister, none of Agenor's obedient children ever returned.

Phineus ended up in Thynia, where he married Boreas' daughter, Cleopatra, with whom he had a few sons. Phineus was eventually blinded by the gods for prophesying too well, and also was haunted by the Harpies. This was his situation when the *Argo* arrived at his kingdom, Salmydessus. Phineus told Jason that he would give the Argonauts the vital information they needed to reach Colchis safely if they would rid him of the Harpies.

The Argonauts Calais and Zetes, who were the brothers of Phineus' first wife, the late Cleopatra, flew off and drove the Harpies far from Salmydessus. In exchange, Phineus suggested that the Argonauts release a dove as they neared the Crashing Rocks at the mouth of the Bosphorus. If they followed closely behind, they too might make it safely through the menacing strait.

In some versions Phineus was not blinded by the gods until after he gave Jason and his companions the information that would help them reach Colchis.

Phocus The son of Aeacus and the Nereid Psamanthe and the half-brother of Telamon and Peleus, Phocus cured Antiope of the madness Dionysus had brought upon her in revenge for the murder of Dirce, and then married her. When Phocus' stepmother, Endeis, exacerbated his brothers' jealousy over his being favored by Aeacus, Phocus' brothers killed him. Aeacus believed that Telamon was the driving force in the plot and laid the most blame on him.

Phoebe In the Pelasgian Creation myth, Phoebe was created by Eurynome as one of the Seven Planetary Powers. Phoebe was Titaness of the Moon, sharing control with Atlas. In some later versions, Phoebe came to be known as the mother of Leto, who went on to conceive Apollo and Artemis with Zeus.

There are several other mythological characters who were given the name Phoebe, including one of the Leucippides.

Phoenix One of the sons of Agenor and Telephassa who went out searching for their sister Europe after she had been abducted by Zeus, Phoenix traveled past Libya to Carthage, where he remained until after Agenor's death. At that point Phoenix returned to Canaan, which was renamed Phoenicia in his honor. Phoenix then conceived Adonis with Alphesiboea.

Phoenix was also the name of a mythological bird that was most famous for its unusual mode of reproduction: as it neared death, the Phoenix built a special nest. It then set fire to the nest and a new Phoenix rose from the ashes.

The Phorcids The children of Ceto by Phorcys and the cousins of the Nereids, the Phorcids included Ladon, Echidne, the three Graeae, and the three Gorgons: Stheino, Euryale, and Medusa.

Phorcys A wise old sea deity, Phorcys was the son of Pontus and Mother Earth, and the brother of Nereus. Phorcys married Ceto, with whom he conceived the Phorcids. Phorcys is also said to have fathered the Sirens on either Sterope or the Muse Terpsichore. There are also versions in which Phorcys is said to have fathered the once-beautiful Scylla upon Hecate.

Phorcys made his home in a harbor on the island of Ithaca. It was into Phorcys' harbor that Alcinous' men brought Odysseus when he finally returned from his journeys. It was in a double-mouthed cave overlooking the harbor where Phorcys oversaw the practice of the rites of death and divine rebirth and where Odysseus rested before crossing the island to his home.

Phoroneus The son of Inachus and Melia, and the brother of Io, Phoroneus was the first man to found and people a market town; he was also the first to discover the use of fire after Prometheus had stolen it from the gods. Phoroneus married the nymph Cerdo, and ruled over all of Peloponnesus.

Phrixus The son of Athamas and Nephele, and the brother of Leucon and Helle, Phrixus was a handsome young man whose aunt, Biadice, made improper advances toward him. When Phrixus spurned Biadice, she claimed that he had tried to ravish her. With the help of Ino, Biadice nearly convinced Athamas to sacrifice Phrixus. Heracles intervened at the last moment, and a winged, golden ram came to carry Phrixus off to Colchis.

As Phrixus prepared to depart, his sister, Helle, grabbed hold of the ram in the hope of accompanying her brother. Helle fell along the way. Phrixus safely reached Colchis, where he sacrificed the golden lamb whose fleece became the object of the quest of Jason and the Argonauts a generation later. There are some versions of Phrixus' story in which it is suggested that his and Helle's ride on the ram was brought about when Nephele discovered the two of them participating in a Bacchic frenzy.

When Phrixus died in Colchis he was denied a proper burial, which caused his ghost to return to his home, Iolcus, and decree that it would not prosper until his remains were brought back and buried in Greek soil. Phrixus' ghost also indicated that the Golden Fleece should be returned to Iolcus. Pelias, who had usurped the throne of Iolcus, used this as an excuse to send Jason on a seemingly impossible mission. The Argonauts retrieved the Fleece, but there is little mention of whether Phrixus' remains were ever obtained.

Phrixus' sons, Cytisorus, Argeus, Phrontis, and Melanion, were rescued by the Argonauts after having been shipwrecked on their way to Greece, and became allied with Jason despite their allegiance to Colchis.

Phylacus The King of Phylace whose cattle were the focus of a border dispute with Neleus. Melampus, wishing to win over Neleus, allowed himself to be captured by Phylacus, and then impressed the king with his prophetic skill. Phylacus told Melampus that he would reward him handsomely if he could cure his son Iphiclus' impotence. Melampus did so, and was given all Phylacus' cattle in payment. This paved the way for Melampus to give Pero to his brother, Bias, in marriage.

Phyleus

The eldest son of Augeias, Phyleus was called upon by his father to witness Heracles' promise to clean his stables. Heracles accomplished the task by diverting two local rivers, which Augeias considered trickery. When Phyleus was called upon in the argument that ensued, he testified in Heracles' favor, after which his father banished both him and Heracles.

Phyleus went to Dulichium, and was later restored to his father's throne by Heracles. In some versions, Phyleus killed Augeias and his brothers, while in others it is suggested that he merely banished them.

Phyllis

A Thracian princess who fell in love with Acamas, Phyllis anxiously awaited Acamas' return, but died of grief one day before his return to Enneodos. Athene transformed Phyllis into an almond tree, which was said to have burst into flower when Acamas touched it upon his return.

Another Phyllis, a Bisaltian princess, fell in love with Acamas' brother Demophon when he visited Thrace on his way home to Athens. The two were married, and Demophon was made the King of Thrace, but he eventually tired of it and wished to travel. When he announced his desire to visit his mother, Phyllis told him that it was unlawful for the king to absent himself from the kingdom for more than a few months at a time.

Demophon swore before all of the Olympians that he would return, and Phyllis, who was skeptical, gave him a casket that she said contained a charm and should be opened only when he had abandoned all hope of returning to her. Despite his oaths, Demophon never had any intention of returning to Thrace and instead settled in Cyprus.

When a year had passed and Demophon had not returned, Phyllis cursed him in the name of Rhea and then committed suicide with poison. At the same time, Demophon was driven insane and killed after looking in the casket.

Pittheus

The son of Pelops and Hippodameia, Pittheus became the King of Troezen when his brother (also named Troezen) died. Pittheus built many shrines and altars, taught oratory and rhetoric, and was considered by some to be one of the most learned men of his age.

Pittheus had a daughter, Aethra, who ended up sleeping with her father's old friend Aegeus, who had come to talk to Pittheus about his inability to conceive an heir. Poseidon lay with Aethra as well, shortly after Aegeus did so, and Theseus, the son that was eventually born, was raised by Pittheus. Poseidon graciously granted Aegeus paternity of the child, but Pittheus spread rumors that Theseus was Poseidon's child since Aegeus' enemies sought to punish him for his role in Androgeus' death.

The Head of Medusa, **Flemish, 16th century.**

Planetary Powers
The name given to the Titans and Titanesses in their roles as overseers of the seven known astrological entities.

Pleiades
The name given to the seven daughters of Atlas and Pleione—Alcyone, Merope, Maia, Electra, Taygete, Celaeno, and Sterope. The Pleiades either took their own lives, out of grief for the fate of their sisters the Hyades or were set among the stars to escape the hunter Orion, who was himself later placed nearby, continuing his pursuit of them across the heavens. The use of their constellation for guidance during the peak sailing months forged a connection between sailors and the Pleiades.

Plutus
The product of Demeter's affair with Iasius, Plutus went on to become Tyche's assistant, and it was to him that Heracles gave the famed Cornucopia filled with golden fruit.

Podaleirius
A son of Asclepius, Podaleirius, who was well schooled in the art of healing, went with his brother Machaon to Troy. Together, Podaleirius and Machaon diagnosed Great Ajax's madness, but when they went with Calchas to confine him they found that he had already taken his own life. Podaleirius is sometimes credited with curing Philoctetes' wound.

Following the fall of Troy, Podaleirius traveled by land with Amphilochus, Calchas, and others. When Podaleirius consulted the Delphic Oracle to determine where he should settle, the Pythoness, who was irritated by Podaleirius' actions, told him to go wherever he might be safe even if the skies were to fall.

Podaleirius eventually decided on a city in Caria named Syrnos, situated with a ring of mountains about it. It was Podaleirius' feeling that even if Atlas were to falter and let the firmament slip, the mountains would still be able to support it. The Italians eventually built a shrine to Podaleirius on Mount Drium.

Podarces
A name given to two well-known figures, the best known of whom was a son of Laomedon. When Heracles sought to collect two divine mares from Laomedon in payment for having rescued his daughter Hesione, Podarces was the only one of Laomedon's sons to support Heracles' claims. Heracles eventually avenged himself by killing Laomedon and all of his sons except Podarces. Hesione was then married to Heracles' ally Telamon, and was allowed to ransom her brother out of slavery, after which Podarces became known as Priam, "the redeemed."

Under this name Podarces became the King of Troy.

In some versions of this myth Podarces is said to be as an infant at the time Hesione ransomed him, in which case he could not have played a role in the dispute between Heracles and Laomedon.

Another Podarces was the son of Iphiclus who accompanied his brother Protesilaus to Troy.

Poliporthis
A son born to Odysseus and Penelope, Poliporthis was conceived during his father's brief return to Ithaca. Following Telemachus' banishment during Odysseus' absence, Penelope ruled Ithaca in the name of Poliporthis, but relinquished control to Odysseus when he returned nine years later.

Polybus
The King of Corinth whose wife, Periboea, never produced a child. Eventually, Polybus and Periboea became the adoptive parents of Oedipus, who eventually killed his true father and became King of Thebes. After Polybus died, Periboea, who had never told him that Oedipus was not his natural son, made the truth known, and this led to Oedipus' downfall.

Polybutes
One of the giants who fought against Zeus and his Olympic allies, Polybutes was killed when Poseidon broke off a part of Cos and threw it at him. The result was the creation of Nisyros, an island beneath which Polybutes is said to be buried.

Polycaste
A sister of Daedalus whose son, Talos, was killed by his uncle. When Polycaste heard about her son's death she hanged herself. According to some versions, her soul was eventually responsible for avenging Talos' death by causing that of Daedalus' son, Icarus.

Polydectes
A king who took Danaë and the infant Perseus into his home after their abandonment by Acrisius, Polydectes became enamored of Danaë. As Perseus became more capable of defending his mother from Polydectes' advances, the king sent him on the seemingly impossible mission of bringing back the head of Medusa.

When Perseus returned from his mission, his mother and Dictys were in hiding, and Polydectes and his companions mocked Perseus and heaped abuse upon him. The hero showed them Medusa's head, which turned all who gazed upon it to stone, and then established Dictys as the new king.

In some versions Polydectes is portrayed as a peacemaker who marries Danaë under less forceful conditions.

Polydeuces
A son of Leda by Zeus, or by Leda's husband, King Tyndareus. Along with his half-brother Castor, Polydeuces (also known as Pollux) was one of the Dioscuri. Polydeuces, who was renowned as the best boxer of his day, is best known individually for his boxing exploits during the course of the Argo's voyage. When the Argonauts arrived on the island of Bebrycos and were challenged by King Amycus to a boxing match, Polydeuces was the Argonauts' obvious choice to represent them. Polydeuces fought carefully, and the bout was long and even until Polydeuces eventually gained the upper hand. In the end, Polydeuces killed Amyclus with a series of powerful, well-directed punches.

Polydorus
The youngest of Priam and Hecabe's sons, Polydorus was sent to live with Iliona, who is described alternately as Hecabe's sister and as another of Priam and Hecabe's daughters. Iliona was married to Polymnestor, King of the Thracian Chersonese, and the two raised Polydorus. They also guarded a large portion of Priam's gold, which the King of Troy had given them either as payment or because he felt he might lose it to the Greeks during the war.

Some time late in the course of the Trojan War, Polymnestor killed Polydorus. In some versions, this happened when Polymnestor learned of Priam's defeat and decided he could keep the gold as long as Polydorus was out of the way. In accounts of the Trojan War, however, it is stated that Polymnestor was either bribed or forced by the Greeks to kill Priam's son. There are some versions in which Polymnestor tricks the Greeks into thinking he has killed Polydorus by killing his own son Deiphilus in his place. This is sometimes offered as the reason for Iliona leaving Polymnestor, which led Polydorus to consult an oracle.

The message from the oracle confused Polydorus, who had grown up thinking that Polymnestor and Iliona were his real parents. Polydorus was told that his home was being reduced to ashes, his father butchered, and his mother taken captive. Polydorus ran "home" and found Iliona and their home untouched. Iliona explained the oracle's statements by revealing the truth of his birth. Polydorus then killed Polymnestor for having sacrificed his own son.

In some versions, Polydorus is taken alive by the Greeks and offered to Priam in ex-

Priam (Podarces) *and the Amazons,* Etruscan relief, 2nd century B.C.

change for Helen. When Priam offers the city of Antandrus in exchange for his son, the Greeks kill the boy.

Polyeidus

A seer who was employed by Minos to find the king's missing son, Glaucus, who had been lost within the Labyrinth on Cnossus, Polyeidus managed to find the boy's dead body, and Minos confined the two of them (in accordance with a prophesy) until Polyeidus revived the child. After watching a snake revive its mate with a particular herb, Polyeidus used the same plant to bring Glaucus back to life.

In reward for this accomplishment, Minos bestowed a great number of gifts on Polyeidus but also insisted that the seer teach Glaucus the secrets of divining the future. Against his will, Polyeidus shared his secrets with Minos' son, but caused him to forget them as he was departing.

Polymele

The name most commonly given to Aeson's wife, the mother of Diomedes. Polymele pretended that the baby had been stillborn because Aeson's half-brother, Pelias,

had vowed to kill any of his children since they might avenge their father. Diomedes was entrusted to Cheiron the Centaur, who raised him under the name Jason.

When Jason came of age and returned to Aeson and Polymele's home, Iolcus, Pelias sent Jason on a seemingly impossible task to prevent him from claiming the throne that Pelias had usurped from Jason's father. When rumors that the Argonauts had failed reached Iolcus, Pelias threatened to kill Polymele and Aeson, who took their own lives rather than allowing Pelias to do so.

Polymnestor

The King of Thrace, Polymnestor was an ally of Priam, and was married to Priam's sister Iliona. When the Trojan War began, Priam sent his son Polydorus to be raised by Polymnestor. He also sent a good deal of gold to Polymnestor, either to pay for Polydorus' care and education or to be hidden from the Greeks.

Toward the end of the Trojan War Polymnestor killed Polydorus. In some versions this is described as a simple case of greed, with Polymnestor feeling confident that no one

could avenge Polydorus' death since Priam and his remaining sons had been killed by the Greeks; in other versions it is said that Agamemnon sent messengers informing Polymnestor that if he killed Polydorus he would be given Agamemnon's daughter Electra in marriage and an enormous dowry of gold.

In some of these versions Polymnestor agrees to these terms and kills his nephew. In other accounts, however, it is suggested that Polymnestor, not certain that Priam had lost the war, sacrificed his own son, Deiphilus, and convinced the Greek messengers that he had slain Polydorus. This soured relations between Polymnestor and Iliona, and Polydorus consulted the Delphic Oracle to determine what might be bothering the couple he thought to be his natural parents. After Polydorus learned the truth of his parentage and was made aware of Polymnestor's murder of Deiphilus, Polydorus blinded and killed his "father."

There are other versions in which Polymnestor is not bribed to kill Polydorus but is forced to do so by the Greeks. In most cases, however, it is agreed that Polydorus is killed by Polymnestor and that when Hecabe eventually

139

learns of her son's fate, she entraps Polymnestor by convincing him that she knows the whereabouts of a secret treasure Priam had left behind. When Polymnestor comes to consult with her, Hecabe kills two of his sons and tears out Polymnestor's eyes. When Agamemnon refuses to punish Hecabe for what she has done, Polymnestor prophesies Agamemnon's future betrayal and murder and also suggests that Hecabe will be punished.

Polyneices

A son of Oedipus and Iocaste, and the twin brother of Eteocles. The twins were destined to fight over control of Thebes because of a curse Oedipus had placed upon them for being disrespectful toward him following the revelation of his true identity.

Polyneices escaped to Argos, where King Adrastus gave him his daughter Aegeia in marriage and promised to help overthrow Eteocles and place Polyneices on the Theban throne. Adrastus gathered together his seven champions and led the attack on Thebes. The battle was turning against the Argive forces when Polyneices and Eteocles agreed to meet in combat to decide the issue. In the course of their battle, each dealt the other a mortal wound, and their uncle, Creon, went on to lead the Theban forces to victory.

Ironically, Polyneices became best known in death, when Creon announced that none of the vanquished Argive troops could be given a proper burial. One of the twins' sisters, Antigone, defied Creon's edict, and this aspect of Polyneices' story was made famous upon the Greek stage.

Polyneices was also the father of Thersander, who was killed by King Telephus during the course of the Trojan War.

Polypemon

The father of Sinis, Polypemon lodged travelers on beds that were either too big or too small for them and then stretched or shortened the unsuspecting lodgers to fit their accommodations. When Polypemon, whose surname was Procrustes ("he who stretches out"), made the mistake of attempting to treat Theseus as he did his other guests, Theseus killed Polypemon using methods Polypemon had used on others.

Polyphemus

One of the giant Cyclopes born to Poseidon and the nymph Thoösa, Polyphemus loved to dine on human flesh, and it was his cave that Odysseus and his men unknowingly entered. While Odysseus and his crew feasted on the food they had found in the cave, Polyphemus returned and captured them all. He ate a handful of sailors with each meal,

The Blinding of Polyphemus,
black-figured hydria, c. 530 B.C.

until Odysseus managed to trick him and blind him. Odysseus and the remaining sailors escaped as Polyphemus prayed to his father, Poseidon, for revenge.

Polyxena

The daughter of Priam and Hecabe with whom Achilles fell in love during the course of the Trojan War. When Achilles, who probably first saw Polyxena in a sacred grove where the Greeks and the Trojans maintained a truce, expressed his desire to marry Polyxena, he was told by Hector that he could marry her only if he betrayed the Greeks or at least murdered Ajax. Achilles refused and fought even harder than before.

When Achilles killed Hector and took possession of his corpse, Priam offered the body's weight in gold as ransom. Achilles offered to exchange Hector's corpse for Polyxena; Priam agreed on the condition that Achilles convince the Greeks to leave without Helen. In the meantime, Priam paid the gold for Hector's corpse and Achilles was left desiring Polyxena.

In some versions, once the gods decided that Achilles must die, Polyxena conspired to trick Achilles into an ambush; in other versions, it is Polyxena who tells Paris of Achilles' vulnerable ankle. In either case, in his dying breaths, Achilles blames Polyxena for his fate and makes his fellow Greeks promise to sacrifice her on his tomb once Troy has fallen.

Following the sack of Troy and the capture of Polyxena, Agamemnon attempted to save Polyxena's life since Agamemnon's own spoil, Polyxena's sister Cassandra, would therefore be more grateful to him. But a contingent of warriors that included Calchas, the ruling council, and Achilles' son Neoptolemus demanded that Achilles' wishes be honored. Achilles' ghost also made frequent appearances to press his request.

In some versions, the Greeks leave Troy with Polyxena still alive, but are halted by Achilles' ghost, who threatens to prevent their passage back to Greece until Polyxena is killed. In other versions, her sacrifice takes place in Troy where she is murdered upon Achilles' tomb, with Neoptolemus serving as priest. In some versions Polyxena goes to her death willingly, out of guilt for the wrongs she had done (this probably refers to the involvement she may have had in Achilles' murder), while in others it is suggested that Polyxena's noble bearing simply prevented her from begging for mercy.

Poseidon

A son of Cronus and Rhea, Poseidon is usually thought to have been swallowed by his father at birth so that he would not grow to overthrow him. (In some versions, Rhea replaced the newborn Poseidon with a foal, which Cronus ate.) Poseidon was later freed when Zeus gave Cronus an emetic that caused him to vomit up the children he had swallowed.

Although Zeus was the leader of their rebellion against Cronus, Hades and Poseidon were also essential to the overthrow of Cronus. Hades used his helmet of invisibility and Poseidon his trademark trident to capture Cronus, setting the stage for Zeus to strike him dead. Lots were then drawn to see who would control the various realms, and Poseidon became the god of the sea.

As the reigning power over all sources of water, Poseidon was capable of both great fury and life-sustaining refreshment. He flooded fertile plains and ruined them, or caused springs to gush up where they were most needed. As an active participant in wars among gods and among mortals, Poseidon used his powers whenever possible, often with grave consequences. As a result of his association with the seas, Poseidon was credited with affecting the outcome of battles by controlling everything from tides to winds to storms.

It is said that Poseidon created the horse and that he rode a golden chariot pulled by white horses, at whose approach it was said storms ceased and sea creatures frolicked about it. He originally possessed a thunderbolt, much like Zeus', but his signature weapon became the trident, a weapon that was directly linked to maritime cultures.

Poseidon supported Hera's coup against Zeus, and when the coup failed, Poseidon and Apollo were both made to work as bond servants in the employ of King Laomedon of Troy for one year. During that time, with the help of Aeacus, they constructed the wall around Troy that would be breached a generation later. When Laomedon attempted to cheat Poseidon and Apollo out of their pay he suffered their wrath; Heracles laid waste to the city and killed Laomedon and all but one of his sons.

Much like his brother Zeus, Poseidon had countless affairs and is frequently mentioned in regard to matters of paternity. Poseidon originally wanted to marry Thetis, but when warned that a son born to the two of them would grow to overthrow him, he decided that it would be better if Thetis were to marry the mortal Peleus instead. Poseidon then courted Amphitrite, who fled to the Atlas Mountains. Poseidon sent a dolphin named Delphinus to

Amphitrite, and this messenger managed to convince her to come back and marry the god. In gratitude, Poseidon set Delphinus' image among the stars.

Amphitrite and Poseidon eventually became the parents of Triton, Rhode, and Benthesicyme. Poseidon was no more faithful to Amphitrite than Zeus was to Hera, and Amphitrite, much like Hera, often took out her jealousy on her husband's partners.

Nothing Amphitrite did, however, could put an end to Poseidon's philandering. While Demeter was tearfully pursuing her daughter, Core, Poseidon became attracted to her. He assumed the form of a horse, as did Demeter, and the result of their union was the birth of Despoena, a nymph, and Arion, a wild horse who reappeared in many mythological tales.

Poseidon is also thought to have been the father of Halirrhothius, and of Athene, though she preferred to believe that Zeus was her father. Poseidon may have been the father of Asopus, and maybe Augeias. He was the father of Orion and Parnassus, for whom the mountain and city are named. Poseidon forced him-

self upon Aethra right after Aegeus had lain with her. (When Aethra discovered that she was pregnant, Poseidon graciously conceded paternity of the child to Aegeus.) He fathered Eumolpus, and rescued the child when its mother threw it into the sea to avoid the wrath of her husband, Boreas. Poseidon then entrusted Eumolpus to Benthesicyme.

When Hephaestus caught his wife, Aphrodite, in bed with Ares, and called for all the Olympians to witness their crime, Poseidon was overwhelmed by Aphrodite's beauty and argued in her defense. In gratitude for his assistance in getting her released, Aphrodite slept with Poseidon and eventually bore him two sons, Rhodus and Herophilus.

When Cycnus, another of Poseidon's children, was killed by Achilles, Poseidon helped arrange the Greek hero's death. Despite this particular vendetta, Poseidon otherwise supported the Greeks against the Trojans. Despite his active role in the Trojan War, Poseidon eventually found himself tormenting another member of the Greek alliance. When Odysseus blinded Poseidon's son Polyphemus, the Cyclopes beseeched his father to avenge his injury. For the rest of Odysseus' wanderings, Poseidon worked against him at all turns.

Priam A son of the Trojan King Laomedon, Priam was originally named Podarces; under this name, Priam is known for siding with Heracles when the great warrior had a dispute with Laomedon during which Heracles killed Laomedon and all of his sons except Podarces. Laomedon's daughter Hesione was taken captive and given to Heracles' ally Telamon, who allowed her to ransom one of the Trojan prisoners. Hesione chose her sole surviving brother and bought his freedom, which led to his subsequently being renamed Priam, "the redeemed," and then being enthroned as the new King of Troy.

Priam's first wife was Arisbe, by whom he became the father of Aesacus. Priam eventually passed Arisbe along to Hyrtacus, and took Hecabe as his second wife. With Hecabe, Priam fathered nineteen of his fifty sons (the balance were in all likelihood born to his concubines) and several daughters.

Troy prospered under Priam's rule, but Aesacus warned Priam that an impending royal birth was bound to lead the kingdom to ruin. When Priam's sister Cilla delivered a son, Priam killed both mother and newborn child. Later that day Hecabe delivered Paris, but Priam chose not to kill Hecabe, and, as he could not bring himself to kill his infant son with his own hands, he entrusted the task to

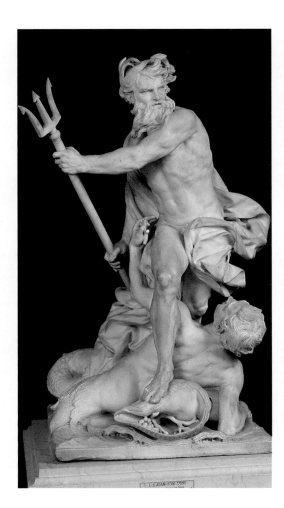

Neptune Calming the Waves,
Lambert-Sigisbert Adam, 1757.

Poseidon, **marble statue,** c. 200 B.C.

his herdsman Agelaus, who ended up taking the child in and raising him himself.

When Paris had grown to manhood he returned to Troy and competed in the annual funeral games Priam had instituted in honor of the infant son that had supposedly been abandoned on Mount Ida. Paris won several events, angering Priam's other sons. A fight eventually erupted, and Agelaus revealed the truth of Paris' origins. Priam embraced his son warmly and insisted that he come to live with him in Troy, despite warnings from his advisors.

Some years earlier, Priam's sister Hesione had been abducted by Telamon and brought to Greece. Priam wanted to use force to ensure her return, but the ruling council recommended that persuasion be given a chance. With this in mind, Priam sent his brother-in-law Antenor and a cousin, Anchises, to Greece to deliver Priam's demands for Hesione's return. The Greeks refused, and the two messengers were fortunate to return to Troy alive.

With Hesione still in Greek hands and Paris secretly lusting for the Greek princess Helen, the wife of Menelaus, Paris volunteered to lead a mission to Greece to bring Hesione home. When Paris and Helen ran off together, Menelaus sought revenge. Agamemnon attempted to settle the problem through diplomatic channels, but as Priam knew nothing of Helen's "abduction"—Paris and Helen were still sailing in southern waters—Priam reiterated his demands regarding compensation for Hesione's kidnaping.

When Paris and Helen finally arrived in Troy, Priam gave his word that she would never be turned over to the Greeks and that she would stay in Troy as long as he ruled over it. Each side then began to prepare for war. (The true motive for war probably revolved around the city's position overlooking the Hellespont. Troy's ability to control commerce between the Black and Aegean seas made it strategically crucial.)

Priam was fairly old by the time the Trojan War began and his role on the battlefield consisted mostly of rooting from the sidelines. Priam enlisted allies such as the Amazons and the Mysians, and there were also occasional dealings between Priam and the Greeks, including the time Hermes led him to Achilles' tent to negotiate a ransom for Hector's corpse.

When the Greeks constructed the Trojan Horse and gave the appearance of having abandoned their quest, many warned that the horse should be burned, but Priam insisted that the offering be brought inside the city walls and taken to Athene's temple, so as not to offend a goddess who had supported the Greeks throughout the war.

Laocoön recognized Odysseus' involvement in all of this and urged Priam time and again to burn the Trojan Horse. Laocoön then went away, where he met a grisly death at the hands of Apollo, who was angry with him for other reasons. Priam took Laocoön's death to reflect divine displeasure with him for having earlier thrown his spear into the horse and made up his mind to bring it into the city.

Some of the allies, such as Aeneas, withdrew from the city upon hearing of Priam's decision, while the majority remained to join in the celebration over the Greeks' apparent departure from the fields of Troy. That night a handful of Greek warriors emerged from the belly of the Trojan Horse and began the final

Helen and Priam, red-figured kylix, 5th century B.C.

attack on Troy. Priam, Hecabe, and their daughters took refuge in front of an altar in Zeus' courtyard. Hecabe restrained Priam from joining the remaining Trojans' desperate defense until their son Polites was killed before their eyes.

When Priam could control himself no longer, he threw a spear at Neoptolemus, who then captured the Trojan King. Priam was brought to the steps of his own palace and butchered. His headless body was set atop Achilles' tomb, where it was left to rot.

Priapus
Born to Aphrodite and Dionysus, Priapus was an ugly child with enormous genitals. His deformity was caused by Hera as an expression of her disapproval with Aphrodite's promiscuity. Priapus, a gardener by trade, tried to violate Hestia, an avowed virgin, following a bit of drunken revelry, but the braying of an ass (a symbol of lust) woke Hestia in the nick of time.

Procne
A daughter of Pandion and Zeuxippe. When Procne's husband, Tereus, fell in love with her sister, Philomela, he misled her into believing that Procne was dead. He then violated Philomela, and imprisoned her in his court. Procne, whose tongue Tereus had cut out to prevent her from shouting for help, eventually let Philomela know of her circumstances by weaving a message into a bridal robe being made in preparation of Tereus' marriage to her sister. Philomela freed Procne, who murdered her son by Tereus, Itys, and served the child's remains to his unknowing father. When Tereus learned what had happened he chased after both sisters with his ax until the gods intervened and turned all three of them into birds, with Procne being transformed into a swallow.

Procris
A daughter of King Erechtheus and Paxithea, Procris was married to Cephalus. Procris' favors were easily obtained, and Minos was one of her suitors; he gave her the famous hound Laelaps, as well as a dart that would never miss its target.

Meanwhile, Cephalus was having an affair with Eos, and feeling guilty for his infidelity. But Eos set out to prove to him that Procris was just as unfaithful. Fearing reprisal from Minos' wife, Pasiphaë, for their adultery, Procris had disguised herself as Pterelas. It was in this guise that she encountered Cephalus, with whom she reconciled when each realized that both were guilty. Procris was later killed by her husband—through the machinations of Artemis—when he mistook her for an animal.

Proetus
A son of Abas and Aglaia, Proetus shared rule of Argolis with his twin brother, Acrisius. After he lay with his brother's daughter Danaë, Proetus was banished, and he sought refuge with Iobates, the King of Lycia. There he was married to Iobates' daughter, Stheneboea.

With Lycian support, Proetus regained his half of the throne and raised a family that included Lysippe, Iphinoë, and Iphianassa. When these daughters offended Dionysus (or Hera), they were driven insane. Melampus offered to cure them in exchange for one third of Proetus' kingdom, but their father thought the price too high.

In time the madness spread to all of the women in the kingdom, who wantonly slaughtered babies and animals. Proetus once again sent for Melampus, who now asked for two thirds of the kingdom in payment. Proetus accepted the inflated rate, and Melampus ended the madness. In addition to handing over a large portion of his kingdom, Proetus married Lysippe to Melampus and Iphianassa to his brother, Bias.

In some accounts of Proetus it is suggested that his true name was Anaxagoras.

Prometheus

The son of Clymene and Iapetus (or Eurymedon). In some creation myths, Prometheus is said to be the creator of mankind, using the clay and water of Panopeus to form humans in the likeness of gods; Athene breathed life into these mortals, who went on to populate the Mediterranean.

As an early companion of the Olympian gods, Prometheus was persuaded by Hermes to breach Zeus' skull so as to allow Athene to emerge from it fully armed. Prometheus had been an ally of Zeus during the latter's overthrow of Cronus, and that kept Prometheus in Zeus' good graces for some time. From Athene, Prometheus learned about architecture, astronomy, mathematics, navigation, metallurgy, and other useful arts. Prometheus also was adept at prophecy, and he sought to share all of his knowledge with mankind, a desire that was not met with approval from the gods.

When Prometheus tricked Zeus into giving him the fire that Prometheus then shared with mankind, Zeus became so angry that he created Pandora and entrusted her with a jar that contained a host of horrible evils. Prometheus learned of Zeus' intentions and warned his brother Epimetheus to beware any presents from Zeus. This further enraged Zeus, who punished Prometheus by chaining him to a rock, where his liver was eaten daily by a vulture, and grew back nightly, only to be eaten again the following day.

After thirty years (or one thousand or thirty thousand), Heracles encountered Prometheus, still bound to his rock, and pleaded Prometheus' case with Zeus, who by now was ready to pardon Prometheus. Zeus eventually pardoned Prometheus, but ruled that Prometheus would have to wear a ring with a stone from the mountain to be reminded of his punishment. This represented the first ring to have a setting, and it was in Prometheus' honor that mankind wore rings (in gratitude for all that he had given to them). And in imitation of Heracles' shooting with an arrow the vulture that had tormented Prometheus, some mortals killed or burned whatever vultures they encountered as well.

The Torture of Prometheus, **Gustave Moreau, 1868.**

143

Prometheus married Hesione before his divine punishment, and is said to have conceived Oceanus with her. He is also thought to have been the father of Deucalion, and in most versions is described as the brother of Atlas and Menoetius as well as Epimetheus.

The dark-winged hound of Zeus will come, the
savage eagle,
An uninvited banqueter, and all day long
Will rip your flesh in rags and feast upon your
liver,
Gnawing it black.
—Hermes, Prometheus Bound, Aeschylus

Protesilaus
The son of Iphiclus, Protesilaus was originally known as Iolaus, by which name he was married to Laodameia and subsequently went off to fight with the Greeks in the Trojan War. The first Greek to leap ashore at Troy, Protesilaus killed many Trojans until he was struck down by Hector (or Euphorbus or Achates).

There are many variations of several aspects of Protesilaus' story, including those in which it is suggested that he survived the Trojan War and captured Priam's sister Aethylla, who had set fire to a number of Greek ships. In some versions, it was the burning of Protesilaus' ship that drew Achilles back into the battle.

Proteus
A name meaning "first man" that was applied to several progenitors. The first Proteus was the cousin of Arethusa who was interrogated by Aristaeus. When Aristaeus asked why his bees were dying, Proteus told him that it was because he had caused the death of Eurydice.

Another Proteus, an Egyptian King who lived in Pharos, received Dionysus with great hospitality and in some versions is described as at some point being entrusted with the care of Helen. This Proteus was the father of the nymph Eidothea, who told Menelaus what he needed to do in order to obtain favorable winds for his voyage home from Troy. This advice included capturing Proteus himself and forcing him to provide the required information. Proteus transformed himself into a lion, a serpent, a panther, a boar, running water, and a leafy tree, but the Greeks held onto him and eventually forced him to tell them what they needed to know. At this point Proteus informed Menelaus that Agamemnon was dead and that he needed to go to Egypt and propitiate the gods with hecatombs (sacrifices of a hundred cattle) before he would be able to return home.

***Pygmalion and Galatea**, Etienne Falconet, 18th century.*

Psamathe A Nereid who was the mother of Phocus by Aeacus. When Peleus, Aeacus' son by another woman, killed Phocus, he ran off to Actor's court, where he eventually killed Eurytion. When Peleus attempted to atone for this second murder by sending a herd of cattle as a peace offering, Psamathe sent a wolf to kill Peleus. The beast was distracted by the cattle, upon which it became sated. The wolf made a feeble attempt on Peleus, and was turned to stone by Thetis.

Another Psamathe, who was the daughter of Crotopus, also conceived a son with Apollo. She exposed the child, Linus, upon a mountain, where he was rescued by shepherds. But Crotopus had the child ripped apart by his hounds, and then deduced that Psamathe had been the mother and had her killed as well. Apollo then sent the Harpy Poene to punish Crotopus; he also cast a plague over Argos until proper sacrifices were made to Linus and Psamathe.

Pygmalion A son of Belus, Pygmalion fell in love with Aphrodite, who refused to lie with him. Pygmalion then created her image in ivory and slept with it. Aphrodite took pity on him, brought the image to life, and called it Galatea. Pygmalion then conceived Paphus and Metharme with Galatea.

Pygmalion was the father of the seer Phrasius, also known as Thrasius or Thasius, who was sacrificed by the Egyptian King Busiris.

Pylades The son of Strophius and Astyochea, Cyndragora, or, most likely, Anaxibia (the sister of Agamemnon and Menelaus). Pylades was a playmate of his cousin Orestes, who was raised by Strophius after the murder of Agamemnon. Once the boys became full-grown, Pylades accompanied Orestes to avenge his father's death. Various plays depict Pylades' role in the murders of Clytaemnestra and Aegisthus differently. In Sophocles' *Electra*, for example, he is simply Orestes' mute companion, but in Euripides' play of the same name he is a speaking ally who helps entrap Aegisthus on his way to prayer.

Pylades also accompanied Orestes in his attempt to take possession of the Taurian statue of Artemis in order to pacify the Erinnyes. The two were caught by the severe Taurians, but rescued by Orestes' sister Iphigeneia, who had become a priestess there.

During the course of their return trip from Taurus, Iphigeneia suggested that Pylades propose marriage to his cousin Electra, Orestes'

Agamemnon's Ghost with Orestes and Pylades, **marble relief from a sarcophagus,** A.D. **3rd century.**

other sister. Pylades and Electra were married and returned to his home in Phocis.

Pylas When Pandion was expelled from Athens he took refuge with Pylas (whose name is alternatively listed as Pylus and Pylon), the Lelegian King of Megara. Pandion married Pylas' daughter, Pylia, and had four sons with her: Aegeus, Pallas, Nisus, and Lycus. When Pylas killed his uncle, Bias, he fled Megara, entrusting the throne to Pandion, and took refuge first in Messenia and then in Elis.

Pyrrha The wife of Deucalion and the mother of Epimetheus, Pyrrha survived the flood named for her husband, and the two then pleaded with the gods to repopulate the earth. Pyrrha and Deucalion threw stones over their shoulders, from which sprang a new generation of men and women.

Python/Pythoness A monster of the darkness that lived in Delphi long before the ascent of the Olympians, the Python is depicted in some versions as a serpent sent by Hera to pursue Leto for having coupled with Zeus. When Apollo later sought to avenge his mother's treatment, he wounded the snake at Ortygia, then finished the Python off at the Delphic Oracle.

Some say that Zeus instituted the Pythian Games in the serpent's honor, since Apollo had exceeded his mandate by slaying the Python inside a temple. In later versions, however, it is suggested that the Games were to celebrate Apollo's actions, which had made the Oracle accessible once again.

Since the Python is often interpreted as being female, it is sometimes referred to in classic literature as the Pythoness. In this incarnation, the Pythoness is the name given to Pythia after she became the priestess of the Delphic Oracle. For one month a year the Oracle answered the questions of those able to provide it with lavish gifts (the many characters who consulted the Delphic Oracle were usually kings, generals, and wealthy men).

The Pythoness was seen as the prophet of Apollo and the vehicle through which he made his wishes known. In the Oracle, which was situated at the foot of Mount Parnassus, the Pythoness sat on a three-legged stool straddling a stream of vapor that rose from a cleft in the rock beneath her. She fell into a trance before revealing what Apollo had imparted to her. The Delphic Oracle was often thought to be the center of the world, and was visited by pilgrims from around the known world. As priestess of this unrivaled shrine, the Pythoness enjoyed a similarly exalted status.

Rhadamanthys

A son of Europe by Zeus, Rhadamanthys, together with his brothers, Minos and Sarpedon, were adopted by their mother's husband, Arestius, who raised them as his own. Rhadamanthys remained in Crete along with Minos, while Sarpedon traveled. They split their father's kingdom into thirds, and Rhadamanthys became widely respected as a just man and an upright lawmaker.

Rhadamanthys eventually married Heracles' mother, Alcmene, although it is not clear when this occurred. In some versions it is suggested that after killing a kinsman he had fled to Boeotia, where he lived in exile and met Alcmene. It may also be that they were mated after death in the Elysian Fields, where Rhadamanthys became best known as one of Tartarus' three judges. (The other two were his brother Minos and Aeacus.) Rhadamanthys was responsible for judging Asiatics for their proper afterlife assignments.

Rhea

In most Pelasgian creation myths, Rhea is simply one of the seven pairs of Planetary Powers, created by Eurynome as the Titaness of Saturn with her partner Cronus. In Orphic creation myths, however, she is described as a daughter of Uranus and Mother Earth. She is often depicted as the inescapable mother who banged a brazen drum in front of the cave in which Night and Phanes lived. Rhea drummed in order to draw the attention of mortals to the oracles that they might honor her and the gods.

After Cronus overthrew Uranus, Rhea and Cronus married and went to live in Elis, from which Cronus ruled and where Rhea bore him several children. Much to Rhea's dismay, however, Cronus swallowed each child at birth because he had been warned that one of his sons would overthrow him in much the same way that he had overthrown his own father.

Rhea became pregnant again, and delivered Zeus. In some versions it is suggested that the Dactyls came to be at this time when Rhea dug her fingers into the ground during the pain of childbirth. Tired of having Cronus swallow her children, Rhea wrapped a stone in swaddling blankets for Cronus to swallow and spirited Zeus off with Mother Earth so that he might be reared in safety. When Zeus became old enough, Rhea established him as Cronus' cup-bearer and helped Zeus obtain the emetic that would cause Cronus to expel the other children he had swallowed.

Zeus and his siblings overthrew their father and killed him. They realized their debt to their mother and treated her with great honor, with the exception of Zeus, whom Rhea announced should not be allowed to marry on account of his dangerous lust. Zeus became furious, violated Rhea, and then engaged in a spree of similar offenses.

Once Zeus became established as the leader of the Olympians, Rhea's role became increasingly diminished. She is credited with having reconstituted the young Dionysus after the child had been butchered by Hera and the Titans and then entrusting him to Persephone's care. Rhea later purified Dionysus of the blood sins committed during his mad travels around the world. Rhea even initiated Dionysus into her mysteries, but Dionysus quickly returned to his rough and rowdy ways. Rhea also played a role in bringing Tantalus' son Pelops back to life.

As Zeus and Hera became increasingly prominent in the Hellenic world, Rhea's worship became isolated to specific areas such as Crete and Arcadia.

Rhode

The daughter of Poseidon and the nymph Halia (although some versions posit Amphitrite as the mother), Rhode had six brothers who were turned into the Eastern Demons by Poseidon. Rhode then became the sole heir to Rhodes, and married Helius, with whom she conceived seven sons and a daughter, Electryo. The sons, with the exception of Actis, who was banished for fratricide and went on to teach the Egyptians astronomy, later ruled Rhodes.

Salmoneus

The son of Aeolus and Enarete, Salmoneus was the brother of Sisyphus and Athamas. When Aeolus died and Salmoneus tried to usurp the throne, Sisyphus seduced and impregnated Salmoneus' daughter, Tyro. After she learned Sisyphus' true motives, Tyro murdered her two sons by him. Sisyphus took this tragedy as an opportunity to accuse Salmoneus of incest and murder, and caused him to be expelled from Thessaly. Salmoneus went to Elis with a group of followers and built Salmonia, where he was a most unpopular ruler. Salmoneus began to take credit for things usually ascribed to the handiwork of Zeus, who became angry and eventually struck Salmoneus dead and burned down his entire city.

Sarpedon

The name given to two prominent characters. The first Sarpedon was the son of Europe born after his mother was ravished by Zeus. Sarpedon and his brothers, Minos and Rhadamanthys, were adopted by Asterius when he married Europe. When they were older, the brothers quarreled over the affections of a pretty young man named Miletus, who was asked to choose among them. Miletus chose Sarpedon, which angered Minos and caused him to chase Miletus out of town. Later, when Asterius died, Minos seized control of the throne and later banished Sarpedon.

Sarpedon went to Cilicia, where he allied with Cilix against the Milyans and came to rule a kingdom of his own. Zeus permitted Sarpedon's line to reign for three generations.

The second Sarpedon was a son of Zeus and Laodameia who led the Lycians against the Greeks in the Trojan War. This was the same Sarpedon that Laodameia volunteered to sacrifice when her father, Isander, and Hippolochus were on the verge of battle. The two were so impressed by Laodameia's actions that they agreed to make Sarpedon a co-king along with Hippolochus' son Glaucus. This Sarpedon was eventually cut down by Patroclus during the defense of Protesilaus' ship against the Trojans.

Satyrs

Creatures renowned for their carnal appetites and drunken revelry. As companions of the Maenads in Dionysian revelry, Satyrs

A Satyr Playing the Flute, **Roman copy after Greek original, 4th century** B.C.

became the embodiment of unrestrained Nature. Although originally human, the Satyrs eventually came to be depicted as beings whose lower parts were those of a goat and whose torso and head were human.

In many tales, Satyrs are anonymous stock figures on the verge of violating various maidens whose saviors usually end up doing what the Satyrs were attempting in the first place.

Scamander

A Cretan prince who is frequently credited with colonizing an area in Phrygia near Hemaxitus at the base of Mount Ida, Scamander married the nymph Idaea, upon whom he fathered Teucer. In a battle between Scamander's transplanted Cretans and their neighbors, the Bebrycians, Scamander leapt into the river Xanthus, which subsequently was renamed in his honor. Following a Cretan victory over the Bebrycians, Teucer succeeded his father, although in some versions it is suggested that it was Teucer who first settled the colony that was eventually incorporated into what came to be known as the city of Troy.

The river Scamander was credited with fathering Glaucia, who eventually became the partner of Heracles' ally Deimachus. When Deimachus was killed in battle, Heracles took care of Glaucia and the son of Deimachus, who was also named Scamander, she delivered after his death. This Scamander became the King of Boetia and later renamed the river Inachus for himself, the city of Glaucia for his mother, and the city of Acidusa for his wife.

Scylla

A hideous barking monster who lived in the sea, Scylla was once the beautiful daughter of Phorcys and Hecate Crateis. (Echidne and Typhon, Triton, and Tyrrhenus are all named in various versions as being Scylla's parents.) Scylla was changed into a dog-like sea monster with six imposing heads and twelve feet either by Circe, when Circe became jealous of Glaucus' attention toward Scylla, or by Poseidon's wife, Amphitrite, who had discovered that Scylla and Poseidon were having an affair.

Nisus, the King of Nisa, also had a beautiful daughter named Scylla. When Minos laid siege to her father's kingdom, Scylla fell in love with him. To gain Minos' favor, Scylla cut off a lock of her father's hair, which was said to have made him invulnerable. Scylla brought Minos the keys to the city, which she made conditional on his promise of reciprocating her love.

Minos quickly conquered Nisa, and lay with Scylla as he had promised. But despite Scylla's pleas that Minos take her home with him, Minos refused since he hated those who were capable—for any reason—of committing patricide. Scylla clung to the stern of Minos' ship as he left Nisa, but the soul of her father assumed the form of a sea eagle and swooped down at Scylla. She started at the sight of the imposing bird, lost her grip on Minos' ship, and drowned. In some versions, this Scylla is then transformed into the famous sea bitch.

> Female shall murder male: what kind of
> brazeness
> Is that? What loathsome beast lends apt
> comparison?
> A basilisk? Or Scylla's breed, living in rocks
> To drown men in their ships
> —Cassandra, Agamemnon, Aeschylus

The Seasons

Daughters of Themis who hastened to clothe Aphrodite when she emerged naked from the sea. The Seasons, who had been fathered by Zeus during the rampage that followed his fight with Rhea, had been nurses to Hera in Arcadia. The Seasons were often personified as Thallo and Carpo, names that translate, respectively, to "sprouting" and "withering."

Scylla and Charybdis from *The Ulysses Cycle*, Alessandro Allori, 1560.

Scylla, **terra-cotta relief, 5th century** B.C.

Selene A young woman who didn't recognize Pan, and willingly rode on his back, allowing him to treat her as he pleased, Selene is best known for having fallen in love with Endymion, whom she spied sleeping on Mount Latmus. When she asked the gods to give Endymion perpetual youth, they granted him a dreamless, ageless sleep. Selene lay with her sleeping lover and conceived as many as fifty children with him.

Some say that Selene may have given birth to the Nemean Lion on Mount Tretus and set it upon the Bambinaeans for failing to fulfill a promised sacrifice.

Selene is the sister of Helius and Eos, and her parents are thought to be Hyperion and either Euryphaessa or Theia.

Semele The daughter of King Cadmus of Thebes, Semele had an affair with Zeus while he was disguised as a mortal. When Hera became jealous, she purposely gave Semele bad advice, which angered Zeus and caused him to strike her dead. Hermes was able to save the six-month-old fetus Semele was carrying, and sewed it into Zeus' leg for the remainder of its term. From these inauspicious beginnings Dionysus was born.

Once Dionysus became established as one of the twelve Great Ones on Olympus, he bribed Persephone to release Semele, whom he then brought to Artemis' temple in Troezen and established under the name Thyone.

Seven Planetary Powers This is the name given to the Titans and Titanesses created by Eurynome to oversee the seven known astrological entities: Sun, Moon, Mars, Mercury, Jupiter, Venus, and Saturn. In the original Pelasgian creation myth, there were fourteen members, although this number was eventually cut to twelve to match the signs of the zodiac, and further reduced in other versions when it became limited to one overseer for each unit. In the end, Zeus swallowed all of the Titans, thus assuming all of the planetary powers they possessed. The planetary powers represented illumination (Sun), enchantment (Moon), growth (Mars), wisdom (Mercury), law (Jupiter), love (Venus), and peace (Saturn).

Silenus The leader of the Satyrs and a devout follower of Dionysus. Silenus and his Satyrs, together with the Maenads, accompanied Dionysus on his far-flung travels and participated in many of the god's wildest revels. Silenus claimed to have fought alongside Dionysus in the battle between the giants and

Drunken Silenus, Rubens and Jan Brueghel the Elder, c. 1612.

the Olympians, and also figured in Dionysus' granting of Midas' wish that everything he touched would turn to gold.

Sinis The son of Sylea by Pemon, or Polypemon (whose surname was Procrustes), and the father of Perigune. Sinis was an evil character who killed passersby in one of two ways: by bending two trees to the ground and tying the individual's legs to one and head to the other, thus causing the person to be ripped in half when the trees were released; or by bending one tree and using it to catapult the person into the air. Theseus encountered Sinis during the course of the former's efforts at making travel safe; Theseus then gave Sinis a dose of his own medicine.

Sinon There was a son of Sisyphus and Merope whose name was Sinon, but the most famous character with that name was the grandson of Autolycus and first cousin of Odysseus. Sinon was assigned the task of remaining in the Greek camp after the Trojan Horse was constructed and the rest of the troops had sailed off to give the appearance of having retreated. Once the horse was brought into the city it was Sinon's job to light the signal beacon to alert the remaining Greek troops that the final attack on Troy had begun.

As part of the plan, Sinon allowed himself to be "captured" by the Trojans, and he "admitted" that he had been singled out by Odysseus for sacrifice until fair winds provided

the Greek fleet a quick opportunity for their escape. Sinon claimed to have escaped in the confusion, at which point, he said, the Trojans had found him.

Priam believed Sinon, and asked him about the Trojan Horse. Sinon reported that the Greeks had lost Athene's support when they had stolen her Palladium from Troy and that the horse was a placatory offering. Sinon suggested that the horse had been built so wide so that the Trojans could not fit it through the city gates. The Trojans fell completely into the trap by proceeding to tear down a portion of the city's wall and bring the Trojan Horse within.

That night, after much revelry, Sinon was able to slip away. He went straight to the tomb of Achilles, from which he signaled the Greek fleet that everything was proceeding as planned. The remaining troops joined the invasion that night and Troy fell quickly thereafter.

Sirens Female creatures whose beautiful voices enchanted passing sailors and often caused them to wreck their ships upon the rocky coast of the Sirens' island. The daughters of Achelous or Phorcys by either Terpsichore or Sterope, the Sirens supposedly had the faces of girls but the feet and feathers of birds. In some versions, these physical properties were the result of Demeter's anger at their not having gone to Core's aid when she was abducted by Hades. In other versions it is suggested that

Aphrodite turned them into birds because of their unwillingness to yield to the romantic desires of men. They became flightless after losing a contest to the Muses, who plucked their wing feathers in order to fashion themselves crowns.

The Sirens were terribly alluring and their coastline was littered with the bones of sailors who had been drawn to their deaths. When the Sirens failed to lure Odysseus and his men to their deaths—Odysseus had devised a plan whereby he could listen to their song but not steer toward it—they became distraught and committed suicide.

The number of Sirens varies greatly, and is often said to be as few as two, three, or four. A list of names variously ascribed to the Sirens includes Aglaope, Aglaophonos, Leucosia, Ligeia, Molpe, Parthenope, Peisinoë, Raidne, Teles, Thelxepeia, and Thelxiope.

Autolycus, an unsavory sort who had the power to transform beasts. Sisyphus outsmarted his neighbor by marking his livestock's hooves, by which he was later able to identify them. While gathering witnesses to confirm his claims, Sisyphus secretly seduced Autolycus' daughter, Anticleia. From this union Odysseus was born. (In his visit to the underworld, Odysseus saw Sisyphus, but did not recognize him as his father.)

Sisyphus was given Corinth by Medea following her murderous rampage and preceding her departure from the region. But Sisyphus is best known for his actions following Zeus' abduction of Aegina. When the girl's father, Asopus, went looking for her, Sisyphus provided some useful information in exchange for Peirene, an eternal spring in Corinth. After Asopus failed in his attack on Zeus, the supreme god commanded that Sisyphus be

Sisyphus Punished, **vasepainting, 4th century** B.C.

the Sixteen Matrons represented the different cities of Elis, and covered a wide range of ages. Their competition was a single race among virgins, which was handicapped according to age. The women ran in short tunics with their right breasts bared, and their first champion was Chloris.

Smyrna

The daughter of King Cinyras, who boasted that Smyrna was more beautiful than Aphrodite. Cinyras was punished by the goddess by having Smyrna fall in love with her father and trick him into sleeping with her. When Cinyras realized what had happened, and that Smyrna was carrying a child by him, he chased after her. Aphrodite took pity on the girl and turned her into a myrrh tree, which Cinyras split in half. The newborn Adonis emerged from the tree, and Cinyras took his own life shortly thereafter.

Solemn Ones

The name given to the Erinnyes after they were finally pacified by Orestes.

Part of the Erinnyes' willingness to leave Orestes in peace came from Athene's offer of a grotto haven and numerous worshipers. The Solemn Ones settled in Athens, and served on the Areiopagus at times. In their grotto, the Solemn Ones had three underworld gods standing behind them: Hades, Hermes, and Mother Earth. It is said that their rites were performed silently.

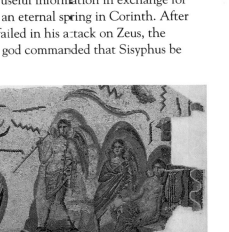

Ulysses and the Sirens, **Roman mosaic,** A.D. **3rd century.**

Sisyphus

A cunning businessman and a well-respected navigator, Sisyphus also was a robber and murderer of passersby.

Sisyphus was the son of Aeolus, and the brother of Salmoneus and Athamas. When Aeolus died, Salmoneus tried to usurp the throne that rightfully belonged to Sisyphus, who consulted the Delphic Oracle. Sisyphus was told to seduce his niece, Tyro, whose children would avenge him on Salmoneus. After bearing Sisyphus two sons, Tyro eventually learned Sisyphus' true motives, and killed her children. Sisyphus claimed that the sons were actually Salmoneus', and that he was responsible for their deaths. Salmoneus was quickly expelled from the kingdom by those who believed the charges.

Later, Sisyphus came to believe that portions of his cattle herd were disappearing from the Isthmus of Corinth. He suspected

taken to Tartarus by Hades. The wily Sisyphus, however, managed to trick Hades and hold him captive. Ares, whose warmongering was adversely affected by Hades being thus held, freed Hades, and returned Sisyphus to Tartarus. But Sisyphus again escaped, this time eluding Persephone.

Finally, Hermes brought Sisyphus back to Tartarus once and for all. There Zeus created a boulder the size of the one he had transformed himself into when Asopus surprised him. It was this boulder that formed the basis of Sisyphus' eternal punishment: he was forced to push the boulder up one of two hills, and each time he reached the top, the boulder would roll back down and Sisyphus would have to start anew.

Sixteen Matrons

A group assembled by Hippodameia to institute the Heraean Games, which occurred before the Olympic Games,

Sown Men [Sparti] The armed giants who sprang up when Cadmus sowed the teeth of the great serpent he had killed at the Spring of Ares. At Cadmus' instigation, the Sparti fought amongst themselves until only five were left: Echion, Udaeus, Chthonius, Hyperenor, and Pelorus. This group offered their services to Cadmus and served him well.

Sphinx A monstrous creature born to Echidne and her son Orthrus, to Echidne and Typhon, or maybe to Orthrus and the Chimaera, the Sphinx was a composite beast with the head of a woman, the body of a lion, the tail of a serpent, and the wings of an eagle.

When the Sphinx was sent by Hera to punish King Laius for his abduction of Chrysippus, it settled atop Mount Phicium, where it asked each passerby a riddle given it by the three Muses: What creature has only one voice, walks sometimes on four legs, sometimes on three, and sometimes on two, and is weakest when it walks on four? Those who failed to give the correct answer were throttled and devoured on the spot.

The Victorious Sphinx, **Gustave Moreau, 1888.**

When Oedipus guessed the answer to the riddle, the Sphinx leaped to its death into the valley below and Oedipus was subsequently proclaimed the new Theban King. (The riddle's answer? Man.)

Strophius A King of Phocis who became allied with Agamemnon by marrying his sister, Anaxibia (also known as Astyochea or Cyndragora), Strophius was entrusted with Orestes, either when Agamemnon was murdered or just before. Orestes was raised by Strophius and Anaxibia with their own son, Pylades.

Stygian Nymphs The nymphs in whose care the magic tools Perseus needed to overcome Medusa—the magic wallet with which Perseus would carry Medusa's head, a pair of winged sandals, and Hades' helmet of invisibility—were kept.

Stymphalian Birds Large, man-eating birds with brazen wings, beaks, and claws, the Stymphalian Birds were the subject of Heracles' sixth labor. Named for the Stymphalian Marsh near Mount Cyllene, where they took up residence, the Birds were blamed for ruining the region's crops. Heracles drove the Birds off to the Isle of Ares in the Black Sea, and some escaped to the Arabian Desert. In some versions of this labor of Heracles, the Birds are personified as women and are said to be the daughters of Stymphalus and Ornis.

Styx A nymph conceived on Persephone by Zeus during the rampage that followed his fight with Rhea, Styx was said to have perched atop the pillar to which the Aloeides were bound in Tartarus to remind them of their crimes.

In some versions, Styx is the daughter of Oceanus who aided Zeus in his battle with the Titans. She consequently was honored as the protector of oaths and became the goddess of the river Styx, which surrounds Hades.

Syrinx A chaste female who was pursued by Pan. To escape Pan, Syrinx turned herself into a reed in the river Ladon. When Pan could not identify which one she was, he cut several and made them into his trademark instrument, the panpipe.

> *…she ran, ran till*
> *She caught herself up short at Ladon river…;*
> *There, shaken at the sight of Pan behind her,*
> *She begged the sisters of the stream to change*
> *A hamadryad's figure into less*

> *Alluring shape to hasty gods like Pan,*
> *Who as he seized her held a sheaf of reeds…*
> —The Metamorphoses, *Ovid*

Talos The son of Daedalus' sister, Polycaste, Talos is occasionally described as the father of Hephaestus.

During his apprenticeship with his uncle, Talos is said to have invented the saw, the potter's wheel, and the compass, and was considered by some to have exceeded his uncle in skill. When Daedalus grew extremely jealous, he pushed Talos to his death from a roof, and claimed that he was motivated by the allegations that Talos had been having an incestuous affair with his mother, Polycaste.

Talos was also the name of the bronze, bull-headed sentinel, created by Hephaestus, that Zeus gave to Minos to protect the southern shore of Crete. The guardian killed many Sardinians, but met its match when the Argonauts encountered it. Medea told Talos that she possessed a potion that would make him immortal, which she would give him in exchange for safe passage.

The potion made Talos fall asleep, and Medea sneaked up to Talos and removed the pin that kept his vital juices contained within the single vein that ran the length of his

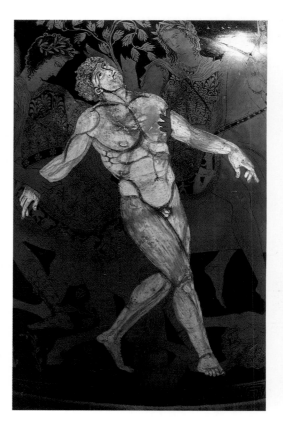

The Death of Talos, **red-figured krater, 5th century** B.C.

bronze body. Talos "bled" to death, and the *Argo* continued its journey.

In some versions it is suggested that Talos was attracted to Medea, and accidentally knocked his own stopper out when he bumped into a rock, and in one story one of the Argonauts, Poeas, shoots an arrow that hits Talos in the heel and kills him.

> . . .*Talos, for all his brazen fame, was brought down by the force of Medea's magic. He was hoisting up some heavy stones with which to keep them from the anchorage, when he grazed his ankle on a sharp rock and the ichor ran out of him like molten lead. He stood there for a short time, high on the jutting cliff. But even his strong legs could not support him long; he began to sway, all power went out of him, and he came down with a resounding crash.*
> —The Voyage of Argo, Apollonius of Rhodes

Tantalus

Thought to be the son of Pluto and either Zeus or Tmolus, Tantalus may have been the King of Argos, Corinth, or Paphlagonia. His wife is often listed as being Euryanassa, although Eurythemista, Clytia, and Dione are also possible candidates. Tantalus is also said to be the father of Pelops, who may actually have been the son of Atlas and Linos, Niobe, or Broteas.

A friend and confidant of Zeus, Tantalus first fell into disfavor by sharing Olympus' divine nectar and ambrosia with mortals. In an attempt to propitiate the gods, Tantalus held a banquet for them on Mount Sipylus. Discovering that he was running short of food, Tantalus killed and butchered Pelops and served him to the gods.

Except for Demeter, who was still distracted by the recent kidnapping of her daughter, Core, all of the gods quickly realized what Tantalus had done. Subsequently Tantalus' kingdom was laid waste, and Tantalus was killed by Zeus and subjected to eternal punishment: he was suspended from a fruit tree and made to suffer eternal thirst and hunger. The fruits are kept just out of reach, and the river above which he is hung never rises high enough to allow him to slake his thirst.

In addition to this aspect of Tantalus' torment, there is an enormous stone from Mount Sipylus that hangs perilously above his head. This is said to be payment for Tantalus' role in the theft of the golden mastiff Hephaestus had fashioned to protect the infant Zeus.

Tecmessa

A daughter of the Phrygian King Teleutas, Tecmessa was claimed by Great Ajax as an early spoil of the Trojan War.

Tantalus in the Underworld, **vasepainting, 4th century** B.C.

Tecmessa became Ajax's concubine, and bore Eurysaces during that time. Tecmessa attempted to temper Ajax's madness when he was denied a share of Achilles' armor, but could not prevent him from taking his own life. Tecmessa joined Teucer, Ajax's half-brother, in the search for Ajax's corpse, which she covered with her robe once they had found it.

Teiresias

The son of Everes and Chariclo, Teiresias was out hunting one day when he accidentally came upon Athene bathing. Athene, a modest goddess, reacted by blinding Teiresias instantly. Since Chariclo was one of her companions and Teiresias had not meant to see her, Athene compensated Teiresias, with the help of Erichthonius, by giving him inward sight. It is said that Teiresias spent some time as a woman after seeing snakes couple on Mount Cyllene. When Teiresias killed the female, he changed gender, and when seven years later he encountered another pair of snakes, he killed the male and was transformed back into a male.

In some versions a very different explanation is offered for Teiresias' becoming a seer and experiencing gender transformation. In these accounts, Teiresias is made to decide who is the most beautiful of the three Charites and Aphrodite. When Teiresias chose Cale,

Odysseus and Teiresias, **red-figured vase, 5th century** B.C.

one of the Charites, as the most beautiful, Aphrodite turned him into an old woman. Later, Hera and Zeus argued over which of the sexes received greater pleasure from lovemaking and, because he had spent time as each sex, decided to let Teiresias resolve the issue. Teiresias proclaimed that nine tenths of the pleasure from sex was the woman's, in response to which Hera, who had argued that men received the greatest pleasure, blinded him. In compensation, Zeus then granted him inward sight and a long life.

Teiresias eventually became one of the most famous and prominent seers in all of mythology, and many Greek dramas included him as a helpful foreshadowing device.

Teiresias figures quite prominently in Sophocles' dramatization of Oedipus' tragedy. When Oedipus was insistently trying to uncover the reasons for his predicament, Teiresias was hesitant to reveal the facts since he knew they would ruin Oedipus, not to mention anger him greatly. Oedipus assumed that Teiresias was misleading him for other reasons and became abusive toward the seer, who

eventually revealed the truth of Oedipus' parentage. In *Oedipus the King*, Teiresias warns Oedipus that "This day shall show your birth and shall bring you ruin," and later reveals that Oedipus is "the slayer of the man [Laius] whose slayer you seek."

The nature of Teiresias' death is uncertain, but his ghost was present in Tartarus by the time Odysseus made his visit to the underworld. Among the warnings Teiresias gave Odysseus were those concerning Hyperion's cattle in Sicily and the current goings-on in Ithaca.

Telamon

The brother of Peleus and the son of Aeacus and Endeis. Aeacus was also the father of Phocus by another partner, the Nereid Psamathe, which caused Phocus to be the target of Endeis' jealousy. After Phocus was murdered, Telamon proclaimed his innocence only after having taken refuge on Salamis. Aeacus permitted Telamon to argue his case from a ship off the coast of Oenone, but found Telamon's defense insufficient and informed his son that he should return to Salamis.

In Salamis, Telamon married Glauce and eventually succeeded her father, Cychereus, to the throne. Telamon represented Salamis in the hunt for the Calydonian Boar, during which he tripped on a tree root and was rescued from the charging beast by Peleus, Atalanta, or both. After Glauce's death, Telamon married Periboea, with whom he conceived Great Ajax.

Telamon was an ally of Heracles, whom he accompanied on his ninth labor. On their way back from accomplishing this labor, Telamon and Heracles came upon Laomedon's daughter Hesione chained naked to a rock on the coast of Troy, awaiting sacrifice. Heracles and Telamon rescued Hesione, which led to a battle with Laomedon and his forces. When Heracles' side prevailed, he gave Hesione to Telamon.

Telamon took Hesione back to Greece with him, where he fathered Teucer upon her. The Trojans objected to what they perceived as her abduction, and this became the initial conflict in a series of events that eventually led to the Trojan War.

After Ajax committed suicide and Teucer returned without his remains, and without Ajax's wife and son, Telamon refused to let Teucer's ship dock. He forced Teucer to plead his case from the deck of his ship, as he himself had once been made to do; and like his father before him, Telamon ruled against his son, declaring that Teucer was guilty for having failed to support Ajax's claims, as well as for

his failure to bring back his remains and surviving family.

Telchines

Nine dog-headed, flippered Children of the Sea who were entrusted by Rhea to young Poseidon, the Telchines forged the latter's trident and made the toothed sickle that Cronus used to castrate Uranus.

The Telchines originated in Rhodes, and founded several cities across the island. They were also said to have been the first inhabitants of Crete. When Zeus grew tired of their meddling with the forces of nature and weather, he decided to flood their lands. Artemis warned the Telchines, and they scattered throughout the Mediterranean. Some went to Teumessus, where they built a temple to Athene, while others went to Orchomenus, where they tore Actaeon to pieces. In the end, most were destroyed by Zeus' floods, and many others succumbed to Apollo in the form of a wolf. A handful, however, were rumored to have survived in Sicyon.

Telegonus

The last of three sons born to Odysseus and Circe during the former's stay on Aeaea. When Telegonus set out to find his father, he and his crew raided Ithaca, having mistaken it for Corcyra. Telegonus fulfilled Teiresias' warning that Odysseus' death would come from the sea when, using a spear made of the spine of a stingray, he mortally wounded his own father.

Despite the accidental nature of the killing, Telegonus was banished from Ithaca for a year. Once the year passed Telegonus returned and married his father's widow, Penelope. At the same time, Odysseus and Penelope's son Telemachus married Circe, thus uniting two separate branches of Odysseus' family tree.

Telemachus

The son of Odysseus and Penelope, Telemachus was an infant when the Trojan War broke out. When Odysseus was warned that it would take him twenty years to return home if he went to Troy, he feigned insanity when Agamemnon's allies came to enlist his support. The allies did not believe that Odysseus was truly mad, and Palamedes forced Odysseus to reveal his clarity of mind by threatening the life of Telemachus.

Telemachus grew to manhood during his father's absence, and grew increasingly distressed by the presence of the suitors who tried to convince his mother to accept that Odysseus was not coming back and that she should marry one of them. When Telemachus heard of Menelaus' return from Troy he went off to Sparta to see if there was any news concerning his father. While in Sparta, Telemachus was instructed by Athene to return to Ithaca as soon as possible; she also directed him safely past an ambush set by Penelope's suitors.

When Telemachus returned to Ithaca, he landed near the hut of Eumaeus. There Telemachus encountered an old beggar who eventually revealed himself to be Odysseus in disguise. Father and son shared a touching reunion, but kept Odysseus' secret between themselves. Telemachus returned home as if nothing had happened, and Odysseus followed closely behind, disguised once again as a beggar. The next day, after Odysseus revealed himself, Telemachus fought alongside his father in the ensuing battle.

After the relatives of the slain suitors brought legal action against Odysseus, and Odysseus was banished from Ithaca for another ten years, Telemachus assumed his father's throne. When an oracular warning suggested that Odysseus would be killed by his own son, the Ithacans assumed that this referred to Telemachus and banished him to Cephallenia.

The prophesy actually referred to Telemachus' half-brother Telegonus, who, after a year-long banishment from Ithaca, returned and married Penelope. At the same time, Telemachus married Telegonus' mother, Circe, thus uniting two branches of Odysseus' family.

Hercules Finding His Son Telephus,
Roman wallpainting, A.D. **1st century.**

Telephus

The illegitimate son of Auge and Heracles. When an oracle warned Auge's father, Aleus, that the son she was carrying would grow to kill her maternal uncles (Neaera's brothers), Auge was sold into slavery. Along the way to Teuthras, her new owner, she delivered Telephus on Mount Parthenius, where he was abandoned.

Telephus was suckled by a doe and eventually rescued, at which time he was entrusted to King Corythus. Telephus grew to manhood under Corythus' care, until an oracle told him to seek out Teuthras the Mysian, to whom Auge had been sold.

When Telephus reached Mysia, he found Teuthras and Auge happily married, and was himself given Teuthras' daughter, Argiope, in marriage and made heir to the kingdom. In other versions, however, it is suggested that Teuthras welcomed Telephus into the family to secure his support for Teuthras' defense of his kingdom against Idas. In still other versions Auge becomes Teuthras' stepdaughter and is the one offered to Telephus in exchange for his allegiance. In these versions, Auge and Telephus are about to commit incest when they recognize one another as mother and son.

Ulysses and Telemachus, **Roman mosaic,** A.D. **1st century.**

**Telephus and His Companions in Mysia,
from the frieze of the Zeus Altar of
Pergamon, 2nd century** B.C.

Once Telephus assumed control of Mysia, he was forced to defend it against Odysseus, who attacked thinking that he had reached nearby Troy. The Greeks were repelled, but Telephus was wounded when he tripped on a vine, leaving him vulnerable to Achilles, whose spear cut through Telephus' thigh. Telephus' wound festered, and an oracle suggested that only the instrument that caused the wound would be able to cure it. So Telephus got Clytaemnestra to make a deal with Agamemnon, who promised to cure Telephus in exchange for his allegiance against the Trojans. Telephus helped the Greeks reach Troy safely, but would not take up arms since his wife, whose name is given alternately as Laodice, Hiera, and Astyoche, was said to be a daughter of King Priam.

Tenes The son of Cycnus and Procleia (though it is suggested that Apollo may have been Tenes' true father). When Cycnus took Phylonome as his second wife, she became attracted to her stepson, Tenes. When Tenes spurned her, Phylonome told Cycnus that he

had tried to violate her. Cycnus believed his new wife and banished Tenes, as well as Tenes' sister Hemithea. Tenes eventually settled and ruled over Tenedos, and Cycnus eventually learned the truth regarding Phylonome's claims against Tenes. Cycnus divorced Phylonome and set out to apologize to his children. At first Tenes was unforgiving, but he eventually accepted Cycnus' apologies and established a home for his father nearby.

When the Greeks passed Tenedos on their way to Troy and Tenes hurled boulders at their ships, Achilles responded by killing him.

Tereus A son of Ares, Tereus acted as a mediator for Pandion and subsequently married his daughter, Procne. She bore him a son, Itys, whom it was prophesied would die by a relative's hands. Eventually, Tereus came to fall in love with Procne's younger sister, Philomela. He imprisoned Procne, led her sister to believe she had died, and had his way with her. Shortly thereafter, Tereus went out and killed his brother Dryas, whom he suspected of plotting to kill Itys in fulfillment of the prophecy. Taking advantage of Tereus' absence, Procne wove a message into some needlework (Tereus had cut out her tongue to keep her from crying out for help) to alert Philomela, who freed her. Procne then killed Itys, and served pieces of him to Tereus upon his return. Tereus chased after the sisters with murderous intent until the gods turned them all into birds. Tereus is said to have been turned into either a hoopoe or a hawk.

Teucer The name of two characters, one of whom was instrumental in the establishment of the city of Troy and the other of whom contributed to its downfall. The first Teucer was a son of Scamander and the nymph Idaea. In some versions, Scamander is described as founding one of the earliest settlements that would become part of Troy and Teucer is described as succeeding him. In other versions, however, Teucer is welcomed by Dardanus to Phrygia, and proceeds from there, along with Dardanus' daughter, to settle the fledgling Trojan community on his own.

The other Teucer was the son of Telamon and Hesione and the half-brother of Great Ajax, one of the best of the Greek warriors. Teucer was considered to be the best archer in all of Greece and often fought in tandem with Ajax, hiding behind his half-brother's shield before darting out and launching his well-aimed arrows. Teucer is also credited with winning the archery competition held at the funeral games for Achilles.

When Ajax committed suicide, Teucer was away in Mysia. When he returned, Zeus informed him of Ajax's fate, and directed Teucer and Ajax's wife, Tecmessa, to his corpse. After learning that Agamemnon had decreed that Ajax would not be allowed an honorable cremation, but should be left as carrion, Teucer left Tecmessa and Ajax's son, Eurysaces, to guard the body while he angrily petitioned Agamemnon. In the end, Agamemnon permitted Ajax to be buried in a coffin, the standard procedure with suicides. Odysseus offered to assist Teucer, who politely declined, probably because of Odysseus' part in Ajax's death.

Teucer left a few short locks of his hair on Ajax's grave and headed back to Salamis, where he was blamed for not supporting Ajax's claims on Achilles' armor, as well as for having left a vainly small amount of hair. There were also claims that he failed to bring Tecmessa and Eurysaces home with him. Teucer was forced to defend himself against these charges from his ship while the judges listened from shore. The judges ruled against Teucer, who was then banished. He received the assistance of King Belus of Sidon and went to Cyprus, where he founded his own Salamis.

Teumessian Vixen A creature that harassed Theban subjects until King Creon enlisted Amphitryon to kill it. The Vixen was fated never to be caught, however, so when Amphitryon sent Laelaps the hound, who was fated to catch any quarry he chased, after it, a paradox resulted. To circumvent this paradox, Zeus turned both creatures to stone.

Teuthras The son of Leucippe, Teuthras was the King of Teuthrania, the Mysian city named for him. Teuthras is best known for purchasing a slave named Auge, who turned out to be the daughter of Aleus and the mother of Telephus by Heracles. When Telephus came looking for his mother, he found her happily married to Teuthras, who offered his own daughter, Argiope, to Telephus in marriage, and subsequently made Telephus his heir.

There are some versions in which Teuthras presented Auge as his stepdaughter, and told Telephus that he could marry her if he protected Teuthrania from Idas' forces. Telephus was successful defending Teuthras' kingdom, and realized just before marrying her that his betrothed was in fact his mother.

Teuthras' story is sometimes extended to include an incident in which he angered the goddess Artemis by killing a boar in her temple. Artemis punished Teuthras by giving him leprous scabs and making him crazy. At some point his mother, Leucippe, had the seer Polyeidus tell her how she could appease Artemis, who eventually allowed Teuthras to be cured.

Teuthras was eventually killed by Great Ajax during the course of the Trojan War.

Thamyris
One of the preeminent musicians of his day and a poet who was one of the first to proposition one of his own sex, the beautiful young Hyacinthus, Thamyris was slain by Apollo. Thamyris, along with Minos and Laius, is considered one of the first pederasts.

Thea
The daughter of Cheiron. Shortly after Thea (also known as Thetis) and Poseidon coupled in the form of horses (in which form Thea was known as Euippe), Thea dropped a foal, Melanippe. Poseidon eventually transformed this foal into a baby girl who was named Arne and became the mother of Aeolus and Boeotus.

Theano
The wife of Metapontus, the King of Icaria. Theano's marriage (and life) were in jeopardy when it appeared that she was barren. Metapontus warned her that if they did not have children soon she would be sent away. Around that time a shepherd brought the foundlings Aeolus and Boeotus to Theano, who announced that they were her own. Metapontus was happy, and shortly thereafter Theano became pregnant with children of her own, another set of twins.

Theano eventually grew jealous of Metapontus' preference for Aeolus and Boeotus (over their own sons). She could not reveal these emotions to Metapontus, who still believed the foundlings to be his own progeny, and instead conspired with her sons to kill Aeolus and Boeotus. Their attempt was unsuccessful, and resulted in the deaths of the younger twins. When Theano saw the foundlings carrying her dead sons back to the palace she stabbed herself to death with a hunting knife.

Theia
A Titaness created by Eurynome to rule over the Sun with Hyperion as her partner. One of the Planetary Powers, Theia and Hyperion are said to be the parents of Eos, Selene, and Helius, who drove the Sun across the sky each day.

Theia is also paired with Oceanus as the mother of twins, alternatively named Passalus and Acmon, Olus and Eurybatus, and Triballus and Sillus, who became known as the Ephesian Cercopes.

The Goddess Themis, **Chairestratos, 3rd century** B.C.

Themis
One of the Titanesses created by Eurynome to serve, along with Eurymedon, as the Planetary Power overseeing Jupiter, Themis was also the Great Goddess who ordered the year into the thirteen-month calendar employed by the Greeks. During the course of Zeus' debauchery following his fight with Rhea, he fathered the Seasons and the three Fates on Themis.

When Poseidon wished to marry Thetis the Nereid, Themis prophesied that any child born to them would grow to overthrow his father. As a result, Poseidon instead had Thetis to marry Peleus, a mortal. Thetis helped rear Apollo, and was sent by Zeus to Deucalion (following the flood that bears his name) to help him and his wife, Pyrrha, repopulate the earth.

Theonoë
A sister of Leucippe and Calchas, and the daughter of Thestor, Theonoë was kidnapped by Carian pirates and later became King Icarus' mistress and prisoner. When Thestor set out to rescue his daughter, he too became Icarus' prisoner.

Years later, Leucippe, who had been a child when Theonoë disappeared, was instructed by an oracle to visit Icarus' kingdom in disguise. First Thestor and Leucippe encountered and recognized one another, and later Theonoë also was reunited with her father and sister. King Icarus was moved by the reunion and sent the three home laden with presents.

Thersander
The son of Polyneices, Thersander copied his father's ploy of bribing Eriphyle with one of Harmonia's divine wedding presents. Thersander gave Eriphyle a divine robe in payment for her convincing Alcmaeon to lead the Epigoni to avenge Polyneices' death. Later, Thersander made the mistake of bragging that he was responsible for the Epigoni's success, and was overheard by Alcmaeon, who in this way learned of his bribing Eriphyle. Alcmaeon killed Eriphyle for her treachery.

When Odysseus was marshalling forces to march on Troy, Thersander joined and participated in a premature attack in which Mysia was mistaken for the outskirts of Troy. The Mysians and their king, Telephus, turned back all of the Greeks except Thersander, who stood his ground. Thersander was killed in the fighting that followed. Thersander was buried in Elaea, and was succeeded by his son Tisamenus, who assumed command of the Boeotian forces marching on Troy.

Theseus
The son of Aethra and Poseidon, Theseus is sometimes known as the Athenian Heracles, based on the tasks he accomplished and his preeminence in any list of Attic heroes.

Shortly after Aegeus lay with Aethra, Poseidon did so as well, but the god graciously deferred any claims of paternity to Aegeus, who kept the birth of the son that was born to Aethra a secret. Aegeus worried that his nephews (the fifty sons of Pallas) might harm the child who would become Aegeus' heir in their place.

The infant Theseus was entrusted to Aethra's father, Pittheus, who raised him in Troezen. Theseus became a strong, intelligent, and prudent youth, and was eventually told the truth of his conception and birth. When the time had come for Theseus to travel to Athens and make his existence known as

History of Theseus, **panel painting, Italian, 15th century.**

Aegeus' rightful heir, Aethra and Pittheus warned him not to make the journey overland. Theseus insisted on making the trip on foot, in emulation of similar journeys made by Heracles.

The road between the two cities was a dangerous one, and Theseus vowed to make it safe. He instigated no battles along the way, but promised to treat in kind any who attempted to harm him. When Theseus encountered Periphetes, he killed the murderer with his own club, a weapon that Theseus carried with him for the rest of his life. Theseus then killed Sinis and chased after his daughter, Perigune, on whom he fathered Melanippus. Cercyon, who took pleasure in dropping people on their heads, was himself dropped upon his head, for which Theseus is often credited with inventing the art of wrestling. Theseus then went to Corydallus, where he killed Sinis' father, Polypemon.

After completing his self-assigned task, Theseus went to be purified by the sons of Phytalus alongside the river Cephissus. He then proceeded to Athens and his father Aegeus' palace. Aegeus' new wife, the troublesome Medea, was jealous of Theseus, who was the heir to Aegeus' throne, displacing Medus, Medea's son by Aegeus. Medea attempted to poison Theseus, but Aegeus prevented it at the last moment. Aegeus celebrated his reunion

with Theseus with an enormous banquet that ended with Theseus chasing after Medea for having tried to kill him.

After Theseus was warned of a trap being set by the sons of Pallas, Theseus ambushed them and killed half of Pallas' fifty sons. Pallas surrendered and Aegeus' throne was, for the time being, secure.

Once things settled down in Athens, Theseus went and captured the ferocious white bull Poseidon had unleashed on the region from Argos to Marathon. Theseus seized the bull by its horns and dragged it throughout Athens.

Theseus is also said to have confronted Minos over the sacrifices he demanded that Athens make to the Minotaur. In the second or third year that the sacrifices were to be made, Theseus volunteered to be one of them on the condition that the sacrifices be ended if he could conquer the Minotaur barehanded.

Theseus beseeched Aphrodite to join him on the journey to Crete, and she aided him by causing Minos' daughter, Ariadne, to fall in love with him. With Ariadne's help, Theseus found his way through the Labyrinth in which the Minotaur was hidden and eventually overcame the beast. Theseus then left Crete, bringing with him both the intended sacrifices and Ariadne, whom he abandoned on the island of Dia (later known as Naxos).

There are countless variations on the entire chain of events regarding Theseus' voyage to Crete and his battle with the Minotaur, who is occasionally personified in the form of one of Minos' generals, Taurus. In some versions Minos dies at sea chasing after Theseus' ship, and in some Ariadne dies in childbirth on Naxos.

On his return to Athens, Theseus forgot to hoist the white sails that would signal the successful completion of his tasks. When Aegeus saw the black sails that had accidentally been left up, he either fell or leapt to his death into the sea that still bears his name. It was said that this tragic mistake was Ariadne's revenge on Theseus for leaving her behind.

Theseus assumed Aegeus' throne, and quickly consolidated control by executing the majority of his opponents. During his reign, Theseus was perceived by many of his subjects to be a ruthless, evil man. Acts like the abduction of Anaxo and his many affairs greatly embarrassed his fellow Athenians. After a few generations, however, as his personal habits were forgotten, Theseus' political accomplishments came to be considered great. He was credited with federalizing the Attic peninsula and centering control over the region in Athens, encouraging the city's development as a metropolis. Theseus is said to have been the first king to found a commonwealth, and is also credited with becoming the first Athenian to employ printed currency.

Theseus later fought the Amazons (alongside either Heracles or Peirithous) and abducted Antiope, whose sister, Oreithyia, swore revenge against him. Oreithyia led the Amazons in an attack on Athens, but Theseus engaged the skilled warriors in a long battle that ended with the Amazons offering to make peace. It was the first time Athens had ever repulsed a foreign invasion, and an indication of the strength of the system Theseus had established during the course of his reign.

Following his battle with the Amazons, Theseus prepared to marry Phaedra, the sister of King Deucalion. The marriage was arranged for political reasons, which did not assuage Antiope, who felt wronged since she had conceived a son, Hippolytus, with Theseus, and had never lain with another man. Antiope came to the wedding and battled the guests until Theseus was forced to kill her.

Some time later Phaedra managed to anger Artemis, who punished her by causing Phaedra to fall in love with her stepson, Hippolytus. When Hippolytus rejected Phaedra, she accused him of trying to ravish her. Theseus responded by banishing Hippolytus, and used up one of the three wishes Poseidon had given him by wishing that Hippolytus would die that very day. Hippolytus was killed in a chariot wreck, but was subsequently revived by Asclepius at Artemis' direction. Theseus learned what had really hap-

Theseus and Procrustes, red-figured bell krater, 5th century B.C.

pened and begged Hippolytus to return to Athens and live with him again, but Hippolytus refused.

When the truth regarding Phaedra's lies about Hippolytus became known, Phaedra hanged herself. At this point, Theseus and Peirithous set out to abduct the young Helen. Helen was successfully abducted, and Theseus and Peirithous drew lots to see who would marry her when she became old enough. Theseus won, and this eventually led to Theseus and Peirithous being captured in Hades' Chairs of Forgetfulness, from which they could not extricate themselves without fatal self-mutilation. As long as they remained in the chairs, the two were constantly attacked by the Furies, Cerberus, and countless serpents.

More than four years passed before Heracles, in the course of his twelfth labor, recognized Theseus and pulled him from the Chair of Forgetfulness, leaving behind a good deal of flesh. In most versions Heracles leaves Peirithous behind, since he was the cause of their being trapped by Hades, but in some he also is freed.

When Theseus finally returned from Tartarus, he discovered that the Dioscuri had taken control of Athens and established Menestheus as their regent. Theseus took his children to Euboea, where Elpenor sheltered them, and then headed off to Crete, where Deucalion had promised him refuge. A storm blew Theseus' ship to Scyros, where King

Lycomedes, an ally of Menestheus, pushed Theseus from a cliff, claiming it was a drunken accident.

It was said that Theseus' spirit inspired the Athenian troops during the course of the Battle of Marathon, and that Theseus' bones were eventually brought back to Athens by Cimon.

There are scores of other attributes and accomplishments credited to Theseus. He was said to have been a skilled lyre player, and a patron—along with Heracles and Hermes—of gymnasiums and wrestling schools. During the course of his reign in Athens, Theseus helped avenge the champions who fell at Thebes, defeating Creon in the process. Theseus is credited with giving a proper burial to Oedipus after he was hounded to death by the Erinnyes, and after Heracles' apotheosis, Theseus remained allied with the Heraclids, whom he supported after Eurystheus attempted to expel them from Greece.

Stung by the pricks of that goddess most hateful to us who delight in virginity, your wife became enamored of your son. . . As became a righteous man, he yielded not to her proposals. But neither did he repudiate the oath he had sworn, though vilely treated by you, for a pious man he was. But she feared an investigation, and wrote lying writings, and destroyed your son by guile. Yet you believed her.

—Artemis, Hippolytus, *Euripides*

Theseus Killing the Minotaur, Roman floor mosaic, A.D. 4th century.

Thestius

A King of Aetolia, Thestius was closely allied with Heracles. Thestius was a neighbor of Amphitryon and the husband of Megamede, with whom he is said to have conceived fifty daughters, the eldest of whom was Procris.

When Heracles slew the Lion of Cithaeron, Thestius implored his daughters to grant their favors to their savior, and all but one complied. Later, Thestius purified Heracles after Hera brought about the insane rage that caused Heracles to kill his own family. And it was at Hera's directions that Thestius sent his sons to colonize Thebes and Sardinia.

Thestor

A son of Idmon the Argonaut, Thestor was the father of Calchas, Theonoë, and Leucippe. When his daughter Theonoë was kidnapped by Carian pirates, Thestor went in search of her, little knowing that she had become the prisoner and mistress of King Icarus. During the search, he also became a prisoner of King Icarus. Thestor and Theonoë were eventually freed when Leucippe came to their aid.

Thetis

A Nereid who is sometimes described as the daughter of Cheiron and a mortal woman, although Cheiron is accused of trying to claim that her mother was a deity. More often, Thetis' parents are said to have been Nereus and Doris. Thetis had fifty attendants who were known collectively as the Nereids.

Thetis was courted by Poseidon and/or Zeus until it was prophesied that a child of hers would grow to outshine its father. When the Olympians decided that Thetis should marry a mortal instead, they instructed Peleus to claim her. Thetis resisted Peleus by changing forms, transforming herself into many creatures, but Peleus maintained his grasp upon her and Thetis eventually yielded to his passionate embrace.

Hera was relieved that Zeus had not slept with Thetis and personally hosted the wedding that followed, which took place on Mount Pelion and was attended by nearly all of the Olympians. Unfortunately, Eris was not invited to the event, and sought to avenge this slight by tossing into the crowd a golden apple with the inscription "To the Fairest." This caused an argument between Hera, Aphrodite, and Athene that led to Paris running away with Helen.

Thetis became best known for the events that surrounded the birth, life, and death of her most famous child, Achilles. Thetis and Peleus had had six sons before Achilles, each of whom had been destroyed during Thetis' attempts to make them immortal by burning off their mortal parts in the hope of leaving only the immortal. When Peleus discovered her trying to make Achilles immortal via the same process, he snatched the infant away moments before the process would have been finished. All of Achilles had been made immortal, with the exception of one heel, which remained vulnerable. (In some versions it is suggested that Thetis dipped the infant Achilles in the river Styx to make him invulnerable, and that the portion of his heel left vulnerable was where she had held him.)

Thetis was so angry with Peleus that she disowned the child and refused to let it feed from her breast. The boy was named Achilles, a name that refers to the fact that the child's lips never touched his mother's breast. Achilles was entrusted to Cheiron the Centaur for upbringing, but Thetis kept an eye on her son as he grew older. When the Trojan War became inevitable, she became wary because of her knowledge that Achilles would be a hero if he went to Troy, but just as surely would die before the fighting had ended. Thetis wished to prevent her son's death, and attempted to disguise him.

After Achilles was discovered by the Greek leaders, Thetis resigned herself to her son's fate, but gave him two warnings: the first Greek to step ashore at Troy was sure to die, and if Achilles ever killed one of Apollo's sons, Apollo was sure to kill him.

Thetis aided Achilles as much as possible during the course of the war. She brought him new armor when he rejoined the battle, knowing all along that he would die before the war ended. When Paris' arrow mortally wounded Achilles, Thetis, the Muses, and many of the Greek warriors mourned him for seventeen days. On the eighteenth, he was cremated and his ashes were mixed with those of his companion, Patroclus. Thetis is said to have snatched Achilles' soul from the pyre and brought it to the island of Leuce.

"Now you will not have forgotten that I brought you up myself and loved you more than any other Lady of the Sea because you rejected the amorous advances of my consort Zeus. . . . But you were frightened and out of your regard for me you would not let him have his will. In return for which he took a solemn oath that you should never be the bride of an immortal god. Yet in spite of your refusal he did not cease to keep his eye on you, till the day when the venerable Themis made him understand that you were destined to bear a son who would be greater than his father. When he heard this, Zeus gave you up though he still desired you. He wished to keep his power for ever. . . . Then, in the hope of making you a happy bride and mother, I chose Peleus, the noblest man alive, to be your husband."

—Hera, *The Voyage of Argo,*
Apollonius of Rhodes

Thoas

The name Thoas, which translates to mean either "impetuous" or "nimble," was given to a large number of mythological characters. The first Thoas was one of the giants who challenged Zeus and the Olympians.

Another Thoas was a child of Ariadne and Dionysus who was King of the Taurians when Orestes came to retrieve the wooden image of Artemis. King Thoas planned to sacrifice Orestes and his companion, Pylades, but Iphigeneia, who had been serving as a priestess in a Taurian temple, helped them escape with their lives and the statue.

Thoas was also the name of Hypsipyle's father, the King of Lemnos. Hypsipyle spared Thoas' life when the Lemnian Women killed all the men on their island. Thoas escaped by sea, and Hypsipyle was sold into slavery when her treachery was revealed.

Thyestes

A son of Pelops and Hippodameia, Thyestes was Atreus' twin brother. The two were enlisted by their broth-

Thetis Bringing Weapons to Achilles,
red-figured krater, 5th century B.C.

King Thoas, engraving, 1894.

er-in-law, Sthenelus, to guard his Mycenaean kingdom while he and Eurystheus continued their battle with Amphitryon. Eurystheus was killed in battle, and Sthenelus either succumbed to his advanced years or was also killed in battle.

This left Thyestes and Atreus in control of the kingdom, and fulfilled the prophesy that said they were fated to fight for succession to a throne. While the brothers were trying to wrest the throne from one another, Atreus came into possession of a gold-fleeced, horned lamb of divine origins. Atreus put the animal's stuffed and mounted remains in hiding, and proclaimed that anyone who might produce such a divine object should surely be given full control over the throne.

Atreus did not know, however, that his wife, Aerope, was secretly in love with Thyestes, and had promised to steal the animal for him in return for his affections. The day after Atreus' statement, Thyestes produced the divine lamb and was made king.

In response, Atreus claimed that anyone who could make the sun set in the east the next day should be king. With the help of Zeus and Eris, who convinced Helius to ride his chariot backwards this one time, Atreus regained control of the Mycenaean throne, and banished Thyestes.

When Atreus finally learned about Aerope and Thyestes' treachery, he invited his brother back to Mycenae, and welcomed him with a great banquet. Atreus killed three of Thyestes' sons—Aglaus, Orchomenus, and Callileon—and a Naiad, and served them to him. Only when Thyestes was finished did

Atreus tell him what he had eaten, for which Thyestes cast a curse upon him.

After Thyestes was again banished, he went to Sicyon, where he raped his daughter Pelopia and immediately fled. Atreus arrived in Sicyon shortly thereafter, and met Pelopia, whom he mistook to be Thesprotus' daughter. Atreus married Pelopia and brought her back with him to Mycenae, where she gave birth to a son whom he believed to be his, but was in fact Thyestes'. When the child, Aegisthus, had grown to the age of seven, Atreus lured Thyestes back to Mycenae and imprisoned him. Atreus sent Aegisthus to kill the prisoner, but Thyestes survived.

Thyestes then revealed the whole truth to Pelopia, who immediately killed herself. Thyestes then sent his son to kill Atreus, and in this way regained control of the Mycenaean throne.

Thyestes was eventually forced to relinquish the throne when Agamemnon and Menelaus, with the support of King Tyndareus and his armies, demanded he do so.

The feud between Thyestes and Atreus passed on to the next generation when Thyestes' son, Aegisthus, allied with Clytaemnestra to kill Atreus' son, Agamemnon.

[Thyestes], in ignorance,
At once took that which prompted no close
*   scrutiny,*

And tasted food from which, as you now see,
*   our house*
Has not recovered. Then he recognized, in all
Its loathsomeness, what had been done. With
*   one deep groan,*
Back from his chair, vomiting murdered flesh, he
*   fell;*
Cursed Pelops' race with an inexorable curse;
With his foot sent the table crashing wide, and
*   screamed,*
'So crash to ruin the whole house of Tantalus!'
*   —Clytaemnestra, Agamemnon, Aeschylus*

Thymoetes One of Priam and Hecabe's older sons, Thymoetes figured in the circumstances that surrounded the birth of Paris. After it was prophesied that a royal birth on a specific day would lead to the fall of Troy, Priam killed his sister Cilla and her newborn son, Munippus, whose father was Cilla's nephew Thymoetes. Paris was born later that same day.

Titans and Titanesses In the Pelasgian creation myth, a group of beings, referred to as the Planetary Powers, created by Eurynome to oversee the seven known astrological entities. In other versions it is suggested that they were fathered by Uranus upon Mother Earth, who later encouraged their overthrow of Uranus. The pairings of the Titans, and their assigned powers, were as follows: Theia and Hyperion, the Sun; Phoebe and Atlas, the Moon; Dione

Zeus and a Titan, stone engraving, 18th century.

and Crius, Mars; Metis and Coetus, Mercury; Themis and Eurymedon, Jupiter; Tethys and Oceanus, Venus; and Rhea and Cronus, Saturn.

Under Cronus' leadership, the Titans and Titanesses fought against Zeus and his allies, who included Hades, Poseidon, the Cyclopes, and the Hundred-handed Ones. Zeus prevailed, but he spared the Titanesses for the sake of Metis (who had helped him during his overthrow of Cronus) and Mother Earth. The Titans, except for Atlas, were banished to either Tartarus or the British Isles, where they were guarded by the Hundred-handed Ones.

The Titans, severely weakened, later followed Hera's instructions to rip young Dionysus to pieces. The revived Dionysus then allied with the Amazons and defeated the Titans in battle. The Titans are also said to have committed similar savagery on Zeus' son Zagreus, whom they lured out of the Idaean Cave. Athene managed to save Zagreus' heart, bring him back to life, and make him immortal, while Zeus struck all of the Titans dead with his thunderbolts.

Tithonus

Along with his brother Ganymede, Tithonus was abducted by Eos. Zeus took an interest in Ganymede, whom he took from Eos in exchange for making Tithonus immortal. Zeus, however, forgot to include perpetual youth with his gift and Tithonus became increasingly feeble. Eos eventually tired of nursing him and locked him inside her bedroom, where he turned into a cicada, an insect that had always been associated with dawn.

Tityus

One of Zeus' giant offspring, Tityus made the mistake of attacking Leto in one of her sacred groves. Her children, Apollo and Artemis, killed Tityus, and sent him to Tartarus, where he was eternally tortured by being stretched out with his arms and legs secured to the ground—covering acres of the underworld—and having two vultures eat at his liver.

Tlepolemus

A son of Heracles and either Astyoche or Astydameia, Tlepolemus was invited to settle in Argos when the Heraclids were expelled from Greece by Eurystheus. Shortly thereafter, Tlepolemus accidentally killed his great uncle, Licymnius, and fled to Rhodes, where he divided the island into three parts and founded the cities of Lindus, Ialysus, and Cameirus.

As King of Rhodes, Tlepolemus led nine ships to support the Greeks in the Trojan War,

Triptolemus on a Chariot with Winged Serpents, **red-figured kylix, 5th century** B.C.

during which he was killed. In some versions it is suggested that Tlepolemus' wife, Polyxo, avenged his death by sending some of her women disguised as Erinnyes to hang Helen, whom she blamed for having caused the situation that led to her husband's death.

Tmolus

A river god who is best known for his role in judging the musical contest between Apollo and Marsyas, Tmolus wisely awarded the prize to the divine participant, Apollo. (Tmolus is also said to have judged a musical contest between Pan and Apollo.) Tmolus and his wife, Omphale, were the parents of Ares and Theogone.

Triptolemus

One of the sons of King Celeus and Metaneira, Triptolemus reported to Demeter that his brother Eubuleus had seen Hades carrying Core down to Tartarus. Demeter rewarded Triptolemus with seed-corn, a wooden plough, and a serpent-drawn chariot. She sent him all around the world to introduce the art of agriculture wherever possible. Since Triptolemus gave many agricultural lessons on the Rarian Plain, he is sometimes thought to have been a son of King Rarus.

Triton

Part man and part dolphin, Triton was the son of the sea deities Poseidon and Amphitrite. As Poseidon's messenger, Triton had the ability to calm turbulent seas. Triton aided Jason and his Argonauts by directing them to the Tacapae River so that they might return to the Mediterranean.

Troilus

The son of Hecabe and Apollo, Troilus was one of the most popular members of the Trojan alliance. It was said that Troy would survive the Greek attack as long as Troilus reached twenty years of age. Of course, this kind of prophecy had a way of shortening life-spans, and Troilus became the subject of much Greek attention.

Troilus had been in love with Calchas' daughter Briseis, who was caught in Troy at the outbreak of the war. Agamemnon won her release from Priam, and Briseis ended up falling in love with Diomedes, after which Diomedes made every possible effort to kill Troilus.

The circumstances surrounding Troilus' death are uncertain. In some versions it is suggested that Achilles fell in love with young Troilus and killed him when Troilus rejected him. In these versions, Achilles kills Troilus in the same sanctuary in which Achilles was later betrayed by Polyxena. There are also versions in which Troilus set out to avenge the death of Memnon, only to be killed by Achilles. And Achilles' role in Troilus' death is sometimes depicted as an indirect one; that is, the Greek

Triton, Nereids, and a Sea-Antelope, Roman mosaic, A.D. 1st century.

he married Deipyla, Adrastus' daughter. Adrastus promised to return Tydeus to his throne as soon as they had restored Tydeus' brother-in-law Polyneices to his throne in Thebes.

When Adrastus sent Tydeus to inform their Theban enemies of their intentions, Tydeus challenged and successively defeated each of Eteocles' chieftains. Once the battle began in full, however, Tydeus was wounded in the stomach by someone who was also named Melanippus.

Athene, who favored Tydeus, went to obtain an elixir that would cure him; during this time, Amphiaraus, one of Tydeus' more tenuous allies, offered him Melanippus' skull, from which he partook of his enemies' brains. Athene, returning to the scene, dropped the vial of elixir in horror and fled, allowing Tydeus to die.

Tyndareus The son of Gorgophone and Oebalus. Tyndareus and his brother Icarius were Spartan princes who eventually succeeded their father to the throne as co-rulers. The two were eventually expelled from Sparta by Hippocoön and his twelve sons, after which Tyndareus took refuge with King Thestius in Aetolia.

Tyche, Roman copy after Greek original, after 300 B.C.

commander did not slay Troilus himself, but simply ordered his capture and execution.

Tros Successor of his father, Erichthonius, as King of Troy (which was named for him), Tros expanded the realm to include all of Troad. During his marriage to Callirrhoë, Tros fathered Cleopatra the Younger, Ilus the Younger, Assaracus, and Ganymede. He is also said to be the father of Tithonus, although it is not clear who the mother was.

When Zeus abducted Ganymede to join him on Olympus, he had Hermes present Tros with two divine horses and a golden vine fashioned by Hephaestus.

Tyche A daughter of Zeus, Tyche had the power to decide the fortunes of mortals. As such, she is depicted as being completely irresponsible (it is said that she ran about juggling a ball). It was at Tyche's temple that Palamedes dedicated the first set of dice, and it was her assistant Plutus who received the Cornucopia filled with golden fruit from Heracles.

Tydeus The son of Oeneus who was prophesied to die at the hands of his brother Melanippus. Instead, Tydeus "accidentally" killed Melanippus, for which he was banished. He ended up in the court of Adrastus, where

The Castration of Uranus by Cronus, Giorgio Vasari, c. 1555–1559.

Tyndareus married Thestius' daughter Leda, who was the mother of Castor, Clytaemnestra, Helen, and Polydeuces. In most cases, Tyndareus is mentioned as the father of Castor and Clytaemnestra, while Zeus is credited with siring Polydeuces and Helen.

Once Heracles had reestablished Tyndareus as the King of Sparta, Tyndareus helped Agamemnon regain his father's throne. The Dioscuri fought against Agamemnon, while Tyndareus supported the latter and sanctioned his marriage to Clytaemnestra. Despite his sons the Dioscuri being killed in their defense of Thyestes' kingdom, Tyndareus continued to support Agamemnon, and even gave his remaining daughter, the heavily courted Helen, to Agamemnon's brother Menelaus. During the courtship of Helen, Tyndareus took Odysseus' advice that he make all who sought Helen's hand in marriage swear to defend whomever was lucky enough to win it. In repayment for Odysseus' sage advice regarding Helen's suitors, Tyndareus later aided Odysseus in his quest to marry Penelope.

Unfortunately, Tyndareus had neglected Athene during the course of one of his sacrifices years earlier, an act of negligence for which the goddess caused all of his daughters to have ill-fated marriages.

Following the conclusion of the Trojan War, Tyndareus was grieved to learn of Orestes and Electra's murders of Clytaemnestra and Aegisthus. Despite having helped raise Orestes, Tyndareus called for the Athenians to stone Orestes and Electra to death for their crimes. Tyndareus tried to convince Menelaus to join him in his request, but Orestes escaped first. Tyndareus nonetheless continued to press the case against Orestes, and eventually received a hearing before the Areiopagus. Athene cast the deciding vote in Orestes' favor, and Tyndareus returned to Sparta to live out his later years.

Typhon

The product of the union between Mother Earth and Tartarus, which took place when the earth goddess slept with Tartarus to avenge Zeus' annihilation of her sons the giants, Typhon was the largest, most dangerous, and most grotesque of all creatures. Nothing but coiled serpents from the thighs down, Typhon possessed the head of an ass and arms that stretched one hundred leagues in each direction, with serpents' heads where hands should be.

So frightening and intimidating was Typhon that when he rushed Mount Olympus all of the gods ran off to Egypt and hid themselves by assuming the forms of various animals. Only Athene stood firm, and goaded Zeus into action. Zeus struck Typhon with a thunderbolt and used Uranus' castrating sickle to wound the enormous creature.

Typhon retreated to Mount Casius, where he and Zeus resumed their struggle. Typhon got the upper hand and immobilized Zeus by removing all of his sinews. The monster entrusted them to Delphyne, his sister, who was tricked by Pan and Hermes into relinquishing them. These two returned the sinews to Zeus, allowing him to again use his muscles. Typhon and Zeus began hurling mountains at one another, which eventually resulted in Typhon being crushed beneath what is now known as Mount Aetna.

Typhon is credited with fathering the Sphinx on Echidne, with whom he may also have conceived the Lernaean Hydra and Ladon.

> *I pity Typhon, that earth-born destroying giant,*
> *The hundred-headed, native of the Cilician*
> * caves;*
> *I saw him, all his fiery strength subdued by*
> * force.*
> *Against the united gods he stood, his fearful jaws*
> *Hissing forth terror; from his eyes a ghastly glare*
> *Flashed, threatening to annihilate the throne of*
> * Zeus*
> *—Prometheus, Prometheus Bound, Aeschylus*

Tyro

The daughter of Salmoneus and Alcidice, who died during childbirth, Tyro was seduced by her uncle, Sisyphus, as part of his plot against Salmoneus, with whom he was fighting for control of the Thessalian throne. When Tyro became aware of her uncle's true motives, she killed the two sons she had conceived with him.

Tyro went to live with her father and his second wife, Sidero, who blamed her for getting them banished from Thessaly. When Tyro fell in love with the river Enipeus and her love went unrequited, Poseidon disguised himself as Enipeus and seduced her. Tyro was appalled when she learned what had happened, and feared Sidero's wrath if she were to learn of the pregnancy brought about by Poseidon's trickery. When she gave birth to twin sons, Tyro abandoned them to die, but they were saved by a horseherd and raised as Pelias and Neleus.

The twins grew to rescue Tyro from Sidero's cruel treatment. Tyro then married her uncle Cretheus and gave birth to Aeson. Cretheus also adopted her sons Pelias and Neleus. When Pelias went on a rampage, killing as many Aeolians as possible (because of a prophecy that said that one would kill him), he spared his half-brother Aeson for Tyro's sake.

Universal Egg
In some creation myths, this is the object laid by Eurynome in the form of a dove, from which sprang all things that exist: the sun, the moon, the earth and all the other planets, the stars, and the mountains, rivers, trees, herbs, and all living creatures. The Egg plays a prominent role in some of the earliest myths.

Uranus
In the later, patriarchal creation myths, Uranus is born to Mother Earth in her sleep, and then showers his "fertile rain" upon her to create all living things. Uranus became Mother Earth's husband, and fathered the Hundred-handed Ones, the Cyclopes, and the Titans upon her. (These patriarchal versions often focus exclusively on the Titans, disregarding their female counterparts.)

Uranus seems to signal the supremacy of a masculinized creation scenario. Before his arrival, Mother Earth or some other all-encompassing female being was credited with the formation of life. As patriarchal tribes began to take control of Greek land and Greek thought, however, it became necessary to create a male creator figure.

Xanthus
A river god who is credited with having fathered a number of daughters, among them Eurythemista, Psophis, and Glaucippe.

Xanthus was also the name of the horse used by Achilles to drag Hector's corpse after Achilles had slain him. The horse was originally one of two given by Poseidon to Peleus as a wedding present upon his marriage to Thetis.

Xuthus
A son of Hellen and Orseis, and the brother of Dorus and Aeolus, Xuthus was accused of theft by his brothers and fled to Athens, where he married Creüsa and sired Ion and Achaeus. (There are versions of Xuthus' story in which Apollo was Ion's true father.) In the end, Xuthus' time in Athens was cut short with his unpopular selection of his brother-in-law Cecrops to succeed Erechtheus. Xuthus and Creüsa were banished from the city and died in Aegialus.

Zagreus
A son of Zeus and Persephone, Zagreus was given to the Curetes to be raised in the Iaedian Cave. Zagreus was lured from the cave by the Titans, who were then at war with Zeus. They ripped the youth to shreds and ate his flesh, but Athene rescued Zagreus' heart, enclosed it in a gypsum figure, and breathed life into it, thus making the boy immortal. Zeus avenged his son by striking the Titans dead with his thunderbolts.

Zetes
The twin brother of Calais. Both of the twins grew wings when they reached manhood, and both joined the crew of the *Argo*. During the Argonauts' visit to Salmydessus, Calais and Zetes drove off the Harpies, who had been tormenting their brother-in-law, Phineus, the local king. Phineus repaid their assistance by giving the Argonauts information that would help them reach Colchis safely.

While in Salmydessus, Calais and Zetes also managed to free the children of their sister, Cleopatra, Phineus' first wife.

When Jason decided to abandon Heracles, Calais and Zetes supported their captain. Years later, Heracles avenged this treatment by killing them on the island of Tenos.

Zethus
A son of Antiope and Zeus and the twin of Amphion. When the brothers were abandoned by their uncle Lycus on Mount Cithaeron, they were discovered by cattlemen, who raised them. Despite initially turning their unrecognized mother out of their house, they eventually rescued her from Lycus' abusive wife, Dirce, whom they then killed.

The twins went on to expel Laius from Thebes, and came to rule over the lower city. Zethus married Thebe, for whom the city was named, while Amphion married Niobe.

Zethus later married Aëdon, who bore him Itylus. Before Niobe made disparaging remarks about Leto, Aëdon was jealous of the many children she had produced, and attempted to kill her oldest son. In the process, she instead managed to accidentally kill Zethus' son, Itylus.

Zeus
The greatest and most powerful of all the Olympians, Zeus was born the third son of Cronus and Rhea. Cronus had been warned that one of his offspring would dethrone him, so he swallowed each of his children immediately following their births. Rhea saved the infant Zeus by replacing him with a stone wrapped in swaddling clothes, then sent him to Mother Earth to be raised.

Mother Earth took the infant Zeus to Lyctos on Crete, and hid him in Dicte's cave on the Aegean Hill. The ash nymph Adrasteia and her sister Io were placed in charge of the baby's care, and were aided by some of Hephaestus' finely crafted toys and sentinels. Once Zeus set out on his own he went to Metis, who sent him on to Rhea so that Zeus could be made Cronus' cup-bearer. With Metis' help, Zeus laced one of Cronus' cups with an emetic that caused him to vomit up Zeus' brothers and sisters. The siblings assembled under Zeus' leadership, and while Poseidon held Cronus captive with his trident, Zeus struck him dead with a bolt of lightning.

When Cronus' death was followed by an attack from Atlas and the Titans, Zeus freed the Cyclopes and the Hundred-handed Ones from Tartarus. This turned the tables against the Titans and allowed the Olympians to prevail.

The stone that Cronus expelled along with Zeus' siblings became the centerpiece of the Delphic Oracle and Zeus' preeminence

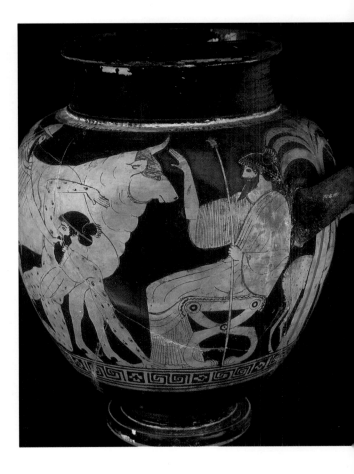

Zeus and Io, red-figured stamnos, 5th century B.C.

Zeus, **marble statue, Hellenistic period.**

the gods fled, with the exception of Athene, who goaded Zeus into returning and facing the beast. Zeus and Typhon engaged in combat and Typhon quickly gained an advantage and proceeded to strip Zeus of the sinews in his hands and feet. Typhon entrusted the sinews to his sister Delphyne; she in turn was tricked out of the sinews by Pan and Hermes, who then returned them to Zeus. Zeus eventually crushed Typhon beneath what is now known as Mount Aetna.

Once Zeus felt reasonably secure in his position, he sought out his twin sister, Hera, came to her in a disguise, and ravished her. The two were married and spent a wedding night that was said to have lasted three hundred years. When Zeus' mother, Rhea, advised her son against marriage, to Hera or anyone else, Zeus ravished Rhea in the form of a snake, and then engaged in a frenzied debauch throughout the known world.

The other Olympians grew increasingly distressed by Zeus' actions and conspired to overthrow him. Poseidon, Apollo, and Hera led a group that eventually managed to capture Zeus and bind him with one hundred knots. But Thetis convinced Briareus, one of the Hundred-handed Ones, to free Zeus and help him capture all those who had opposed him. Zeus sold Poseidon and Apollo into temporary bondage, but reserved his greatest punishment for Hera, who was bound with chains and weighted down with anvils. Only when all of the Olympians swore never to revolt again did Zeus finally release Hera.

Zeus went on to conceive Hermes on Maia; father Apollo and Artemis on Leto; and impregnate Demeter, Io, Dione, Persephone, or Lethe with Dionysus. Zeus coupled with Nemesis in the form of a swan, conceiving Helen, and also fathered Zagreus on Persephone. The list of Zeus' other progeny is extensive and uncertain.

Of all Zeus' children, none was conceived with expectations equal to those held for the child Zeus conceived with Amphitryon's wife, Alcmena. While Amphitryon was off fighting, Zeus lay with Alcmena and convinced Helius to rest for two days and not cause the sun to rise or travel across the sky during that time, since the procreation of such an important individual could not be accomplished hastily. In fear of rousing Zeus' jealousy, Amphitryon never again was intimate with his wife.

When the birth of Alcmena's child came near, Zeus boasted of all that this son would accomplish. Hera tricked Zeus into promising that the next divinely conceived delivery would be made a High King and then delayed

among the Olympians was established. Initially his reign was a rocky one, full of conflict and sexual conquest. Zeus first sought out Metis, who continually changed form in efforts to escape him, and impregnated her. When an oracle assured Zeus that Metis was carrying a female, but that any son of theirs would dethrone Zeus, Zeus swallowed Metis.

Eventually Zeus developed a desperate headache that caused him to scream and howl. Hermes diagnosed the problem and fetched either Prometheus or Hephaestus. A crack was made in Zeus' skull, and Athene, daughter of Zeus and Metis, emerged fully armed. This story is one of many examples of the quickness with which the conception of the various Olympians was ascribed to Zeus. Gods and goddesses who had enjoyed high status in scattered regions of ancient Greece quickly found themselves adopted into the fold and minimized by being assigned a secondary role.

When Typhon later attacked Olympus, all

Zeus and Ganymede, Correggio, 1530.

Alcmena's labor and hurried that of Nicippe, who gave birth to Eurystheus after a seven-month pregnancy. Zeus was enraged and eventually made Hera promise that if Alcmena's son, Heracles, were able to perform ten labors for Eurystheus, he would be allowed to join the Olympians and be made a deity.

Zeus also was known for the severity of the punishments he meted out, the most extreme of which rank among the best known of all stories in the mythological canon. For passing the secret of fire to mortal men, Prometheus was chained to a rock, his insolence further punished by a vulture daily consuming his liver, which regenerated each night. Ixion was bound for eternity to a fiery wheel for trying to seduce Hera, and Asclepius was struck dead when he interfered with the powers of the Olympians by successfully bringing mortals back to life.

There are countless other stories in which Zeus figures prominently. As the supreme deity among all the Olympians, Zeus is invoked constantly, and his interventions in all manner of undertakings are numerous. One of the greatest changes that occurred with Zeus' usurpation of Cronus' throne was the lessening of human sacrifices. Zeus and his messengers (specifically Hermes) are frequently depicted saving the lives of those about to be sacrificed, and while a good deal of tribute was still expected by the Olympians, it did not as frequently include human blood.

As Zeus' status as the supreme Olympian solidified, he was increasingly given credit for the accomplishments of others. As patriarchal monotheism took hold of the Mediterranean world, Zeus took on the properties of many of the gods who had come before him, and much of Hellenistic religious belief was consolidated in the worship of this one figure.

These are new laws indeed
By which Zeus tyrannically rules;
And the great powers of the past he now
  destroys.
  —Chorus, Prometheus Bound, *Aeschylus*

His fierce fire-breathing thunderbolt—that will
  not save him:
His fall will be sure, shameful, unendurable!
  —Prometheus, Prometheus Bound, *Aeschylus*

With ease he strengthens any man; with ease
He makes the strong man humble and with ease
He levels mountains and exalts the plain
Withers the proud and makes the crooked
  straight
  —Works and Days, *Hesiod*

FOUNDING FATHERS AND OTHER FAMOUS FOREBEARS

Achaeus
The son of Xuthus and Creüsa, Achaeus was the father of the Achaean race.

Aeolus
The eldest son of Hellen and Orseis, Aeolus was the progenitor of the Aeolian nation.

Arcas
The son of Callisto and Zeus, Arcas was the ancestor of all Arcadians. Arcas was also the grandfather of Xanthus and the great-grandfather of Psophis.

Dorus
Most often said to be the son of Hellen and Orseis, Dorus emigrated to Mount Parnassus, where he founded the first Dorian community.

Hellen
The son of Deucalion and the brother of Orestheus and Amphictyon, Hellen is considered the father of all Greeks. The four most famous Hellenic nations—the Ionian, the Aeolian, the Dorian, and the Achaean—are all considered to have descended from him. Hellen married Orseis, with whom he conceived Aeolus, Xuthus, and Dorus.

Ion
The son of Apollo and Creusa, Xuthus' wife, Ion married Helice and later became King of Eleusis. Ion was the father of the Ionian nation.

Pelasgus
One of the characters considered to be the first man, Pelasgus is the ancestor of the Pelasgians, who are thought to have sprung up from Ophion's teeth after they were dislodged by Eurynome. The term *Pelasgian* has come to be applied to nearly all the pre-Hellenic inhabitants of Greece.

THE PANTHEON IN GREEK AND ROMAN

Roman mythology is, for the most part, identical with Greek mythology. In fact, the Romans usurped the Greek stories and characters (granted, with some variation—Mars, the Roman god of war, for example, is of much higher status than his Greek equivalent), Latinized the names, and called this "new" mythology their own. The following table presents the names of the major characters in both their Greek and Roman forms.

Greek to Roman

Aias – Ajax
Aphrodite – Venus
Apollo/Helios – Sol
Ares – Mars
Artemis – Diana
Athene – Minerva
Boreas – Aquilo
Chloris – Flora
Cronus – Saturn
Demeter – Ceres
Dionysus – Bacchus
Eos – Aurora
Eros/Amor – Cupid
Hades/Pluto – Dis
Hephaestus – Vulcan
Hera – Juno
Heracles – Hercules
Hermes – Mercury
Hestia – Vesta
Leto – Latona
Odysseus – Ulysses
Pan – Faunus/Silvanus
Persephone/Core – Proserpïna
Polydeuces – Pollux
Poseidon – Neptune
Rhea – Bona Dea/Cybele
Uranus – Coelus
Zeus – Jupiter

Roman to Greek

Ajax – Aias
Aquilo – Boreas
Aurora – Eos
Bacchus – Dionysus
Bona Dea/Cybele – Rhea
Ceres – Demeter
Coelus – Uranus
Cupid – Eros/Amor
Diana – Artemis
Dis – Hades/Pluto
Faunus/Silvanus – Pan
Flora – Chloris
Hercules – Heracles
Juno – Hera
Jupiter – Zeus
Latona – Leto
Mars – Ares
Mercury – Hermes
Minerva – Athene
Neptune – Poseidon
Pollux – Polydeuces
Proserpïna – Persephone/Core
Saturn – Cronus
Sol – Apollo/Helios
Ulysses – Odysseus
Venus – Aphrodite
Vesta – Hestia
Vulcan – Hephaestus

ROMAN MYTHOLOGICAL CHARACTERS

While most of the characters in Roman mythology were derived from the Greek, the following figures are uniquely Roman. None of the gods are repeated here, for their stories are essentially the same as they appear in the Greek accounts.

Amulius
A descendant of Aeneas, Amulius usurped the throne of Alba Longa from his brother Numitor. Amulius attempted to prevent Numitor's daughter, Rhea Silvia, from having heirs who might avenge their father's treatment, but Mars impregnated her with the twins Romulus and Remus, who eventually killed Amulius.

Brutus
A member of the Roman aristocracy, Lucius Junius Brutus—who had been informed by the Delphic Oracle that either he or one of his brothers was destined to become the next King of Rome—feigned stupidity to avoid arousing the suspicions of the reigning Tarquinius. Brutus eventually led a successful popular revolt against the royal family. When it was over, Brutus served as co-Consul until his own death in battle with the exiled previous ruler, Tarquinius Superbus, whom Brutus killed at the same time. Brutus went on to be revered as the founder of the Roman Republic. It is unclear whether Brutus was a historical or purely mythological figure.

Caeculus
Because he was conceived by a spark that flew into his mother's lap, Caeculus is said to have been the son of Vulcan. Caeculus supported Turnus in his battle with Aeneas and is best known as the founder of the city of Praeneste.

Camillus
A historical figure who probably served as the dictator of Rome at the start of the fourth century B.C., Camillus was instrumental in the Roman victory at Veii, and later helped defend Rome against the Gauls. Following the latter event, Camillus oversaw the restoration of Rome and instituted reforms that included the admission of plebeians to the upper ranks of government.

Canens
A nymph who was betrothed to Picus, a son of Saturn. After Circe turned Picus into a woodpecker for having spurned her, Canens wandered far and wide in search of Picus, and eventually grieved for so long that, like Echo, Canens wasted away until only her voice remained.

Cardea
A virgin huntress with aspects similar to those of Artemis, Cardea tricked each man who tried to force her into having sex with him by sending him into a cave, where she said she would soon join him, and running off. Janus eventually outsmarted Cardea and lay with her, in exchange for which Janus made her goddess of doorways.

Cincinnatus
A historical figure who appeared in many mythological stories, Cincinnatus, who was also known as Lucius Quinctius, was a farmer selected by the Roman Senate to lead the defense against a tribe of Aequians. Cincinnatus quickly resigned his dictatorship and returned to his fields until another political crisis forced him out of retirement, despite his being more than eighty years old at the time.

Coriolanus
A hard-line conservative, Coriolanus led the Romans to victory at Corioli and opposed the feeding of the lower classes who had seceded from the Roman empire. The plebeians eventually exiled Coriolanus, who went on to lead an army of Volscians against Rome. When Coriolanus' wife and sons pleaded with him to relent in his attack, he did so; because of this, the Volscians put him to death.

Curiatii
A set of triplets who represented Alba Longa against Rome's Horatii, the Curiatii killed two of the Horatii, but were then killed by the surviving triplet.

Daunus
The son of Pilumnus, a minor deity, and Danaë, the daughter of Acrisius, Daunus grew to become the King of the Rutulians in Latium. He married Venilia and was given a sword by Vulcan; this weapon was later used against Aeneas by Daunus' son Turnus, after the latter was refused the hand of Lavinia.

Dido
A Queen of Carthage, Dido became famous in Virgil's *Aeneid* because of her love for Aeneas. Dido and her sister Anna fled to North Africa when their family was attacked by their brother, Pygmalion. In Africa, Dido met Aeneas and fell in love with him as he recounted his story. The gods convinced Aeneas he must move on, and Dido was crushed when he left without her. She ordered a pyre to be lit, supposedly in order to burn the presents Aeneas had left her, then stabbed herself and threw herself on the fire. In the underworld, it was said that her spirit snubbed Aeneas' when it arrived.

Dido and Aeneas, Giambattista Tiepolo, 1757.

Egeria
A water nymph who was the lover of Numa Pompilius, Egeria counseled Numa on matters of statecraft and religion until his death, at which she became so distraught that Diana turned her into a spring in Aricia.

Fabula
A famous whore who slept with Hercules, among others, and accumulated a great deal of wealth, which she left to the Roman people. Fabula is sometimes said to have been Acca Larentia, the wife of the shepherd Faustulus, who found the abandoned twins Romulus and Remus.

Faustulus
The shepherd credited with discovering Romulus and Remus after they had been abandoned by Amulius, Faustulus suspected the twins' royal origins and preserved the cradle in which they had been abandoned to later prove their identity.

Horatii
A set of triplets chosen to defend Rome against the Curiatii. Two of the Horatii were killed, but the third managed to dispatch the three wounded Curiatii. This surviving Horatii, Horatius, went on to kill his sister when she mourned one of the Curiatii to

The Oath of the Horatii, **David, 1784.**

having lain with her, but these were not enough to prevent Aeneas from prevailing.

Lara After the nymph Lara informed Juno about Jupiter's adulterous adventures, Jupiter pulled Lara's tongue from her mouth and instructed his son Mercury to bring her to the underworld. Along the way Mercury fell in love with her and fathered the Lares—Roman household gods—upon her.

Lavinia A daughter of Amata and Latinus. When Amata wanted Lavinia to marry a prince named Turnus, Latinus objected, and the difference of opinion led to a war in which Turnus was killed. Latinus then arranged it so that Lavinia was married to Aeneas, which made her the stepmother of Ascarius.

Liber A god of the countryside who is identified with Dionysus in many ways, particularly the extent to which Liber was credited with the introduction of viniculture.

Lucretia The wife of the Roman leader Lucius Tarquinius, Lucretia was the only wife found to be behaving honorably while the Roman army was away. Sextus Tarquinius found Lucretia's beauty and fidelity arousing and returned a few days later, eventually raping her at dagger point. Lucretia reported this to her husband and her father, and then took her own life. Legend suggests that these events set into motion the revolt of the Roman nobles against their king and the subsequent founding of the Roman Republic.

whom she had been engaged. Horatius was tried for his sister's murder, but was acquitted by the Assembly of the People in gratitude for his defense of Rome.

Janus A uniquely Roman deity, Janus was considered to be the god of beginnings, doors, gates, and passageways. Janus is depicted as having two faces looking out in opposite directions. (He is sometimes endowed with four faces.) This ability allowed him to ensnare the nymph Carna, and father Proca upon her.

Janus is credited with many accomplishments in Roman mythology, including defending Rome against the Sabines. Janus is sometimes described as a King of Latium and is said to have welcomed Saturn after Zeus had usurped his throne. It was a son of Janus, Tiberinus, who was drowned in the river that was subsequently renamed the Tiber in his honor.

Juturna Daughter of Ardean King Daunus, Juturna was the sister of Turnus, whom she supported in Turnus' battle with Aeneas. Juturna used her power over springs and rivers, which Jupiter had bestowed upon her after

Janus, **Etruscan sculpture, 4th century** B.C.

Manlius A Roman consul who may have been a historic figure, Manlius is credited with defending Rome's garrison against Gauls who had managed to evade the night guards. Manlius became known as Capitolinus for his exploit, while the Captain of the Watch was thrown from a cliff.

Mezentius An Etruscan King who Virgil claimed was a victim of Aeneas, while Cato the Elder suggests that Mezentius survived the battle as an ally of Turnus and was later defeated by Aeneas' son Ascanius.

Numa Pompilius A mythological king, Numa Pompilius was said to have succeeded Romulus some time around the year 715 B.C. Numa was a Sabine known for his piety, and his rule was said to have been as peaceful as Romulus' had been warlike. Jupiter himself sent talismans from above to ensure Rome's safety, and Numa honored him greatly. In

Aeneas and Anchises (with the Penates),
Bernini, 1619.

addition to its tranquility, Numa's reign
included the discouragement of human
sacrifice.

Numitor A son of Proca, Numitor was the
King of Alba Longa and the father of Rhea
Silvia. Numitor was unseated by Amulius, but
eventually was restored to his throne by his
grandsons, Romulus and Remus.

Ocrisia The mother of Rome's sixth legendary king, Servius Tullius, Ocrisia was a
slave-woman taken as a spoil of war. When
Servius became king, Ocrisia was suddenly said
to have been of royal birth. Servius himself was
said to have been divinely conceived when

Ocrisia stood before a fire in which a phallic
image mysteriously appeared.

Palinurus The helmsman on Aeneas' voyage home from the Trojan War, Palinurus died
at Elyma on Sicily when Juno became angry
that the ship had survived the storm she had
sent to wreck it. Aeneas met with Palinurus'
ghost in the underworld and promised to give
his remains a proper burial, an event that
eventually took place on a cape that was subsequently named in his honor.

Penates Originally Roman gods of the
stone cupboard, the Penates eventually came
to be credited with the protection of the entire
Roman nation. The Penates were associated
with Aeneas, and were said to have been
brought by him to Italy from Troy.

Picus A Roman character whose name
means woodpecker, an animal whose form
Picus is said to have assumed for different reasons. In one version Picus is described as the
son of Saturn and the father of Faunus and it is
suggested that Circe turned him into a woodpecker when he refused her. In another version
Picus is described as a country god with the
power to change his shape, preferring that of
Mars' sacred bird, the woodpecker.

Pomona A goddess of fruit and its cultiva-
tion, Pomona was courted by Vertumnus, who
assumed the form of an old crone and spoke so
well on his own behalf that Pomona gave herself to him when he resumed his natural form.

Psyche The youngest of three sister
princesses, Psyche was so beautiful that people
stopped worshiping Venus and adored Psyche
instead. When Venus sent her son Cupid to
cause Psyche to fall in love with the ugliest
creature he could find, Cupid too was won
over by Psyche's beauty and immediately fell in
love with her.

Remus One of the twin sons born to Mars
and Rhea Silvia and eventually abandoned by
their mother. Rhea Silvia's uncle Amulius,
who had usurped her father's throne, feared
any rightful heirs to the throne and sent the
twins to be drowned. Amulius' servants set the
twins adrift in the flooded Tiber, along which
they eventually washed up at the base of a fig
tree when the high waters receded.

Remus and his twin brother, Romulus,
were protected by Mars' sacred familiars, a she-
wolf and a woodpecker, until the shepherd

Pomona, **Roman marble sculpture,** A.D.
1st–2nd century.

Faustulus discovered them. Faustulus and his
wife, Acca Larentia, raised the boys until they
were fully grown and Remus was captured by
Amulius' men for stealing cattle. Remus was
recognized by Numitor, his grandfather, and
led a rebellion in which he finally reclaimed
the throne.

Remus and Romulus set out to found a
city of their own but then argued over who
should assume command of the undertaking.
The two eventually agreed to settle the conflict by finding out which of them might see
more vultures from two different hills. Remus
spotted six from the Aventine Hill, while
Romulus saw twelve from the Palantine Hill.
Remus contested the result and mocked
Romulus by stepping over the stones Romulus

had laid to mark the place where the walls would be, thus implying that Romulus may rule but Remus would return and conquer the city no matter how high its walls were built. Romulus or his foreman Celer then picked up a spade and killed Remus with a single blow to the head. In some versions it is suggested that Faustulus was also killed in the fighting. Romulus made it clear that threats from anyone else would be similarly handled, but wept sincerely at his brother's funeral.

Rhea Silvia

The only child of Numitor, the King of Alba Longa, Rhea Silvia was forced to become a Vestal Virgin when her uncle Amulius usurped Numitor's throne. Rhea Silvia was spotted by Mars, who came down and raped her. The result of this was the birth of twin sons, Romulus and Remus. Amulius sent the twins to be thrown into the river Tiber and imprisoned Rhea Silvia. The twins were rescued and eventually grew to free their mother while restoring Numitor to his throne. In some versions, however, it is suggested that Amulius did not spare Rhea Silvia when the twins were born, but had her either drowned or beheaded.

Romulus

The mythological founder of Rome. Romulus and his twin brother, Remus, were born to Rhea Silvia. Rhea Silvia's uncle, Amulius, had usurped her father's throne, and

Romulus and Remus Given Shelter by Faustulus, Pietro Berettina da Cortona, c. 1643.

fearing any potential rivals for the throne, sent the twins to be drowned. When the high waters receded, Romulus and Remus were discovered first by Mars' familiars, a woodpecker and a she-wolf, and then by Faustulus, a shepherd. Faustulus brought the twins home and raised them with his wife, Acca Larentia.

Eventually the twins went to attend a festival, where they were ambushed and Remus was captured. This led to Remus being recognized by his grandfather, Numitor, from whom Amulius had usurped the throne. Numitor enlisted Romulus and Remus in a successful rebellion against Amulius, during which the twins are said to have killed Amulius.

Romulus and Remus set out to found a city of their own, but argued over who would command their mission. The brothers chose to settle the matter by means of augury and divination. By spotting twelve vultures from the Palatine Hill, while Remus tallied only six from the Aventine Hill, Romulus was declared the victor. Remus contested his brother's victory, and then made threatening remarks while Romulus was beginning the construction of a wall around the new city. Romulus or his foreman Celer responded by picking up a spade and killing Remus with it. Romulus proclaimed that anyone else who tried to cross his walls would receive similar treatment, but he then wept sincerely at his brother's funeral.

Romulus' city became populated with rogues and fugitives, most of them male. This led to the entrapment of the Sabines and the subsequent rape of their women. This resulted in a war, which ended in a truce that merged the Romans and the Sabines into a single federation with Rome as its capital and Romulus sharing control with Titus Tatius. It is said that the federation experienced forty years of peace and prosperity before Romulus, while reviewing his army, vanished in a cloud during a violent thunderstorm.

Romulus' divinity was quickly acclaimed, and his spirit made visits to subsequent rulers of the city. The twins were said to be related to Aeneas through Rhea Silvia and Numitor.

Scaevola

A war hero who defended a siege of Rome by disguising himself as an Etruscan and infiltrating their camp. Scaevola, also known as Gaius Mucius, hoped to kill the Etruscan King, Lars Porsenna, but killed the wrong person. Mucius was brought before Lars and demonstrated his resolve by sticking his right hand into a fire and holding it there. Lars returned his sword, which Mucius was now forced to take in his left hand; this resulted in his nickname, Scaevola, which was derived

Scaevola Before Porsenna, terra-cotta plate, Piatto, c. 1560.

from *scaeva,* meaning "a left-handed person." Scaevola went on to ingratiate himself to Lars and eventually negotiated a peace between the Romans and the Etruscans.

Servius Tullius

The sixth of Rome's legendary kings, Servius Tullius was said to have ruled in the sixth century B.C. Servius was the son of a slave woman, Ocrisia, and either the god Vulcan or a prince who was also named Servius Tullius. Young Servius was adopted by and came to be the favorite of King Tarquinius Priscus and his wife, and was established as king when he led the revolt against the forces that had unseated his adoptive father. Servius increased the size of the city, building the Servian Wall in the process, and introduced the worship of Diana to Rome. Servius' progressive and peaceful reign pleased the masses but rankled the patricians, who eventually rallied behind his daughter, Tullia, when she plotted Servius' assassination in the forty-fourth year of his reign. Tullia went so far as to ride his carriage over her father's corpse.

Sibylla

A mythological character who served Apollo for having given her the gift of prophesy, which she expressed in oracular riddles. Sibylla, also known as Sibyl, became Apollo's mistress, but forgot to ask for perpetual youth to go along with the immortality he bestowed upon her. Sibylla aged to the point where she became shriveled up, after which she was kept in a bottle that hung from a ceiling in a cave. Sibylla kept telling visitors that she wished to die, and once accompanied Aeneas to the underworld. Later, Sibylla offered to sell her nine books of prophesies to

Tarquinius Superbus, who allowed her to burn six of them before being made aware of their value and salvaging the remaining three.

Tanaquil

The wife of Tarquinius Priscus who persuaded him to move to Rome, where he became king, Tanaquil was credited with supporting her adopted son Servius Tullius after Priscus was murdered and helping him gain control of the throne.

Tarquinius Collatinus

The husband of Lucretia, who was brutally raped by an unknown prince, Collatinus avenged his wife's treatment by helping to establish a new republic. Although Collatinus served well, his name associated him with the royal family and caused him to resign his position and go into exile at Lanuvium.

Tarquinius Priscus

The fifth king of Rome, Tarquinius Priscus was the son of a Greek immigrant in Tarquinii. Priscus was originally known as Lucumo but changed his name to Lucius Tarquinius Priscus when he came to Rome with the divine omen that he was destined to rule. Priscus came to serve King Ancus Marcius, and was elected to succeed him when the king died. Priscus is thought to have reigned for thirty-eight years, during which he founded the Circus Maximus and expanded Rome's borders. Priscus was eventually killed by order of the natural sons of Ancus Marcius. The murderers were caught and Marcius' sons fled into exile while Priscus' adopted son, Servius Tullius, succeeded him.

Tarquinius Sextus

The youngest of Tarquinius Superbus' three sons, Sextus gained control of Gabii for his father. But Sextus then went on to rape Lucretia, which upset the populace to the point where they overthrew his father and expelled the entire family. Sextus took refuge in Gabii, where he was eventually assassinated.

Tarquinius Superbus

The seventh and last of Rome's legendary kings, Tarquinius Superbus straddles the cusp between mythology and history. Superbus was either the son or grandson of the powerful Tarquinius Priscus. Servius' daughter, Tullia, saw potential in Superbus, known at the time as Lucius, and incited him to kill his wife and his brother, who was married to Tullia, so that Tullia and Superbus could marry. Tullia then convinced Superbus to kill her father and seize his throne. When Superbus' men killed Servius, Tullia rode her carriage over his corpse.

Superbus was a ruthless ruler, but he nonetheless accomplished much during his reign. His son Sextus helped him conquer the town of Gabii, and Superbus also managed to bring the remaining Latin states under Roman rule. It was, however, Sextus' rape of Lucretia during the siege of Ardea that led to revolt. Lucius Junius Brutus led a citizens' revolt and forced Superbus to flee to Caera, where he organized Etruscans and Tarquinii unsuccessfully against his former kingdom. Superbus' personal property was laid open to the populace, and he continued his attempts at revenge by trying to organize others against Rome. He was wounded by Romans at the battle of Lake Regillus, and died a few years later in Campania.

Titus Tatius

The Sabine King who laid siege to Rome after the Sabine women were seized by the Romans. Tatius and the Sabines were on the verge of victory before Romulus appealed to Jupiter for assistance. This resulted in the Sabine women running between the two armies and asking them to make peace, which resulted in the creation of a single federation with Rome as its capital and Titus Tatius ruling alongside Romulus.

Turnus

A prince of the Rutulians and the son of Daunus and Venilia, Turnus came to vie with Aeneas for the hand of Lavinia. Lavinia's mother, Amata, supported Turnus, but Turnus ended up trying to escape Aeneas' Trojans. Venus put a stop to Turnus' escape and Aeneas killed him.

Vestal Virgins

The priestesses who served as the superintendents in the worship of Vesta, the Roman goddess of the hearth. The Virgins, who usually came from Rome's most powerful families, carried a great deal of power. They were allowed to relinquish their virginity after thirty years, but those who broke their vows before that time were given a funeral service and then buried alive.

Vestal Virgins, Joan Raoux, 1727.

BIBLIOGRAPHY

Classical Drama

Aeschylus. *The Oresteia*. Translated by Philip Vellacott. New York: Penguin Books, 1959.

Aeschylus. *Prometheus Bound and Other Plays*. Translated by Philip Vellacott. New York: Penguin Books, 1961.

Apollonius of Rhodes. *The Voyage of Argo*. Translated by E.V. Rieu. New York: Penguin Books, 1971.

Aristophanes. *The Complete Plays of Aristophanes*. Edited by Moses Hadas. New York: Bantam Books, 1962.

_____. *The Wasps; The Poet and the Women; The Frogs*. Translated by David Barrett. New York: Penguin Books, 1964.

Callimachus. *Aetia, Iambi, Hecale and Other Fragments*. Translated by C.A. Trypanis. Cambridge, Mass.: Harvard University Press, 1958.

Euripides. *Alcestis and Other Plays*. Translated by Philip Vellacott. London: Penguin Books, 1953.

_____. *The Bacchae and Other Plays*. Translated by Philip Vellacott. London: Penguin Books, 1954.

_____. *Euripides II*. New York: The Modern Library, 1958.

_____. *Four Tragedies*. Various translators. Chicago: University of Chicago Press, 1955.

_____. *Medea and Other Plays*. Translated by Philip Vellacott. New York: Penguin Books, 1963.

_____. *Ten Plays*. Translated by Moses Hadas and John McLean. New York: Bantam Books, 1960.

Herodotus. *The Histories*. Translated by Aubrey de Sélincourt. New York: Penguin Books, 1987.

Hesiod. *Theogony/Works and Days*. Translated by Dorothea Wender. New York: Penguin Books, 1973.

Homer. *The Iliad of Homer*. Translated by Richmond Lattimore. Chicago: The University of Chicago Press, 1951.

_____. *The Iliad*. Translated by Robert Fitzgerald. Garden City, N.Y.: Anchor Books, 1963.

_____. *The Odyssey*. General editor, Harry Shefter. New York: Washington Square Press, 1969.

Ovid. *Metamorphoses*. Translated by Mary M. Innes. New York: Mentor Books, 1958.

_____. *The Metamorphoses*. Translated by Horace Gregory. New York: Mentor Books, 1958.

Pindar. *The Odes of Pindar*. Translated by Sir John Sandys. Cambridge, Mass.: Harvard University Press, 1978.

Seneca. *Four Tragedies and Octavia*. Translated by E.F. Watling. New York: Penguin Books, 1966.

Sophocles. *The Complete Plays of Sophocles*. Translated by Sir Richard Claverhouse Jebb. New York: Bantam Books, 1967.

Theognis. *Elegies*. Translated by Dorothea Wender. New York: Penguin Books, 1973.

References

Boardman, John, Jasper Griffin, and Oswyn Murray, eds. *The Oxford History of the Classical World*. New York: Oxford University Press, 1986.

Bowra, C.M. *Classical Greece*. New York: Time Incorporated, 1965.

Bullfinch, Thomas. *Mythology*. Abridged by Edmund Fuller. New York: Dell Publishing, 1959.

Frazier, Sir James George. *The Golden Bough: A Study in Magic and Religion*. Volume I, Abridged Edition. New York: Macmillan Publishing Co., 1963.

Graves, Robert. *The Greek Myths*. Volumes I and II. New York: Penguin Books, 1960.

Grant, Michael. *Myths of the Greeks and Romans*. New York: Mentor Books, 1986.

_____, and John Hazel. *Gods and Mortals in Classical Mythology: A Dictionary*. New York: Dorset Press, 1979.

Hamilton, Edith. *Mythology*. Boston: Little, Brown & Company, 1942.

Hawkes, Jacquetta. *Dawn of the Gods*. New York: Random House, 1968.

Hendricks, Rhoda A. *Classical Gods and Heroes: Myths as Told by the Ancient Authors*. New York: Morrow Quill Paperbacks, 1974.

Kirk, G.S. *The Nature of Greek Myths*. Woodstock, N.Y.: Overlook Press, 1974.

Lattimore, Richmond. *The Poetry of Greek Tragedy*. New York: Harper Torchbooks, 1958.

Murray, Alexander S. *Who's Who in Mythology: A Classic Guide to the Ancient World*. New York: Bonanza Books, 1988.

Pinsent, John. *Greek Mythology*. London: Paul Hamlyn, 1969.

Rose, H.J. *A Handbook of Greek Mythology*. New York: E.P. Dutton, 1959.

Walker, Barbara G. *The Woman's Dictionary of Symbols and Sacred Objects*. San Francisco: Harper & Row, 1988.

Zimmerman, J.E. *Dictionary of Classical Mythology*. New York: Bantam Books, 1964.

PHOTO CREDITS

Allanari/Art Resource: 24, 33bottom, 53, 57top, 70bottom, 71, 104, 128top, 135, 139

Art Resource/New York: 56, 89left, 146

Bridgeman/Art Resource: 47bottom, 51top, 88, 107, 110, 127left

Foto Marsburg/Art Resource: 29

Gardner/Art Resource: 69, 82

Giraudon/Art Resource: 12top, 30top, 32, 74, 109both, 123bottom, 127right, 141left, 143, 149bottom, 156, 167, 171

Erich Lessing/Art Resource: 10, 11, 13, 14top, 17, 18, 23, 26, 28top, 34bottom, 38bottom, 41left, 41right, 42, 45both, 48, 49both, 50, 52both, 67, 75bottom, 78, 80, 81both, 92, 93, 94, 98bottom, 100left, 101, 103, 105, 108top, 112, 113, 116both, 118, 119bottom, 120, 121bottom, 124, 126, 129, 132top, 136, 144, 145, 147both, 149top, 151, 152, 153bottom, 155, 157both, 161both

Natural Museum of Americ. Art/Art Resource: 144bottom

Nimatallah/Art Resource: 28bottom, 40, 68, 85, 89, 95bottom, 99, 41right, 170top

Scala/Art Resource: 4, 15, 21, 25, 27, 30bottom, 31, 33top, 35, 39, 41middle, 43, 47top, 51bottom, 54, 55, 57bottom, 60, 61, 62, 63right, 64, 65, 70top, 72both, 73, 76, 79both, 83, 84right, 86, 87, 95top, 96, 98top, 106, 108bottom, 114both, 115, 117, 119top, 121top, 122, 123top, 128bottom, 131, 132bottom, 133both, 140, 142, 153top, 158, 164, 168bottom, 169both, 170bottom

Tate Gallery/Art Resource: 36, 125

Vanni/Art Resource: 100right

Victoria & Albert Museum/Art Resource: 12bottom

New York Public Library: 159top

Palubniak Studios Inc.: 159bottom

Missing chromes: 14top, 20, 22, 34top, 37, 38top, 44, 46, 58, 59, 63left, 75right, 77, 90, 91, 97, 102, 111, 130, 134, 137, 148, 150both, 160, 162, 165, 168top

INDEX

Abderus, 10, 82
Acamas, 10, 19, 60, 105
Acastus, 10, 49, 53, 94
Achates, 17
Achelous, 10, 25, 45, 59, 83
Achilles, 10–12, *10*, *11*, *12*, 20, 22, *22*, *23*, *23*, 31, 32, 40, 42, 43, 44, 45, 49, 59, 60, 61, 64, 71, 75, *75*, 76, 77, 79, 91, 97, 98, 104, *104*, 105
Acrisius, 13, 56, 57, 61, 94, 102
Actaeon, 13–14, *14*, 37
Actor, 71, 107
Admetus, 14
Adonis, 14–15, *15*, 33, 44, 50, 68
Adrasteia, 15, 26, 54
Adrastus, 15, 28, 46, 53, 66, 68, 86, 98, 103
Aeacus, 15, 34
Aëdon, 15
Aeëtes, 15–16, 42, 48, 50, 78, 93, 100, 101
Aegeus, 16, 19, 30, 66, 101, 105
Aegialeus, 66
Aegina, 15, 16, 38
Aegisthus, 16–17, *17*, 20, 21, 25, 40, 51, 52, 66, 77, 85, 105
Aegyptus, 17, 57
Aeneas, 17–18, 30, *30*, 33, 39, 49, *75*
Aeolus, 18, *18*, 25, 37, 43, 46, 60, 99, 105, 106
Aerope, 18–19, 41, 104
Aesacus, 19, 74
Aeschylus, 15, 17, 38, 41, 52, 57, 65, 68, 91
Aeson, 19, 54, 62, 92
Aethra, 10, 16, 19, 33, 60, 76
Aetolus, 19, 65
Agamemnon, 10, 11, 12, 16, 18, 19–21, *19*, *20*, 22, 23, 31, 38, 40, 43, 44, 45, 46, 50, 51, 52, 60, 61, 63, 64, 76, 77, 89, 90, 91, 94, 104, 105
Aganippe, 13
Agave, 21, 99
Agelaus, 21
Agenor, 21, 44, 69, 88
Aglauros, 21, 66
Aias, 21
Ajax, 11, 12, 20, *21*, 22–23, *22*, *23*, 40, 46, 75, 85, 104
Alcathous, 23–24, 51, 102
Alcestis, 14, 24, *24*, 71
Alcinous, 24, 93, 101
Alcippe, 36, 55, 100
Alcithoë, 85
Alcmaeon, 10, 24–25, *25*, 28, 37, 45, 53, 66, 100
Alcmena, 25, *25*, 29, 78, 79, 80
Alcmene, 64, 72, 91
Alcyone, 25, 48, 71
Alcyoneus, 72, 73
Aletes, 25, 66
Aleus, 25, 42, 83
Aloeides, 25, 66

Aloeus, 78, 92
Alope, 25–26, *26*, 48
Althaea, 26, 51, 58
Amazons, 26–28, *26*, *27*, *28*, 42, 43, 62, 66, 69, 82, 86, 90, 99
Amphiaraus, 15, 24, 28, 66
Amphictyon, 60
Amphilochus, 24, 28, 53, 66, 100
Amphion, 28, 32, 33, 63, 98
Amphissa, 46
Amphissus, 35, 63
Amphitrite, 28–29, *28*, *29*
Amphitryon, 25, 29, 47, 48, 52, 64, 80, 81, 91, 94, 97
Anchinoë, 47
Anchises, 30, *30*, 33, 78
Androgeus, 16, 23, 30, 37
Andromache, 30, 38, 64, 75
Andromeda, 30–31, *30*, 46, 47, 57
Antaeus, 31, *31*, 82
Antenor, 31–32, 39, 66
Antigone, 32, 53, 74, 90, 92
Antilochus, 32, 100, 104
Antiope, 28, 32–33, *32*, 63, 69, 86, 94, 98
Aphareus, 88, 97
Aphidnus, 33, 76
Aphrodite, 14, 15, 17, 26, 30, 33–34, *33*, *34*, 39, 40, 44, 45, 50, 51, 61, 63, 64, 65, 66, 68, *68*, 72, 73, 74, 76, 78, 79, 85, 86, 99, 103, 105
Apollo, 10, 11, 12, 14, 15, 24, 28, 31, 34–35, *34*, 37, 38, 40, 42, 46, 49, 50, 52, 53, 55, 57, *57*, 58, 59, 63, 66, 71, 74, 75, 76, 77, 84, 85, 86, 88, 89, 94, 95, 97, 99, 100, 102, 105, 106
Apsyrtus, 16, 35, 50
Arachne, 35, *35*
Archippe, 41, 71, 79
Architeles, 83
Areiopagus, 35, 36, 40, 106
Ares, 14, 26, 33, 35–36, 40, 44, 55, 62, 65, 66, 68, 71, 74, 78, 79, 82, 86, 103
Arete, 24, 93
Argonauts, 15, 24, 28, 29, 36, 40, 44, 45, 48, 55, 58, 63, 68, 69, 70, 81, 88, 89, 92, 93, 94, 96, 100, 101
Argos, 17, 25, 29, 46, 52, 57, 62, 66, 79, 97, 98, 102, 103, 105
Argus, 36, 64, 89
Ariadne, 16, 36, *37*, 56, 60, 107
Aristaeus, 13, 37, 55, 63, 89
Arne, 18, 37, 43, 60, 103, 105, 106
Arsinoë, 24, 25, 37, 45
Arsippe, 85, 96
Artemis, 12, 13, 14, 20, 24, 25, 26, 27, 28, 34, 35, 37–38, *38*, 41, 44, 46, 47, 48, 52, 58, 63, 64, 66, 86, 91, 96, 101, 103
Ascalaphus, 38
Ascarius, 39
Asclepius, 35, 38, *38*, 49, 52, 55, 72, 85, 86, 98, 99, 102
Asopus, 16, 33, 38
Asterius, 38, 69, 106, 107

Asterodeia, 15, 48
Astynax, 38–39, 75
Astyoche, 39, 50, 70
Atalanta, 39, *39*, 51, 53, 88, 103
Athamas, 39, 62, 78, 89
Athene, 18, 19, 20, 21, 22, 23, 31, 33, 34, 38, 39–41, *40*, *41*, 43, 44, 45, 53, 54, 55, 57, 59, 61, 62, 65, 69, 73, 74, 77, 79, 80, 85, 89, 94, 100, 102, 104, 105, 106
Athens, 16, 21, 37, 40, 47, 48, 53, 60, 63, 66, 86, 90, 96, 101, 105, 106
Atlas, 41, *41*, 46, 66, 82, 84, 85, 94, 105
Atreus, 16, 18, 19, 41–42, 47, 71, 78, 86, 104
Auge, 25, 42, 53
Augeias, 42, 107
Autolycus, 32, 42, 80, 82, 85
Autolyte, 18, 43, 106
Automedon, 11
Autonoë, 13, 37

Bellerophon, 19, 31, 42–43, *42*, 49, 90, 94
Bias, 43, 91, 102, 103
Boeotus, 18, 37, 43, 60, 105, 106
Boreas, 43, *43*, 45, 51, 65, 66
Briseis, 11, *19*, 20, 43–44
Britomartis, 37, 38, 44, 96
Broteas, 44, 69
Busiris, 31, 44, 82
Butes, 44, 66, 68, 86

Cacus, 44, *44*
Cadmus, 21, 44–45, *45*, 59, 66, 69, 74, 88, 89, 90, 93
Calais, 45
Calchas, 12, 23, 28, 38, 39, 43, 45, 91
Cale, 33, 45, 48
Calliope, 14, 97
Callirrhoë, 10, 25, 37, 45, 49, 62, 72
Callisto, 37, 46
Calyce, 65, 71
Calydonian Boar, the, 14, 24, 26, 28, 38, 39, 45, 46, 47, 51, 63, 88, 91, 98, 103
Calypso, 46
Canache, 46
Capaneus, 15, 46
Caphnis, 58
Carmanor, 10
Cassandra, 12, 16, 20, 23, 46, *46*, 52, 77
Cassiopeia, 30, 46–47
Castor, 47, *47*, 63, 76, 80, 89, 96, 99
Catreus, 47
Cecrops, 47
Celeus, 60, 69
Centaurs, 10, *10*, 12, 19, 38, 45, 47, *47*, 49, 53, 58, 59, 61, 63, 68, 71, 81, 83, 84, 86, *86*, 92, 107
Cephalus, 29, 47, 65, 94
Cepheus, 25, 30, 46, 47
Cerberus, 47–48, *48*, 64, 70, 82
Cercopes, 48
Cercyon, 48

Ceryneian Hind, the, 37, 48, 81
Ceryx, 69
Ceto, 48, 73, 85
Ceyx, 48
Chalciope, 15, 16, 48, 70
Chaos, 48, 70
Charites, 33, 45, 48–49, *49*, 73
Charon, 49, *49*, 70, 82
Charybdis, 49
Cheiron, 10, 12, 18, 19, 38, 49, 55, 62, 81, 92
Chimaera, the, 42, 49, *49*, 58, 64, 90
Chione, 35, 42, 43, 69
Chios, 105
Chrysaor, 49–50
Chryse, 50, 58
Chryseis, 11, 20, 43, 44, 50, 77
Chrysippus, 39, 41, 50, 94
Chrysothemis, 50, 51, 52, 64
Cilla, 50
Cinyras, 50
Circe, 50–51, *50*, 70, 73, 93
Cithaerian Lion, the, 24, 51, 80
Cleopatra, 26, 51, 103
Clio, 97
Clotho, 51
Clymene, 39, 41, 47, 88, 106
Clymenus, 65
Clytaemnestra, 16, 19, 20, 21, 25, 34, 40, 50, 51–52, *51*, *52*, 63, 64, 66, 76, 77, 85, 88, 90, 91, 94, 96, 104, 105
Coeus, 96
Colchis, 15, 16, 24, 29, 35, 36, 45, 48, 50, 58, 70, 81, 86, 92, 93, 96, 100, 101, 108, 136
Comaetho, 52
Cometes, 62, 86
Core, 38, 52, 59, 60, 74, 75, *79*
Coronis, 52–53
Coronus, 45
Corybantes, 35
Corythus, 53, 58
Creon, 15, 29, 53, 73, 74, 93, 97, 98, 100, 101, 102
Cretan Bull, the, 53, *53*, 81, 107
Crete, 26, 38, 45, 53, 56, 61, 81, 82, 89, 101, 105
Cretheis, 10, 53
Cretheus, 19, 38, 43, 54
Cronus, 15, 26, 33, 40, 41, 49, 54, 55, 59, 66, 73, 79, 86, 106
Curetes, the, 54, 55
Cyclopes, the, 18, 35, 37, 54–55, *55*, 57, 86
Cycnus, 55, *55*
Cyrene, 35, 37, 55, 62, 89
Cythera, 33
Cyzicus, 55

Dactyls, the, 54, 55, 58, 88
Daedalus, 55–56, *56*, 88, 106, 107
Danaë, 13, 56–57, *57*, 61
Danaids, the, 17, 29, 57, 87, 98
Danaus, 17, 29, 57, 62, 87, 88, 98
Daphne, 35, 57–58, *57*, 97
Daphnis, 85

Dardanus, 50, 53, 58, 88
Dascylus, 58
Deianeira, 10, 58–59, *58*, 61, 82, 83, 87, 90, 97
Deidameia, 11, 59, 91, 98
Deimachus, 73
Deimus, 33, 36
Deiphilus, 89
Deiphobus, 12, 40, 59, 76, 77, 105
Deipyle, 61
Delphic Oracle, the, 15, 16, 40, 42, 44, 54, 59, 64, 66, 81, 97
Delphinus, 29
Delphyne, 59
Demeter, 38, 48, 52, 54, 57, 59–60, 62, 69, 74, 88
Demophon, 10, 19, 60, 105
Demophoön, 60
Desmontes, 18, 37, 43, 60
Deucalion, 60–61, *61*
Dexamenus, 61
Dictys, 57, 61
Diomedes, 10, 18, 19, 20, 22, 37, 43, 49, 55, 61–62, 66, 82, 92, 98
Dionysus, 12, 21, 27, 31, 33, 36, 39, 45, 58, 59, 62–63, *62*, *63*, 73, 74, 78, 85, 89, 90, 92, 96, 97, 98, 99, 102, 106
Dioscuri, the, 16, 19, 33, 47, 51, 63, *63*, 76, 77, 88, 89, 97, 99, 100, 104, 105
Dirce, 28, 32, 33, 63, 98
Discordia, 68
Dryads, 37, 63
Dryope, 35, 63, 74, 87, 97

Eastern Demons, the, 64, 74
Echenus, 71, 87
Echidne, 49, 64, 94, 96
Echo, 64, *64*
Eëtion, 11, 64
Electra, 20, 50, 51, 52, 53, 58, 64, 74, 77, 88, 89, 91, 94, 105
Electryon, 25, 29, 64
Elysian Fields, the, 12
Empusae, the, 65, 75, 94
Endymion, 19, 65, *65*, 91
Eos, 33, 35, 43, 47, 65, 77, 78, 85, 87
Epaphus, 65
Epeius, 65–66
Ephialtes, 66
Ephyra, 83
Epicaste, 51
Epigoni, the, 15, 24, 28, 57, 61, 66, 99, 100
Epimetheus, 66, 79
Erebus, 72
Erechtheus, 44, 66, 69
Eriboea, 25, 66
Erichthonius, 21, 39, 66, 79
Erigone, 66, 99
Erinnyes, the, 66–67, *67*, 68, 72, 74, 105
Eriphyle, 24, 25, 28, 66, 67
Eris, 33, 68, 78, 79, 86
Eros, 15, 68, *68*, 100
Erymanthian Boar, the, 68, 81

Erystheus, 25, 53
Erytheis, 85
Eryx, 68
Eteocles, 15, 32, 53, 68, 90
Eubuleus, 69
Euippe, 37, 38, 62, 68, 103
Euippus, 24, 102
Eumaeus, 68
Eumenides, the, 66, 68
Eumolpus, 66, 68–69, 80
Euneus, 69, 93
Euphemus, 69, 93
Euripides, 29, 38, 74, 84, 93, 99, 101, 102
Europe, 21, 38, 44, 53, 69, *69*, 74, 106
Euryanassa, 44, 69
Eurybius, 82
Eurycleia, 69–70, *70*
Eurydice, 32, 37, 49, 63, 70, *70*
Eurylochus, 50, 70
Eurynome, 38, 41, 48, 54, 66, 70, 73, 78, 87, 106
Euryphaessa, 77
Eurypylus, 46, 70–71
Eurystheus, 70, 71, 79, 80, 81, 82, 99
Eurytion, 10, 47, 58, 71, *71*, 82
Eurytus, 71, 73, 80, 82, 92, 107
Evadne, 46, 71
Evander, 71–72

Fates, the, 26, 42, 51, 72, 93, 103
Furies, the, 26, 52, 54, 66, 72, 103

Ganymede, 72, *72*, 95
Geryon, 44, 49, 50, 71, 72, 82
Giants, the, 72–73
Glauce, 53, 73, 93, 101
Glaucus, 22, 38, 42, 73, 105, 106
Golden Fleece, the, 15, 16, 24, 36, 40, 42, 48, 50, 92, 93, 100, 101
Gordius, 73, 106
Gorgons, the, 27, 40, 49, 57, 73, 102
Gorgophone, 73, 88, 97
Graces, the, 70, 73

Hades, 14, 24, 35, 38, 47, 48, 49, 52, 54, 59, 69, 70, 72, 73–74, *74*, 75, 82, 84, 96
Haemon, 32, 53, 74
Halia, 64, 74
Hamadryads, the, 63, 74, 103
Harmonia, 21, 26, 28, 33, 45, *45*, 59, 66, 74, 88
Harpies, the, 45, 51, 74, 75
Hebe, 79, 83
Hecabe, 11, 21, 46, 59, 74–75, 77, 94, 99
Hecate, 65, 72, 74, 75
Hector, 11, *13*, 18, 22, 30, 38, 59, 64, 70, 75–76, *75*, 99, 104
Helen, 10, 12, 17, 19, 20, 31, 33, 34, 40, 51, 53, 59, 60, 63, 74, 76–77, *76*, *77*, 85, 95, 96, 99, 104, 105
Helenus, 11, 46, 76, 77
Helius, 15, 42, 50, 56, 58, 65, 73, 77–78, 85, 87, 89, 101, 102
Hellas, 93

Helle, 39, 78, 92
Hellen, 60
Hemera, 65, 78
Hephaestus, 12, 26, 33, 40, 44, 66, 72, 74, 77, 78–79, 78, 85, 103
Hera, 23, 25, 33, 36, 37, 39, 40, 41, 45, 46, 48, 53, 54, 58, 62, 63, 64, 65, 68, 71, 72, 73, 74, 78, 79–80, 79, 85, 86, 89, 90, 91, 92, 93, 94, 96, 98, 99, 102, 103
Heracles, 10, 14, 15, 22, 23, 24, 25, 27, 29, 31, 38, 39, 40, 41, 41, 42, 44, 44, 45, 47, 48, 48, 49, 50, 51, 53, 53, 55, 56, 58, 59, 60, 61, 62, 64, 66, 68, 69, 70, 71, 72, 73, 78, 79, 80–84, 80, 81, 83, 85, 86, 87, 88, 90, 91, 92, 93, 94, 95, 96, 97, 98, 99, 100, 101, 102, 107
Heraclids, the, 25, 84, 87, 90, 97
Hermaphroditus, 33, 84, 84
Hermes, 11, 21, 25, 25, 26, 33, 34, 35, 36, 37, 40, 41, 42, 46, 47, 50, 51, 58, 59, 61, 62, 63, 63, 66, 69, 70, 71, 72, 74, 78, 84–85, 84, 85, 89, 92, 97
Hermione, 85, 105
Hesione, 20, 31, 82, 85, 95, 105
Hespera, 65, 85
Hesperides, the, 10, 80, 85
Hestia, 54, 63, 85, 85
Hippasus, 85–86
Hippocoön, 38, 88, 97
Hippodameia, 23, 41, 45, 47, 50, 59, 63, 68, 71, 86, 86
Hippolyte, 66, 82, 86
Hippolytus, 38, 72, 73, 86
Hippomenes, 39, 102
Homer, 23, 32, 49, 73, 76, 77, 79, 83, 93
Hope, 86, 87
Hundred–handed Ones, the, 54, 55, 86
Hyacinthus, 35, 86, 106
Hylas, 63, 81, 86–87
Hylius, 87
Hyllus, 59, 83
Hyperion, 65, 70, 77, 78, 87
Hypermnestra, 57, 87–88, 98
Hypsipyle, 69, 88

Icarius, 66, 88, 99
Icarus, 56, 56, 88, 88, 89, 97
Idaeus, 58
Idas, 35, 63, 88–89
Idmon, 55, 89
Idomeneus, 89, 97, 100
Ino, 39, 62, 89
Io, 36, 62, 65, 89–90, 89, 90
Iobates, 42, 43, 49, 90
Iocaste, 32, 53, 90, 92, 94
Iolaus, 56, 80, 81, 82, 90
Iolcus, 92, 93
Iole, 59, 71, 82, 83, 87, 90, 92
Iphianassa, 19, 43, 64, 65, 90–91, 91, 92, 103
Iphicles, 25, 80, 83, 90, 91, 103
Iphiclus, 43, 91, 102

Iphigeneia, 11, 20, 45, 51, 52, 90, 91, 91, 105
Iphimedeia, 25, 66, 91–92
Iphinoë, 42, 56, 92, 102, 103
Iphitus, 71, 82, 92
Ismene, 32, 53, 90, 92
Ithaca, 21, 24, 32, 46, 68, 70, 92, 103
Ixion, 47, 78, 85, 92

Jason, 15, 16, 24, 36, 42, 45, 49, 50, 53, 62, 69, 71, 73, 81, 82, 88, 92–93, 92, 93, 96, 100, 101
Jupiter, 18, 32

Ladon, 79, 80, 82, 85, 94
Laius, 28, 39, 50, 90, 94
Lamia, 94
Laocoön, 94, 95
Laodice, 10, 19, 94–95
Laomedon, 35, 39, 50, 73, 82, 85, 95
Leda, 47, 51, 63, 76, 95–96
Lemnian Women, the, 88, 96
Lernaean Hydra, the, 80, 81, 96
Leto, 12, 28, 34, 37, 38, 44, 96
Leuce, 96
Leucippe, 45, 85, 96–97
Leucippides, 63, 88, 89, 97, 98
Leucippus, 96, 97
Leucon, 39, 78
Leucothea, 74, 89, 97
Leucus, 89, 97
Lichas, 97, 97
Licymnius, 97
Linus, 35, 80, 97
Lycaon, 61, 64, 97
Lycomedes, 11, 59, 97–98, 98
Lycurgus, 25, 38, 88, 98, 98
Lycus, 16, 28, 29, 32, 33, 58, 62, 63, 82, 98, 102
Lynceus, 57, 63, 88, 89, 97, 98–99
Lysippe, 26, 92, 99, 103

Macareus, 99
Macaria, 99
Machaon, 99
Madness, 99
Maenads, the, 63, 99, 99
Maera, 99
Maia, 84
Manto, 53, 99–100
Marathon, 100
Marathus, 100
Marpessa, 100
Marsyas, 100
Meda, 89, 97, 100
Medea, 12, 15, 16, 24, 36, 48, 50, 53, 71, 73, 82, 93, 100, 100–102, 100, 101
Medon, 23, 64
Medus, 16, 101
Medusa, 13, 27, 38, 40, 44, 49, 57, 61, 66, 73, 82, 102, 102, 137
Megapenthes, 102
Megara, 53, 82, 87, 90, 91, 98, 102
Megareus, 24, 51, 102
Melampus, 43, 91, 92, 99, 102–103
Melaneus, 71

Melanion, 39, 103
Melanippe, 103
Melanippus, 103
Melantheus, 68, 103
Melas, 97
Meleager, 26, 51, 53, 58, 82, 83, 103, 103
Meliae, the, 103
Melicertes, 39, 89
Melisseus, 15
Melite, 16
Memnon, 32, 103–104, 104
Menedemus, 81
Menelaus, 17, 18, 19, 20, 22, 31, 40, 59, 76, 77, 85, 104–105, 105
Menestheus, 105
Menodice, 86
Menoeceus, 51, 53, 68, 90
Menoetius, 66
Merope, 19, 56, 73, 105
Metapontus, 18, 43, 105–106
Metion, 47, 66, 106
Metis, 40, 106
Metope, 16, 38
Midas, 73, 100, 106
Miletus, 35, 38, 106
Minos, 10, 16, 23, 30, 36, 37, 38, 44, 47, 50, 56, 61, 66, 69, 73, 81, 88, 94, 102, 106–107
Minotaur, the, 16, 36, 38, 53, 56, 66, 81, 106
Minyans, 102
Minyas, 62, 96
Mnemon, 11
Moliones, 107–108
Mopsus, 28, 35, 45, 100, 108
Mother Earth, 15, 31, 35, 37, 40, 47, 48, 49, 54, 55, 57, 66, 72, 74, 75, 79, 85, 86, 94, 106, 108–109
Munippus, 50, 74
Munitus, 10, 19, 95
Muses, the, 12, 14, 37, 108, 109, 109
Mycenae, 16, 18, 25, 29, 41, 42, 48, 53, 64, 68, 72, 78, 81, 82, 104
Myrmidons, the, 15, 109
Myrtilus, 85, 86, 110

Naiads, 88, 110
Narcissus, 64, 64, 110–111, 111
Naupiadame, 42
Nauplius, 16, 18, 25, 42, 47, 51, 62, 89, 97, 100, 111
Nausinous, 46
Nausithous, 46
Nebrophonus, 69
Neleus, 43, 54, 102, 111
Nemean Lion, the, 64, 71, 73, 80, 81, 81, 111
Nemesis, 95, 111
Neoptolemus, 18, 20, 30, 39, 59, 71, 77, 85, 91, 98, 111–112
Nephele, 39, 47, 78, 89, 92, 112
Nereids, the, 112
Nereus, 46, 82, 112
Nessus, 58, 59, 83, 112
Nestor, 11, 20, 32, 99, 105, 108, 112–113

Nicippe, 71, 113
Nicostrate, 71, 113
Niobe, 15, 28, 34, 69, 96, 113–114
Nisus, 24, 114
Nymphs, 15, 26, 28, 35, 37, 39, 41, 45, 57, 58, 62, 63, 64, 65, 71, 74, 85, 86, 96, 97, 103, 105, 150

Oceanus, 10, 38, 46, 48, 70, 85, 114
Odysseus, 11, 18, 19, 20, 21, 22, 23, 24, 31, 32, 38, 39, 40, 41, 42, 46, 50, 55, 59, 61, 65, 69, 70, 74, 75, 76, 77, 87, 92, 94, 98, 103, 104, 114–119, 114, 115, 116, 117, 118
Oedipus, 32, 53, 66, 68, 74, 90, 92, 94, 119–120, 119, 120
Oeneus, 10, 26, 38, 46, 62, 103, 104, 120
Oeno, 31
Oenoë, 30
Oenomaus, 86, 97, 120
Oenone, 15, 16, 53, 120
Oenope, 102
Oenopion, 105, 120
Oeonus, 97
Olympics, the, 83
Olympus, 25, 40, 43, 47, 55, 65, 66, 69, 70, 72, 77, 78, 79, 80, 83, 84, 85, 105
Omphale, 82, 120–121, 121
Opheltes, 88
Ophion, 70, 121
Oracles, 13, 21, 25, 39, 42, 58, 59, 69, 77, 85, 89, 90, 94, 95, 99
Oreithyia, 43, 45, 51, 121
Orestes, 16, 17, 17, 20, 25, 40, 41, 50, 51, 52, 64, 66, 68, 77, 85, 88, 97, 105, 121–122, 121, 122
Orion, 35, 37, 38, 65, 105, 122–123
Orpheus, 37, 49, 55, 64, 70, 70, 97, 99, 106, 123, 123
Orthrus, 71, 123–124
Otus, 124
Ovid, 48, 53, 58, 61, 65

Pactolus, 69
Palaemon, 124
Palamedes, 20, 31, 61, 124
Palladium, the, 18, 20, 22, 23, 31, 40, 61, 75, 77, 89
Pallas, 16, 30, 40, 73, 89, 124
Pan, 26, 58, 59, 63, 64, 68, 74, 75, 85, 99, 124, 124
Pandareus, 15, 105, 124–125
Pandion, 16, 44, 66, 106, 125
Pandora, 66, 79, 86, 125
Panopeus, 65, 125
Paris, 12, 17, 20, 33, 34, 50, 53, 59, 74, 76, 77, 85, 99, 104, 105, 125–126, 125
Parthenopaeus, 15, 53, 126
Pasiphaë, 10, 30, 36, 47, 50, 53, 56, 73, 88, 106, 126, 127
Patroclus, 11, 12, 22, 61, 105, 127, 127
Pegasus, 42, 43, 49, 102, 127–128, 127
Peirithous, 63, 68, 128
Pelasgus, 79, 88, 97

Peleus, 10, 12, 39, 49, 53, 68, 71, 128–129, *128*
Pelias, 10, 14, 19, 24, 49, 54, 71, 92, *92*, 93, 101, 129, *129*
Pelopia, 16, 42, 55, 129
Pelops, 19, 20, 23, 39, 41, 46, 50, 51, 59, 60, 65, 69, 71, 77, 86, 94, 130
Penelope, 21, 32, 69, 70, 92, 94, 130–131, *130*, *131*
Penthesileia, 131
Pentheus, 45, 99, 131
Penthilus, 66
Periander, 131
Periboea, 22, 88, 131–132
Periclymenus, 132
Perigune, 132
Perilaus, 88
Perimedes, 82, 97
Periphetes, 132
Pero, 38, 43, 102, 132
Perse, 15, 50
Persephone, 14, 15, 24, 33, 38, 39, 52, 62, 63, 69, 74, 75, 76, 96, 132, *132*
Perses, 16, 101
Perseus, 13, 29, *30*, 40, 46, 47, 49, 56, 57, 61, 64, 73, 102, 132–133, *133*
Phaedra, 10, 86, 133
Phaëthon, 78, 133–134, *134*
Phanes, 134
Phegeus, 24, 25, 45, 66, 134
Pheneus, 90
Philammon, 35, 42
Philoctetes, 61, 80, 83, 99, 105, 134–135, *135*
Philoetius, 103, 135
Philomela, 44, 66, 135
Phineus, 21, 45, 51, 69, 136
Phlegra, 72
Phobus, 33, 36
Phocus, 71, 136
Phoebe, 41, 96, 97, 136
Phoenix, 20, 21, 29, 98, 136, *136*
Phorcids, the, 64, 73, 94, 136
Phorcys, 48, 73, 85, 136
Phoronus, 88, 136
Phrixus, 15, 39, 43, 48, 78, 89, 92, 93, 136
Phylacus, 71, 102, 136
Phylas, 100
Phyleus, 42, 81, 137
Phyllis, 60, 137
Pittheus, 16, 19, 137
Planetary Powers, the, 54, 70, 106, 138, 148
Pleiades, the, 105, 138
Pluto, 74
Plutus, 59, 88, 138
Podaleirius, 99, 138
Podarces, 82, 85, 91, 95, 138
Podes, 64
Poliporthis, 138
Polybus, 138
Polybutes, 73, 138
Polycaste, 56, 138
Polydectes, 13, 57, 61, 138
Polydeuces, 29, 47, 63, 89, 96, 99, 138

Polydorus, 74, 139
Polyeidus, 43, 73, 106, 139
Polymele, 19, 49, 53, 62, 92, 93, 139
Polymnestor, 74, 75, 89, 139–140
Polypemon, 140
Polyphemus, 81, 87, 140, *140*
Polyxena, 11, 12, 20, 59, 60, 75, 140
Porphyrion, 73
Poseidon, 12, 15, 16, 18, 19, 21, 23, 24, 25, 26, 28, 28, 29, 30, 31, 36, 37, 38, 40, 42, 43, 44, 45, 46, 48, 54, 64, 66, 68, 69, 70, 73, 74, 75, 76, 78, 85, 88, 89, 90, 91, 94, 95, 100, 102, 106, 140–141, *141*
Priam, 11, 17, 19, 20, 21, 23, 31, 38, 39, 43, 45, 46, 50, 59, 64, 74, 75, *75*, 76, 77, 82, 85, 89, 94, 95, 97, 99, 103, 105, 141–142, *142*
Priapus, 33, 63, 85, 142
Procne, 44, 65, 142
Procris, 47, 94, 142
Proetus, 13, 31, 42, 90, 92, 99, 102, 103, 142–143
Promachus, 93
Prometheus, 15, 40, 41, 49, 60, 61, 66, 79, 85, 86, 90, 143–144, *143*
Protesilaus, 11, 144
Proteus, 37, 105, 144
Psamathe, 145
Purification, 10, 25, 29, 37, 50, 66, 71, 93
Pygmalion, 72, *144*, 145
Pylades, 25, 52, 64, 91, 145, *145*
Pylas, 43, 99, 145
Pylia, 16
Pyraechmus, 80
Pyrrha, 60, 61, *61*, 145
Pyrrhus, 59
Python/Pythoness, the, 45, 58, 59, 81, 82, 100, 145

Rhadamanthys, 23, 25, 31, 38, 69, 106, 146
Rhea, 36, 48, 54, 55, 59, 60, 62, 72, 73, 74, 79, 98, 146
Rhode, 29, 74, 146
Rhodes, 44, 57, 78, 93

Sarpedon, 69, 73, 94, 106, 146
Satyrs, 29, 34, 63, 74, 99, 100, *146*, 146–147
Scamander, 73, 147
Scylla, 52, 64, 94, 147, *147*
Selene, 65, 77, 87, 148
Semele, 62, 63, 85, 148
Silenus, 106, 148, *148*
Sirens, the, 33, 44, 51, 74, 148–149, *149*
Sisyphus, 32, 38, 42, 73, 74, 94, 101, 149
Sixteen Matrons, the, 86, 149
Smyrna, 14, 33, 50, 149
Soloön, 69
Sophocles, 32, 53, 59, 74, 84
Sown Men, the, 44

Sparta, 19, 47, 53, 60, 63, 76, 77, 83, 88, 95, 104, 105
Sparti, 44, 150
Sphinx, 49, 64, 74, 90, 94, 150, *150*
Spites, the, 66
Stymphalian Birds, the, 150
Styx, 25, 150

Talos, 56, 78, 79, 150–151, *150*
Tantalus, 19, 44, 51, 58, 59, 63, 69, 72, 76, 104, 151, *151*
Tartarus, 12, 14, 18, 21, 23, 24, 25, 32, 38, 42, 47, 49, 50, 52, 55, 58, 59, 63, 66, 70, 72, 74, 82, 105, 107
Tecmessa, 22, 151
Teiresias, 15, 29, 33, 35, 40, 53, 57, 66, 68, 99, 151–152, *152*
Telamon, 15, 22, 23, 39, 85, 95, 152
Telchines, the, 152
Telegonus, 152
Telemachus, 152–153, *153*
Telephassa, 44, 69
Telephus, 11, 39, 42, 53, 70, 83, *83*, 94, 153–154, *153*, *154*
Temenus, 79
Tenes, 154
Tereus, 154
Tethys, 70
Teucer, 22, 58, 85, 154
Teumessian Vixen, the, 29, 47, 94, 154
Teuthras, 42, 154–155
Thalia, 35
Thamyris, 155
Thea, 18, 37, 60, 68, 155
Theano, 18, 43, 155
Thebes, 15, 24, 25, 28, 29, 32, 36, 44, 45, 46, 47, 50, 51, 53, 57, 62, 66, 68, 71, 81, 82, 87, 90, 94, 97, 98, 99, 101, 102, 103
Theia, 48, 65, 77, 155
Themis, 61, 72, 155, *155*
Themisto, 39
Theonoë, 155
Thersander, 24, 66, 155
Thersites, 12, 61
Theseus, 10, 15, 16, 19, 26, 30, 33, 36, 48, 53, 56, 60, 61, 63, 66, 69, 71, 82, 86, 87, 90, 97, 98, 101, 103, 105, 107, 155–157, *156*, *157*
Thestius, 81, 158
Thestor, 89, 158
Thetis, 10, 11, 12, 26, 46, 49, 53, 68, 78, 79, 97, 158, *158*
Thoas, 69, 73, 158, *159*
Thyestes, 16, 18, 19, 41, 42, 78, 86, 158–159
Thymoetes, 159
Timandra, 51
Tiphys, 69
Tisamenus, 66
Tisiphone, 53
Titan, 54, 62, 66
Titans/Titanesses, 41, 55, 72, 77, 86, 87, 96, 106, *159*, 159–160
Tithonus, 103, 160
Tithys, 38
Titias, 58

Tityus, 34, 160
Tlepolemus, 39, 160
Tmolus, 160
Trachis, 83
Triptolemus, 160, *160*
Triton, 29, 69, 93, 160, *161*
Troilus, 11, *11*, 43, 160–161
Trojan Horse, the, 10, 20, 45, 59, 66, 77, 94, 105
Trojan War, the, 10, 11, 12, 15, 17, 19, 20, 22, 28, 30, 31, 32, 40, 43, 50, 55, 59, 60, 64, 65, 68, 69, 70, 73, 74, 75, 76, 79, 84, 85, 89, 94, 97, 100, 103, 104, 105
Tros, 39, 72, 161
Troy, 10, 11, 15, 16, 18, 19, 20, 21, 22, 23, 27, 31, 32, 34, 35, 36, 38, 39, 42, 43, 45, 46, 50, 51, 53, 58, 59, 60, 61, 66, 70, 71, 73, 74, 75, 76, 77, 85, 89, 90, 94, 95, 97, 98, 99, 105
Tyche, 161, *161*
Tydeus, 15, 61, 68, 161
Tyndareus, 20, 38, 47, 76, 88, 161–162
Typhon, 40, 47, 49, 59, 64, 72, 85, 94, 96, 162
Tyro, 19, 54, 162–165

Underworld, the, 18, 23, 38, 47, 55, 59, 69, 70, 73, 75
Uranus, 33, 54, 55, 66, 72, 103, 106

Virgil, 18, 40

Xanthus, 42

Zeus, 10, 12, 13, 14, 15, 16, 18, 20, 21, 22, 23, 25, 25, 26, 28, 29, 30, 32, 33, 34, 36, 37, 38, 39, 40, 41, *41*, 43, 44, 46, 47, 48, 49, 51, 52, 53, 54, 55, 56, 58, 59, 60, 61, 62, 63, 64, 65, 66, 68, 70, 71, 72, 73, 74, 75, 76, 77, 78, 79, 80, 83, 84, 85, 88, 89, 90, 92, 94, 95, 97, 100, 103, 104, 105, 106